Study Guide

Leigh Anderson and David A. Hennes

Principles of Microeconomics

Eugene Silberberg

Prentice Hall, Englewood Cliffs, NJ 07632

Project Manager: Nancy Proyect
Acquisitions Editor: Leah Jewell
Manufacturing Buyer: Ken Clinton
Assistant Editor: Teresa Cohan

Printed in the United States of America

10 9 8 7 6 5 4 3 2 1

ISBN   0-13-157703-4

Prentice-Hall International (UK) Limited, *London*
Prentice-Hall of Australia Pty. Limited, *Sydney*
Prentice-Hall Canada Inc., *Toronto*
Prentice-Hall Hispanoamericana, S. A., *Mexico*
Prentice-Hall of India Private Limited, *New Delhi*
Prentice-Hall of Japan, Inc., *Tokyo*
Simon & Schuster Asia Pte. Ltd., *Singapore*
Editoria Prentice-Hall do Brazil, Ltda., *Rio de Janeiro*

Table of Contents

Introduction

Over two hundred years ago, in the great philosophic tradition of rational inquiry, the Scottish philosopher Adam Smith began contemplating the nature and causes of the wealth of nations. Smith, like generations of philosophers and economists who have followed him, was trying to order and make sense of the complex society he lived in -- to derive principles or generalities that could explain the diverse and seemingly random economic activities that without central coordination, held these societies together.

Economists today are still involved in this pursuit, though specialization has led most of us to contemplate far narrower questions than the relative prosperity and workings of whole societies. (An explanation of the benefits of specialization, by the way, was one of the many topics Smith touched upon in his 1776 treatise.) And while our understanding has progressed significantly from the classic diamond water paradox you will read about in chapter 2, we are still unable to adequately explain many things, for example, problems of development in many poorer countries.

Nonetheless, the legacy of economic thought to date has left us with one of the most consistent, powerful, and enduring theories for explaining human behaviour. The principles of microeconomics, and the underlying economic paradigm are the roots from which all these inquiries stem. Whether you are studying this material because you have to, or because you want to, with a little effort and a lot of thought you can develop a way of thinking that can give you insight into an amazing number of phenomena.

Gene Silberberg's text, *Principles of Microeconomics*, is your gateway to this way of thinking. Your instructor should be another source. Our study guide is intended to complement both these sources. The goal of the study guide is threefold: to answer what we have found are the most commonly asked questions in introductory microeconomics courses and to anticipate where we think you may have problems; to provide alternative explanations and additional examples; and most importantly, to give you practice answering questions and working through problems.

We have broken each study guide chapter into three sections. The first section contains chapter objectives with examples and questions for you to study and work through. These objectives should serve as intermediate goals for you to master along the way toward understanding the whole of microeconomic principles. This section records the regular study session between two college students, Ginny Hill and Mo Gibson. Ginny and Mo met last summer while working at Jim's Diner in Seattle. Ginny is a freshman. She has yet to declare her major though she is leaning towards history, and contemplates teaching as a career. Mo is a sophomore and a business major. Both are taking their first microeconomics class from Gene Silberberg at the University of Washington, and working through his text.

We choose to have Ginny and Mo take you through the objectives of each chapter for two reasons. First, Ginny and Mo are more interesting than we are, and we have to keep you reading to entice you to work through problems. Second, Ginny and Mo will encounter many of the same difficulties as some of you, and we think you will gain more from working through the problems with them, rather than having us just restate the results.

Some of you will identify with Ginny, who is a good conceptual thinker but has pretty rusty math skills. In fact, Ginny has developed a bit of a math phobia which she hopes to overcome by working through this course. Ginny grew up in rural Washington and spent a lot of time reading, so she already has a pretty impressive vocabulary. Her facility with words will be useful as Silberberg doesn't hesitate to throw some large ones your way.

Mo likes numbers and is a logical thinker. She lacks Ginny's ability to link subtle ideas and make esoteric associations, but she has strong analytical and problem solving skills. Mo grew up in the city influenced by an energetic and entrepreneurial mother. Mo plans to blast through a business degree and start her own business when she finishes. Her older brother Adam is a senior majoring in Economics. Adam has promised to give Ginny and Mo some help with their studies, partly because he is a nice guy, and partly because he has a crush on Ginny.

Section two gives you the big picture. This is our attempt to help you rise above all the jargon, rules, and numbers. By standing back from all these details we hope you will be better able to see how all the parts fit together, why they are important, what purpose they serve, and ultimately your path through the economic paradigm.

Understanding economics and mastering the economic way of thinking requires some conceptual, analytical, and technical skills. But mostly it requires a lot of work. That's where section three comes in: practice problems. We cannot stress enough the importance of disciplining yourself to work through these problems. You cannot learn economics just by reading a textbook, even one as good as Silberberg's. Only by applying the concepts, through problem solving, can you assess your understanding. Moreover, it is only through problems on homework assignments, quizzes and exams that you can demonstrate your ability and understanding of the concepts.

Another great economist, John Maynard Keynes remarked that "the ideas of economists and political philosophers both when they are right and when they are wrong, are more powerful than is commonly understood. Indeed the world is ruled by little else." Whether or not you go on to inspire others with your economic ideas, the seeds of which can begin in this course, you will, we hope, gain the ability to critically analyze and appreciate others' ideas that are influencing your life.

CHAPTER 1
But Will It Work In Theory?

PRINCIPAL GOALS

1.0 Recognize the basic elements of social science methodology and their relationship to economic inquiry. (Objectives 1.1, 1.2)

2.0 Identify the main elements of the economic paradigm and their basic relationship to one another. (Objectives 2.1, 2.2, 2.3, 2.4)

3.0 Understand the graph of the basic supply and demand model. (Objective 3.1)

OBJECTIVES
Answers to bold-faced questions appear at the end of the dialogue.

"Did you understand it?"

"Sort of. Did you?"

"Sure, sort of."

They looked at each other and laughed.

"I always feel like this when I start reading a textbook," Mo said. "I'm excited about learning something new, but this doesn't exactly look easy."

"I know, it sounds so scientific," said Ginny. "Like what is all this about human behavior and theories and refutable propositions?"

"And what does it mean to *'mitigate ... the adverse consequences of constraints'*?" asked Mo.

Ginny looked back across the table, "I don't know exactly, but I know you had better start convincing me why I should take this course rather than art history."

"Well, haven't you ever wondered about how it is that when you go to the store to buy a CD or some particular kind of cereal, you find what you want?

"Not really."

"Well you should," Mo said. "We take for granted that if we want chicken for dinner we can go to the supermarket and find some. But in economies like the former Soviet Union, with central planners deciding how many chickens to raise, the shelves were often bare. Think about how amazing it is that with no plan whatsoever, with everybody just doing their own thing, somehow all this economic activity takes place. All these goods are produced. And when we want to buy a new music disc, there it is waiting for us."

"That is pretty amazing, how all the different activities get coordinated so that a Pearl Jam CD is sitting at the record store for me to buy when the mood is right."

"Studying economics is the key to explaining things like that. Adam told me what he really likes about economics is that its a way of thinking that gives him insight into almost everything we do, and that it helps him understand history and current world events. He actually said that economic thinking is a 'clear and powerful lens through which to view the world'."

"Your brother is a nerd Mo."

"Absolutely, but he's also an A student with great career prospects. There's nothing nerdy about that. Besides you don't want to be one of these people passing your day watching sit-coms and soap operas and only reading the horoscopes and people sections in the paper because you can't follow the news and business reports; and ending up in the same stupid arguments about things you don't really understand where you just repeat your opinion over and over again. No! You want to stride the world stage and understand the complexities of current and historical trends; you want to win influence through the compelling logic of your arguments; you want to..."

"Compel you to stop this speech. O.K. Mo, you've convinced me. I should take the course and work hard at it for my own enrichment. But why are you so concerned about my life?"

"That's simple. I want a study partner."

"Alright, I'll take the course," Ginny laughed. "But I think we need a plan. I say we figure out what's important from each chapter and make sure we understand it by trying to work through some problems."

Mo agreed, and they each went through the chapter, making up a list of what they believed to be the most important things.

"What's the first thing on your list?" Ginny asked.

"I want to understand all of this social science stuff -- like theories, postulates, positive and normative statements, and refutable propositions. I don't *really* know what most of those words mean, let alone what they're for."

"Well, I guess I'm not too sure about some of them myself", Ginny said. "I do know that we have to be careful with our words, because I think economists have their own jargon just like everyone else. So we want to make sure we use them in the right way, and understand how Silberberg uses them."

OBJECTIVE 1.1 Recognize definitions for the important new vocabulary.

Question 1. Match the term with its definition(s). Write out definitions for any undefined terms.

a. theory   b. postulates

c. propositions
e. normative statements
g. refutable propositions
i. confirmed theory
k. causality

d. positive statements
f. ad hoc (theory)
h. proven theory
j. correlation

_____ A prediction which is intended to either affirm or deny something about the subject at hand.

_____ The observation or demonstration that without the occurrence (or non-occurrence) of one event, a second event would not occur.

_____ A statement which asserts the way things ought to be.

_____ The observation or demonstration that as one event occurs more frequently, a second event is more likely or less likely to occur.

_____ A statement which can be classified as either true or false.

_____ A theory that is based on significant support from gathered evidence.

_____ A theory that cannot be consistently used and confirmed as a general explanation of the occurrence of an event.

_____ A basic principle, which is assumed in order to pursue a course of reasoning.

_____ A proposition that could in principle be wrong.

_____ A statement which asserts the way things are.

_____ A collection of assertions or propositions that have been verified through testing, which explain or establish a relationship between observed events.

_____ The observation or demonstration of a relationship between two ideas and/or events.

_____ A statement which is based in one's ethical values.

_____ A theory that is generally accepted as true.

* * * * * * *

"Okay. So now for the tricky part Ginny, what does all of this have to do with studying economics?"

OBJECTIVE 1.2 Identify the parts and confirm the validity of a theory.

"I think that this is the way economists and social scientists think when they try to explain what's going on in the world. These are their tools and materials, and their approach for asking and answering economics questions. They can't just say whatever they think. They have to methodically build their case, based on specific postulates and theories, then they have to prove that their explanation is right."

"You mean confirm."

"Right, and it seems as though they confirm their explanations with tests or experiments. I don't really understand how they test these theories or explanations. Its not like a science experiment in a lab."

"I don't know either exactly", Mo said, "but I remember Silberberg saying something about testing the assertions of the theory against specific facts to confirm it. Maybe we should think through an example."

"Okay, I've got one", Ginny said. "You remember that guy Bob who ate at the Diner every Saturday night?"

"You mean Bob with the black glasses? I liked him. He seemed like a normal guy."

"He did. Anyway, a couple of Saturdays ago he stopped coming in. My theory is that he doesn't come in anymore because he lost his job."

Question 2. Is this really a theory? _____ Is it an ad hoc theory? _____ Why or why not?

Question 3. On what postulates might this theory be based?

Question 4. What is the proposition of the theory?

Question 5. Is the proposition a refutable proposition?

* * * * * * *

"Wait a minute", Mo said. "How do you know he hasn't joined some cult or maybe he got involved with some woman who doesn't eat meatloaf?"

"I don't, but that's my theory."

"Has Jim raised prices at the Diner?"

"No."

"Hmm, I thought maybe he'd gone somewhere cheaper. Maybe he got tired of Karl's cooking?"

"Maybe, but how could I know that?" Ginny asked. "Look, I know there are lots of other explanations, but how do we test <u>my</u> theory?"

"Maybe he's dead."

"Mo -- he's not dead! I've seen him around a couple of times."

"Sorry, I was just thinking. We could just ask him why he doesn't come in anymore."

"That's true, but I guess I'd rather not", Ginny said. "Suppose that it's because he's given up hoping you'd return to work. In that case, he might not tell me the truth. Besides, we won't always be able to test our theories just by asking someone."

"So let's follow him around to see if he goes to work."

Question 6. Is their observation of Bob's activities a valid test for confirming or refuting the theory?

_____

Question 7. If Ginny and Mo observed that Bob was going to work, but that he was also not eating dinner on Saturday nights at the Diner, does this refute their hypothesis or proposition? _____

* * * * * * *

"If he does go to work, then we can refute my theory and move on to one of yours."

"So you start with the basic assumptions or postulates as your foundation, then relying on these for guidance you develop a refutable proposition, which is essentially why you think whatever has happened or not happened, has happened or not happened. Am I right so far?" Mo asked.

"I would say yes. The refutable proposition just has two parts to it really. The first part is what you are trying to explain, like Bob not eating at the Diner anymore. And the second part is the proposed reason."

"Right, but the reason is the testable part too: if Bob lost his job, which we could observe, then we might conclude that that's why he doesn't eat at the Diner anymore. You test the proposition, and the overall theory really, against your observations. I feel like an economist already."

Ginny laughed, "Hey that's just the social science part, we haven't even talked about economics yet."

"I know," said Mo. "I have a few questions about this economic paradigm. Like, what is a paradigm?"

"Twenty cents."

"Please Ginny, I get enough lame econ humor at home from Adam."

"I thought it was funny."

"This paradigm is supposed to be the roots of economic theory right?"

"I think so, a paradigm is basically a model, so the economic paradigm would be the basic model of economic theory", Ginny said.

"I understand a model as a simplified version of the real thing, but beyond that I need to work with this a little bit more."

"Me too", Ginny said. "Should we start with the vocabulary again?"

OBJECTIVE 2.1 Recognize definitions for the important new vocabulary.

Question 8. Match the term with its definition(s). Write out definitions for any undefined terms.

a. goods   b. scarcity
c. opportunity cost   d. constraints
e. opportunities   f. tastes/preferences
g. demand   h. supply

_____ A measurable condition that limits our behavior.

_____ The highest price one can receive for a resource.

_____ There are not enough of the items humans find desirable to satisfy everyone's wants.

_____ Choices (behavior) of people involved in the production of goods.

_____ That which limits (represses) our behavior.

_____ Anything that is bought and sold by humans.

_____ An unmeasurable condition that affects our behavior.

_____ The value of a foregone opportunity or alternative resulting from choosing.

_____ Things you like or don't like.

_____ Choices (behavior) of people involved in the consumption of goods and services.

_____ A measurable condition that allows us to do more.

OBJECTIVE 2.2 Observe the prevalence of scarcity in your own life.

"So it seems pretty logical to me Ginny, that because of scarcity there is competition for resources and there is choice; and because there is choice there is always an opportunity cost to using that resource. I think those are the roots of the paradigm."

"We should try to think of some real examples then, before getting into choice and supply and demand. When I was reading this last night I wrote down some goods. I'm not sure I know whether these are all scarce goods or even whether they are all goods for that matter. So which of the following are scarce goods for you?"

water	text books
nuclear weapons	music cd's
clean water	the AIDS virus
leisure time	broccoli

"Water - yes. Nuclear weapons - for me, definitely not, but for the country maybe yes. That's a tricky one in a way because we'd all prefer not to have them, but we also want a national defense. Clean water - hey wait a minute, clean water versus just water. Well, clean water is a definite yes and water is...well."

"I ended up thinking both were scarce just because I think the water everywhere, including the ocean, is polluted -- it's killing ocean life which is a big problem to me."

"I agree but then you're talking about clean water again. This is just like his example of air not being scarce. The ocean, for example, is there in all its abundance. Ask yourself if you'd want more of the good than you currently consume, if it was given away free."

"The ocean is basically free -- at least for sailing a boat on it."

"And do you find yourself wanting more?"

"No. Okay, all water is not scarce. Let's go on."

"Okay, leisure time - any time is scarce for me. Text books - yes, though I would probably pass by a "Challenges in Trigonometry" text lying on the sidewalk."

"So what we are really talking about is what we consume every day. These are scarce goods and we make choices about how to use them. Just think of what you did today Mo."

OBJECTIVE 2.3 **Identify the constraints and opportunities you face. Observe how they stem from scarcity and guide the choices you make. Identify the opportunity costs of your choices.**

"Let's see, what did I do today? I guess I got up and took a shower, ate a bagel..."

"Stop right there. I took a shower too."

"Well congratulations Ginny."

"Seriously, we could have taken baths, which I really love, or no shower at all. So the choice was to shower, though I guess I didn't really think about it like that this morning."

"Yes, but that's important, don't you think? Why did you really choose to take a shower over a bath?" asked Mo. "I did because I'm constrained by time, and bathing takes longer."

"I also take showers because I think it saves water, and clean shower water is a scarce good. I'm constrained by guilt."

"So we would predict that I would take a bath on Sundays, when I have more time, but that you would continue to shower, unless your guilt takes the weekend off. If it doesn't, there's no change in your constraints, so no reason to expect a change in your behavior."

"So what are the costs, or opportunity costs, of us taking showers rather than nothing at all?"

"I would have eaten breakfast. I sacrificed breakfast in the dorms for a shower. That seemed like a clear choice at the time."

"I guess I gave up another 15 minutes of sleep," Mo said.

"Wow, this really makes me think about the CDs I buy," Ginny said. "What is the opportunity cost of buying a CD?"

"That would be the other goods you don't buy with the money, or the time you spend working to earn the money in the first place."

"Exactly. I figure it costs me one hour of work - and that's wages and tips before taxes - to get a CD."

"But you are constrained by your income and other bills to being able to buy only one or two CDs a month right?"

"Yes. I am a constrained young woman," lamented Ginny.

Question 9. Fill out the chart below as you work through the following exercise.

Choices	Opportunity Cost	Constraints

1. Think back over the last couple of days. Write down some choices you have made -- as many as you can remember, but NO LESS THAN FIVE CHOICES. These are choices about what clothes, food, books or other things you bought, wore, ate or used. Did you buy those new boots, what did you choose for breakfast, lunch or dinner, books (new or used), the economy sized laundry soap or the little one, did you take the bus or did you drive yourself? How did you spend your time? Did you go to class, go to work, read a novel, practice your music, work out, see a movie, study hard, talk to people? Write down each one in the choices column.

2. In the next column, beside each choice, write down what you gave up to choose as you did (i.e. the opportunity cost). That is, what else could or would you have bought or done with the money or time, if you hadn't bought or done what you did? What did your choices really cost you? Did the two-hour workout cost you two hours worth of study or two hours with your friends or family? Maybe it cost you two hours worth of pay? Remember also that inactivity is a choice.

3. Now think about constraints and opportunities (a constraint being relaxed). Why did you buy and do what you did? Why did you eat chicken instead of tofu or steak? Why did you make your lunch rather than eat out? Why did you eat your salad with no dressing? Why did you choose to go to economics class, instead of taking an extra shift at work? Did you buy a new computer because the prices dropped? Write down the major influence(s) (constraint) on your choices in the appropriate column.

OBJECTIVE 2.4 From your own experience of the constraints you face and choices you make, derive an explanation for the changes in your behavior (your choices) when there is a change in your situation (i.e. your constraints).

"So is this it then?" Mo asked. "Is this the economic paradigm?"

"To me the crux of the whole thing is Section 1.3 where he talks about how things change when constraints change," said Ginny. "That's the economic paradigm: a model of how they will change."

Question 10. For each of the choices you listed in the exercise above change the related constraint in column three, if possible, in a positive and a negative direction, then reevaluate your choice from column one. Tip - When you change the constraints, make a big change.

* * * * * * *

"Like you with CDs; you would buy more if you earned more money. Of course that explains the graph too. For demand you have a negatively sloped or inverse relationship between quantities demanded and the price, and for supply there is a positive slope and relationship between quantities supplied and the price."

"Whoa, whoa, whoa Mo! Where did you get all that?"

"Reading the chapter, but also the graphs. I just put the two together when you said that about the economic paradigm. The graphs really make it clear to me what all those words are actually trying to say."

"You're amazing", Ginny said. "All this stuff about negative and positive slopes, and all of these cryptic symbols in the place of words. I can follow the descriptions below the graphs, but when I look at them I don't really understand what they say."

[Note: You may want to go over the material in the Supplement on Graphs first then come back to this objective.]

Mo laughed. "The first step to understanding and using graphs is to start drawing them yourself. That way you know what all the pieces are. My high school algebra teacher used to torment us -- making us draw out hundreds of these graphs. It's not hard; you just have to use them enough so that you're comfortable with what they mean -- come on, draw out the axes."

"Is this your fantasy? To become your math teacher?"

"My fantasy is to finish this chapter before the Sonic's game starts. So put your pencil to the paper."

OBJECTIVE 3.1 **Draw and label a set of axes for graphing supply and demand curves. Transfer and represent data on the graphs.**

Demand   Supply

(Circle the appropriate answers below).

Demand
Question 11. Would you buy (more, fewer, or the same amount of) tie-dyed t-shirts if the price went from $5.00 to $20.00 per shirt and your income and all other factors remained the same?

On the axes above mark off prices of $5.00 per shirt and $20.00 per shirt. Also show on the quantity axis how many t-shirts you would buy at each of these prices.

Mark the points out in the graph space (i.e. the space between the axes) representing the quantity of t-shirts you would buy at the $5.00 and $20.00 prices. You should have two points. Connect them with a line.

This is your demand curve for tie-dyed t-shirts. Is it negatively sloped? _____

Supply
Question 12. Now suppose you make tie-dyed t-shirts that you sell at weekend markets. The first week you made and sold 20 shirts at $5.00, the next week you made and sold another 30 shirts but you raised the price to $10.00 because you had to hire help. For the next weekend would you make (more, fewer, or the same number of) shirts to sell? Would you try (raising, lowering, or keeping the same) price? Why?

On the axes above mark off prices of $5.00, $10.00 and your final price per shirt. Show on the quantity axis the corresponding quantities of t-shirts you made for the third weekend.

Mark the points out in the graph space representing the quantity of t-shirts you would make at $5.00, $10.00 and your final price. You should have three points. Connect these points with a line.

This is your supply curve for producing tie-dyed t-shirts. Is it positively sloped? _____

Question 13. Draw out supply and demand curves for mountain bikes purchased in Seattle so that there is an equilibrium at a price of $350.00 and a quantity of 12,000 per year.

Question 14. According to the law of demand, would Seattleites buy (more, fewer, or the same number of) mountain bikes if the price of all mountain bikes rose to $400.00? Show this increase in price on your graph then show the number (the quantity) of mountain bikes demanded. Mark the quantity demanded with a Q_d.

Question 15. According to the theory of supply, would the suppliers of mountain bikes sell (more, less, the same amount of) bikes if the price rose to $400.00? Show this increase in price on the same graph, and mark the quantity supplied with a Q_s.

Question 16. Do the same for supply and demand for a price decrease to $300.00.

ANSWERS TO DIALOGUE QUESTIONS

Question 1. Vocabulary: c or g, k, e, j, d, i, f, b, g, d, a, j, e, i.
There is no answer for h, because theories cannot be logically proven.

Question 2. Yes. Silberberg in *"The Structure of Economics: A Mathematical Analysis"* writes that a theory is comprised of three parts: a set of behavioral assertions or postulates, a set of assumptions or test conditions, and the predicted events. "The theory says that the behavioral assertions…imply that if the test conditions…are valid (realistic), then certain events…will occur." Ginny and Mo's theory states, if Bob lost his job (the test condition), he will no longer eat at the Diner on Saturday nights (the event). Unbeknownst to them, there are behavioral assertions implicit in their theory. See the answer to Q-3.

This is not an ad hoc theory because its predictive ability extends to many different observable events (i.e., it is a general statement about behavior). In this case, that people who experience a decrease in income reduce their spending on luxuries, like eating in restaurants.

Question 3. Postulates are fundamental assertions that allow you to pursue a course of reasoning or to propose an explanation. They are essential to constructing theories. The postulates of behavior underlying economic theory are presented in Chapter 2, and they amply serve as the behavioral postulates (the foundation) for Ginny and Mo's theory. What is the underlying logic governing Bob's sudden change in outward behavior? For now, Mo said Bob seemed like a normal guy. They might hold as a postulate then, that Bob's behavior is rational -- it takes place within reasonable expectations. In other words, he was coming in for a rational reason and he stopped coming in for a rational reason.

Question 4. The proposition in the theory is that Bob no longer eats at the Diner because he lost his job.

Question 5. This is a refutable proposition, because it could in principle be wrong. Bob could have stopped eating at the Diner for another reason.

Question 6. Yes. The observed action's (or inaction) conformance to the theory is the test of the theory.

Question 7. Yes. The theory would be refuted and they would have to find a new explanation.

Question 8. d, None, b, h, d, a, f, c, f, g, e

Question 9. The table might look like this.

Choices	Opportunity Cost	Constraints
Slept extra 1/2 hour	Didn't get to go jogging	Time
Packed a lunch	Cafeteria sloppy joes	Income and sustenance needs
…		

Question 10. For example, I chose to pack a peanut butter sandwich, a carrot, some cookies and a banana for lunch. My constraint is my income. If I change (increase/decrease) the constraint, first by only $200 a month, I don't know if I would change my behavior all that much. But if I topped it up by about $20,000 a month, I'd be eating out every day.

Question 11. Fewer, because they are more expensive and I can no longer afford them at the higher price. The demand curve is negatively sloped.

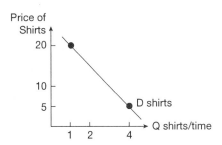

Question 12. More shirts; raise the price. I want to sell the most shirts at the highest price. The supply curve is positively sloped.

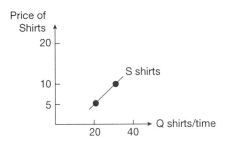

Question 13.

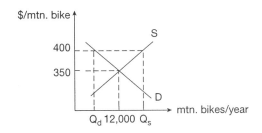

Question 14. Fewer, see Q-13 graph.

Question 15. More, see Q-13 graph.

Question 16.

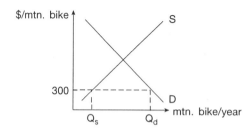

THE BIG PICTURE

There are two important things from this chapter for you to think about and somehow internalize for the rest of your studies. The first is that Chapter 1 is the big picture of economics, presenting its methodology for approaching the study of human behavior and a distilled version of the basic assumptions and working model of economic theory. The remainder of the book expands on and qualifies the basic framework presented here.

As you progress through the course you will learn the basic postulates about human behavior, and these assertions underlye the choices we make confronting scarcity. You will study how people respond to changes in constraints, and how to measure, manipulate and communicate this knowledge. The key word is change; choice, and therefore economics, is a fluid process.

The second thing is that social scientists (i.e. your econ professors) practice this method. They value it; and they reward their peers and students who apply it creatively and well. Why? Because this basic methodology, when combined with the working theories and postulates of economics creates a powerful way of looking at and explaining why, every day, people choose to use their own, their companies, and the world's resources as they do.

A crucial distinction to consider as you work through this course and others is that this social science method is based on logical thought and positive analysis: on reason, not emotion or intuition -- though these things might help you find the answers. Normative statements, i.e. opinions, cannot be measured, they cannot be confirmed or refuted. Therefore they do not add to the base of knowledge from which predictions of human behavior come.

A confirmed theory or hypothesis implies that each layer of the explanation from its foundations in the behavioral postulates to its final prediction has been rigorously examined and tested. If any part does not hold up it must be reworked or abandoned. The explanations that stand up over time are well crafted, thoroughly researched and a little bit inspired, but more than anything they are well reasoned, logical and as defensible as current knowledge and testing allow.

For the remainder of the course you will be filling in pieces of the economic model, with these first few chapters providing a framework and the foundation of the behavioral postulates. From these few early assertions, if you take the time to really understand them, you can derive almost everything you face later on -- just as from the condition of scarcity we infer choice which in turn leads us to understand that the demand curve is negatively sloped. This simplicity and generality, though it may not seem simple to you yet, is what makes economic theory such a powerful predictor and explainer of human behavior.

REVIEW QUESTIONS

Answers to all review questions appear at the end of this chapter.

PROBLEMS AND EXERCISES
Write your answer in the space(s) provided.

1. You are walking down the street one day and a sort of half-way crazy looking guy comes up along side of you and says, "I'll give you ten dollars if you give me five." You look at him with a side-ways glance, like, is this a trick or what? But you pull out a fiver and exchange it for his ten. Two blocks later a wealthy looking woman coming out of a bank stops you and says, "I'll give you either this five dollar bill or this ten dollar bill. Which do you want?" What is with these people you wonder? "Which do you want", she says? You take the $10.00. What is the opportunity cost of your action in each case?

Case I: $5 for $10: _____   Case II: $5 or $10: _____

What is the change in your wealth level in each case?

Case I: $5 for $10: _____   Case II: $5 or $10: _____

2. The President appears one day at Old Macdonald's farm. And on this farm for the same amount of effort and resources he can grow either 40 bushels of corn or 100 bushels of wheat. The President talks to Old Macdonald about what crop he will grow. As intelligent people they talk about the cost of growing wheat or corn.

a.   What is the opportunity cost to society of producing 40 bushels of corn on Old Macdonald's farm? _____

b.   What is the opportunity cost to Old Macdonald of producing corn? _____

The President confides in Old Macdonald that there is a shortage of corn this year and that the government is going to pay farmers $1.00 per bushel of corn produced, in addition to what they can sell the corn for.

c.   What is the opportunity cost to Old Macdonald of producing wheat? _____ of corn? _____

In addition to the President's offer, Old Macdonald knows he can sell his corn for $1.50 per bushel and his wheat for $1.00 per bushel.

d.   What is the opportunity cost to Old Macdonald of producing the 40 bushels of corn to serve his country? _____

e.   From an economic perspective, which crop would Old Macdonald grow? Explain why?

3. Which of the following are goods for society? Which are scarce goods for you?

_____economics lectures   _____money
_____lawyers   _____basketball season tickets
_____desert sand   _____theater season tickets
_____sewage   _____honest lawyers
_____time   _____education

4. Classify the following statements as either positive or normative propositions regarding the causes of increasing homelessness.

_____ a. If people had a greater sense of community and morality, then there would not be the number of homeless people there are today. People would be more willing to help the needy, as we have in the past.

_____ b. Reductions in funding to mental hospitals have forced hospital administrators to release patients who don't always have a place to live.

_____ c. Interviews of the homeless indicate that increasing worker layoffs from companies over the past six years was a major factor in putting them on the street.

_____ d. They don't want to work to support themselves. They should take any job they can get.

5. Look at the following pairs of variables and think about which of them are correlated. Indicate correlation with a C or no relationship with a N in the blank in front of the pair. For those where you think there is a causal relationship indicate with an arrow in the blank space between the pairs, the direction of causality.

a.   _____ lung cancer _____ smoking
b.   _____ the sighting of Elvis _____ the advent of world peace
c.   _____ the warmer temperatures of spring _____ the renewal of the growing cycle
d.   _____ the number of people who drive while under the influence of alcohol _____ severe drunk driving penalties
e.   _____ consuming more calories than your body can burn _____ gaining weight
f.   _____ crime _____ poverty
g.   _____ extreme wealth _____ happiness
h.   _____ education _____ poverty
i.   _____ burning your hand _____ putting your hand in a fire
j.   _____ the use of computers _____ quality writing
k.   _____ foreign car sales _____ domestic car makers' profit

6. Read the following theory and respond to the directions that follow.

Scarcity is a condition of the natural world. All living creatures must struggle and compete to maintain life against their own species, against other species - either predatory or those which compete for the same sources of sustenance - and with the physical conditions of life. A species possessing some variation in physical or mental attribute which is advantageous to the maintenance of its life will have a greater probability of surviving and procreating. According to the principles of genetic inheritance, species attributes will be passed along through subsequent generations of offspring. If a species possesses an attribute that gives it an advantage, then that attribute will be passed along through the offspring and help ensure the survival of the species over time. The results of this continuous process of adaptation can be seen in the multitude of species in the world, each possessing unique and beneficial attributes that allow it to compete successfully for scarce resources.

1.   Circle and number the postulates upon which this theory is based.

2.   Underline the propositions of this theory.
3.   Indicate with an **A**, the assumptions of the proposition (i.e., identify the condition that must be present or absent, or that changes in order for the predicted event to occur); and with an **O**, the predicted outcome or event that we would observe in confirming the theory.

7. Place the following labels in the correct places on the graph below. There is only one correct answer for each space on this graph.

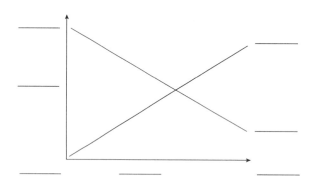

a. demand   f. Quantity
b. supply   g. cans of chili peppers/week
c. $/case of chili peppers   h. Qe
d. cans of hot sauce/week   i. O
e. Pe   j. Pesos/can of chili peppers

8. Draw a graph to depict the following relationship between the price of steak and the amount of steak Alfred Packer buys in a month. Suppose we know that if the price of steak is $2/lb. Alfred will buy 14 lbs. per month. At prices of $4, $6, $8, $10, $12, and $14 he will buy 12, 10, 8, 6, 4, and 2 pounds respectively. Don't forget to label the axes and label this curve D_1.
a.   What is the slope of this line?
b.   What is the p- (or y-) intercept and the q- (or x-) intercept for this line?
c.   Express this linear relationship in algebraic form (an equation).

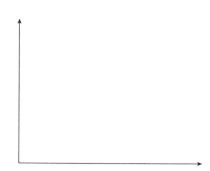

Suppose Alfred's income falls (a change in constraint) and he decreases his consumption to one-half the previous quantity at each price (i.e. 7 lbs/month at $2.00/lb, etc.).

d.   Draw this new relationship on the same graph and label it D_2.
e.   What is the slope of this line? _____
f.   Express this linear relationship in algebraic form. _____
g.   What is the p-intercept and the q-intercept for this line?
         p: _____   q: _____
h.   Describe the position of D_2 relative to D_1, and relative to the origin of the graph.

TRUE - FALSE QUESTIONS
Provide a one or two sentence explanation with your answer.

1.   Events that consistently occur together may be causally unrelated.

2.   The past several years when the Toronto Blue Jays have made the playoffs the demand for tickets to playoff games has increased significantly over the demand for regular season tickets. Therefore we can say that playoff tickets are more scarce than regular season tickets.

3.   Scarcity only exists during bad economic times in wealthy countries and in low-income countries.

4.   A theory is an abstraction of reality.

5.   Inaccessible old growth forest is not a good, but legally protected (e.g. in a national park) old growth or old growth purchased for logging is a good.

6.   The theory of demand is based on scarcity.

7.   The theory of demand is based on choice.

8.   The theory of supply is based on choice.

9.   The theory of supply is based on scarcity.

10.   The theories of supply and demand apply to all people's behavior at all times.

MULTIPLE CHOICE QUESTIONS
Choose the best answer.

1. In a market economy people decide whether to produce and exchange goods based on
a.   government policy
b.   the price of the good.
c.   tradition
d.   society's needs

2. Economists would say that people engage in production and exchange in a free market because:
a.   of their fear of poverty.
b.   of the requirement of providing basic needs.
c.   of the fundamental characteristic of greed.
d.   of mutual benefit to the people involved.

3. Suppose your car depreciates at $5.00 per day if it is not driven, and $10.00 per day if it is driven (assume depreciation includes all maintenance and other costs). The minimum payment per day that would induce you to lend out your car if you were going on holidays is:
a. 1 cent b. $5.01 c. $10.00 d. $10.01

4. The opportunity cost theory suggests that the cost to an airline of letting its employees fly at no charge
a.   depends upon the alternatives available to the employees.
b.   will depend upon the value employees place upon travel.
c.   is zero.
d.   is greater during the holidays than at most other times.

5. The opportunity cost of going to college includes
a.   both tuition and the value of the student's time.
b.   tuition, the value of the student's time and the monthly grocery bill.
c.   only tuition and the grocery bill, since the value of the student's time is highest obtaining an education.
d.   only the value of the student's time, since tuition and the grocery bill are explicit costs.
e.   none of the above.

6. Jim and Midge each have a 15 minute drive to work. Jim drives the company car. Midge has a company chauffeur drive her. After getting onto the freeway, however, both are slowed by traffic. While Jim curses the traffic, Midge pulls out her work. It takes them each 1 hour to get to work. Nobody likes being stuck in traffic but what did it really cost Jim and Midge?

a.   It cost Jim 1 hour of work and it cost Midge zero.
b.   It cost them both the same, because they were both in traffic for 1 hour.
c.   It cost Jim 45 minutes of work and it cost Midge zero.
d.   None of the above, because we don't know the value of their time.

7. A market system based on voluntary exchange provides a way to
a.   allow specialization and exchange to work together.
b.   improve the well-being of humankind.
c.   allocate resources to their highest valued use.
d.   all of the above.

8. The negative slope of a demand curve shows that
a.   a higher price is associated with a higher quantity.
b.   a higher quantity consumed is associated with having less money.
c.   price is not associated with quantity.
d.   a lower price is associated with a higher quantity.

9. The supply curve has a positive slope because
a.   it provides an equilibrium with the demand curve.
b.   lower prices are associated with additional units produced.
c.   higher costs are associated with additional units produced.
d.   tradition.

10. At the point of equilibrium
a.   sellers want a higher price for that quantity.
b.   buyers want a lower price for that quantity.
c.   buyers and sellers are willing to adjust the price for that quantity.
d.   buyers and sellers are willing to exchange that quantity at that price.

Two baseball players, S. Musial and T. Williams, have the capacity to produce within the following ranges:

Musial		Williams	
Fielded balls	Hits	Fielded Balls	Hits
200	0	100	0
0	150	0	100

11. What is the opportunity cost of producing one hit for Williams?
a.   100 fielded balls
b.   2 produced hits
c.   1/100 fielded ball
d.   1 fielded ball

12. What is the opportunity cost of producing one hit for Musial?
a.   1 and 1/3 fielded balls
b.   3/4 fielded ball
c.   200 fielded balls
d.   1 fielded ball

SHORT ANSWER QUESTIONS

1. Hennes is bringing the basketball down court guarded by Anderson. Hennes tries to blow past Anderson with a nifty cross-over dribble, but Anderson anticipates it perfectly. Anderson steals the ball, goes down court and scores two points on the lay up. What is the cost of Hennes' turnover? Is this the same thing as opportunity cost?

2. Various utopian philosophers throughout history have envisioned a society in which scarcity would not exist. All wants and needs of each member would be provided for freely. Bearing in mind the meaning of scarcity, what would be required for such a society to exist?

3. We often hear economists discuss their graphs in terms of negative or positive relationships. For example, the demand curve demonstrates a negative relationship and the supply curve a positive relationship. What are they relating? Why is it positive or negative?

4. Over the past half century per capita income in the United States has been rising fairly steadily. Does this imply an end to scarcity in America in the future? Explain.

ANSWERS TO REVIEW QUESTIONS

Answers to PROBLEMS AND EXERCISES

1. Opportunity Cost -- Case I: $5.00   Case II: $5.00
$5.00 and $5.00. In the first case the cost of taking the ten is paying $5.00 - pretty straightforward. In the second case the cost is not as clear, but you must forgo taking the $5.00 bill (clearly the highest forgone alternative) when you choose the $10.00. A common answer to the second question is zero, because people think they gave up nothing and gained $10.00. This is an incorrect understanding of opportunity cost, because in fact you gave up the $5.00 bill.

Change in wealth -- Case I: $5.00   Case II: $10.00

2. a. 100 bushels of wheat
    b. 100 bushels of wheat
    c. 40 bushels of corn + $40.00; and 100 bushels of wheat
    d. $100.00 for the 100 bushels of wheat
    e. Either. Old Macdonald's cost is the same either way.

3. Answers will vary for these items, but keep the definitions of a good and of scarcity in mind. For me **economics lectures** are not scarce. Although at one point I paid a lot of money to sit in class, right now I would not pay to attend. Well, I might. But for this example suppose I would not. For you, however, they are a good and they are almost certainly scarce, since you are paying for the lectures you now attend (in your time or money).

   Lawyers are a difficult one. They are a good, because I have had need of lawyers in the past. But they are not currently scarce. For society as a whole lawyer's service are certainly in demand and therefore are a good. They are also scarce because if they offered their services for free, there would not be enough lawyers to serve everyone's needs or wants. Some people may argue that its only **honest lawyers** that are scarce.

4. a. Normative - the statement implies that people **ought** to have a greater sense of community and morality, and that the loss of this unmeasurable sense has resulted in a failure to help.
b. Positive - this statement asserts a refutable proposition that homelessness **is** a result of hospitals having insufficient funds to support and house all former patients. It may be right or it may be wrong. It may need further substantiation, but it is a statement of the way things are rather than ought to be.
c. Positive - Again this statement asserts a direct link between the information gathered from homeless people about the reasons they are homeless. It asserts that homeless people **are** homeless because of increasing layoffs from jobs over the last six years.
d. Normative - This statement clearly suggests what people **ought** to do and is therefore a value judgement.

5. C = correlation N = no relation → = direction of causality
a.   C: lung cancer ← smoking
b.   N: the sighting of Elvis_____ the advent of world peace
c.   C: the warmer temperatures of spring → the renewal of the growing cycle
d.   C: the number of people who drive while under the influence of alcohol ← severe drunk driving penalties

e.   C: consuming more calories than your body can burn → gaining weight

f.   C: crime ← poverty

g.   N: extreme wealth_____happiness

h.   C: lack of education ⇄ poverty

i.   C: burning your hand ← putting your hand in a fire

j.   N: the use of computers_____ quality writing
          (this is debateable)

k.   C: foreign car sales → domestic car makers' profit

6. Postulates in italics, (A in brackets, O outside brackets) *Scarcity is a condition of the natural world.(1) All living creatures must struggle and compete to maintain life against their own species, against other species - either predatory or those which compete for the same sources of sustenance - and with the physical conditions of life.(2)* [A species possessing some variation in physical or mental attribute which is advantageous to the maintenance of its life] will have a greater probability of surviving and procreating. *According to the principles of genetic inheritance, species attributes will be passed along through subsequent generations of offspring.(3)* [If a species possesses an attribute that gives it an advantage], then that attribute will be passed along through the offspring and help ensure the survival of the species over time.

7.

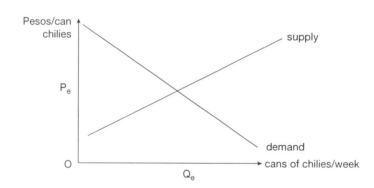

8.   a. slope = $\frac{\$14 - \$12}{2 - 4} = \frac{2}{-2} = -1$

      b. p-intercept = 16; q-intercept = 16

One way to solve this is by putting values for p and q into the equation of a line y = mx + b or in this case p = mq + b, where b is the p-intercept (y-intercept) and m is the slope.

$$14 = (-1)2 + b$$
$$14 = -2 + b$$
$$16 = b$$

Once you have the equation, then replace p with 0 to get the q-intercept.

$$p = (-1)q + 16$$
$$0 = (-1)q + 16$$
$$(1)q = 16$$
$$q = 16$$

      c. p = -q + 16

d.

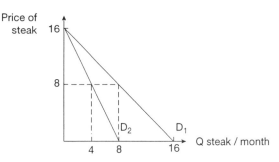

e. slope = $\dfrac{\$14 - 12}{1 - 2} = \dfrac{2}{-1} = -2$

f. $p = -2q + 16$

g. p-intercept = 16   q-intercept = 8

      $p = mq + b$ $p = mq + b$

      $14 = (-2)1 + b$ $p = (-2)q + 16$

      $14 = -2 + b$ $0 = (-2)q + 16$

      $16 = b$ $2q = 16$

                        $q = 8$

Answers to TRUE - FALSE QUESTIONS

1. True. Simultaneous occurrence does not necessarily imply causal relationship (See Silberberg p.12). For example, every time I have left the country for more than six months the St. Louis Cardinals have played in the World Series. Clearly my leaving the country does not cause St. Louis' baseball success.

2. True. Scarcity is a condition that exists when excess demand exists at a price of zero (if given away free, quantity demanded would exceed quantity supplied). It implies enough cannot be produced or found in nature to satisfy everyone who wants some. In this view if the supply of a good were to decrease (or the demand to increase) then the unmet demand of the world's population would increase and therefore that good would be considered more scarce.

3. False. Scarcity exists as a basic condition all humans face. Various goods may be more or less scarce in certain countries or settings, such as water in the desert versus the rain forest, electric garage door openers in the U.S. versus in Mongolia.

4. True. A theory is constructed of only those postulates, propositions and variables that the theorist believes are necessary to explain the predicted event. The theory making process is one of eliminating and holding constant unnecessary or potentially confusing real world phenomena so that the theorist can test specific parts of the theory. It is not the real world.

5. False. Since a good is anything that humans find useful then it would hold that all three of these stands of old growth forest would be considered goods, even the inaccessible one.

6. True. Our behavioral postulates, the foundations of economic theory which operate from supply and demand, stem from scarcity and choice.

7. True. See above.

8. True. See above.

9. True. See above.

10. False. Individual actions may not conform to the theories of supply and demand. The theories are generalizations about behavior that provide a foundation for making predictions about the behavior of individuals.

Answers to MULTIPLE CHOICE QUESTIONS

1. b	6. c	11. d
2. d	7. d	12. a
3. b	8. d	
4. d	9. c	
5. a	10. d	

Answers to SHORT ANSWER QUESTIONS

1. Two or three points and massive humiliation. Yes.

2. This utopian society would require a world in which resources were unlimited, so that resources would exceed the demand by the consumers of those resources. Alternatively, consumers' wants would have to become limited, thus changing what according to all historical evidence is basic human nature.

3. The curves of a graph show the relationship between the two variables measured on the horizontal and vertical axes. It is positive when the change in the value of the variables is in the same direction and negative when the change in the value of the variables is in opposite directions. So if the variable on the vertical axis gets larger, say from 3 to 5 (a change of +2), then this causes the variable on the horizontal axis to change. For the relationship to be positive the value of the horizontal variable would have to change in the same direction, say from 20 to 30 (+10). The identical sign (+ or -) for the direction of change in both variables indicates a positive relationship. A negative relationship would be if the horizontal variable changed from 20 to 10 (-10) when the vertical variable changed from 3 to 5 (+2). The opposite signs indicate a negative relationship.

4. No. Scarcity is a condition that will exist regardless of per capita income, because it is based on the fact that supplies of resources relative to demand for those resources is small. The ability to pay for things does not eliminate the existence of the underlying condition. VCR's may not be that scarce anymore if most people already have one per TV, but CD Rom players and high definition TV's are.

SUPPLEMENT ON GRAPHS
Part I: The Basics

THE NATURE AND PARTS OF GRAPHS

Graphs are pictorial representations of information and of relationships between variables you want to measure and understand. You use similar pictorial and visual representations every day: the arrow on a road sign, the map of stores in a shopping mall, or the fuel gauge in your car. Each of these things conveys with visual images or pictures some kind of information. For example, you are low on gas, or you are on the opposite side of the shopping mall from the store you are seeking.

Because graphs are drawn on paper they are limited in what can be represented. At best they can depict three dimensions clearly (Fig. 1). For this course, however, graphs are only drawn in two dimensions (Fig. 2) with a horizontal axis and a vertical axis, though more advanced economic analysis might use the third dimension.

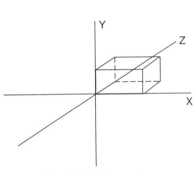

Fig. 1 Three Dimension

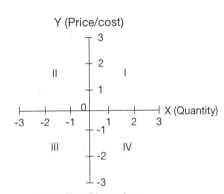

Fig. 2 Two Dimensions

The point in the middle where the axes cross is called the origin and is frequently marked with the letter O. If the axes are to be used for counting or numerical measurements -- which they almost always are -- then the origin is 0 (zero) and the numbers count outward along the axes with positive numbers to the right and upward, and negative numbers to the left and downwards (Fig. 2 above).

Economics is interested, virtually without exception, in the relationships of **positive** quantities of goods being supplied or demanded and the **positive** prices or costs of those goods. If you think about it, it doesn't make sense to talk about some good with a negative price; or producing a negative quantity of something. Therefore, economics graphs all appear in quadrant I, where both axes represent positive numbers (Fig. 2).

To understand the information of a graph and the relationship depicted, the axes must be assigned and labelled. Standard practice is to assign the quantity of a good, or workers, or whatever you're measuring to the horizontal axis and price or cost of that good, those workers (which would be wages), or whatever else to the vertical axis. Often these are quickly labelled Q for quantity and P for price. To be accurate, however, quantities and prices always come in measured units and these units should appear on the graph. In economics quantities are usually measured as a physical unit per unit of time, for example, pizzas per week, movies per month, or kilowatts per hour. Prices are measured as monetary units per physical unit or unit of time, for example, dollars per pizza, Yen per hour (as in wages), or dollars per kilowatt.

The first rule of reading graphs is to always check the axes for their assignment and label so you know what is presented by the graph. You should also check the units being used to measure quantity and price. If you are drawing the graph, you should consider the size and kind of units that would best convey your information. Will a simple Q and P suffice? Or would it be better to provide a short descriptive title such as "Income in thousands of US $" or "deli's per city block"? Be attentive to labelling because it can mislead you or your reader if it is not clear and accurate.

Exercise 1. Assign and label the axes to convey the relationships below. You will have to supply the appropriate units for measurement:

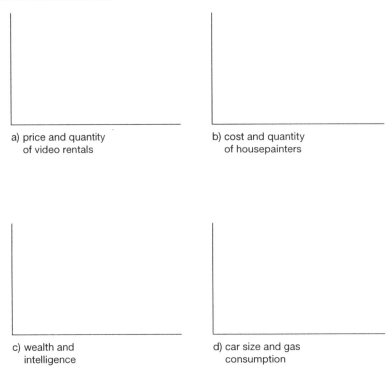

a) price and quantity
   of video rentals

b) cost and quantity
   of housepainters

c) wealth and
   intelligence

d) car size and gas
   consumption

RELATIONSHIPS

Because of the limits of a two dimensional (horizontal and vertical) graph, we are limited in what we can graph to points, lines, and areas. Each of these reveals something about the relationship between the variables presented on the axes. The meaning of the points, lines and areas of a graph are found on two different levels but both levels depend on the information contained on the axes. The first is the units and labels measured on the axes. A point out in the middle of the space indicates that there is some relation between whatever is assigned to the vertical and horizontal axes. It could be the number of computers purchased (from the horizontal axis) at a given price (from the vertical axis).

Each point represents a separate observation of the relationship between, in this case, the prices charged for computers and the quantities of computers purchased at each of those prices for a consumer or a company or some other group of purchasers. For the person making the graph, the numerical values of computers and prices would be determined beforehand and generally recorded in a table of data then transferred to the graph (Figure 3). For the graph reader, in Figure 4 they would look from the point to the axes to determine the numerical values represented by the point.

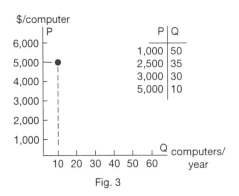

Fig. 3

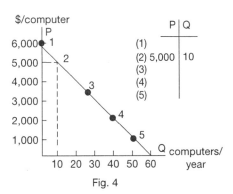

Fig. 4

Exercise 2. Finish entering the data from the table onto the graph in Fig. 3. Interpret the points from the graph in Fig. 4 and record the prices and quantities suggested into the table.

If we have enough points (two at a minimum) we can fit or draw a line to represent the points in a more continuous and general way. A line, or curve as lines on graphs are often called, allows the user of a graph to examine and predict potential relationships between the variables assigned and measured on the axes. For example in Fig. 3 above, we don't have any data on how many computers the consumer would buy if the price were $4000. If you fit a line (as in Fig. 4) linking up the data points that we do have, however, you can estimate a best guess by eye-balling across from $4000 on the Price axis to the line, then down from the line to the numbers on the Quantity axis. In this case you should estimate that this company would buy 20 computers if the price were $4000.

The second level of meaning comes from the variety of ways the variables on the axes are related. Generally, this level of understanding is achieved by observing the direction, shape and steepness of the curves and by comparing a section of a curve to another section, or one curve to a second, third or even fourth curve all on the same graph. For example, the following diagrams (Fig. 5) are all graphs that you will see in this course. What each curve represents is not important right now. For now focus your attention on the variety of shapes you see (straight, bending, etc.), and how flat (horizontal) or steep (vertical) sections of lines or entire lines are. Notice how some of the curves begin higher on the left and move downward to the bottom right, while others do the opposite and some do both or neither. Notice also how your perception of the direction, shape or steepness of the curves is dependent on the axes. The axes are your guide to knowing what is straight and what isn't, what is steep and what isn't. It takes a standard to make meaningful comparisons and measurements. Also remember, the lines are continuous representations of points of data and that each point has a numerical or other value that can be determined by reading across or down to the axes.

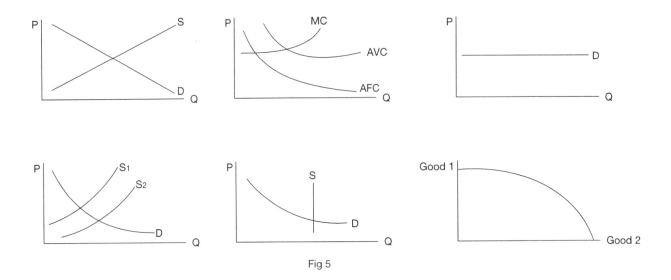

Fig 5

SLOPE

Aside from the axes, the key to understanding the meaning contained in the direction, shape and steepness of the curves is in your ability to understand *slope*. Slope is the measurement of these properties of a line. Slopes come in positive, negative or neutral (zero) directions and in an infinite number of steepnesses between flat (horizontal) and straight up (vertical). All lines have slopes. Generally, slope is a measurement of change. More specifically it is a measurement of change in vertical distance compared to a change in horizontal distance; or how far we move up or down the vertical axis for a given movement along the horizontal axis.

Fig. 6   Fig. 7

To see what this means, imagine that you are standing on flat ground, and you take two steps forward. We draw a line connecting where you are to where you were as in Fig. 6. How would you describe this line? Since the ground is flat, we could say the line is horizontal and it is two steps long. But what is its slope? Leave the first line there for a minute and go back to your starting point. Imagine that there is now a set of steps before you, and you again take two steps forward, but this time for each step you move both forward and upward. Again draw the line from where you are to where you were as in Fig. 7. How would you describe this line? It's not flat like the first one but you did move forward two steps, just as far as with the first line. Given that we are working in only two dimensions or on two axes (horizontal and vertical) we can say that in the first case you moved horizontally two steps and vertically zero steps (2,0). In the second case, you moved two horizontally and two vertically or (2,2).

Now, to figure out the slope you want to compare the vertical change to the horizontal change. Mathematically, this is represented by the following symbols:

$$\text{Slope} = \frac{\Delta Y}{\Delta X} = \frac{\text{Rise}}{\text{Run}} \qquad \text{(Eq. 1)}$$

The Δ is the greek letter delta and is the symbol for change. Y is the letter used to represent the vertical axis and X the horizontal. This formula could be spoken as "delta Y over delta X" or "the change in Y divided by the change in X". The formula for slope is also often described as measuring the rise over the run. In the first case above your rise (vertical change) was zero and your run (horizontal change) was two steps. So you have zero divided by two, which is zero - a slope of zero is a flat line. In the second case your rise was two steps compared to your run of two steps: two divided by two equals one.

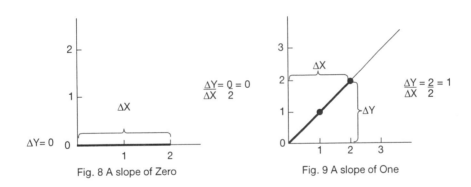

Fig. 8 A slope of Zero   Fig. 9 A slope of One

What does that tell us? At this point not much because you are just out there walking up and down stairs. Like most things they are only meaningful in a context, such as when the MEGAGIANT Food Corporation wants to know how high they can actually raise their cereal prices before consumers balk and their revenues fall. Or more appropriately for now, when you have the price per box of cereal on the vertical axis and the quantity of boxes per year purchased by Sarah Smile on the horizontal axis and you want to predict Sarah's reaction to an increase in cereal prices.

We can, however, tell a few things from a slope just by looking at it, regardless of context. First of all, the more vertical the line, the farther the slope is from zero and the more horizontal the line, the closer the slope is to zero. Think about this. Since slope is a ratio or a comparison of change in the vertical dimension to change in the horizontal dimension, the larger the numerator relative to the denominator the larger the outcome and the larger the slope. If for every one foot forward you stepped horizontally, you rose 100 vertical feet, that is a pretty steep slope (100/1 = 100). Conversely, the larger the denominator relative to the numerator, the smaller or the closer to zero the outcome will be. If for every 100 feet you move forward you only rise one vertical foot, then that is a pretty flat slope (1/100 = .01).

Second, lines have direction. They either move in a positive, negative or neutral direction. In this last example you rose 100 positive feet for every one positive step forward. If you fell 100 feet for every one step forward the slope would be negative since the change in your vertical dimension was -100 feet (-100/1 = -100). So just by looking at slope figures you can judge roughly if it is a steep or flat line and if it is moving in a positive or negative direction.

Exercise 3. Calculate the slopes of the lines in graphs a and b below. In graphs c and d number the axes and draw a line that represents the given slope.

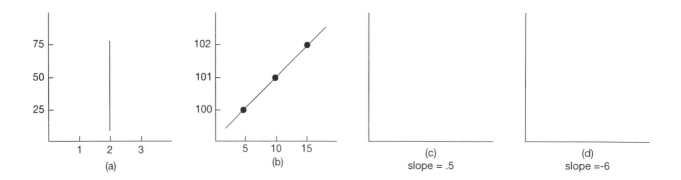

The two extreme cases of lines are the line with a slope of zero and a line with an infinite slope. In both of these cases what is happening is that no matter what the change in one of the variables (on one of the axes) there is no change in the other (i.e. a zero change for delta Y or delta X). For example, if we put the price per pound of lard on the Y (vertical) axis and the quantity of guitar strings purchased per week on the X (horizontal) axis, it is highly unlikely a change in the price of lard would affect guitar players' decisions to purchase guitar strings, unless the guitar player is a starving artist who lives on lard sandwiches. Therefore you could see a large ΔY and a ΔX of zero. Because the denominator would equal zero, the formula would yield a result of infinity - a vertical line with an infinite slope.

Earlier we said that a graph is a pictorial representation of a relationship between what is assigned to the vertical and horizontal axes. In both the case of a zero and an infinite slope the relationship demonstrated is no relationship; no matter how much one variable changes the other does not change. The variables are *independent* of each other. In all other cases whether the slope is -2,000,000 or 1, there is a relationship between the two variables. This relationship is usually referred to as a *direct relationship*, meaning that if you change one of the variables, you will see a change in the other one.

CURVED LINES

As you can see from the graphs above in Fig. 5, economics relies heavily on curved lines. Curved lines also have slopes. The difference is that straight lines have a constant slope. No matter where on the line you decide to measure the vertical and horizontal changes the ratio will always be the same - constant. If it is not the same then it is not a straight line. On a curve this is not the case. The slope changes at every point along a curve. Look at Fig. 10(a) below and notice how the upper reaches of the curve (around point a) are steeper than the lower sections (around points b and c). Also note how the direction of the slope changes from negative at point a, to zero at point b, and to positive at point c.

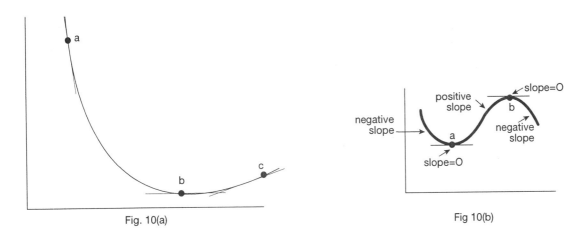

Fig. 10(a)

Fig 10(b)

There is a way, however, to get an approximation of the slope of a curved line by using straight lines tangent to the curve at the chosen point. Recall that a tangent line touches a curve (or is tangent to the curve) at a single point, as the tangent lines touch the curve at points a, b, and c in Figs. 10(a) and 10(b). For each point on a curve there is only one tangent line, therefore to measure the slope of the tangent line is to measure the slope of the curve at the point of tangency.

One important use of this knowledge about slope and tangent is that at the point where a curve bottoms out or peaks before beginning to rise or fall (points a and b in Fig 10(b)), the slope at that point is zero. Both tangent lines are completely flat at these points. As you know the slope of a flat line is zero. Keep this in mind as you move through the course. Also keep in mind that it is also at this zero-slope point that the curve's slope changes from positive to negative or vice versa.

We can eyeball or draw tangents to curves to estimate the steepness and confirm the direction of the slope, but to determine the slope exactly we must use calculus, which is not part of this course. You will notice that Silberberg will occasionally make reference to curves and calculus in the footnotes of his text.

Part II: More on Graphs and Some Other Things You Should Know

NUMBERS, EQUATIONS AND GRAPHS

From which of the following do you understand or learn the most? Which means the most to you?

a) $y = -2x + 12$
or $P = -2Q + 12$

b)

x	y
1	10
2	8
3	6
4	4
5	2

c)

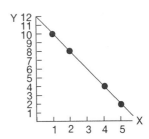

Most people say the graph in c). Each of these three, however, are representations of the same relationship and information. a) is an algebraic equation expressing a relationship between the variables x and y. b) is the same relationship in the form of a table of data and, of course, c) is a pictoral or graphic representation. They each have advantages and disadvantages and they each have a function.

Throughout the course you will be working with all three of these forms: numbers, equations and graphs. You must be able to work with any of these forms, and be able to move fluently from one form to the other, to the third and back again. Specifically you must be able to *derive* either of the other two forms when given the third. If the problem contains tables of data you'll need to be able to convert that data into an equation or into a graph. All three represent the same information or at a minimum the same relationship between the two variables you are analyzing.

An important part of being able to use and create all three is determining slopes. The algebraic equation in a) is the equation of a line. The basic form of an equation of a line is y = mx + b. Y and x are variables, m is the slope and b is the Y-intercept.[1] The slope as discussed above is the change in the vertical dimension compared to the change in the horizontal dimension (rise over run). This can be calculated using the following equation,

$$m = \frac{y2 - y1}{x2 - x1} . \qquad \text{(Eq. 2)}$$

When given an equation for a line, we will not immediately know what the points y2, y1 and x2, x1 are, but if we manipulate the equation so that it takes the form y = mx + b, we know that the number before the x (called a coefficient) is the slope. Thus, in the equation above y = -2x + 12 we know that the slope is -2. Otherwise we can enter numbers for x (or y) into the equation arriving at values for y (or x) and converting the equation into a table of numbers. For example, we enter 1 for x,

$$y = -2(1) + 12$$
$$y = -2 + 12$$
$$y = 10$$

Our table thus begins to take shape x   y, and we can continue to
                                      1   10
enter values for x (2, 3, 4, ...) to solve for y until the table is reasonably full as in b) above. From the table of numbers calculating the slope is simple arithmetic. Pick any two sets of values for x and y then put them into their respective places in the equation for slope (equation 2).

m = 6 - 8 which equals m = -2 or m = -2.
    3 - 2   1

Remember to assign the later set of values for x and y to x2 and y2 and the earlier set of values in the table to x1 and y1 as follows:

---

[1] A variable is a symbol, such as the letters x and y, P and Q, that represents any actual number you wish to put in its place. They are called variables because their value *varies* as you substitute actual quantities (numbers) in for them while working with the data and the equation. M and b are symbols representing numbers that, once calculated for a given set of data, will not change, such as the slope of a straight line and the point at which that line crosses the Y or X axis. These fixed numbers are called constants.

$$
\begin{array}{cc}
\underline{\text{x}} & \underline{\text{y}} \\
1 & 10 \\
\text{x1} = 2 & 8 = \text{y1} \\
\text{x2} = 3 & 6 = \text{y2}
\end{array}
$$

The y-intercept, or b in the equation, is the value of y when the value of x is zero. Likewise the x-intercept would be the value of x when the value of y is zero. On a graph the y-intercept is the point where the line (or the curve) in the graph touches or crosses the vertical axis. At this point you are at zero on the horizontal axis and some number on the vertical axis. In the graph above in c) this is the point (0,12). In the equation this can be calculated by putting zero in for x and seeing what y is.

$$y = -2(0) + 12$$
$$y = 12$$

From a table of data it may be a little more difficult to determine the y-intercept if it is not already given. For a linear equation (a straight line) you may be able to figure it out simply by using the slope. In our example, with a slope of -2, an increase of one in the value of x results in a decrease of two in the value of y. This indicates that by decreasing the value of x from 1 to 0, we would see an increase in the y value from 10 to 12 (see Fig. 11).

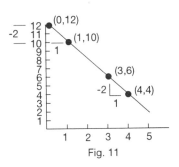

Fig. 11

To be certain, or if you can't figure it out this way, another solution requires entering one set of values for x and y (for example in our case x = 1 and y = 10) and the slope (-2) into the basic algebraic equation for a line then solving for b.

$$y = mx + b$$
$$10 = -2(1) + b$$
$$10 = -2 + b$$
$$12 = b$$

DEPENDENT AND INDEPENDENT VARIABLES

As mentioned, a dependent variable is a variable that *depends* on the value of another variable for its own value. An independent variable does not. It is assigned a value, specifically to determine what the resulting dependent variable's value will be. The two are causally related. Most frequently this relationship is expressed in equation form, such as the following example.

$$y = 4x + 3$$

The custom with equations in mathematics, science, economics, etc. is that the variable on the left-hand side of the equal sign is the dependent variable and the variable on the right-hand side is the independent variable. In equation 1 therefore, y is the dependent variable and x is the independent. Indeed, if you want to know the value of y, you have to plug in some values for x. Of course if you want to know the value of x you can simply plug in some values for y too. The difference is that you would have to manipulate everything from the right-hand side to the left-hand side to isolate x. The equation, because of custom, is set up to produce values of y given changing values of x.

This custom carries over into graphing as well. The dependent variable (the left-hand side of the equation) always goes on the vertical axis and the independent (the right-hand side of the equation) on the horizontal. When you calculate the slope of a line what you are measuring is for a given change in x how much does y change. This is contained in the formula for slope $\Delta Y/\Delta X$.

Occasionally you will get, however, or want to use, the equation of a line in the form: $x = 1/m*y + b/m$, with the variable on the horizontal-axis written on the left hand side. This equation is identical to $y = mx + b$, but must be interpreted differently. $1/m$ is now the inverse slope, and b/m is the horizontal-axis intercept, the value of x when y is equal to 0.

For example, in Chapter 2 Silberg introduces and discusses dependent and independent variables with respect to demand curves versus marginal value curves (pp. 48-49). He states that when price is the independent variable and quantity the dependent variable the curve is a demand curve. When the reverse is true the curve is interpreted as a marginal value curve.

As you can see moving between a table of numbers, an algebraic equation and a graph requires you to frequently borrow from a basic set of mathematical knowledge, such as the equation of a line and the formula for slope. Being able to move fluently among the three forms will not only help your grade but it will also equip you to better understand the concepts behind the mathematical manipulations you will encounter throughout the course.

SOLVING SIMULTANEOUS EQUATIONS

Economists are concerned with equilibrium prices and quantities in markets -- meaning a point of equality or balance. Specifically, economists are interested in what values of the price and quantity variables simultaneously satisfy the demand and supply equations; thus making them equal at that value. Visually the point of equilibrium is the point on both lines, or where supply and demand curves cross.

Anytime you have two equations, such as Q = 12 - P and Q = 2P, a value of P and Q can be found that makes the two equations equal. (To solve for three variables you would need three equations, because two equations cannot intersect in three dimensions. The rule is to have as many equations as there are unknown variables).

Two equations can be solved simultaneously in a couple of ways. One way is simply to set the two equal, and solve first for the one remaining variable, then for the other. In the equations above, since both of the right-hand sides are equal to Q, we can set them equal to each other:

$$12 - P = 2P$$
$$3P = 12$$
$$P = 4.$$

Now substitute the value for the first variable, P, into either original equation, and solve for the second:

$$Q = 12 - (4)$$
$$Q = 8.$$

A second, similar method is to substitute one equation into the other. This requires having at least one variable isolated in one of the equations. For example, if the supply equation above was written $P = .5Q$, this equation could be sustituted into the demand equation producing: $Q = 12 - (.5Q)$. Solving for Q yields $1.5Q = 12$, $Q = 8$. Substituting $Q = 8$ back into either original equation produces $P = 4$. Use the method that you are most comfortable with, or that is easiest given the structure of the question.

AREAS UNDER CURVES AND UNITS OF MEASUREMENT

A graph depicts the relationship between the two variables assigned and measured on the vertical and horizontal axes. This relationship is described in terms of the units of measurement provided on the axes and in the axes' labels. 6,000,000 barrels of oil per year at $17.50 per barrel - that is a relationship of quantity consumed or produced at a given price. Information of this sort is portrayed by a point or a line (a collection of points) within the axes of a graph. As you learned in Chapter 2, however, there is more to graphs than just points and lines. For example, to measure total expenditure, total value and consumers surplus you need to look at the area beneath and between the curves or lines.

To find the exact area under a curve requires calculus, which you will not be using in this course. What you must know, however, is how to calculate the areas under lines (straight lines). With only rare exceptions, you will be running into areas that can be broken down into rectangles and triangles. The formulas for calculating areas are:

1/2 base x height for triangles, and
base x height for rectangles.

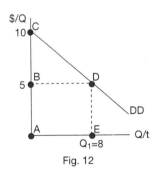

Fig. 12

In Fig. 12, the area of triangle BCD is one-half the base dimension of 8 times the height of 5.

$$1/2(8) \times 5 = \text{area}$$
$$4 \times 5 = 20$$

The area of the rectangle ABDE in Figure 1 is base x height or, $8 \times 5 = 40$. Thus, the total area under the line DD up to quantity Q_1 is $20 + 40 = 60$.

Exercise 4 Calculate the areas of the shaded portions of the figures below.

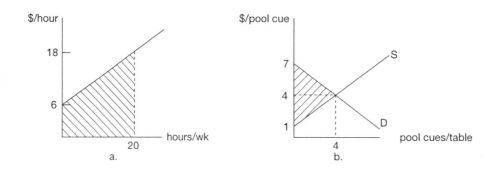

a.   b.

The question now from the example above is 60 whats; what are the units of measurement for an area? What are the units of total revenues, total value, consumers' surplus? The answer is contained in knowing that measurements made and the units provided on a graph are nearly always a rate. One unit of measurement is given *relative* to some other unit of measurement. Thus, we do not measure sales of oil at just $17.50; it is $17.50 *per* barrel. Likewise, we do not measure our consumption of oil without some reference to the amount of time it took us to consume that amount: 6,000,000 barrels *per* year. Nearly everything is measured *per* something else. Therefore, on a graph, regardless of what you might see - for example, just a P for price and a Q for quantity - the labels nearly always represent a rate. In general these are monetary unit per unit of physical quantity ($/Q) or unit of time ($/t) for the price axis, and physical quantity unit per unit of time (Q/t) for the quantity axis.

Suppose then that we have $/Q (dollars per quantity) on the vertical axis and Q/t (quantity per time) on the horizontal. Or to make it more real $/movie ticket on the price axis and movie tickets/month on the quantity axis. A data point representing the relationship between our two variables would bring together the units of both axes, $5.00/ticket and 8 tickets/month. But what if you want to know how much you spend on movies each month, that is your total expenditures on movies per month? Well, that is $5.00 per ticket x 8 tickets each month. That equals $40/month on tickets. This would indicate that the units of measurement for total expenditures - the area ABDE under the line in Fig. 12 - is dollars per month or monetary unit per unit of time ($/t). What is happening there is that when you multiply the base dimension, 8 tickets per month, times the height dimension, $5.00 per ticket, you are effectively multiplying 8 x 5 to get 40 and you are multiplying

$$\frac{\text{tickets}}{\text{month}} \cdot \frac{\text{dollars}}{\text{ticket}}$$

The "tickets" in the numerator and denominator of these two expressions when multiplied together cancel each other out and you are left with dollars/month.

UNITS AND SLOPE

Before leaving units of measurement, when visually evaluating the slope of a line always check the units marked on the axes. In many cases a line that appears to have a steep slope or gradual slope may not. This is usually due to the magnitude of the units measured on the horizontal and vertical axes. For example, in Fig. 13 there are two positively sloped lines that appear to have the same slope. Closer examination of the units on the axes reveals that in (a) price is measured in 10 cent increments and quantity by the hundreds, while in (b) price is measured in 10 dollar increments and quantity by ones.

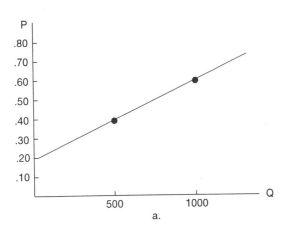 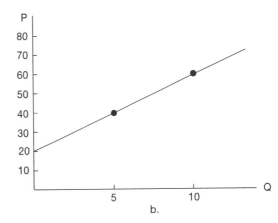

The slopes of the two lines are:

a) $\dfrac{.2}{500} = .0004$

b) $\dfrac{20}{5} = 4$

If you turn to pages 21 and 22 in Silberberg you should now be better able to intuitively understand the demand and supply curves. Are they positively or negatively sloped? Is either of the curves' slopes zero or infinity? What does all this mean about the relationship between Quantity and Price for each curve? What do the areas of the curves mean? On the demand curve a positive change in quantity results in what kind of change for price? Now reread Silberberg's description on pages 21 and 22.

Finally you will observe that there are frequently letter symbols instead of numbers on the axes in the diagrams. This is an abstraction, or a representation of reality, that allows us to work at a general level. Rather than providing a specific example of real prices and quantities using dollar values, etc., the P_1s and Q_2s and so forth can stand for any numbers that fit the general relationship indicated by their position on the graph. For example, we would not accept that q_2 is a smaller number than q_1 if q_2 is farther from the origin along the axis of the graph than q_1. Just as we would not accept that four tons of mustard is less than two tons. The use of letter symbols is not just to make things complicated or to appear more important, they are used to portray a concept or relationship at a general level so people don't get bogged down in specific numbers or examples. The alphabet, numbers, mathematics these are all abstract symbolic representations of spoken or otherwise understood ideas; some are just more familiar than others. Economics uses a fairly small set of such symbols at this level, and fairly frequently. But you will see that there is a consistency in which ones are used and how they are used.

ANSWERS TO SUPPLEMENT EXERCISES

Exercise 1.

Exercise 2.

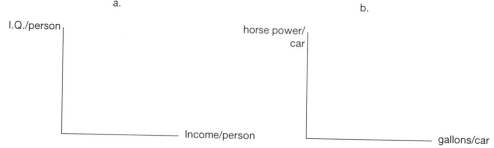

Exercise 3. a. slope = 25/0 = ∞   b. slope = 1/5 = .2

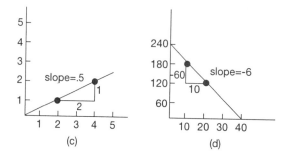

Exercise 4.

a. Total Area = 240 dollars per week

Upper triangle: = 1/2(20) x (18-6)   lower rectangle: = 20 x 6
                   = 10 x 12   = 120
                   = 120

b. Total Area = 12 dollars per table

Triangle: = 1/2(7 - 1) x 4
             = 3 x 4
             = 12

PROBLEMS AND EXERCISES
Graphs

Answers to all questions appear at the end of this supplement. Write your answer(s) in the space provided.

1. Create a table of data from the following graph. Calculate the slope of the line and describe the relationship between Q/t and $/Q in an algebraic equation.

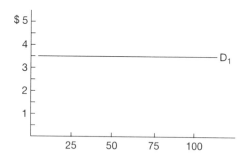

2. Draw a graph to represent the data in the following table. Put P on the vertical axis. Calculate the slope of the line and write an equation describing the relationship between P and Q.

P 1 2 3 4 5
Q 2 4 6 8 10

3. Graph (sketch) the relationship between the following pairs of variables. Be attentive to the slopes. Do you anticipate positive or negative, big or small changes? Indicate clearly which variable is represented on which axis.

a. The proportion of seniors in a community and the number of heavy metal compact discs purchased.
b. The price of wheat and the price of a dozen bagels.
c. The number of car chase scenes in a movie and the number of people who buy tickets and see the movie.
d. The starting salaries for lawyers and the number of students who choose to go to law school.

e. U.S. environmental policy and the attendance at major league baseball games.
f. The unemployment rate and the incidence of property crime.

a. Seniors & Heavy Metal

b. Wheat & Bagel Prices

c. Car Chases & Tickets

d. Salary & Law Students

e. Env. Pol. & MLB

f. Unemployment & Crime

4. Between line A and line B in the graph below, which one implies a greater change in Quantity for an equal change in Price? Which line has the greater slope? _____ and _____.

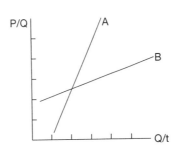

5. Between line A and line B in the graph below, which one implies a greater change in Quantity for

an equal change in Price? Which line has the greater slope? _____ and _____

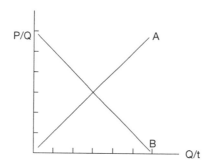

6. What is the slope of a line that is half way between zero and infinity (that is between being horizontal and vertical)? _____

7. The graph on the left has a slope of 100 the graph on the right has a slope of .001. How is this possible given that the graphs appear identical? Show your solution on the graphs.

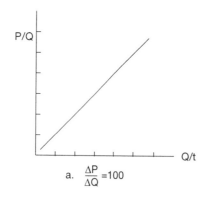

a. $\frac{\Delta P}{\Delta Q}$ =100

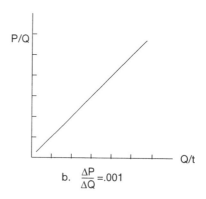

b. $\frac{\Delta P}{\Delta Q}$ =.001

8. Rank the following slopes from the steepest to the flattest.
a.   delta Y = 457, delta X = 456
b.   delta Y = -10, delta X = .25
c.   delta Y = 39, delta X = 1
d.   delta Y = 1, delta X = 0

9. What is the slope of the line Y = X?
    What is its Y-intercept?

10. Calculate or otherwise determine the p-intercept of this line.

P	23	19	15	11	7
Q	2	4	5	6	8

11. Determine an appropriate label (physical, monetary, time, or other units) for the axes of graphs depicting relationships between the price and quantities of the following.
a. wild salmon
b. old growth forest
c. computer memory
d. diamonds
e. music

12. Rank the following shaded areas from smallest to largest.

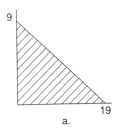

a.

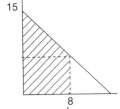

b.

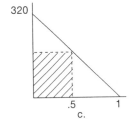

c.

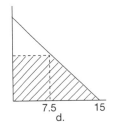

d.

13. At what quantity and price on the graph below is the area greatest?

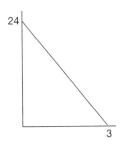

14. Solve the following pairs of simultaneous equations for the two unknown variables:

a. $Y = 2X + 12$
    $Y = 3X$

c. Demand: $Q = 6 - .5P$
    Supply: $Q = P$

b. $R = -.5M$
    $M = 2R + 3$

d. Demand: $Q = 20 - P$
    Supply: $Q = 2 + 2P$

ANSWERS TO PROBLEMS AND EXERCISES
Graphs

1.
$/q	q/t
3.50	25
3.50	100
3.50	∞

The slope of the line is 0, since the change in $/q (the rise) is always 0. There is no relationship between $/q and q/t; $/q is a constant.

2. The slope is 1/2. The equation of the line is P = 2Q. There is no intercept since the curve passes through the origin.

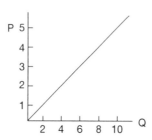

3.

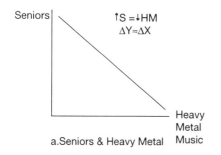

a. Seniors & Heavy Metal Music

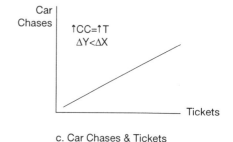

b. Wheat & Bagel Prices

c. Car Chases & Tickets

a. Positive change in seniors leading to approximately equal negative change in heavy metal sales.
b. Positive change in wheat price leading to smaller positive change in bagel prices.
c. Positive change in car chases leading to greater positive change in movie ticket sales.
d. Positive change in lawyer salaries leading to smaller positive change in number of law students.
e. Positive change in amount of environmental policy leading to no change in baseball attendance.
f. Positive change in unemployment rate leading to smaller positive change in crime.

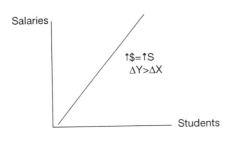

d. Salary & Law Students

e. Env. Pol. & MLB

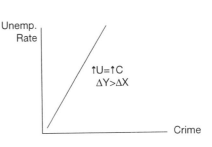

f. Unemployment & Crime

4. B, A

5. same, same

6. one (a forty-five degree line)

7. The units on the axes differ. One solution is in graph a. with slope = 100, the vertical axis is measured in hundreds (i.e. 100, 200, 300, etc.) and the horizontal axis is measured in ones (i.e. 1, 2, 3, etc.); while for b. the vertical axis is marked in hundreths (i.e. .01, .02, .03, etc.) and the horizontal axis in tens (i.e. 10, 20, 30, etc.).

8. d, b, c, a

9. 1, 0 (the origin)

10. When Q = 0, P = 27.

11. a. price per lb. of wild salmon and lbs. of wild salmon per season.
b. price per linear feet of old growth and linear feet of old growth per month.
c. price per megabyte and megabytes per computer life
d. price per caret and carets per purchase
e. chords per sheet and sheets per week.

12. (c), (a), (d), (b)

13. P = 12, Q = 1.5

14.   a. X = 12, Y = 36   c. P = 4, Q = 4
b. R = 2, M = 7   d. P = 6, Q = 14.

CHAPTER 2
The Postulates of Behavior

PRINCIPAL GOALS

1.0 Understand the behavioral postulates' relationship to the refutable propositions. (Objectives 1.1, 1.2)

2.0 Understand value and the difference between total and marginal value. (Objectives 2.1, 2.2, 2.3, 2.4)

3.0 Distinguish between marginal value and demand. (Objectives 3.1, 3.2)

4.0 Recognize the influence of time. (Objectives 4.1, 4.2)

OBJECTIVES
Answers to bold-faced questions appear at the end of the dialogue.

"Where does all my money go? I work 20 hours a week at the Diner, but I'm always broke. Do you think this course will help me balance my budget?"

"I doubt it", Mo said. "That's more like accounting -- a course, by the way, that makes economics seem like a ton of fun. Besides, remember what Silberberg said in chapter 1, economics is not about how to shop wisely (p.4). I don't think it has much to say about the wisdom of you spending every paycheck on CD's. Your parents might, but from my reading, economics just gives us a way to predict how your CD purchases will change if their price changes, or if you lose your job, or if your rent goes up, or...."

"You're right. But let's face it, according to postulate 2 - more CDs are preferred to less."

"Sure, but that includes more food to less food, more education to less education...don't forget Ginny, that scarcity forces us to make choices, and those choices have costs."

"Now you're sounding like my parents. There's never a scarcity of advice."

OBJECTIVE 1.1 Distinguish between the behavioral postulates and refutable propositions.

"There's never a scarcity of people complaining about money either. But let's move on. I understood how these four assertions about choices are the same thing as 'maximizing behaviour', but what confuses me is the difference between postulates and refutable propositions."

"Yes, let's move on," Ginny said. "The behavioral postulates are the foundation of a theory. But we can't get inside someone's head to see these postulates working, we can only make refutable propositions -- statements about observable actions that are based on the underlying assertions or postulates."

"So in essence then, the refutable propositions put the assertions into an observable form. That sounds reasonable, but can you give me an example?"

OBJECTIVE 1.2 Formulate a refutable proposition.

"Sure. Suppose the price of plums rises a lot relative to the price of peaches and knowing that you regularly buy both, I want to predict what you will do. If I could read your mind I might read that you prefer more to less and that you are willing to substitute between plums and peaches."

"But fortunately you can't read my mind."

"Fortunately. So I make a refutable proposition like, 'Mo will buy fewer plums and more peaches when the relative price of plums rises.' I would expect this from someone whose behaviour was governed by our postulates. But in this form, the statement is measurable, because I can observe your actions at the store, and it's refutable -- you could buy more plums. If you do as I predicted, though, and buy fewer plums, then your action is consistent with the underlying assertions, and supports them."

"Okay. And we can only support or confirm our theory, rather than prove it?"

"Yes, because there may be another set of underlying assertions or behavioral postulates that your actions are also consistent with, such as you suddenly associating plums with some unpleasant event -- like visits from your annoying aunt Anita. Maybe you irrationally became convinced that the more plums you ate, the more likely it was that Anita would appear on your doorstep."

"That would definitely curb my appetite for plums, regardless of the price."

"Yes, but it's not exactly rational, and your reduced plum purchasing is for reasons not stemming from our behavioral postulates. Since these postulates are never directly observable, we can't rule out the possibility of some other postulates that would lead to the same type of behaviour."

Question 1. You cannot prove propositions, but you can disprove them. True or False?

OBJECTIVE 2.1 Recognize definitions for important new vocabulary.

"It seems like half of every introductory course in University is about learning a new vocabulary. At least a lot of these terms are familiar from my business courses."

"You're lucky, consumers' surplus hasn't appeared yet in my Chinese history course. You have to be careful, though, that all the terms are used in exactly the same way. That's what makes jargon, jargon: it's a specialized vocabulary."

Question 2. Match the term with its definition(s). Write out definitions for any undefined terms.

a. maximizing behavior
b. substitution
c. value
d. marginal value
e. total value
f. diminishing marginal value
g. consumer surplus

_____ The amount of other goods an individual would be willing to give up in order to obtain an additional unit of a specific good.

_____ The tendency to reduce the impact of constraints or enhance the impact of opportunities.

_____ The amount of other goods an individual would be willing to give up in order to obtain some amount of a specific good rather than getting none of that good whatsoever.

_____ The difference between what an individual pays for a good and the maximum amount he or she would be willing to pay to obtain that good.

_____ The principle that two or more goods may satisfy an individual's wants and that the individual will make trade-offs among all of the available alternatives.

_____ The benefits individuals may receive when they make an exchange to obtain goods.

_____ An expression of preference for a good, observable only during trade for that good and measured in terms of the maximum amount of other goods that an individual is willing to give up to obtain it.

OBJECTIVE 2.2 Give an example of the difference between marginal value and total value.

"Let's try a few problems from Adam's old exam on this marginal and total value idea," Ginny said.

> **Problem:** Why do newspaper dispensers on the street allow you to take as many papers as you want, but soda pop machines only let you take one at a time?

"Well, who would take more than one paper anyway, unless you were planning on selling them? You only read the paper once. But everyone would take as many soft drinks as they could, don't you think?"

"I do," Ginny said. "So in terms of the marginal value of newspapers and soft drinks your marginal value of newspapers falls to zero after the first one."

"Meaning a second newspaper is worthless to you."

"Right, but your marginal value of a second soda is still likely to be positive. Even if you didn't want to drink a second one right away, you can drink it later. So it's more likely people would help themselves to more than one soda, than more than one newspaper."

"O.K., so that's marginal valuation. How about total valuation?" asked Mo.

"I think about the difference between marginal and total value as whether you can buy one unit at a time, or if you have to buy a package of goods, so that it's an all-or-nothing choice. At the Diner, remember, if we want to buy our favorite butterscotch sundae sauce we have to buy a case of four large cans. Jim says he would only buy one every 3 months, but the distributor doesn't sell individual cans. That must mean Jim's marginal value for the second can is below its price, right?"

"That's right, he wouldn't use more than one can, and the upfront expenditure takes away money for other purposes. But Jim has to make an all-or-nothing choice, and he chooses to buy the four cans."

"Apparently his total value of the four cans is still greater than what he actually pays for them -- his total expenditure -- because he buys the case."

"Just in case the postulates don't apply to Jim because he isn't rational, which I've sometimes suspected, let's look at another problem from Adam's exam."

> **Question:** Bill values his first muffin of the day at $1.00, and his second at $.85. Elaine values her first muffin at $.90, and her second at $.65. The bakery charges $.75 per muffin. How many muffins do they sell daily to these two, and what are Bill and Elaine's consumer's surplus on the exchange?

"Ah, a numbers problem. Mo -- Why don't you start?"

"Don't panic," Mo said. "Sometimes these are the easiest types of questions. Just try to group all the relevant information together, like the book does. In this case, I would list for each person, their marginal value of each muffin. Then beside that we can put the price of the muffins."

		BILL				ELAINE	
Q	$MV	Price	CS		$MV	Price	CS
1	1.00	.75	.25		.90	.75	.15
2	.85	.75	.10		.65	.75	
	-----	----	----		----	----	----
	TV=1.85	TE=1.50	CS=.35		TV=$1.55	TE=$.75	CS=$.15

"Now we can see that Bill will buy 2 muffins, because his marginal value ($MV) is above the price of 75 cents for each muffin."

"How did you figure out consumers' surplus?" asked Ginny.

"That's just the difference between their marginal values ($MV) for each muffin, and the muffin's price. For Bill's first muffin it is $.25 ($1.00 - $.75), and for the second muffin it is $0.10 ($.85 - $.75). His total consumer surplus (CS), therefore, is $.25 + $.10 = $.35. His total expenditure (TE) is 2 x $.75 = $1.50. Elaine would only buy one muffin, because her marginal valuation for the second muffin is only $.65, below the price. Her consumer's surplus on that one muffin is $.90 - $.75 = $.15."

"I get it. Let me read the rest of the question."

> **Problem:** One day the bakery stopped selling individual muffins, and only sold muffins in packages of two for $1.50. How many muffins would they sell daily now to Bill and Elaine? Could either of them possibly be worse off since the average price of a muffin is still $.75?

"Ah, I get what they're doing," Ginny said. "Bill and Elaine must now make an all-or-nothing choice."

"Right, so we can't compare the price to their marginal value for individual muffins any more, since muffins are only sold in packages of two."

"Then it's meaningless to ask how much Bill or Elaine are willing to pay for one more muffin. We can only look at their marginal value for two muffins."

"I think you've got the right idea Ginny, but their marginal value for two muffins is their total value. Since their choice is two muffins or nothing, we would look at their total value for two muffins and compare it to $1.50, their total expenditure for two muffins."

	BILL		ELAINE	
Q	$MV	$TV	$MV	$TV
1	1.00	1.00	.90	.90
2	.85	1.85	.65	1.55
	-----	----	----	----
		TV=1.85		TV=$1.55

"Right. So in this case, both Bill and Elaine would buy the package of two muffins because their total value of two muffins exceeds their total expenditure. And surely neither can be worse off since the average price of a muffin is still 75 cents?"

"No, Elaine is worse off having to buy two together than one at a time. Remember that Elaine's marginal value of a second muffin was below 75 cents. So she would not buy the second muffin if she could buy one at a time. Her consumer's surplus having to buy the package is still positive, or she wouldn't have done it. But now it is only $1.55 - $1.50 = $0.05, when before it was $.15."

"But for Bill it shouldn't matter, right?" Ginny asked. "Because he bought two in the first place."

"That's right, his consumer surplus is $1.85 - $1.50 = $.35 regardless of how they package the muffins."

Question 3. Suppose the customers had become angry and the bakery decided to lower the package price. The two muffins would have to be offered at a price of _____ to leave Elaine with the same consumer surplus as when she could buy individual muffins.

Question 4. At this price you would expect Bill's consumer surplus to rise/fall?

* * * * * * *

"This muffin example is making me hungry Ginny. Want to order a pizza?"

"Sure, I'll call Little Cleopatra's. They have a two-for-one deal: 2 pizzas for $11.99."

"They always have that deal on," Mo said. "And I almost always end up buying the two pizzas and spending $11.99. But I would rather have just one pizza for $6.00, an option that's never available."

"This is just like what we've been studying isn't it? The sellers sell more, but we end up with a lower consumer surplus than if we were allowed to buy individual pizzas one at a time for the low average price. I'm surprised that you're so easily manipulated Mo."

"Yes, but what about the CD club you belong to? You get the first seven for nothing, but you have to buy five more at higher than store prices. The average price is lower than the store, but you still have to buy the package."

"Touche. I guess we're still better off, but it's embarrassing that we're not getting as good a deal as we thought. Let's move on while we wait for this consumer-surplus capturing pizza."

"Okay. Oh, you know the diamond water paradox at the end of the chapter? It seems to me that it's really about this marginal value-total value distinction."

OBJECTIVE 2.3 Identify the confusion behind the diamond water paradox.

"I agree," Ginny said. "I asked Silberberg about that and his answer was a history lesson about Adam Smith, David Ricardo and Karl Marx, political economists in the mid- to late-1700s and 1800s. Their work was classical economics, and it was based largely on the value of inputs."

"Inputs?"

"Yes, Silberberg called them the factors of production: essentially the land, labor, capital (machinery), energy and other materials that go into producing things. Well Smith, Ricardo and Marx could apparently explain a lot just by looking at input values, but they couldn't explain why a luxury like diamonds was more expensive than a necessity like water. It wasn't until later, when other economists came along -- Silberberg mentioned these guys Jevons, Walrus, Marshall and Pareto -- that this paradox was really explained. These new guys used what we are now studying, the marginalist approach -- and their theory became known as neoclassical economics. Neo, by the way, means new."

"So", Mo said, "these guys determined that although the marginal value of diamonds may exceed the marginal value of water (meaning how much you would be willing to pay for one more unit of either), the total value of water, given an all-or-nothing choice, would far exceed the total value of diamonds."

"That's right. It seems sort of obvious now, so I guess you had to be there at the time to appreciate what a revelation it was."

"Maybe, but people still confuse total and marginal value judging by the book's labor market examples."

OBJECTIVE 2.4 Give an example of the difference between total value and total expenditure/revenue.

"People also confuse total value and total expenditure," Ginny said. "Do you remember a few years ago when the media reported the Governor of California saying that restricting Mexican farm labor from entering California had raised the value of the crops, and thereby benefited consumers? I remember my Dad saying the Governor didn't know what he was talking about, and now I think I understand my father's point. The Governor confused total value and total revenue."

"How do you mean?" Mo asked.

"Well, the Governor is really talking about farm revenues, not value. Presumably crop prices rose with the loss of the migrant labor. And since there are very few substitutes for the crops, consumers can't just stop buying. So the higher prices mean higher consumer expenditures, and higher farm revenues."

"Sure, because total revenue is the same thing as total expenditure, price times quantity, just from a different perspective. A consumer's total expenditure of $5 on oranges, not counting taxes, is $5 in total revenue for the producer of those oranges. So you're saying the farmers' total revenue and consumer' expenditures increased. That's tough for the consumer, but isn't the farmer better off?"

"Not likely. Their revenues may have risen slightly, but their costs increased by more. Don't you think you'd be more profitable with cheaper rather than more expensive labor?"

"I get your point. So revenue, but not profit, has increased. If prices have risen, wouldn't this imply that the total value of the crop had decreased?"

"Exactly," Ginny said. "The restriction on labor raises costs, and because it's more expensive to produce, farmers decrease output. With every farmer decreasing output, the market price for that crop will rise. Consumers must buy the same amount of output at a higher price, or a smaller amount of output at the same price -- they have not benefitted."

OBJECTIVE 3.2 Recognize definitions for important new vocabulary.

Question 5: Match the term with its definition(s). Write out definitions for any undefined terms.

a. reservation price   b. independent variable
c. dependent variable   d. demand curve
e. marginal value curve   f. ceteris paribus

_____ A fundamental assumption in economics, that other influences are held constant while an assessment is made of the relationship between the variables in question.

_____ That variable in a relationship which changes in response to a change in another variable.

_____ A curve that represents the amounts an individual is willing to pay for given quantities of a good.

_____ The price of a good beyond which an individual will not enter into an exchange for the good.

_____ A curve that represents the quantities demanded of a good by an individual at given prices.

_____ That variable in a relationship whose change causes a change in another variable.

OBJECTIVE 3.2 Determine a consumer's demand and marginal value for a good.

"Okay, I have a question," Ginny said. "What's the difference between marginal value and price? And why does Silberberg refer to the demand curve as both a demand curve and a marginal value curve?"

"That's two questions", Mo said, "but they're both easy ones. The vertical axis on our graphs generally measures $/Q, some dollar amount per unit of the good or service. More specific expressions of $/Q are price or marginal value. On the graphs you can do two things - at least so far. You can either start from $/Q on the vertical axis then read over to the curve and down to the quantity axis, or you can do the opposite. When Silberberg asks what quantity a consumer would demand given a certain price, you start at that price on the $/Q axis (now interpreted specifically as a price axis) then read across to the curve and down to the quantity axis. So in this case it's a demand curve and price is the independent variable."

"Ah-ha, that's what he meant by causality going from price to quantity."

"Exactly," Mo said. "Now, if you ask how much a consumer would be willing to pay for a certain quantity of goods, you start on the quantity axis, read up to the curve then over to the vertical axis, which still has $/Q on it, but really tells you what the consumer's marginal value is for that quantity of goods."

"So now the curve is a marginal value curve and the numbers on the vertical axis are marginal values."

"Yes, but it plots as the same line on a graph. Mathematically, the marginal value curve is just an inverse demand curve, which is the demand equation solving for P on the left hand side as the dependent variable, instead of Q."

"I can see that I need the supplement on graphs," Ginny said. "But conceptually, isn't an inverse demand curve different from a marginal value curve, because we can only observe prices not marginal values?"

"Yes, which is why in practice, we use the law of demand rather than the law of diminishing marginal value."

"This must be related to why Silberberg didn't list the law of demand as a separate behavioral postulate, even though he refers to it as the 'central behavioral proposition in economics' (p.50)."

"The law of demand embodies all four postulates," said Mo, "but it's the only one that you can truly observe and therefore form refutable hypotheses from. Like you said, if you went out to collect data you wouldn't be able to see peoples' marginal values, just the quantities they buy at certain prices - which is a demand curve. So you collect data on quantities purchased given certain prices. You don't know what their marginal value is, just that it must be at least as high as the price."

"But what about auctions, where there is no posted price?" asked Ginny. "People bid higher and higher amounts, so you start to get some idea about their marginal value."

"I suppose so. You certainly know if the bid has gone beyond their reservation price because they drop out of the bidding. But for the person who finally wins the bid, you still don't know if their marginal value was a little bit higher than their winning bid."

"This must relate to what Silberberg means by 'operational significance.'(p.50) The law of demand is an interpretation of the postulates in terms of measurable, observable, prices and quantities."

"Exactly. The behavioral postulates, and marginal value, will never be observable except by omniscient mind-reading profs who produce marginal value schedules on econ exams and questions. The law of demand is a statement, embodying those postulates, that we can actually use. Ready for a quiz Ginny?"

Problem: You walk into a store to buy jeans and discover a half-price sale -- regularly $35.00 now $17.50. How many pairs of jeans would you buy (have bought) at both prices? Show your jeans purchasing decisions in a graph. Given this question are you determining your marginal value for jeans or your demand for jeans? What are the independent and dependent variables in this question? What is the direction of causality between variables?

"Let's see, at half-price I would probably buy two pairs instead of one. I go through jeans pretty quickly. The graph would show one pair bought at $35.00, and two pairs at $17.50. Like this:

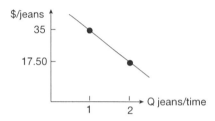

"The question is at some price, what quantity would I buy. So it's about my demand for jeans, rather than my marginal value of jeans," Ginny said.

"Yes. If the question asked what you were willing to pay for one and two pairs of jeans, that would be about your marginal value. And for marginal value curves, price or willingness to pay is the dependent variable <u>given</u> some quantity; for demand curves, quantity is the dependent variable, <u>given</u> some price."

"That's the next part of the question. So the causality here is from price to quantity, from independent to dependent. Oh, of course, causality always runs from the independent to the dependent variable."

"You'll be a quant jock before this course is through Ginny."

Question 6. Elaine's marginal value for squid packed in its own ink (a Mediterranean delicacy) is shown below. Her marginal value for a third can is _____? For a _____ can, Elaine's marginal value is $4. If she could buy all cans at $4/can, Elaine's total consumers' surplus will be _____.

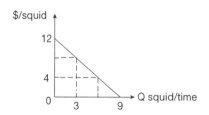

Question 7. In the graph above, the independent variable is in units of _____, and the dependent variable is in units of _____ .

OBJECTIVE 4.1 Think of your own example where choices result in trading off present consumption for future consumption, and vice versa.

"How come you decided not to work part-time at Jim's during school Mo? Aren't you worried about all the student loans you're piling up?"

"Not really, I plan on making a ton of money when I graduate and being able to pay off my loans quite quickly. And according to Silberg, this behaviour is quite rational."

"How so? I don't recall reading anything about debt."

"It's the same thing as trading off present consumption for future consumption (p.53). My future consumption will be slightly lower because I'll be paying off a student loan, but by borrowing those dollars now, my present consumption is higher."

"That's pretty straightforward", Ginny said. "I guess what confused me about consumption over time was that graph, figure 2-5."

OBJECTIVE 4.2 Show graphically the tradeoff between present and future consumption.

"That was pretty tough," Mo said. "Maybe we could recreate that graph from a specific example. Think of something that people can trade off some present consumption for future consumption?"

"Well, almost anything really, unless its something that you can't consume in the future -- like watching a particular match-up in the Super Bowl. But how about this, my Dad gets four weeks of paid vacation a year at the granary. But he can carry unused weeks over to the next year, or borrow weeks from the upcoming year, so really he can take eight weeks of vacation every two years."

"O.K., let's graph that," Mo said. "What is the price of present consumption in this case? What kind, and how many units of present consumption are we measuring along the horizontal axis?"

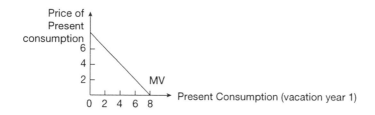

"Let's see. The price of present consumption is foregone vacation weeks next year, so the vertical axis also represents remaining vacation weeks in year two. And the horizontal axis will measure a choice of between 0 and 8 weeks of vacation to be taken in the present year."

"Now," Mo asked, "what does a downward sloping marginal value curve of present consumption mean?"

"It means that my marginal value of a week of vacation time is highest for the first week, and that it falls with each week of vacation that I take. In other words, if I haven't had any vacation, a week off has a higher value than if I have already had a break."

"So how would that affect the way you take your vacation weeks?"

"Like my father, I'd probably take four weeks each year rather than none one year and eight the next."

"Why do you say probably?"

"Well, he saved up for a seven week vacation last year because he and my mom were going overseas. But that was an exception, he found he got too burned out with only one week off the previous year. And he's never gone an entire year with no vacation."

"Still, in general he's tried to smooth the flow of vacation time. Let's put some numbers on the graph and try to determine the gains he gets from consuming 4 weeks each year, rather than 8 weeks the first year and none the next. Since the price of consuming a week in year one is foregoing that week in year two, let's draw this as a line with a vertical and horizontal intercept of 8, and a slope of minus one."

"I'll draw in those numbers," offered Ginny.

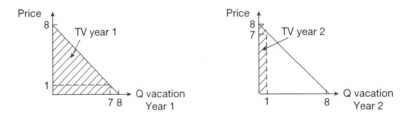

"To figure out total values, suppose he took seven weeks in year one, and one week in year two. Then his total value for year one is this shaded area under the marginal value curve up to seven weeks on the horizontal axis. So first calculate the area of the rectangle at a price of one up to a quantity of seven, so $1 x 7 = $7, then add on the triangle on top with an area of 1/2[($8-$1)(7)] = $24.50. The total for year one is $31.50. For year two you only get one week of vacation, so the total value under the curve up to a quantity of one is the rectangle, $7 X 1 = $7, plus the triangle on top, 1/2[($8-$7)(1)] = $.50, for a total of $7.50. Adding up the two years gives a total value of $31.50 + $7.50 = $39.

Question 8. Draw the graphs below for year one and two when *four* weeks of vacation are taken each year. Shade in and calculate the area representing total value.

* * * * * * *

"Thanks Mo, the graphs are intimidating until you really work through them. I feel confident enough now to enjoy this pizza as I start doing some review problems."

ANSWERS TO DIALOGUE QUESTIONS

Question 1. <u>True</u>. Propositions can be disproved if the observed events refute the predicted outcome.

Question 2. Vocabulary: d, a, e, g, b, g, c. A definition for diminishing marginal value is missing: the assertion that the more you consume of some good, the less you are willing to give up to obtain additional units of that good.

Question 3. CS = TV - TE. Her total value for 2 muffins is $1.55, so for a consumer's surplus of $.15, her total expenditure must be <u>$1.40</u>.

Question 4. Rise. Check this with the numbers in his MV schedule.

Question 5. Vocabulary: f, c, e, a, d, b

Question 6. <u>$8.00</u>, <u>sixth</u>, The triangle of consumer's surplus (CS) is one-half, base x height or CS = ½[($12 - $4)(6), so <u>CS = $24</u>.

Question 7. Quantity per time period (rate of consumption),
willingness to pay in $/q

Question 8. By taking four weeks every two years, his total value is ($4 x 4) = $16, plus 1/2[($8-$4)(4)] = $8, for a total of $24 each year, or $48 for the two years. Clearly total value is higher by smoothing consumption of vacation weeks over the two year period.

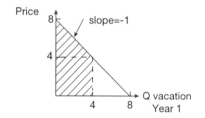

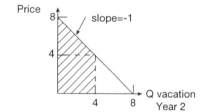

THE BIG PICTURE

Before you go on take a minute to look at the relationship between the main ideas in Chapter 1 and the behavioral postulates in Chapter 2. In Chapter 1 you were introduced to the condition of scarcity. Because goods are scarce, we must make choices, and every choice has a cost (an opportunity cost). You'll notice section 2.1 is titled "Axioms of Choice". The behavioral postulates presented in Chapter 2 are, within economics, the formal recognition and expression of the axioms that guide our choices as consumers. If you analyze the postulates, while looking back to Chapter 1, you can see how they derive from and represent the ideas of scarcity, choice, and cost. This is obviously more than a coincidence; this is the logical, reasoned structuring of the theory of economics.

Also important is that we can begin to see how economics works. By observing the *action* of consumers, i.e. their choices and substitution among scarce goods in response to changes in costs or constraints, economists can come as close as is possible to verifying the behavioral postulates, though, of course, their observations only *confirm* them. Thus, we can observe whether people buy more or less of something, like electricity, as the price changes. And we can offer an economic explanation based on the law of demand, an operational statement of the behavioral postulates reflecting the conditions of scarcity, choice and cost.

This sequence is economic theory at work: asserting behavioral postulates ⇒ forming refutable propositions based on those postulates ⇒ testing these propositions under observable conditions and with measurable phenomena. It seems so simple, but it takes economics from an exercise in the minds of economists about the behavior of humans, out into the street and into the world where the model and its implications can be tested with real observations of people making choices between steak and hamburger, high paying jobs with lousy working conditions and lower paying jobs in nice surroundings, careers and families, and the thousands of other choices that we make every day.

Economics is about explaining and predicting changes in behavior based on changes in the constraints we face, such as prices, income, age, laws, and education, assuming tastes remain unchanged over the period in study. It is about positive (not normative), testable analyses. Chapter three elaborates on the most powerful proposition we have for economic analysis: the law of demand.

REVIEW QUESTIONS

Answers to all review questions appear at the end of this chapter.

PROBLEMS AND EXERCISES
Write your answer in the space provided.

1. It is sometimes argued that used book markets hurt publisher's revenues. Suppose, however, that a professor has been using the same Introductory Economics textbook for years, and has no plans to change. If you (a sophomore) and your brother (a freshman) each have a marginal value of $10.00 for the book, how much could the publisher charge you for a new book given that you could resell it a year later to your brother?

a. Suppose that your brother didn't want the book but you could sell it to a used book store. The store wants to make at least $6 from their sale of the book. The most the used book store would offer you for your book is _____.

b. The most the publisher could charge you for the new book if you knew you would be selling it a year later to a used bookstore would be _____.

c. Why do some people sell their books to used bookstores and lose $6 off the top rather than just trying to sell their books privately?

d. If there were no used book markets, the most the publisher could charge you for a new book would be _____.

e. Why do people sell their Introductory Economics textbooks after they finish the course?

2. If Penelope has had no pizza in a week, she is willing to pay $12 for her first. If she has already consumed one pizza that week, she is only willing to pay $9 for her second. She is willing to pay $6 for her third, $3 for her fourth, but nothing for her fifth. You would have to pay Penelope to eat a sixth pizza in any one week. Record this information below:
$/pizza   Pizzas/week

a. Is this a demand schedule or marginal value schedule? _____ Why?

b. If this information represented a demand curve, it would read, for example: at a price of $6, Penelope would buy _____ pizzas.

c. Graph the information below.

d. Write out the equation for this line:_____

e. Would the graph look any different if it was a demand schedule? Yes or No?

f. Suppose the market price is $3.00. Penelope would buy _____ pizzas, and her consumer's surplus would be _____.

g. Suppose the market price is $5.00. Penelope would buy _____ pizzas.

3. Dudley Do-right discretely observed Sweet Nell's purchase of lemon drops over several weeks. When the price of lemon drops is $6.00/kilo (Dudley and Nell are Canadian, so they use the metric system), Nell buys a half kilo per week (about a pound). When the price falls to $5.00/kilo, Nell buys a kilo per week. Graph Nell's demand schedule below. Don't forget to label your axes.

a. We call this a demand schedule because the quantity of lemon drops are the _____ variable.

b. Assuming this demand curve is completely linear, at a price of $5.50/kilo Nell will buy _____ kilos. At $5.25/kilo she buys _____ kilos.

c. Nell's reservation price is _____.

d. If lemon drops were given away free, Nell would consume _____ kilos per week.

e. Is it likely, given that perfect smile of Dudley's, that his demand for lemon drops is higher or lower than Nell's?

4. Which of the following explain negatively sloped demand curves?
a. People will substitute among goods.
b. People have different tastes and preferences.
c. The more a person has of a good, the less they will give up to get an additional unit.

5. In the mid-1980s when the Jacksons (formerly the Jackson Five) started their "Victory Tour", the ticket price was set at $120 for a package of 4 tickets. Individual tickets were not available.

a. For which fan below would this pricing strategy be successful (i.e. which fan(s) would buy the package of 4, but buy fewer than 4 if they were priced individually at $30/ticket)? _____ (Hint: For package deals look at total value rather than marginal value)

FAN ANNA			FAN BOB			FAN CURT		
$MV	|	Qtks	$MV	|	Qtks	$MV	|	Qtks
----		----	----		----	----		----
60		1	30		1	50		1
50		2	25		2	35		2
40		3	20		3	25		3
30		4	15		4	15		4

b. Calculate each fan's consumer's surplus under the package deal compared to being able to buy individual tickets at $30/ticket.

Consumer's Surplus (CS) under the package deal:

        Anna = _____   Bob = _____   Curt = _____

Consumer's Surplus (CS) with individual ticket purchases:

        Anna = _____   Bob = _____   Curt = _____

c. Would this type of strategy have made sense if the promoter's had known that the concert would have been sold out everywhere? Why or why not?

6. Construct a marginal value schedule for a person who would not buy a second pair of socks if the price per pair was $4.00, but who would buy two pairs if the store they were in only sold them in

packages of two, and their choice was two pairs for $8.00, or no pairs of socks.

Q socks	$MV	$TV
1		
2		

7. Many fast-food restaurants now offer meal packages like the "Full Meal Deal". Suppose that Gene, Theo, and Calum represent three typical customers. Their marginal value schedules for one serving of french fries ($FF), hamburgers ($Hb), and a soft drink ($D) are given below:

	GENE			THEO			CALUM		
Q	$FF	$Hb	$D	$FF	$Hb	$D	$FF	$Hb	$D
1	.75	.65	.50	.50	1.35	.50	.30	1.50	.60

a. If the restaurant priced each item to ensure that they sold at least one to each customer, what prices would they have to charge? _____ for french fries, _____ for hamburgers, and _____ for soft drinks.

b. Their total revenue would be 3 x (_____ + _____ + _____) = _____.

c. Look closely at the marginal value schedules and think about how the restaurant might increase their total revenue. What is the maximum price they could they charge, for example, to get everyone to buy a full meal package consisting of french fries, a hamburger, and a soft drink? _____

d. Can you think of any pricing strategy that might increase revenues further? Think about what makes Gene's schedule different from Theo's and Calum's. Propose a few and see if revenues actually increase.

8. On the graph below, draw a consumer's marginal value curve and indicate some market price. Identify the price (with the letter a) at which the consumer would begin buying the good, a quantity where the consumer's MV > P (with the letter b), a quantity where the consumer's MV < P (with the letter c), and a quantity at which the consumer's MV = 0 (with the letter d).

9. Last year the city of Ottawa (Canada's capital) acquired the triple A baseball team, the Ottawa Lynx (the farm team for the Montreal Expos). Ottawans love the Lynx, and the inverse demand for Lynx tickets has been estimated at P = 100 - .01 Q, where Q is the number of tickets per game, and P is the

price per ticket. The new stadium built for the Lynx has a seating capacity of 9,200. All seats are priced the same.

a. Graph the demand for Lynx tickets.

b. At a price of $5.00 per ticket, _____ tickets would be demanded? (Hint: Plug $5.00 into the equation and solve for Q).

c. How many people wanting a ticket at $5.00 would have to go without? _____

d. If the Lynx owners wanted to sell exactly 9,200 tickets, what price should they charge? _____
Calculate the total expenditure, total value, and consumer's surplus at this price.
TE = _____, CS = _____, TV = _____

e. All seats sell for the same price, but all seats are not equally desirable. How do you suppose the best seats get allocated, if not through the price system?

TRUE - FALSE QUESTIONS
Provide a one or two sentence explanation with your answer.

1.   Scarcity only exists when the price of a good is held below the market clearing level.

2.   The law of demand implies that as more people return to college, more high school students are likely to take SAT review courses.

3.   If the government set up a gasoline rationing system under which equal quantities of gas were allocated to each vehicle, we would expect all cars to be driven about the same number of miles per month.

4.   Economic theory explains social occurrences from the perspective that the value of anything is equal to its price.

5.   The law of demand implies that a prolonged recession will assist the military's recruiting problems.

6.   The law of demand implies that the advent of more home labor-saving appliances, such as self-cleaning ovens and nofrost freezers, could have contributed to the major entry of women into the labor force in the 1980s.

7.   One often hears the expression, "I had no choice." This accords with economic theory.

8.   The published costs of the military draft under estimate the true cost to society.

MULTIPLE CHOICE QUESTIONS
Choose the best answer

1. The behavioral postulates predict that
a.   individuals will try to maximize their income.
b.   rich people will give more to charity than poor people.
c.   wealthier individuals will have a lower marginal value of money than poorer individuals.
d.   an increase in tax deductibility for charitable contributions will lead to an increase in contributions.
e.   all of the above.

2. If a consumer can purchase as large a quantity as he wants at a given price, he will continue to buy units up the point where
a.   marginal value is zero.
b.   total value is maximized.
c.   marginal value equals the market price.
d.   total expenditures are minimized.

3. One behavioral postulate asserts diminishing marginal value for goods. Consider a law of increasing marginal value: the more the consumer has of a good, the higher its marginal value. Then economic theory would predict that the consumer would
a.   refuse to purchase any goods.
b.   spend all their income on only one good.

c.   buy equal amounts of all goods.

d.   have no desire for money.

4. The demand curve for the good with increasing marginal value would be:

a.   positively sloped.

b.   negatively sloped.

c.   horizontal at the good's price.

d.   vertical at the good's quantity.

5. The total value of a certain quantity of a good is

a.   the area under the marginal value curve up to the quantity purchased.

b.   the slope of the marginal value curve at the quantity purchased.

c.   the area of the rectangle inscribed within the marginal value curve at the quantity purchased.

d.   none of the above.

6. Our behavioral postulates suggest that

a.   current consumption is preferred over future consumption.

b.   people save because future consumption is preferred over current consumption.

c.   people with a high marginal value of present consumption relative to future consumption will save.

d.   people with a high marginal value of present consumption relative to future consumption will borrow.

Jane has the following demand schedule for bluegrass CD's:

$/Q|	15	14	13	12	11	10	9	8	7	6
Q/t|	1	2	3	4	5	6	7	8	9	10

7. If the price is $11.00 per CD, how many will Jane buy and what will her total expenditure be?

a. 5 and $65   b. 5 and $55   c. 4 and $54   d. 4 and $48

8. At a price of $11 per CD, what will Jane's consumer's surplus be on her purchase?

a. $10   b. $11   c. zero   d. $9

9. Suppose the store Jane was in only sold CD's in packages, and if Jane wanted any CD's she would have to buy a package of 8 for $88. Would she do it, and why or why not?

a. no, P > MV   b. no, TE > TV   c. yes, TE > TV   d. yes, TV > TE

10. What would her consumer's surplus be?

a. $7   b. $4   c. -$7   d. -$4

11. At a price of $11 per CD, Jane would have zero consumer's surplus if she were forced to buy a package of

a. 5   b. 7   c. 9   d. 8

12. If a consumer voluntarily makes a purchase, we can infer

a.   total expenditure is less than total valuation.

b.   total expenditure is greater than total valuation.

c.   total valuation is greater than or equal to total expenditure.
d.   total valuation is less than or equal to total expenditure.

13. The law of demand predicts that
a.   retired people are more likely to save than the middle-aged.
b.   an MBA student is more likely to borrow than a graduate student doing their Master's in Religious Studies.
c.   that people in jobs with wages based on experience are more likely to save than those in jobs with fixed salaries.
d.   none of the above

14. Consumers' surplus for C units (price B) can be determined using which of the following methods?

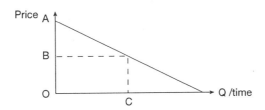

a.   1/2 (AB x OC)
b.   SUM (consumers' marginal value for each unit purchased minus the price).
c.   Total Value of C units minus Total Expenditure of C units.
d.   all of the above.
e.   none of the above.

15. The price of a good and a consumer's marginal value for the same quantity of that good are identical. This statement:
a.   is true.
b.   is false.
c.   can be true or false depending on the purchase.

16. The 'other things held constant' in the statement of the law of demand include all of the following except for:
a.   the price of the good.
b.   income.
c.   the price of related goods (substitutes and complements).
d.   tastes.

SHORT ANSWER QUESTIONS

1. Legend has it that Howard Hughes counted every dollar he made. Does a millionaire having a high

marginal value for an additional dollar contradict economic theory?

2. Although Professor Swimmer's income had risen considerably since he first took his Ph.D., and he could therefore afford more vacations and leisurely pursuits, he indulged in less of such activities compared with the days when he was a student and his income was lower. What economic concept can explain this phenomenon?

3. Silky's bar, the only bar in town, charges certain problem customers on a sliding scale. Silky decides when to increase the per drink price for each customer, but he keeps raising the price for each drink, say from $1 to $2 to $4 to $8 and so on. He calls it his program to prevent drunk driving. Some of his customers think he is just ripping them off and making some fat profits. Upon what economic assumption does Silky base his program?

4. We often hear economists discuss their graphs in terms of negative or positive relationships. For example, the demand curve demonstrates a negative relationship and the supply curve a positive relationship. What is the relationship they are referring to?

5. When the consumer's marginal value equals the price of the good, is it a bad deal to purchase the good? Explain.

6. Describe the relationship between a consumer's marginal value for a good and the price of that good.

7. In 1890 "basic human needs" in the United States were considered to be food, shelter and clothing. In 1990, Senator Ted Kennedy asserted that our "basic human needs" now also include medical care, affordable transportation, and day care. Have human beings become more needy in the last 100 years?

a. If we observe individuals making choices about the quantity of day care they consume, for example, would economists call day care a need?

b. We observe even the very poor making tradeoffs between food and other goods, does this suggest that food is not a need?

ANSWERS TO REVIEW QUESTIONS

Answers to PROBLEMS AND EXERCISES

1. A price between $10.00 and $20.00. The publisher could charge you $10.00 (your current value for the book), plus the amount, in this year's prices, for which you can resell the book to your brother. The value to you today of receiving a dollar one year from now is called the "present value" of a dollar, and is discussed in chapter 10. Intuitively though, if prices rise between now and next year (known as inflation), $10 received one year from now will not buy the same amount as it does today (if a book costs $10 today, you can buy 1 book for $10. If the price rises to $11 next year you can only buy ten-elevenths of the book with $10). So the *present* value (meaning it's real value in today's terms) of the $10 you get 1 year from now is something less than $10 because of inflation. Also, you might lower the price to your brother somewhat, since he is your brother, and it is a used book. Hence the publishers could charge you something close to, but less than, $20.00.

a. $4.00
b. $10.00 + the "present value" of $4.00. So something less than $14.00.
c.   The cost to you in time and inconvenience must exceed $6.00.
d. $10.00
e.   No idea.

2.

pizzas/week	1	2	3	4	5
$/pizza	12	9	6	3	0

a. This is a marginal value schedule because willingness to pay is the dependent variable, and quantity is the independent variable.

b. three

c. To find the vertical intercept, extend the columns up until you get a value for price ($/pizza) when quantity is zero. Likewise, the horizontal intercept is the quantity (5) when price is zero.

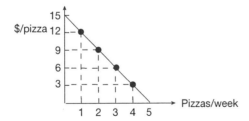

d. The line's equation is P = 15 - 3Q. The vertical intercept is 15 and the slope ($\Delta p/\Delta q$) is -3/1 = -3.

e. No, it would look the same because the price/quantity coordinates are the same. But price would now be interpreted as the independent variable.

f. 4, CS equals {½ [($15 - $3)(4)], CS = $24. Using the numbers rather than the graph, CS = $18.

g. This is not evident from the columns of data. The easiest route is to use the equation, and substitute in $5 for the price: 5 = 15 - 3Q, Q = 3⅓ pizzas.

3.

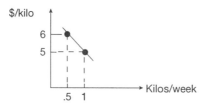

a.   dependent
b.   .75 kilos/week, .875 kilos/week (midway between .5 and 1 is .75, midway between .75 and 1 is .875)
c. $7.00
d.   3.5 kilos/week (convert data to an equation; drops are free so set P = 0 then determine Q)
e.   lower.

4. Behavioral postulates i. and iii. imply negatively sloping demand curves.

5. a. Only Fan **Curt** would buy a package of four tickets for $120, since his total valuation for four tickets is $125. Sold individually for $30/ticket, however, he would only have purchased 2 tickets. **Anna** would buy 4 tickets no matter how they sold (packaged or individually). Her total value is $180. **Bob** would only buy one ticket at $30 if they were available individually. He would not buy the package of four since his total value, equal to $90, is less than the required expenditure of $120.

b. CS for Anna is the same: $180 - $120 = $60. CS for Bob would be -$30 with the package deal (which he would not buy) and 0 if he were allowed to buy just one ticket. Curt's CS is $125 - $120 = 5$ with the package deal. Purchasing tickets individually, he would gain $20 on the first ticket ($50 - $30), and $5 on the second ticket ($35 - $30) for a total of $25, higher than under the package deal.

c. Not really. The goal is to sell more tickets than on an individual basis. If the concert was going to be sold out everywhere anyway, total revenues are the same selling tickets individually or in packages.

6. Any schedule would work where the total value for two pairs of socks exceeds $8.00 but the marginal value for the second pair of socks is less than $4.00. Such a schedule is:

Qsocks	$MV	$TV
1	$5.00	$5.00
2	$3.50	$8.50

Total value is $8.50, which exceeds the total expenditure of $8.00 so the consumer would buy the package. But their marginal value for the second pair of socks is $3.50, less than the price of $4.00.

7. a. $.30, $.65, $.50. The restaurant would have to charge the lowest price that each individual would pay to entice them all to buy all three items.

b. 3 x ($.30 + $.65 + $.50) = $4.35

c. The maximum full meal deal price they could charge would be $1.90, Gene's total for all three items. Total revenue would be 3 x $1.90 = $5.70.

d. Gene's relatively low marginal value for hamburgers brings down the maximum possible full meal price. Another scheme, therefore, might be to charge a price for the full meal just low enough to attract Theo and Calum, and to sell the fries and soft drinks separately at a price that attracts Gene. This also takes advantage of Gene's relatively high marginal value for french fries. A price of $2.35 for the full meal deal would induce Theo and Calum to buy one, and french fries and a soft drink could be sold separately at $.75 and $.50 to Gene. Total revenue would be (2 x 2.35) + .65 + .50 = $5.85.

8.

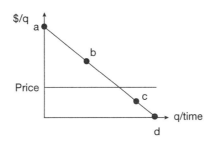

9. a.

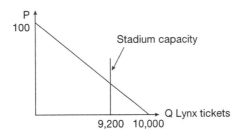

b. Using the inverse demand equation: 5 = 100 - .01Q, <u>Q = 9,500</u>.

c. Stadium capacity is 9,200; 9,500 - 9,200 = <u>300</u> unhappy customers. This is called excess demand.

d. With Q = 9,200, P = 100 - 0.1(9,200), <u>P = $8</u>. Total expenditure is P x Q or $8 x 9,200, so <u>TE = $73,600</u>. Consumer's surplus is ½($100 - $8)(9200), <u>CS = $423,200</u>. Total value is total expenditure plus consumer's surplus, $73,600 + $423,200, or <u>TV = $496,800</u>.

e. Queuing, using connections of "who you know", paying higher prices for prime seats resold outside the ticket office, ticket scalping, etcetera.

Answers to TRUE - FALSE QUESTIONS

1. False. Scarcity exists whenever more of a good would be demanded than would be available if it were given away free. A good selling at a market clearing price is still scarce to some people. Economists use the term "shortage" to refer to the specific case when the price of a good is held below the market clearing level.

2. True. More applicants will increase the demand for college, which raises the entry price in terms of both tuition and entrance standards. High school students can respond to this increased constraint by taking SAT review courses to improve their entrance exam scores.

3. False. People value driving their cars, and hence gasoline, differently. Some people's MV may already be below the price of gas at a quantity below the rationed level. If trading were allowed, these people would exchange some of their gasoline for goods for which their marginal value was higher.

4. False. The value of a good may far exceed the price at which it is sold -- this is consumer's surplus.

5. True. A recession is usually accompanied by higher than average unemployment rates in non-military labor markets. Hence for some of these individuals, the cost of joining the military (in terms of other employment opportunities) falls.

6. True. Labor-saving devices reduced the cost of working outside the home. Many women responded by entering the 'wage' labor force.

7. False. The behavioral postulates assert that people have preferences and that they substitute. What this person means is that their alternatives were less attractive (or more costly) than the route they choose.

8. True. The costs of the draft under estimate the true cost to society because people are not selected, or do not volunteer, based on their opportunity costs. Consider, for example, the cost to society of drafting a gifted cancer researcher to keep track of medical supplies on the warfront.

Answers to MULTIPLE CHOICE QUESTIONS

1. d	5. a	9. d	13. b
2. c	6. d	10. b	14. d
3. b	7. b	11. c	15. c*
4. a	8. a	12. c	16. a

*Marginal value can exceed price; this is where consumers' surplus comes from. But someone's marginal valuation could exactly equal the price on the only unit purchased, and they would be indifferent between purchasing the good and not.

Answers to SHORT ANSWER QUESTIONS

1. No. Economic theory asserts Hughes' marginal value of the millionth dollar he makes will be lower than the millionth minus one. His marginal value (absolutely) may still be high. Economic theory says nothing about comparing marginal values across people, only that for each person, diminishing marginal value is asserted. Hughes' high MV for dollars may be part of the reason he got so rich.

2. Opportunity cost. When Swimmer's income was lower, he gave up less money to engage in leisure. His higher hourly wage means that he must forego more if he wants to take a vacation.

3. Silky is operating on the law of demand. He hopes that as the price increases, the number of drinks demanded per hour will fall as he wants to discourage drinking and driving.

4. The relationship between dependent and independent variables, or the variable on the vertical and horizontal axes. The relationship, for example, between studying and grades, consuming pastry and weight, money and acquaintances.

5. No. The consumer willingly purchases successive units of a good until the difference between their marginal value (MV) of another unit and the price is eliminated or zero. At that point (MV = P) the consumer has gained all possible benefits (i.e., maximum consumers' surplus). For those of you with calculus, in the limit, as Δq approaches zero, MV will equal P and consumer surplus will be maximized. This is occasionally difficult conceptually, for example when goods are discreet, whole units, like a car. The consumer may purchase only one unit every 10 years -- and their MV may exceed the price for that single purchase. But if goods are thought of as divisible units, or as a rate of consumption over a period that includes the purchase of more than one unit (e.g., 1/10th of a stream of car service or as cars per lifetime), the equality makes more sense.

6. There is no necessary relationship between the two, except that the price of the good must be below the consumer's marginal value for that unit or they will not purchase the good.

7. No, basic needs, such as food and water to survive, are the same now as 100 years ago.

a. No, making choices concerning daycare implies it is an economic good that some people want more of. If it was a need, there would be no choice involved.

b. No, some amount of food is necessary to survive, therefore a need. Beyond that amount, when choice is possible, people begin to trade food for other goods implying the extra food is not a need.

CHAPTER 3
The Theory of Demand

PRINCIPAL GOALS

1.0	**Understand absolute versus relative prices.** (Objective 1.1)
2.0	**Derive individual and market demand curves.** (Objectives 2.1, 2.2)
3.0	**Understand and calculate the price elasticity of demand.** (Objectives 3.1, 3.2, 3.3, 3.4, 3.5, 3.6)
4.0	**Understand and apply the Law of Demand.** (Objective 4.1)

OBJECTIVES
Answers to bold-faced questions appear at the end of the dialogue.

"I have to get out of the dorms," moaned Ginny, "some nimrod keeps setting off the fire alarm trying to microwave foil-wrapped submarine sandwiches. Three o'clock in the morning and we all have to evacuate the building until the fire department can confirm, once again, that most university education does not provide training in basic life skills."

"Makes you think twice about your pyjamas choice doesn't it?"

"That's not the point Mo. Have you ever been blasted out of a deep sleep by a mega horn inches from your eardrum?"

"Sure, I grew up in the city. You just have country-pampered ears. But I'm serious about your pyjamas. What would you sleep in at home?"

"A nightgown."

"And what do you sleep in at the dorm?"

"A t-shirt, flannel pyjamas bottoms, and socks."

"You see, your dressing for warmth and modesty is another example of trying to reduce the deleterious effects of a constraint. Is that inconvenience worth the additional time and money it would cost you to move out?"

"Well, that's what I'm trying to figure out. The cost is more than having to give up my favorite nightwear. I'm less productive on the days following the fire alarms because my sleep has been interrupted. And that means that if it takes me six hours to do the work I could have otherwise done in four, the cost is my leisure, or whatever I would have done in those extra two hours."

"I think we're starting to think like economists," observed Mo.

"Does that mean we're going to become as boring as Adam?"

"No, my mom says Adam was born that way. What it does mean, though, is that we should be able to critically examine this choice about moving out."

OBJECTIVE 1.1 State prices in relative and absolute terms.

"It also upsets me," complained Ginny, "that the dorm rates for room and board are going up. I received a notice that the fee for my room and particular meal plan was going up by $80 next year."

"That seems like a lot, but what do you pay now?"

"$400 a month for the eight-month term, so $3,200 for the school year."

Question 1. The $80 fee hike is a _____ percentage increase from $3,200.

* * * * * * *

"So the absolute price will rise to $3,280, or $410 per month. But what about the relative price?"

"You mean the price relative to other goods?"

"Yes. My mom says that housing prices in Seattle have doubled in the past five years, and she's raised rents at the boarding house by 8%. So in terms of the relative prices of other places to live, a 2.5% increase in absolute dorm prices is still a decrease in relative prices."

"That's true. And I read in the paper that this year's inflation rate is expected to average 5%. So I guess that although the nominal price of dorm living will rise, the real price, adjusted for inflation, will actually fall."

Question 2. The nominal price of dorm housing will rise to _____ after the $80 increase, but the real price of dorm housing will fall to _____ with a 5% inflation rate.

* * * * * * *

"What about the meal plan you're on?" Mo asked.

"That's a different scheme. The dorm cafeteria is subsidized, so we pay a flat fee per month to get an entry card, and then we pay the subsidized price for the meals. Right now the lunch and dinner specials cost $2.80 and $4.00 each, with all the bread you can eat and beverages you can drink free. Apparently the average person consumes three slices of bread and two beverages."

"Sounds like a good deal. How is it changing?"

"They've decided to drop the meal prices to $2.10 and $3.30, and charge $.10 per slice of bread, and $.20 per beverage."

Question 3. Under the new pricing scheme, would you expect the average student to change their consumption of bread and beverages? Explain.

* * * * * * *

"Is that good or bad for you?"

"Good actually, since I usually consume only two slices of bread and one beverage. I never thought about it before, but I guess I was subsidizing the heavy eaters, mostly the guys, under the old plan."

"So, the real price of dorm housing, accounting for inflation, is falling, and its relative price, compared to other comparable goods, is also falling. On top of that, your meals will cost you less. Still want to move out?"

"I guess not, especially since Jim's been too cheap to raise our wages. Those are falling in real terms also -- there's no such thing as cost-of-living clauses at the Diner. Fortunately most of my money comes from tips anyway."

"Have those been increasing?"

"Overall I'm not sure. Jim raised most prices on the menu, because he says his costs, with the exception of labor, have all gone up. And since people generally leave 15% of the bill, a higher bill means our tips increase."

"But don't the higher prices mean that people eat at the Diner less often?"

"It depends on what has happened to prices at other Diner's, and restaurants, and the grocery stores, and everything else that is a substitute for eating at Jim's. I suspect that prices at all those places haven't increased as much, so that Jim's relative prices have increased."

"That sounds like a testable proposition to me. What have you noticed?"

"My tips are lower on weeknights, which supports my hypothesis that Jim's relative prices have risen and fewer people are eating at the Diner. But, my tips have increased on the weekends."

"Any explanation?"

"Before the price increases there was always a line-up on Friday and Saturday night -- I guess what you'd call an excess demand for tables. Now there are fewer people in line, but we're still always at capacity. So I serve the same number of people at the higher prices, which means larger bills and therefore larger tips."

"Excellent. Has Jim ever thought about raising prices on the weekends?"

"Sure, but he doesn't really want to have two separate menus. He talks about having a cover charge -- like nightclubs. An additional $5 per table or, $2 per person so we don't get 10 people cramming onto one table."

"But at a nightclub you get some entertainment for your entrance fee. What do you get at Jim's?

"It's the hot place to meet people that you've seen around campus. To see and be seen Mo -- that's what the Diner is about. You don't think people come just for the meatloaf do you?"

Question 4. Table 3-1 gives the CPI for 1960 as 29.6, 1983 as 99.6 (consider this 100), and 1992 as 140.0. In 1960 a hamburger cost $.19 in current dollars. That same hamburger (no change in quality) cost $.59 in 1983 and $.79 in 1992. This means that in real terms, the price of hamburgers rose/fell from _____ in 1960 to _____ in 1983, and rose/fell to _____ in 1992.

* * * * * * *

"Why do you suppose that Seattle housing prices have been rising faster than the rate of inflation?"

"I suspect that it may have something to do with the city being ranked as one of the most livable places in the U.S. It attracts people from all over, especially California."

"I know that the rising crime rate and earthquake fears in L.A. convinced my Uncle Bryan to move," said Ginny. "So what does that mean in terms of the market demand for Seattle housing - is it increasing?"

OBJECTIVE 2.1 Construct a market demand curve from individual demand curves.

"It's pretty straightforward I think. If your market demand curve was originally the sum of 100,000 individual demand curves and then 20,000 more individuals wanting to buy a house move to the area, the market demand curve must increase with the additional 20,000 individual demand curves."

"That seems obvious enough," agreed Ginny. "But why do market demand curves look flatter than the individual demand curves that make them up?"

"Because you add up horizontally, across quantities, or 'laterally' as Silberberg puts it. Think about what you now know about slopes. If we have the same price increase (rise) for an individual demand curve as for a market one, we should have a much greater change in quantity (run) because of all the individuals responding in aggregate. So it will be a flatter curve."

Question 5. Derive a market demand schedule from the individual demand schedules below:

P	Q1	Q2	Q3	Market Price	Market Quantity
3	1	2	3		
2	2	4	6		
1	3	6	9		

Question 6. Graph the three individual demand curves and the market demand curve on the same graph.

* * * * * * *

"Ginny, we've worked through two objectives without you insisting on looking up the key vocabulary. Are we through with the jargon?"

"Hardly."

OBJECTIVE 2.2 Recognize definitions for the important new vocabulary.

Question 7. Match the term with its definition(s). Write out definitions for any undefined terms.

a. nominal (price)   b. real or relative (price)
c. inflation   d. deflation
e. absolute prices   f. constant prices
g. current prices   h. individual demand
i. market demand

__G__   An expression of the general price level.

__C__   An increase in the average price of goods.

_____   The apparent price of a good in terms of the monetary price you would pay to purchase it.

__H__   The sum of the amounts each consumer is willing to purchase of a good at each possible price.

__D__   A decrease in the average price of goods.

__E__   Existing in fact; actual. The actual price of a good relative to and in terms of the prices of other goods.

_____   The nominal or money price of a good in a given time period. The price that consumers face in the given time period.

_____ The lateral sum of all the individual demand curves.

_____ The current price of a good converted or expressed in terms of the general price level of a different time period.

_____ The graphic representation of the amounts an individual consumer is willing to purchase of a good at various prices.

OBJECTIVE 3.1 Get acquainted with the official and unofficial practice of elasticity measures.

"Conceptually I think I understand what elasticities are used for," Ginny said, "but I'm confused by Silberberg's scale and language on page 80 for interpreting them. The scale goes from 0 to -∞, and when talking about elasticity, like the elasticity of meat being less than the elasticity of sirloin, less elastic means closer to zero, right? But technically -0.5 is a larger or greater number than -10."

"That is confusing. I reread that section a couple of times but in the end I had to ask Adam. I didn't know this but there are other kinds of elasticities. Anyway, he said the key is that everyone is taking the absolute value of the price elasticity of demand, although they don't do it with any of the others that we'll eventually learn.

"Although technically the elasticity of demand is always a negative number because of the negative relationship between price and quantity demanded. That's the law of demand."

"That's right, but apparently taking the absolute value is just a practice that makes it easier for people to talk about elasticities. Adam gave us this table to refer to:

Elastic demand	$-\infty < \epsilon < -1$	$|\epsilon| > 1$	more elastic
Inelastic demand	$-1 < \epsilon < 0$	$|\epsilon| < 1$	less elastic
Unitary elastic	$\epsilon = -1$	$|\epsilon| = 1$	

"Okay, so when I read that the elasticity of cabbage or whatever, 'is greater than' or 'increases', that probably means the absolute value is large or getting larger, though technically it means that the number is getting farther away from zero."

"Right," Mo agreed, "after taking absolute values of the actual negative number, the whole scale is talked about as going from zero to $+\infty$. Greater than one means elastic, less than one means inelastic -- though we mean the absolute values.

"Great", Ginny said. "With that a little more vocabulary I'll be ready for anything."

OBJECTIVE 3.2 Recognize definitions for important new vocabulary.

Question 8. Match the term with its definition(s). Write out definitions for any undefined terms.

a. elasticity of demand   b. elastic
c. inelastic   d. unitary elastic
e. total revenue   f. total expenditure

g. price takers   h. second law of demand

_____ The total amount a buyer spends to purchase a good: price per unit x quantity of units consumed.

_____ A given percent change in price induced a larger percent change in quantity demanded.

_____ A measure of responsiveness in quantities demanded to a change in prices.

_____ A given percent change in price induced an equal percent change in quantity demanded. An elasticity of demand measuring -1.

_____ The total amount a seller receives for a good: price per unit x quantity of units sold.

_____ An elasticity of demand measuring between -∞ and -1.

_____ Business firms (producers) which produce an output of goods that is too small relative to the total worldwide production to influence the price at which the good is sold.

_____ The percent change in quantity demanded divided by the percent change in price.

_____ The change in the rate of quantity demanded observed in response to a change in price will be absolutely greater in the long run versus the short run.

* * * * * * *

"Just one more thing math master," asked Ginny, "can you explain what the symbols R(q) and C(q) mean? And why we use them?"

"Yes grasshopper. The symbolic expressions represent a relationship between the two (or more) symbols that make up the function. These examples (p.87) use R to represent total revenues, C to represent total costs, and q to represent quantity of output, or quantity of goods produced. The expression R(q) means that R is dependent on q. This makes sense. The amount of a firm's total revenue depends on the amount of goods it sells - likewise for costs. These expressions allow economists, mathematicians and others to make statements in a symbolic language that can then be manipulated mathematically to test the relationship among the variables."

"That's what I thought."

OBJECTIVE 3.2 Calculate an elasticity of demand

"It's fairly clear to me that the elasticity of demand just measures consumer responsiveness to price changes. The law of demand tells us the direction quantity will go in when the price changes, and elasticity tells us by how much. But I'm afraid I got a little lost, again, in the math," admitted Ginny.

"Well, let's take the formula on page 80 and put in some actual values. Suppose the price of movie admission begins at $5.00 and rises to $6.00, and the theater owner notices that the number of tickets sold drops from 100 to 75. We want to somehow be able to compare the change in dollar terms to the change in the number of tickets -- that's why we compare the percent change in each."

"I understand that elasticity is a ratio of the percent change in quantity to the percent change in price. But why is delta q over q ($\triangle$q/q) the percent change?"

"Suppose that I told you that Sunday newspapers had gone from $1.00 to $1.10. What percent change is that?"

"That's a 10% increase."

"You answered automatically Ginny, but think of what you went through in your head to come up with that. You subtracted $1.00 from $1.10 to get $0.10. Then you divided $0.10 by $1.00 to figure out what percent it was. The first step is $\triangle$p, the change in price -- the new price minus the old price. The second step is taking that result and dividing it by the original price for $\triangle$p/p."

"So in the movie example, $\triangle$q, the change in quantity, is -25. Negative 25 divided by 100, the original quantity, gives me -.25, the percentage change in quantity. And $\triangle$p is $1.00, the change in price. $1.00 divided by the original price of $5.00 equals .2, or 20 percent."

"That's right. So the elasticity of demand is the percent change in quantity -.25, divided by the percent change in price .20, equal to -1.25. It is because the numerator is larger than the denominator that the absolute value of the ratio is larger than one. This provides useful information because it tells us that for any good with an (absolute value of) elasticity greater than one, at those prices the percentage change in quantity will exceed the percentage change in price."

"Are we going to have to say 'the absolute value of...' every time?" asked Ginny. "It's rather cumbersome."

"I don't think so, in fact Adam said that people are pretty sloppy about just saying 'less than' or 'greater than' one. But i think it's important to remember the precise meaning."

Question 9. The elasticity of demand is always negative because of the _____ of _____. The numerator and denominator will always move in _____ directions.

Question 10. If the percent change in quantity is larger than the percent change in price, we call this _____. If the percent change in quantity is less than the percent change in price, the absolute value of the ratio will be _____ than 1 and the demand is called _____. When the percent change in quantity equals the percent change in price, elasticity equals _____ and is called _____.

Question 11. A corner video rental noticed that when it lowered its rental price from $3.00 a video to $2.25 a video, its rentals increased by 30 percent. The elasticity of demand is _____.

* * * * * * *

"Does it make sense to you that a good like theatre tickets would have an elasticity greater than -1?"

"Maybe not twenty years ago," answered Mo. "But today there are lots of alternatives like video rentals, pay-TV movies, and so on. They're not perfect substitutes for the big screen, but as the price of movie admission rises they become more attractive more often."

OBJECTIVE 3.3 List the factors determining the price elasticity of demand.

"So the more substitutes a good has, the greater the elasticity. Do any other factors influence consumer responsiveness?"

"Well, you were considering moving out of the dorms because of a two and a half percent price increase. But last month I remember you took a ferry ride over to the San Juan Islands, despite the paper reporting that fares had increased by 10%. Your demand for room and board seems to be more elastic than your demand for ferry rides."

"That's because I only ride the ferry once or twice a year anyway Mo. But I spend most of my income on food and housing, so if it increases in price, you bet I'm going to respond."

"But the price of a box of toothpicks could double and you'd still buy about one box a year."

"Correct. So that must be another determinant of price elasticity of demand -- all else constant, the greater the proportion of your budget that you spend on the good, the more elastic the demand."

Question 12. Rank the following items from most elastic demand to least elastic demand: ___coffee, ___beverages, ___Folger's coffee, ___hot beverages.

Question 13. All else constant, the broader (more general)/narrower (more specific) the grouping of items, the more inelastic the demand? _____

OBJECTIVE 3.4 Determine changes in total revenue and total expenditure from elasticities, and vice versa.

"An elasticity of -1.25 means that a one percent increase in movie admission at current prices, leads to a 1.25% drop in ticket sales. Wouldn't this lower the theatre owners revenues?" asked Ginny.

"Absolutely, and I bet we would see the price come back down. When elasticity is greater than one, or elastic, total revenues move in the opposite direction of the price change, because the percent change in quantity is larger than the percent change in price."

"That makes intuitive sense. The more elastic the demand, the greater the number of substitutes, so the more likely it is that if you try to raise prices, you'll lose a greater percent of your customers. But if you're selling a good, like cable TV, for which there are few substitutes, the elasticity of demand is likely to be less than one, so chances are you could raise your price and increase revenues since people don't have another product to substitute into. Does this rule hold in general?"

"It must," said Mo. "The equation for total revenue (TR) or total expenditure (TE), is TR = P x Q, from the seller's viewpoint, or TE = P x Q, from the buyer's viewpoint. If price and quantity are moving in different directions, then revenues (expenditures) will follow whichever dominates, P or Q. And elasticity tells us exactly that. If $\epsilon > 1$, the numerator > denominator, or the percent change in Q exceeds the percent change in P so revenues (expenditures) will move in the opposite direction of price.

If $\epsilon < 1$, the numerator < denominator, or the percent change in P exceeds the percent change in Q so that revenues (expenditures) will move in the same direction of price."

Question 14. When $\epsilon = -1$ (unit elastic), a price increase will _____ total revenues or total expenditures.

$$* \; * \; * \; * \; * \; * \; *$$

"Since raising prices when demand is inelastic raises revenues, does this mean that there is no end to price increase from some sellers?" Mo wondered.

OBJECTIVE 3.5 Describe how elasticity changes along the length of a linear demand curve.

"That can't be. At high enough prices revenue must start to fall with further increases. But that means elasticity would have to move from being inelastic at low prices, to elastic at high prices."

"According to Silberberg on pages 81-82, that's exactly what happens."

"But the demand curve is a line, so it has the same slope at all prices. How can elasticity change?"

"Because elasticity is different from the slope of the demand curve, said Mo. "It involves the slope, but it is also determined by the particular price and quantity you are at when you measure it. On page 81, Silberberg rearranges the elasticity formula as: $\epsilon = (p/q)(\Delta q/\Delta p)$. The last expression is run/rise, the _inverse_ of the slope. ($\Delta q/\Delta p$ is the slope of the demand curve when Q is written on the left-hand side of the equation.) So the elasticity formula can be written as: $\epsilon = (p/q)(1/slope)$. This makes it pretty clear that elasticity is determined by the slope, which is the same everywhere along a line, and the price and quantity you are measuring at."

"So when price rises, elasticity becomes a larger number in absolute value. At some point, elasticity will become greater than one, and further price increases would decrease total revenues. It occurs to me that to be perfectly correct, we should always be talking about the elasticity of a good _at a certain price_."

"You're probably right Ginny, but I'm going to assume that you know what I mean. Let's try a question from Adam's exam."

> **Problem:** Mario's corner deli sells 6 lbs./day of hot Italian sausage at a price of $1.80/lb. Mario's son Nick was told in his economics class that someone had estimated the price elasticity of demand for hot Italian sausage at -3. If this estimate is correct, calculate the slope of the demand curve for this sausage. Write out the equation for the inverse demand curve.

"O.K., let's take this in steps. We have P = $1.80, Q = 60, $\epsilon = -3$, and we're asked for the slope of the demand curve. The formula we have linking the slope of the demand curve to elasticity is $\epsilon = (\Delta Q/\Delta P)(P/Q)$. So all we have to do is plug in the numbers: $-3 = (\Delta Q/\Delta P)(1.80/6)$, so $-3 = (\Delta Q/\Delta P)$ x .3, $(\Delta Q/\Delta P) = -10$. The slope of the demand curve is -10."

"How do we know $\Delta Q/\Delta P$ is the slope of the demand curve, and not the inverse demand curve?"

"Because the inverse demand curve writes P on the left-hand side as the dependent variable. And since we plot P on the vertical axis in the supply and demand diagram, the change in P is the rise and the change in Q is the run, so the slope, rise/run, must be $\Delta P/\Delta Q$."

"So if the demand curve is Q = a - 10P, the inverse demand curve is found by solving that equation for P on the left hand side: P = a/10 - 1/10Q, or P = .1a - .1Q."

Question 15. The demand curve for apples sold at a highway fruit stand has been estimated at Q = 1000 - 250P. Currently 100 apples/day are being sold at a price of $0.60 per apple. The owners of the fruit stand could increase their total revenues by increasing price. True or False?

OBJECTIVE 3.6 Provide an example of the second law of demand.

"How come you haven't been downhill skiing as much this winter Mo? I hear the snow in the mountains has been great."

"Lift ticket prices have increased so much in the past few years. At first I just cut back a little, but after awhile I discovered cross-country skiing. It's a lot cheaper and still a lot of fun. So I downhill occasionally, but a lot less than before."

"Sounds like the second law of demand: as time passes, your response to a price change becomes greater."

"It's true. A lot of people think that you react a lot at first to a price increase, but that after awhile you get used to it and go back to consuming the good like before. But that's just not true. You look for substitutes and unless your income rises or something else changes, over time you consume less and less of the good."

Let's try one of Adam's questions on this:

> **Problem:** Suppose new technology lowers the (relative) price of train travel. The elasticity of demand for train travel at current prices is estimated at -1.90. What do you expect to happen to total revenue from train travel? Would the number of weekly customers riding the train be larger or smaller in a one week period a year from now, compared to the week immediately following the price fall?

"Well," volunteered Mo, "-1.90 means that train travel is price elastic at these prices. Using the total revenue rule, since the percent change in quantity will dominate the percent change in price, price and total revenue will move in opposite directions. Since price is falling, total revenue must be rising."

"I agree. And it makes sense intuitively. If you gain more in riders than you lose in fares, revenues should rise. How about the second part of the question?"

"The first law of demand states that if price falls today, quantity demanded will rise. The second law of demand implies that quantity demanded will rise further (i.e the rate of consumption will be greater) as time passes, because people will have had time to discover the lower train prices and adjust their travel habits to take advantage of them."

"So the answer is?"

"The number of weekly customers would be larger one year from now," replied Mo. "Adam showed me this sequence to illustrate the second law of demand:
    If P↓, Q/time ↑ now, and Q/time ↑↑ in the future.
    If P↑, Q/time ↓ now, and Q/time ↓↓ in the future.

OBJECTIVE 4.1 Explain why the "Shipping The Good Apples Out" example is an example of the law of demand.

"My Canadian cousin in Montreal says that she's consuming less and less maple syrup. According to her, the maple tree growers are 'shipping the good syrup' West. She says that 'Le sirop est mauvais.'"

"I understood Silberberg's examples about the apples, the steaks, and so on," said Ginny. "But what if I can't afford the more expensive item? Even if the high quality is relatively less expensive, it's still absolutely more expensive."

"That's true. Some people won't switch, so we're ignoring people's income constraints here and just looking at the effects of substitution based on relative price changes. If you look at Silberberg's example again with numbers the basic idea is clear."

	WA		NOrl	
	$P	Q	$P	Q
High Quality	.40	100	.60	90
Low Quality	.20	100	.40	60
		T = 200		T = 150

"Suppose at $.40 for the higher quality apples and $.20 for the lower quality apples in Washington State (WA), 100 pounds of each kind are sold per day, for a total of 200. When you add the $.20 transportation fee, fewer of both types may be purchased in New Orleans (NOrl). The total falls to 150 in this example, but more importantly, the mix changes: high quality falls from 100 to 90, but the lower quality falls further from 100 to 60."

"I see. So because both types have become absolutely more expensive, fewer of both are purchased, but because the higher quality has become relatively less expensive, proportionately more of it is purchased."

"Well I say that we vacate the library and head to the pancake house in search of high quality maple syrup," suggested Mo. We can work through some more questions over brunch."

ANSWERS TO DIALOGUE QUESTIONS

Question 1. $80/$3,200 = .025, or 2.5%.

Question 2. $3,200 + $80 = $3,280 $3,280/1.05 = $3,124

Question 3. Yes, although one can still consume the same meal with 3 slices of bread and 2 beverages for the same price, the relative price of bread and beverages has risen from 0 to $.10 and $.20.

Question 4. fell, $.64, fell, $.56. Real prices in 1960 were ($.19/29.6) x 100 = $.64, and in 1992 they were ($.79/140) x 100 = $.56.

Question 5. Add up the individual quantities demanded at each price:

Mrkt P	Indiv. Q's	Mrkt Q
3	1 + 2 + 3 =	6
2	2 + 4 + 6 =	12
1	3 + 6 + 9 =	18

Question 6.

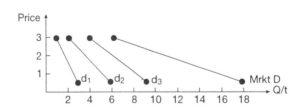

Question 7. Vocabulary: e, c, a or g, i, d, b or f, g or a, i, f or b, h

Question 8. Vocabulary: f, b, a, d, e, b, g, a, h. Inelastic: a given percent change in price induced a smaller percent change in quantity demanded. An elasticity of demand measuring between -1 and 0.

Question 9. law, demand, opposite
Question 10. elastic, less, inelastic, -1, unit elastic
Question 11. ϵ = (.30)/[($2.25 - $3.00)/$3.00] = -1.2
Question 12. Folger's coffee, coffee, hot beverages, beverages
Question 13. broader (more general)
Question 14. not change
Question 15. False. ϵ = ($.60/100)x -250 = -1.5, so raising price would lower total revenues.

THE BIG PICTURE

If you stop and look back you should see clearly the path you have taken through the fundamental condition that for all people, some goods are scarce; and how scarcity inescapably leads to a world of choices and costs. You should also see that the development of economics as a field of inquiry is based on applying a rigorous method of positive (i.e. not normative), logical reasoning centered around refutable propositions. Economists apply this method to explain the choices we make in response to continuous changes in a variety of constraints. These choices are governed by chapter two's postulates of behavior that form the base of economic theory.

From this you were introduced to the means by which economists link their fundamental assertions about human behavior and the world of observable human activity: the law of demand. The law of demand is the most powerful proposition in economics. The series of examples in chapter three of the theory of demand at work are a testament to the leverage one can gain over complex questions by applying its principles.

This brings us firmly into chapter three. The law of demand is about changes in behaviour in response to changes in any price or quantifiable cost related to that behaviour. It often focuses on prices, because prices are the main channel through which consumers and producers communicate. As with most measures, however, prices only take on significance when they are relative prices. Is $12.99 a lot for a pizza? Is thirty minutes a long time to wait for delivery? You can only answer that question relative to the prices of other pizzas, or other meal options. But ultimately, your willingness to buy pizzas, according to the law of demand is dependent on the *relative* price of that pizza.

The law of demand indicates the direction that quantity changes when price changes, and the slope of the demand curve provides a measure of how much -- the rate at which quantity changes for a price change. Chapter three introduces elasticity - a measure that of the magnitude of change that translates that rate of change into a percentage. Without being limited by the dimensions of the variables, elasticity allows for comparison in a way that slope cannot.

At this point you have travelled through a good introduction to the consumer's side of the market: the theory of demand. Looking ahead, you will study supply and exchange more closely. But neither side operates in isolation. You have already had a glimpse of the relationship, for example, by studying how the elasticity of demand affects seller's revenues when price changes. Chapter four and those that follow examine this relationship and exchange more closely.

REVIEW QUESTIONS

Answers to all review questions appear at the end of this chapter.

PROBLEMS AND EXERCISES
Write your answer in the space provided.

1. Assume that during prohibition the fine for being caught selling liquor was the same regardless of whether it was cheap moonshine (sludge water) or high quality moonshine, and there was no fine for consumption. Given this, would you expect to see a higher or lower proportion of high quality moonshine RELATIVE to sludge water offered for sale during prohibition, compared to when alcohol was not illegal? _____

This explanation is based on:
a. The morals of moonshine brewers.
b. The law of demand.
c. The absolute price of high quality moonshine.

2. Full-time (four courses or more) tuition at Carleton University is $3,200. The average student takes four courses per term. Carleton is considering changing full-time to mean three courses, and lowering the flat rate to $2,400, with each additional course costing $800. The number of courses the average student takes is expected to _____. Explain why.

This explanation is based on:
a. The energy of students.
b. The law of demand.
c. The absolute price of courses.

3. Consider the industry for oil (petroleum) and the industry for Golden Delicious apples. Suppose in a recent year technological improvements allowed each industry to produce their old levels of output at a lower cost. The result was an equivalent percentage drop in price for each industry. Is it possible for total revenues to fall in one or both of these industries? _____
If only one, which one and why? (Hint: think about differences in elasticity.)

And if so, would this mean total profits would fall in either industry? _____ Why or why not?

4. The Consumer Price Index (CPI) is calculated by measuring the cost of a set market basket of goods in one year and comparing that cost to a base average cost from a three-year period to determine the change. For one item, the formula for calculating the CPI would be $[(P_1 \times Q_0)/(P_0 \times Q_0)]$, where P_0 and P_1 represent the prices from the two different years and Q_0 represents the quantity of the item purchased. (The actual CPI measurement uses hundreds of items) Based on the Law of Demand, the CPI would under/over estimate <u>increases</u> in the general price level.

What about <u>decreases</u> in the general price level? Explain.

5. One of the two gas pumps in town just closed down, and now on average, a person had to wait fifteen minutes to get gasoline. The pump price is $1.00 per gallon. Both Stu and Emil are waiting to buy ten gallons of gasoline. Stu is an economic consultant who can earn $40 per hour any time he wants to do more work, and he is heading for work right now. Emil is retired.

a.   What is the actual dollar amount Stu and Emil spend on the gasoline?_____

b.   What is the true cost to Stu of the gasoline?_____

c.   If Stu and Emil's elasticity of demand are the same, who will reduce consumption of gasoline by a larger percentage in the long term?_____

6. The Calgary Light Rail Transit System (LRT) operates an above-ground mass transit system. LRT officials at one point raised the basic fare from $1.00 to $1.50. One month after the fare increase ridership had fallen by 15 per cent.

a.   The one-month demand curve was elastic/inelastic over this price range?

b.   The price change raised/lowered LRT's total revenue? Explain.

c.   The monthly percentage reduction in LRT ridership after one year would be larger/smaller than after one week? This is due to the _____ law of demand.

7. Which of the following are relative price measures:
a.   current prices
b.   constant prices
c.   nominal prices
d.   real prices

8. A recent study has shown that the nominal wages of manufacturing workers in the United States have increased over the past twenty years, but the real wages of these workers has declined. Does this mean that manufacturing workers are currently better off or worse off? Explain.

9. Eunice has the following demand for Grateful Dead t-shirts:

$P	10	9	8	7	6	5
Qd		1	2	3	4	5	6

a.   If the price is $7 per t-shirt, how many t-shirts will Eunice buy? _____

b.   What is her total expenditure? _____

c.   What is Eunice's price elasticity of demand over the price range $7 to $8? _____

d.   If the price of t-shirts fell from $8 to $7, producer revenues would: increase/decrease/stay the same.

e.   The price elasticity of demand over this range for Grateful Dead t-shirts is expected to be larger/smaller than for all t-shirts together. Be sure to clearly indicate what you mean by larger or smaller.

10. In the land of taxes to your north, the government added another tax on beer, raising the price from $13.50 to $14.50 for a 12-pack. During the first month sales of each brand was as given below, compared with the same period in 1993.

	1993	1994
Lethbridge Pilsner	450,000	370,000
Labatt's Blue	180,000	100,000
Molson Canadian	360,000	340,000

Using the arc elasticity formula, calculate elasticity and fill in the blanks:
_____ is the beer with the most elastic demand.   For producers of _____ gross (before tax) total revenues will increase.

11. The amount of a commodity that an individual wishes to purchase depends on the price of that commodity, income, the price of closely related goods (i.e. substitutes for the good in question), tastes, etc. With only two dimensions, when graphing the demand curve for that good we choose to plot the price of the good against the quantity, holding all else constant. Suppose instead that you choose to hold the price of the good constant and measure some other constraint? Graphically illustrate a demand curve for steak plotted with the quantity of steak on the horizontal axis and,
a. the price of hamburger meat on the vertical axis.
b. income on the vertical axis.

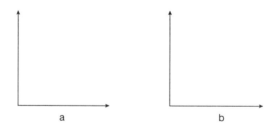

TRUE - FALSE QUESTIONS
Provide a one or two sentence explanation with your answer.

1. Quantity demanded can either rise or fall when price decreases depending on the elasticity of the demand curve.

2. The law of demand is a statement about consumers' responses to nominal price changes.

3. The law of demand implies that if the price of a closer more expensive parking lot and a more

distant cheaper lot both rise by $.50 per day, a greater proportion of drivers will park in the closer lot than before the price increase.

4.   If the University wanted to raise money, revenues would probably increase more by raising tuition to freshmen and sophomores than juniors and seniors. Assume class size is the same.

5.   Elasticity is unitary if a price rise leaves consumer expenditures unchanged.

6.   The elasticity along a straight-line demand curve is higher at higher prices and lower quantities than it is at lower prices and higher quantities.

7.   In 1993 I consumed 50 large pepperoni pizzas for $12.00 a pie. In 1994 nothing has changed in my economic life, but the price of these pizzas increased to $14.00, and I ate 40. My demand for pizzas over this price range is therefore elastic.

8.   The law of demand predicts that I would prefer substantial "inflation" if my employment contract provides for a wage increase equal to the increase in my cost of living (a COLA clause), as measured by inflation.

9.   The elasticity of demand for oil should become more inelastic at current prices as per capita income rises.

10.   The elasticity of demand for oil should become more elastic at current prices as solar energy technology improves.

11.   The elasticity of demand for oil should become more elastic at current prices if a carbon tax is implemented on all fossil fuel products (which includes oil).

12.   The time spent purchasing a good should not be considered part of the cost since the time would have passed anyway.

MULTIPLE CHOICE QUESTIONS
Choose the best answer.

1. How many laws of demand are there?
a.   one
b.   two
c.   not enough
d.   too many

2. The calculation of the CPI restricts the demand for all goods to:
a.   be perfectly inelastic.
b.   be perfectly elastic.
c.   decrease over time.
d.   become more elastic over time.

3. Most provinces in Canada now garnishee the wages (take them directly off the paycheck) of fathers not paying child support. The law of demand predicts the passage of this legislation will:
a.   decrease men's desire for casual sex.
b.   decrease the amount men engage in casual sex.
c.   decrease women's desire for casual sex.
d.   decrease the amount women engage in casual sex.

4. The law of demand predicts that as womens' economic independence and wealth increase:
a.   the age discrepancy between husband and wife will widen.
b.   a man's beauty will become a more valued trait.
c.   the birthrate will increase.
d.   none of the above.

5. The law of demand predicts that property crime rates will increase with:
a.   increases in immigration.
b.   decreases in the populations.
c.   increases in unemployment rates.
d.   none of the above.

6. Disneyland visitors from outside of California are _____ likely to go on the expensive rides than visitors from L.A. because of the _____:
a.   more, the first law of demand.
b.   the same amount, the second law of demand.
c.   less, the first law of demand.
d.   less, the second law of demand.

7. If the price of coffee rose by 9% and the quantity demanded fell by 5%, then over that price interval the absolute value of the elasticity of demand for the good is:
a.   greater than one and total expenditures on coffee are less than before the price change.
b.   greater than one and total expenditures on coffee are more than before the price change.
c.   less than one and total expenditures on coffee are less than before the price change.
d.   less than one and total expenditures on coffee are more than before the price change.

8. The 5% decline in quantity demanded was measured immediately after the price increase. Compared to this, if consumer response had been measured one year from now, one would expect:
a.   the rate of consumption would have declined by less than 5%.
b.   the rate of consumption would have returned to its old level.
c.   the rate of consumption would have declined by more than 5%.
d.   the rate of consumption would have declined by the same amount.

9. The answer for the previous question is based on
a.   the first law of demand.
b.   the second law of demand.
c.   the postulate that more is preferred to less.
d.   the postulate that people have preferences.

10. If the price of vegemite rises by 80% and Australians decrease consumption from 4,500 metric tons to 4,000 metric tons annually, the price elasticity of demand over this price range would be estimated as:
a.   elastic.
b.   inelastic.
c.   unit elastic.
d.   insufficient information to conclude.

11. Assume there is good quality vegemite that sells for $2.00 a jar in Australia and poor quality vegemite that sells for $1.00 a jar in Australia. It costs $4.00 per jar to ship vegemite to the United States. Based on this, we would expect, compared to Australia:
a.   proportionately more poor quality vegemite in the United States.
b.   equal amounts of poor and good quality vegemite in the United States.
c.   proportionately more good quality vegemite in the United States.
d.   no good quality vegemite in the United States.

12. The answer for the previous question is based on:
a.   the first law of demand.
b.   the second law of demand.
c.   the postulate that more is preferred to less.
d.   the postulate that people have preferences.

13. We would predict that the demand for red delicious apples would probably be more elastic than:
a.   the demand for apples.
b.   the demand for food.
c.   none of the above.
d.   both of the above, a and b.

14. "All I know is that on my income I can't afford to live the way I used to. But nothing has changed in my life -- I get the same salary, I've got the same family." As economists, we would predict that this person:
a.   has developed expensive habits.
b.   has developed a taste for more expensive items.
c.   has a poor paying job.
d.   has a salary without a cost-of-living clause.

15. Inflation is most likely to reduce the purchasing power of:
a. the poor.
b. the rich because they consume more.
c. seniors on fixed incomes.
d. teenagers because they are just starting out.

16. For which of these goods would the price elasticity of demand ordinarily be greatest?
a. gasoline
b. unleaded gasoline
c. Mobil regular gasoline

17. A perfectly inelastic demand schedule (vertical demand curve) is inconsistent with
a. the law of demand.
b. the substitution postulate.
c. diminishing marginal value.
d. none of the above.
e. all of the above.

18. If economics professors could be sued for malpractice by students who received credit in Econ 200 despite their failure to learn, we would confidently expect:
a. the quality of teaching to rise.
b. exams to be based more on real-life situations.
c. fewer students to take Econ 200.
d. increased difficulty passing Econ 200.

19. Suppose two couples decide to share their restaurant bill equally (divide the total bill by four). The law of demand would predict that
a. people would order more expensive meals than if they paid individually.
b. people would order the same meal since they have to pay a quarter of the bill anyway.
c. people would order a less expensive meal so they appeared to be more frugal.

20. A $25.00 tax levied on every airline ticket sold to compensate homeowners located near airports would be expected to lead to:
a. more people buying homes near runways.
b. fewer flights.
c. relatively more first-class tickets.
d. none of the above.
e. all of the above.

21. A fall in the general price level, called deflation, would _____ the purchasing power of_____:
a. decrease, the poor.
b. increase, the poor.
c. decrease, seniors on fixed incomes.
d. increase, seniors on fixed incomes.

22. Inflation results from
a. consumers spending more than they earn.

b.   aggressive union leaders.

c.   the money supply increasing faster than the growth of the economy.

d.   all individuals in the private economy.

23. By the law of demand, a decrease in the general price level will induce people to

a.   engage in more transactions.

b.   buy gold and other precious metals.

c.   substitute out of physical capital and into cash holdings.

d.   all of the above.

SHORT ANSWER QUESTIONS

1. a. What does the law of demand imply will happen when a per unit tax is added to two items of varying quality, such as a luxury and compact automobile?

b. Suppose instead of a per unit tax, an ad valorem tax -- a tax that is a percentage of the item's value -- was added. For example, instead of a $2,000 import tax on all automobiles, an ad valorem tax would be a 10% tax on the value of the car. A $20,000 car would have a $2,000 tax, a $12,000 car would have a $1,200 tax added to its price. In the case of an ad valorem tax, what would you expect to happen to the proportion of high and low quality imported cars?

2. Opponents of gun control often say, "Guns don't kill people, people kill people." What would economic theory predict to happen to the homicide rate if handguns became illegal?

3. In the Spring of 1993, the Canadian government raised tobacco taxes yet again, bringing the retail price of a carton of 200 cigarettes to Cdn$48.50. 75% of this price was due to federal and provincial taxes. In the Fall of 1993, the mayor of Cornwall, a small Canadian town on the shores of the St. Lawrence River, was forced into hiding because of threats to his life. The mayor was trying to curb cigarette smuggling across the St. Lawrence -- the Canadian/U.S. border between New York State and the provinces of Ontario and Quebec.

a. Based on this scenario, it is fairly safe to assume that the _____ price of cigarettes coming from the U.S. is _____ than the Canadian price.

b. Cornwall's unemployment rate has been estimated at over 20%. How might this explain why many normally "law-abiding" citizens
also opposed the mayor's war on smuggling?

The government defended the tax increase as an attempt to further reduce cigarette consumption. Critics argue that the elasticity of demand for adult smokers is price inelastic, and that a price increase will not change consumption by much.

c. What will happen to government revenues from the tax on sales of cigarettes to adult smokers?

d. The elasticity of demand for teenagers is estimated to be greater than 1 in absolute value. Is the government's defence more applicable for adult smokers or teenagers?

e. Most of the smuggled cigarettes are actually Canadian exports that are sold legally without the

Canadian taxes in the U.S. and then smuggled back into Canada. What would you expect to happen to the volume of Canadian exports to the U.S. after the tax increase?

f. The actual cost of manufacturing and distributing a carton of cigarettes in Canada is about $12.40. What is the potential profit margin per carton for smugglers of cigarettes? What factors will affect the selling price of smuggled cigarettes?

g. Many people have advocated an export tax on Canadian cigarettes. Why might this temper smuggling the smuggling problem?

h. Why might the tobacco companies be opposed to the export tax?

i. Opponents argue that although most Canadian smokers prefer the tobacco blend used in Canadian cigarettes, at certain prices they would switch to American cigarettes, a carton of which can be purchased at about Cdn$19.00. If this is true, what would you expect in response to an export tax?

j. In February of 1993 the government decided to cut taxes, and the price of cigarettes fell in some provinces by almost 50 per cent. Domestic sales of cigarettes were reported to be 35.8 per cent higher than February 1992. If these numbers are accurate, what is the overall elasticity of demand?

k. Four Eastern provinces have cut their provincial taxes on cigarettes. What does this action do to the relative price of cigarettes sold in the western province of Saskatchewan, for example?

l. It now costs $25 for a legal carton of cigarettes in Ontario. Suppose it costs $3 to transport a carton of cigarettes from Ontario to Saskatchewan. What will cigarettes cost (approximately) at the provincial border? What will happen to cigarette sales in Saskatchewan?

m. After the tax cuts exports fell 75 per cent. Where does this suggest the majority of U.S. exports were headed before?

n. February's rate of inflation was predicted to be 1.5 per cent, up 0.2 per cent from January. Instead, the effect of the tax cut was sufficient to cause a 1.3 per cent drop in the inflation rate to 0.2 per cent, the lowest rate in 32 years. What does this suggest about the proportion of a smoker's budget accounted for by cigarette purchases?

ANSWERS TO REVIEW QUESTIONS

Answers to PROBLEMS AND EXERCISES

1. a. Higher. A proportionate increase in the production of high quality moonshine during prohibition is expected. Since the fine is the same regardless of quality, it becomes a smaller fraction of potential costs with the high quality alcohol, i.e. the relative price of high quality falls.

b. This is an application of the law of demand.

2. Fall, since the relative price of a fourth course per term has risen.

b. This is an application of the law of demand.

3. Yes. It is possible for total revenues to fall in an industry when price falls if the elasticity of demand for that product is inelastic over those price ranges.

This is likely for oil, less likely for Golden Delicious Apples because they have many substitutes.

No. If profits were going to fall, neither industry would adopt the technological improvement. But this improvement lowers costs. For oil, even if revenues fall, costs will fall by more, leading to increased profit. Assuming the demand for Golden Delicious Apples is elastic, revenues would also rise. With rising revenues and falling costs, profits will increase.

4. Over. The CPI would overestimate increases or decreases in the general price level. By holding quantities at their base-year levels, it does not account for consumers substituting away from goods whose price has changed. The quantity response is always in the opposite direction of the price change, so it would mitigate (lessen) the effect of a price increase or decrease. Ignoring this mitigating effect overstates the effect of the price change in either direction.

5. a. $10.00 for 10 gallons at $1.00/gallon
b. $10.00 + $10.00 for 15 minutes of time at $40/hour = $20.00
c. Stu. Their elasticity is the same, but the percentage change in price has been greater for Stu, therefore his percent change in quantity will also be greater.

6. a. inelastic $\{-.15/[(\$1.50 - \$1.00)/\$1.00] = -.3$. Since -.3 is between -1 and 0, the demand is said to be inelastic. Note that if arc elasticity had been calculated using the average of the prices in the denominator for calculating the percent change in price, the formula becomes: $-.15/[(\$1.50 - \$1.00)/\$1.25]$ = -.375, and it is still inelastic.

b. Raised. Total revenues increase, because the inelasticity tells us that at current prices, the percent decrease in quantity will be less than the percent increase in price.

c. Larger, by the second law of demand. Quantity falls immediately following the price increase, and over time as people locate substitutes quantity will fall further.

7. b and d are relative price changes.

8. Worse off because general prices have risen faster than their wages and their purchasing power has fallen. The quantity of goods they can buy at today's price with current wages is less than the quantity they could buy twenty years ago at those wages and prices.

9. a. Four
b. $7 x 4 = $28
c. Using the arc elasticity formula, ϵ = [(3 - 4)/3.5]/[($8 - $7)/$7.5] = -2.14.
d. Increase, because demand is price elastic so price and total revenue move in opposite directions.
e. Larger -- a bigger number in absolute value, more elastic.

10. Labatt's Blue, Molson Canadian because only Molson's has an inelastic demand at those prices.

For every beer, the percent change in price was Δp/avg.p = ($13.50 - $14.50)/$14.00 = .07. For the various beers, the elasticities are therefore (reducing the '000's):
Lethbridge Pilsner ϵ = [(450 - 370)/410]/.07 = -2.8
Labatt's Blue ϵ = [180 - 100/140]/.07 = -8.2
Molson Canadian ϵ = [(380 - 360)/340]/.07 = -.84

11.

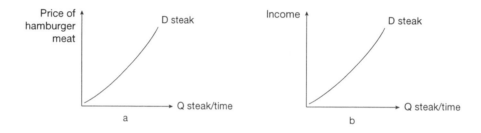

Answers to TRUE - FALSE QUESTIONS

1. False. By the law of demand, quantity demanded will always rise as the price falls. In the exceptional case, if the demand curve is perfectly inelastic, there will be no change in quantity demanded.

2. False. The law of demand is a statement about consumers' responses to relative price changes.

3. True. Although the closer lot is absolutely more expensive, with the tax it becomes relatively less expensive. So the tax represents a relative price fall for the closer lot.

4. False. Revenues would predictably increase more by raising tuition to juniors and seniors. There are fewer good substitutes in your third or fourth year after you have declared a major, fulfilled certain requirements toward that degree, and established networks at a certain school.

5. True. The percentage change in quantity exactly equals the percentage change in price. This is the

definition of unit elastic.

6. True. At higher prices the percent change in prices becomes smaller relative to the percent change in quantity (moving from a price of $9 to $10, for example, is a smaller percent change than moving from a quantity of 2 to 1). So as prices increase, the denominator decreases relative to the numerator and the ratio becomes larger in absolute value.

7. True. The elasticity is [(50-40)/45]/[(12-14)/13] = -1.4.

8. False. If no relative prices are changing then the law of demand has nothing to say. Only if you consume a group of goods whose price traditionally increases at a rate below those goods used to measure the CPI, would you prefer CPI measured inflation and the resulting wage increase that your COLA clause guarantees.

9. True. An increase in income means that oil purchases will constitute a smaller share of the budget, hence consumers will become less price sensitive. Or consider the elasticity formula: $\epsilon = (\Delta q/\Delta p)(p/q)$. An increase in income can be assumed to leave the slope of the demand curve unchanged, but at current prices quantity would increase, decreasing the ratio p/q and hence the (absolute value) measure of the elasticity.

10. True. Increases in the availability of substitutes makes the demand curve more elastic (in this case, it changes the slope).

11. True. A per-unit tax leaves the slope of the demand curve unchanged, but decreases the quantity purchased at each price. Using the formula $\epsilon = (\Delta q/\Delta p)(p/q)$, the decrease in q would increase the (absolute value) of the elasticity.

12. False. Although there is nothing we can do about time passing, we certainly have choices about how we spend that time. If an hour waiting in line to buy something is an hour that would have been spent doing something else, that hour has an opportunity cost. It is the foregone activity that is the cost, not the sixty minutes per se.

Answers to MULTIPLE CHOICE QUESTIONS

1. b	6. a	11. c	16. c	21. d
2. a	7. d	12. a	17. e	22. c
3. b	8. c	13. d	18. d	23. c
4. b	9. b	14. d	19. a	
5. c	10. b	15. c	20. d	

Answers to SHORT ANSWER QUESTIONS

1. a. The law of demand predicts that because the luxury car becomes relatively less expensive, proportionately more luxury cars will be sold after the price change.

b. In the case of an ad valorem tax, relative prices remain unchanged. The $20,000 luxury car "cost" 2 compact cars before the tax, and after the tax. The tax raises the price of the luxury car to $22,000, and the price of the compact to $11,000. One luxury car still costs 2 compact cars. We would expect fewer of both cars to be sold after the tax, therefore, but for the proportions to remain unchanged.

2. Homicides would decline because the cost of killing would rise. The price of contraband guns would be higher than the competitive, legal price that now exists, and there would be additional costs of having to find sellers, conceal the weapon, etcetera. Further, the cost to some individuals of having to commit the crime in a different, and perhaps more "personal" manner would also rise.

3. a. relative, lower

b. The alternative of no job lowers the opportunity cost of those directly involved with the smuggling. For others in the community, the demand for their goods and services may increase if other residents have more income to spend.

c. Government revenues from tobacco taxes will increase if the demand is price inelastic.

d. The government's argument is more applicable to teenagers.

e. The volume of exports is expected to rise. The market for exports now is not just U.S. smokers of Canadian cigarettes, but Canadian smokers of smuggled Canadian cigarettes.

f. The potential profit is $36.10, the difference between the retail price and the manufacturers cost (and the amount of the mark-up in government tax). The actual selling price will depend on how much competition there is between smugglers, what additional distribution and concealment costs the smuggler's incur, smoker's willingness to buy contraband products, etcetera.

g. If the tax is placed on the Canadian cigarettes entering the U.S., the cheap "tax-free" cigarettes won't be available for smuggling back into Canada.

h. The tobacco companies' exports have increased. As long as the tax-free exports are available to be smuggled, cigarette prices in Canada will remain low for many consumers, and by the law of demand, more cartons will be purchased.

i. If the price of Canadian exports rose, proportionaltely more smuggling of U.S. cigarettes would occur. As long as a significant price differential exists between domestically sold cigarettes in Canada, and cigarettes of any origin sold across the border, smuggling activity is expected.

j. About -.7, inelastic.

k. It increases Saskatchewan's relative price. $28.

l. Stores in Saskatchewan that must continue to sell cartons with provincial sales tax added will lose sales. People will simply drive to the border and purchase the cigarettes in the province with no sales tax.

m. Back to Canada via the St. Lawrence river.

n. For most smokers, especially before the tax cut, cigarettes consumed a large part of their budget.

CHAPTER 4
Exchange and Supply

PRINCIPAL GOALS

1.0 Understand and manipulate supply curves. (Objectives 1.1, 1.2, 1.3, 1.4, 1.5, 1.6)

2.0 Understand the theory and mechanics of gains from exchange in a competitive market. (Objectives 2.1, 2.2, 2.3)

3.0 Recognize the implications of gains from exchange, especially the formation of markets, transactions costs, property rights, and middlemen. (Objective 3.1, 3.2, 3.3)

OBJECTIVES
Answers to bold-faced questions appear at the end of the dialogue.

"Hey Ginny. How was Karl's party?"

"Not too bad. He cooked a ton of great food -- no meatloaf mercifully -- but you know what he did? He listed all these different job categories and everybody had to contribute money for beer according to their income. He's really weird, but a great cook."

"A good socialist approach. Of course everyone got to consume according to their appetite."

"Of course! Did you get through the chapter?"

"Yes. Isn't the idea of exchange interesting? Which reminds me, do you have any CD's you don't listen to any more?"

"Well, I've got some that I haven't listened to for awhile", Ginny said. "Why do you ask?

"Oh, I've just started a CD exchange business and I thought that if you had some that you didn't listen to you might want to put them into the exchange."

"Mo, a CD exchange - you never told me you had a business. How long have you had it? You don't even like music all that much do you?"

"Does Wrigley's chew gum? Does Sam Walton's family shop at Wal*Mart? I don't have to be a fanatic about music to run the business. It's really just a service that brings people together to swap discs in an organized way -- like the exchange in this chapter."

"Wow, so what do you do?"

"People send me a list of the CD's they want to get rid of and a list of the ones they would like to buy. I enter the names onto master lists then cross check one against the other. If there is a match then I initiate the swap. It's all done on computer."

"Mo, you're a middleman-person, or intermediary. That's amazing. Are you making any money?"

"Some, by charging a small monthly fee for membership. Right now I'm trying to increase the number of subscribers. Want to join? It's perfect for you Ginny."

"I'll think about it."

"I've got over 300 titles in the pop/rock category."

"I'll think about it. But for now, your Entrepreneurship, let's work on supply curves."

OBJECTIVE 1.1 Recognize definitions for the important new vocabulary.

Question 1. Match the term with its definition(s). Write out definitions for any undefined terms.

a. production   b. marginal cost
c. law of diminishing returns/marginal product
d. supply/demand schedules   e. rent

_____ A table of data representing the relationship between quantities demanded (and/or supplied) and prices of a good for an individual or a market.

_____ The combining of resources to create a new product.

_____ The amount in terms of their alternative value that must be given up in order to create, or produce an additional unit of some good.

_____ Payments in excess of the minimum amount that is necessary to induce a person to relinqush their rights to some good or resource.

_____ The gains in output that result from adding units of a productive input to a fixed amount of other inputs engaged in production eventually diminish.

OBJECTIVE 1.2 Derive an individual supply curve.

"So," Ginny said, "the supply curve represents the amounts of some good an individual is willing to exchange at specified prices. And as the price increases the individual is willing to give up more and more of their stock of the good. Is that right?"

"Yes, because as the price goes up this individual stands to make more money or increase their rents, so they are willing to sell more."

"Is there a supply curve for every different product or good?"

"As I understand it, as long as someone can supply it, we can create a supply curve", Mo answered.

"Okay, what if I supply CD's to your exchange", Ginny said. "What would my supply curve look like?"

"Well, first we would have to know how many CD's you have as your stock. Then we would need to figure out how many discs you would part with as the price changes."

"Hmmm, I can think of about ten or eleven off-hand that I would be willing to trade."

"Allright, how many would you give away for free? Zero?"

"Free! I wouldn't sell any for less than three dollars; I'd sell them all for eight bucks each though."

"Okay, so let's make a supply schedule. I'll put in the extreme values you just mentioned Ginny, and you can fill in the numbers inbetween."

$Price	Supply Schedule
8	11
7	9
6	7
5	5
4	3
3	1
< 3	0

"I want to see how my supply curve looks on a graph", Ginny said, "I'll draw it below."

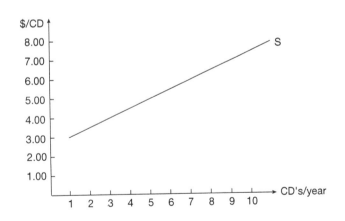

OBJECTIVE 1.3 Derive an aggregate supply curve from individual supply curves.

"Now if I look at the business as a whole", Mo said, "and take the pop/rock supply curves from each individual subscriber I could create an aggregate supply curve for pop/rock discs."

"What would you use that for?"

"For looking at the whole pop/rock market. It would also tell me where your prices lie relative to everyone elses, and with a little more information about demand, what the likely equilibrium price for used pop/rock CD's is. It's easy to derive, you just add the quantities that each individual would supply at each price."

"That is pretty straightforward", Ginny said. "Just like we did with the aggregate demand curve."

Question 2. Calculate aggregate supply and demand schedules for modeling clay based on the following information. Show the resulting aggregate supply and demand curves in a graph.

Demand

Francs	Rodin Kg.	Picasso Kg.	Cezanne Kg.
1	100	50	100
2	90	40	80
3	80	30	60
4	70	20	40
5	60	10	20

Supply

Francs	Paris Clay Kg.	Montmarte Sculptors Supply Kg.	Left Bank Arts Kg.
1	65	50	75
2	75	70	100
3	85	90	125
4	95	110	150
5	105	130	175

* * * * * * *

"Do you think this situation with the clay is the same as the oysters in Chapter 4?", Ginny asked.

"I guess I'm not sure what you're asking", Mo replied.

"With the oysters, she just has this pailful that she won in a contest and she wants to eat the oysters herself. In this clay question these art supply stores have to get the clay somehow before they can sell it and they don't want to use the clay themselves. All they want to do is sell it."

"I see what you're saying", Mo said. "Silberberg talks about that...on pages 117-118 he says:

> 'In most cases of supply, sellers make decisions regarding the amount of some good they offer for sale at a given price on the basis of how much it costs to produce and market those units, rather than merely the cost of relinquishing the rights to already existing units.'"

OBJECTIVE 1.4 **Clearly state the difference between supply curves based on endowments and those based on production.**

"So with the oysters", Mo continued, "he's saying the only decision the woman is making is whether or not she will give up her rights to eat a certain number of her stock as the price changes. When she looks at the price, she doesn't have to factor in the cost of catching oysters, because she just has them."

"But if she were an oyster farmer," Ginny said, "just like the art supply stores, she would have to decide whether the price was high enough to meet her costs of catching and selling oysters or digging up clay, rather than just how much she has to be compensated for not getting to eat them herself."

"It's like she is both a consumer and a supplier, while the clay dealer is just a supplier."

"Another thing", Mo said, "the oysterwoman isn't producing anything; she is simply trading 11 oysters for money. It's just an exchange of existing wealth."

"You're right. It's an exchange that leaves her and her trading partner better off, but doesn't create any new wealth. So her supply curve reflects the cost of her foregoing oysters, but no production costs."

"Silberberg says there will be more on this later."

"Do you have anything else you think we should talk about?, Ginny asked.

"Well, sort of. How come there isn't a Law of Supply?"

"I give up, how come?"

"No, I'm serious."

"I can see that, but I still don't know why..."

"Hey you guys. Hi Ginny."

"Adam! Your sister here was just wondering why there is no Law of Supply like the Law of Demand."

OBJECTIVE 1.5 **Explain why there is no Law of Supply.**

"Oh, that's actually a good question," Adam said.

"Somehow I thought you might say that Adam, but please, continue."

"Well this is a bit ahead of where you are now, but the Law of Demand states that as the price of a good decreases, more of that good is consumed; and as the price increases, less is consumed *ceteris paribus*--"

"*Ceteris what-a-bis*?", Ginny asked.

"*Ceteris paribus*," Adam said. "It means all other things remaining the same; so in this case as price changes, all other variables, like income for instance, remain unchanged. It's fundamental to the study of economics. To analyze the effect of a change in one particular variable you have to hold everything else constant."

"Right, we've had that", Mo said.

"Anyway the Law of Demand holds true in the short- and long-run. No matter what the time frame people will behave according to that principle, which, of course, is expressed in the law of diminishing marginal value."

"Of course."

"Yes, well, for supply its different. It's not regular like demand. Supply is governed primarily by the costs associated with production. In the short-run the cost of producing increases as the quantity produced increases. In other words, marginal costs are increasing with increasing output. That's one reason the supply curve is positively sloped. The problem with formulating a law of supply is that this may only be true in the short term. Over the long-run a producer can employ new technology or other means to lower his production costs. So, while in the short-run a producer's supply curve is positively sloped, over the long-run the supply curve may be positively sloped or flat or, in some cases, negatively sloped, depending on a number of cost factors. Does that make sense?"

"Sort of," Mo said.

"Basically what you're saying", Ginny said, "is that there is no behavioral postulate governing suppliers like the law of diminishing marginal value personally affects consumers."

"That's close enough Ginny. Gosh, it's great to hear you talk like that."

"I imagine we'll get a lot more on costs later on," said Mo.

"A lot more," confirmed Adam, "and it will become clearer as you go on. Well, I've got to go meet the guys at the academic computing center. See you sis, bye Ginny."

"Bye Adam, thanks."

"Your brother is just so darn earnest," Ginny said.

OBJECTIVE 1.6 Calculate a producer's rents, revenues and costs.

"Well I thought the idea of rents, costs, and revenues seemed pretty straight forward, but I wanted to do a few practice problems just to make sure I could work with them."

"Okay", Ginny said, "let's try this one."

> **Problem:** From the graph below showing Bassmaster Lure Co.'s supply curve, determine the quantity supplied, and the producer's total revenue, costs and rent when the price of lures is $9.00. What is the marginal cost of producing the fourth fishing lure?

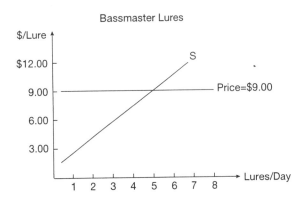

"This doesn't look too hard," Ginny said. "At a price of $9.00 the quantity supplied would be 5."

"Right, which also makes sense if you think about supply as a marginal cost curve. The price would have to be $9.00 to get Bassmaster to relinquish the 5th unit."

"Now the total revenue is price times quantity so that's $9.00 x 5 lures equals $45.00. So the costs and rents would be $22.50 each?"

"Hmm, I don't think so," Mo said. "Your total revenue is right, but you can't just assume that costs and rents are each going to be half of the total revenue. You have to figure them out separately."

"Oh, you're right. Do I make you feel smart sometimes? Don't answer that. Okay, Silberberg says:

> *The areas under the supply curve represent the cost to the sellers of providing this good (p. 117).*

And,

> *The minimum total amount it would take to induce suppliers to sell...[is] the area under the supply curve (p. 116)."*

"So the minimum total amount of money or other goods required to get suppliers to sell some quantity of their stock of goods is the amount that at least covers their costs or equals their marginal value."

"Which is the same thing," interupted Mo, "because they both represent costs -- either wages paid out or foregone consumption."

"And the area under the curve represents that amount. So the supply curve is the line that defines the difference between just covering your costs and having some surplus rent."

"For us then, the area under the supply curve is the area of that little rectangle, which is $1.50 x 5 = $7.50 plus the area of the triangle above it. That's 1/2(5) x $7.50 = $18.75 for a grand total of $26.25. And the producers' surplus or rent would be $45.00 - $26.25 = $18.75." Mo said.

"Sure, or we could calculate the area above the supply curve but below the price line at $9.00. Which would be 1/2(5) x $7.50 = $18.75. So we were right."

"What is the marginal cost of producing the fourth fishing lure?"

"Well, we should be able to just read up to the curve from a quantity of 4 then over to the vertical axis, which is about...yeah it's half-way between $6 and $9. So $7.50."

"Allright!" Mo drawled.

Question 3. Calculate total revenues, costs, and rents for a custom bicycle frame manufacturer with orders for 42 frames. First draw a supply curve representing the following information:

Price	Qsupplied
<$1200	0
$1200	1-30
$1600	31-50

Total Revenue _____
Total Costs _____
Total Rents _____

OBJECTIVE 2.1 Recognize definitions for the important new vocabulary.

Question 4. Match the term with its definition(s). Write out definitions for any undefined terms.

a. mutual benefits　　b. terms of trade
c. transactions costs　　d. competitive markets
e. Pareto efficiency　　f. economic efficiency
g. property rights　　h. private property

_____ The point at which in a competitive economy the seller's marginal cost equals the buyer's marginal value on the last unit exchanged.

_____ The prices (in money or goods) at which goods are exchanged.

_____ A good or property for which an individual has the right to exclude others; claim any income derived from the property; and transfer the property to others at an agreed upon price.

_____ Markets in which many buyers and sellers transact with each other at unique prices that are beyond the direct control of any one trader.

_____ That condition which leads people to engage in exchange because their respective values for a given unit of a good exceed the cost required to carry out the exchange.

_____ In a competitive economy, the condition when the mutual benefits from exchange are exhausted.

_____ The point in a competitive economy at which the market price induces suppliers to offer an amount of the good for sale that is equal to the quantity demanded by consumers at that price.

_____ The legally or otherwise recognized "rules" which govern who is entitled to the benefits from exchange and production.

_____ The costs of exchange that are associated with determining and ensuring the nature and quality of the good or service being transacted.

OBJECTIVE 2.2 Describe the difference between legal and economic rights.

"What did you make of the property rights stuff?" asked Mo.

"Very interesting. Especially how it all fits together: the way the possibility of mutual benefits motivates exchange, but exchange can only occur if individuals or groups have rights over the goods they are exchanging, and if those rights are recognizable and enforceable."

"I agree," Mo said. "The first issue is if a property rights regime exists that gives people the incentive to exchange, and the second is if the political and legal system is strong enough to protect those rights."

"Yes. I was thinking about places like the former Soviet Union when I read this," Ginny said. "They had a clearly defined property rights system: the state owned almost everything. But it would NOT meet the definition of a competitive market."

"Absolutely not," Mo said. "Just look at the three conditions on page 125. Well, exclusion is sort of unclear, but ownership of income and the right to sell property was extremely limited."

"Sure, an individual with the backing of the state had the right to exclude others from using the few things private citizens could own like a refrigerator, or that they had the use of, like their apartment or small garden -- So that was not so different from what we know. But without broad property ownership, private individuals didn't have any income or rents to own, beyond their individual wage."

"No," Mo agreed. "And since they didn't own much property there was precious little to exchange. So on two of three counts, really, the former Soviet economy was not based on private property, which according to Silberberg leads to diminished gains from trade."

"What about a situation or country where an individual can hold private property rights but their rights aren't well protected?" asked Ginny.

"This gets into something that Adam was telling me. He mentioned once that there was a difference between legal and economic rights -- that although a person may have full legal rights to a piece of property, their economic rights are never complete because of transaction costs."

"What does he mean by economic rights? The right to exclude, own income, and transfer?"

"Yes," Mo said. "He used the example of a wallet. You may think you have legal and economic ownership of your wallet and the money inside, but if gun-wielding muggers confront you, you will probably relinquish your economic rights to the wallet and cash. The only ways you can regain your economic rights are either by somehow forcing the mugger to give it back or through legal channels with the help of the police and the court system. You have never relinquished your legal rights of ownership but in an economic sense you lost your rights to the wallet and whatever is inside."

"I see, and you said this is because of transaction costs?"

"Well the transaction costs occur when you try to protect your economic rights. If you were to pay for a bodyguard or self-defense training or a weapon, these would be transactions costs associated with protecting your economic rights to your property."

"Ah, I get it, and you can never really have complete economic rights over something, because there are always those people who will try to take them over for themselves. This is good stuff."

"Something like that," Mo said.

"Is this why economics is called the dismal science?"

OBJECTIVE 2.3 Define and illustrate economic efficiency.

"Do I detect a note of sarcasm?" Mo asked.

"Me? Sarcastic? Come on Mo, I'm from the country. What I am is confused by the explanation of economic efficiency. It sounds like it can exist side by side with complete poverty. It seems contradictory to me that something could be efficient yet completely inequitable."

"I'm not sure I understand that either," Mo agreed. "But he does say that efficiency is not about a value judgement on the distribution of the benefits from trade, it's about a scientific assessment whether the maximum benefits possible have been extracted from the trading opportunity."

"That's true, because earlier he talked about how the total gains would remain the same regardless of the prices agreed upon by the traders. Remember, he said the distribution of the benefits would depend on the prices but the total benefits would stay the same."

"Wait a minute what was this?" Mo asked.

"The gains from exchange are dependent on the marginal values of the two traders, right? Their marginal values don't change as the price changes, so if the total possible gain from exchange is $20 then regardless of the price that the traders finally agree to, the total benefits will remain $20. It's only the distribution that changes."

"Meaning that at one price trader A may get a greater share of the benefit pie, but at another price the benefits would shift toward B, leaving A worse off, or not as well off?"

"Exactly," Ginny said.

"So economic efficiency is simply where all gains from exchange have been exhausted."

"That is so cool," Ginny said.

"Cool?"

"Sure, how these traders are driven to continue trading by their desire to acquire greater benefits for themselves. And that it continues, perhaps unconsciously, toward this point of exhaustion of benefits."

"It sounds almost sexual the way you describe it", Mo said. "Here cool of on this next problem."

Question 5. Which of the following pairs of traders would exchange at a price of $6.00? _____ At $6.00 how many pairs would exchange between 1 and 4 units? _____ Which pair would exchange the greatest quantity at $6.00 and at any price? _____ Which pair could generate the largest total benefits if they are exchanging at the equilibrium price? _____ For each pair, when trading at the equilibrium price and quantity, which partner gains the most from trading? _____

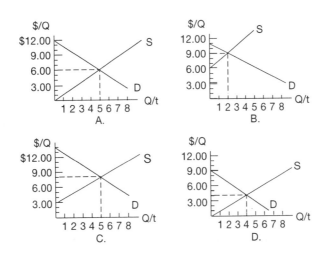

OBJECTIVE 3.1 **Identify the ways in which two people and a society are made better off simply by engaging in exchange, even if there is no production.**

"What I think is cool", Mo said, "is how we can make ourselves and our society better off just by exchanging. We don't even have to produce anything, we can just exchange goods from people who value them less to those who value them more and make both parties better off."

"Like your CD exchange?, Ginny asked.

"Yes, like my CD exchange. But even if I weren't in the middle providing information, if people were to exchange their least valued CD's for more highly valued CD's, they would be better off."

"What form does being better off take? More cash in your pocket?" asked Ginny.

"I think all we know at this point is that it's just value, whether you're talking about a simple trade between two people or the entire economy."

"I know it's value, but what does that mean?"

"For consumers it means the difference between what you would pay for something and what you do pay, and for producers it's the difference between the price you receive for a good and the price at which you would be willing to supply that same good."

"So it's money? Since consumers would pay more to get the good than they actually do pay when they make a trade, the value is some amount of money saved."

"Yes, I guess--"

"For suppliers it's the money they get over and above what they would have accepted for that good."

"Yes, but--"

"There see Mo, that wasn't so hard now was it?"

"Well, no, but I don't think this value is only money. Maybe it's time or some other resource with value."

"But like my father always says, 'Time is money'."

"Sorry Ginny, but your father wasn't the first person to *coin* that phrase."

OBJECTIVE 3.2 **Provide examples of how middlemen and money reduce transactions costs.**

"So clearly there are incentives for people to sign up for your CD exchange Mo."

"Sure, people want to trade into some new CD's. I've just provided the vehicle, the market."

"But you don't set the prices?" Ginny asked.

"No, right now I just put people in touch with one another and they negotiate their own trade. I'm just selling a list, really. But what's kind of interesting is that people can either trade in CD's or in money. When people aren't willing to sell their CD for money it's much harder and it takes way longer to actually make a trade. They've got a Miles Davis that they want to trade for a John Hiatt. Well, there just aren't that many people out there who have the John Hiatt AND want the Miles Davis too."

"That would be a problem. What did Silberberg call that, 'the double coincidence of wants'? But as middleman what are you going to do about it?" Ginny asked.

"Nothing, except encourage them to use money by bringing to their attention the names of people who have what they want. Money is amazing. If they would just use money they could save themselves hours and hours I'm sure. The value of these people's time must be pretty low."

"You know," Ginny said, "when I read section 4.7, I remembered how when Lynn returned from that Club Med resort she told us they used beads for money. I was trying to figure out why they would do that. What transaction costs could they be reducing by using beads for money?"

"I don't know. Maybe it just gets people to spend more. They have these beads and they can only buy things with them at Club Med. At the end of their trip they either take home a pocketfull of worthless beads or they spend them all; Club Med either gets a pure profit or the profit from the sale."

"I guess I assumed they could convert them back into real money at the end, but maybe the idea is that it's easier for people to spend beads than money."

"Maybe it's to prevent the employees from cheating the customers."

"How do you mean?"

"Well if they used real money the employees could overcharge the guests and pocket the extra. But there's no incentive to skim beads off the top because outside of Club Med they're worthless. Club Med just has to have a rule that no employees can convert beads for money and they save themselves the worry and cost of monitoring their employees."

"Clever, though maybe it's just a gimmick, rather than anything to reduce transactions costs."

"You mean they just want the guests to feel like they're transported to a different place with a different currency - have fun, don't worry, be happy, spend beads."

"This is a different subject", Ginny said, "but have you tried to figure out the supply and demand for the CD exchange? Have you graphed it out?"

"No, but I guess we could. I mean it might be hard, because my role is to simply save them the time it would take them each individually to find someone to trade with."

"Lowering their transactions costs", Ginny said.

"Exactly, though I didn't know that that is what I was doing when I began. I just thought it was a service that I could make some money from," Mo said.

"You're saving them time which has a value", Ginny said. "Aha! Now I see what the gains from exchange are. Your service allows them to trade when before they couldn't, or didn't trade, because it was too costly; it wasn't worth their while to spend the time and resources to find trading partners. I think the graph would look similar to the one in Silberberg on page 129."

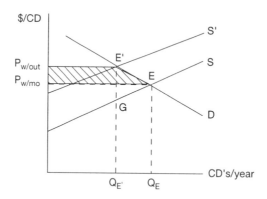

"So we don't know the exact numbers", Ginny said drawing out the graph, "but we know that there is a demand and supply schedule."

"Sure, without my service there is very little exchange, because the costs of transacting are too high. The supply curve (S') lies far to the left, showing trade at quantity $Q_{E'}$ and a price of $P_{w/out}$. But with my service the cost of exchange comes down, the supply curve (S) shifts right, prices fall and quantity increases."

"So the transactions costs have been reduced by the amount between E' and G. But the cost of subscribing to your service, as well as all the other remaining costs, are represented by the supply curve S, right?"

"Yes. Like mailing or the time it takes to make a deal. Or a big thing is they want to know the disc is in good shape. I can't guarantee anything, so there is some uncertainty there. But CD's are pretty durable, and besides, if anybody tries to unload a defective disk word will get around the network pretty quickly. That person would find it difficult making the next deal."

"You know," Ginny said, "if they could lower or eliminate those costs or the cost of your service, their supply curve would move even farther out beyond S to everyone's benefit."

"Your right, but *who* would give them that idea, Ginny?"

"Obviously anyone with basic microeconomics, but until someone figures that out you, as middleman, are earning a little money and everyone else is gaining by however much this shaded area $P_{w/out}E'EP_{w/Mo}$ represents."

"That's right and it's intermediary," corrected Mo.

"Sorry. How about if whenever I say middleman, you just imagine yourself hearing intermediary."

"I'd rather imagine myself hearing, 'with blueberries or chocolate on top?' Let's break for some empty calories before we tackle these questions."

Question 6. Would you expect realtor commissions to be higher in Mexico City or in Kansas City? _____ List a few of the factors that you think would explain why commissions would differ, and a short explanation of their effect.

Question 7. As an agent who represents professional athletes, you have observed the rise of Babe Espinosa, a young pitching prospect out of the Dominican Republic drafted by the St. Louis Cardinals organization. Babe and the Cardinals have to sign a contract before Babe can start playing in the United States. You want to represent Babe, but Babe hasn't yet signed with you. Babe believes the Cardinals value his services at about $500,000 for a one-year contract, which he would be happy with, believing that he could renegotiate for a much higher salary in the second year after he showed his stuff. He would accept a three year deal for $1 million/year, but he doesn't think the Cardinals would want to lock in for that long. You believe the Cardinals are very intent on signing this young phenom, who they have likened to the Cardinal Hall-of-Famer Bob Gibson. Given your experience you believe St. Louis' marginal value of Babe Espinosa appears as in the graph below.

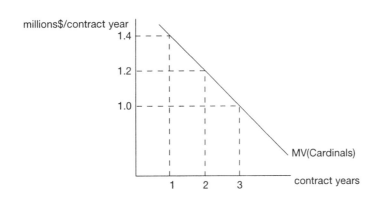

a) On the same graph, add Babe's marginal cost curve given the salaries he would be willing to accept **and** Babe's perception of the Cardinal's marginal value curve.
b) In anticipation of luring Babe into letting you represent him, what can you offer him in terms of salary level and contract years?
c) What is the maximum price you believe you could charge Babe and still make him better off than he would be without you? _____
d) Is it likely Babe would pay you this much for your services? Explain why or why not.

ANSWERS TO DIALOGUE QUESTIONS

Question 1. Vocabulary: d, a, b, e, c

Question 2.

Aggregate Demand		Aggregate Supply	
Francs	Kgs.	Francs	Kgs.
1	250	1	190
2	210	2	245
3	170	3	300
4	130	4	355
5	90	5	405

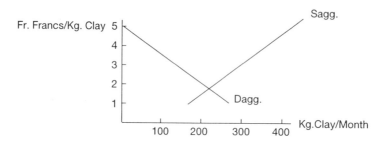

Question 3.   Total Revenues are $1600 each for 42 frames. $1600 x 42 = $67,200.

Total Costs are the areas under the supply curve. $1200 x 30 = $36,000 plus $1600 x 12 = $19,200, for a grand total of $55,200.

Total Rents are total revenues minus total costs. $67,200 - $55,200 = $12,000.

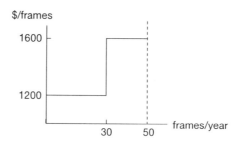

Question 4. Vocabulary: e or f, b, h, d, a, e or f, e or f, g, c

Question 5.
- A, C and D would exchange at a price of $6.00.
- C and D would exchange between 1 and 4 units at $6.00 (C = 3; D = 2).
- A would exchange 5 units (the most) at $6.00, but if the price rose to $8.00 C would also exchange 5 units.
- At any price the largest total benefits are possible in A, where $30.00 is available. B would yield $5.00; C $27.50; and D $18.00.
- In A the benefits are shared equally, $15.00 apiece. In B, the producer receives $3.00 and the consumer $2.00. In C, the producer receives $12.50 and the consumer $15.00. In D, the producer receives $8.00 and the consumer $10.00.

Question 6. I would expect realtor commissions to be higher in Mexico City, because the costs of gathering and producing information on housing would be higher than in Kansas City. My reasons are that Mexico City is a bigger city, with a far greater population, so the basic costs of maintaining a list will be higher (this may also be the case because of differences in the institutional and technological support for the real estate industry). Being a larger city there is probably a higher variability in property quality and values with the geography of mountain sides and the valley floor. There may also be less price and financial stability and other factors increasing costs in the real estate market.

Question 7. a)

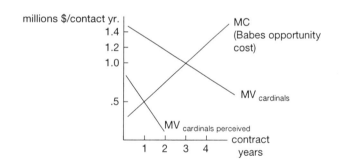

b. You could offer Babe up to $1.4 mill/yr. for a 1-year deal, $1.2 mill/yr. on a 2-year deal and $1 mill/yr. for a 3-year deal.

c. You could charge Babe up to $899,999 for 1 year, $449,999 for a 2 year, and nothing beyond your base fee on a three year contract and still make Babe better off.

d. Babe is not likely to pay these kinds of prices, because there is surely a long line of capable agents ready to serve him. Given this competition for the right to represent Babe, the price of their services to Babe would decrease and Babe would pay a far smaller portion of his salary to his agent.

THE BIG PICTURE

Marco Polo followed ancient trade routes to China and returned to Italy with previously unimagined goods. When Europeans first set foot on North American land they were met by nations of people with long established patterns of trade among themselves. The Bible and other ancient works are filled with references to trading activity. Trade is a primary human activity. Chapter four places this ancient behavior in the framework of the economic paradigm, explaining why people are willing to trade and how trade is the foundation of market economies. As you read through this chapter observe how this explanation of exchange conforms to the behavioral postulates: people have preferences; more is preferred to less; people are willing to substitute one good for another; and for all individuals, the marginal value of a good decreases as more of that good is consumed, *ceteris paribus*.

The crux of this chapter is that through exchange alone we can make ourselves better off, that is, even without production. In future chapters the full complexity of production will be added to this basic model. For now, however, we confirm the ancient understanding that if we exchange portions of our goods for the goods of another, we can be made better off than without the trade.

In a barter economy the price for some quantity of a good is arrived at through negotiation. In markets with thousands of exchanges between buyers and sellers prices are set from the experience of all these exchanges, and are beyond the control of any individual. In such *competitive markets* (which are the only markets Silberberg is describing so far), since buyers cannot adjust the price to match their marginal value for some quantity of the good, to maximize their benefit they adjust the quantity they purchase so that their marginal value for the last unit of the good purchased equals the price.

Every mutually agreed upon exchange of goods or resources produces benefits to be shared by the traders. The market system provides all participants, who desire the maximum benefits possible for themselves, an incentive not to allow these benefits from trade to diminish. Traders find it costly to misallocate resources and goods (i.e., use them in ways that are not their highest valued use) because to do so means the owner will receive less than the highest value for the resource. This implies others will pay (exchange) more to acquire those resources for their own use. In our market economy, countless trades transfer resources from lesser valued to higher valued uses, maximizing economic benefits.

Traditionally economists have viewed exchange as transferring a physical good or property from one person to another. Silberberg introduces another view here that exchange is really a transfer of rights over a particular good. This property rights perspective views ownership and exchange to be not of the good but of the rights to use, sell, make money from, or exclude others from using the property or good.

It is important not to confuse economic rights with legal rights. In general economic rights are protected by legal rights, but it requires the cooperation of society and the coercion of the state to guarantee these rights. A property rights perspective is very useful for explaining development issues around the world. Many people live in societies where their legal rights to own and use property are tenuous and therefore their economic rights to this property are even more tenuous. Chapter Nine discusses property rights further, but it is an interesting perspective to begin thinking about.

REVIEW QUESTIONS

Answers to all review questions appear at the end of this chapter.

PROBLEMS AND EXERCISES
Write your answer in the space(s) provided.

1. Calculate the total benefits at each quantity received by Lupe and Inez when Inez sells earrings to Lupe at the prices listed in the table below.

Quantity Of Earrings	Lupe's Marginal Value	Inez' Marginal Value	Negotiated Sale Price	Total Benefits	
1	$35	$ 5	$25	_____
2	25	10	20	_____
3	15	15	15	_____

What are the total benefits (at each quantity) if at each quantity the final price of earrings falls by $5?

2. Write the letters from the situations described below in the appropriate spaces on the graph.

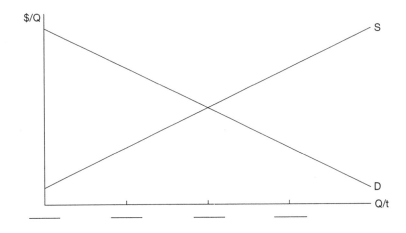

a. at this quantity the marginal value of the producer is greater than the marginal value of the consumer.
b. at this quantity no further exchange will occur, because one or both parties will be worse off.
c. at this quantity further gains from exchange can be realized.
d. at this quantity mutual benefits are exhausted.
e. at this quantity no gains from trade have been realized.

3. Use the following graph for chicken wings at Righteous Robert's Wing and a Prayer Barbecue to respond to questions a - e.

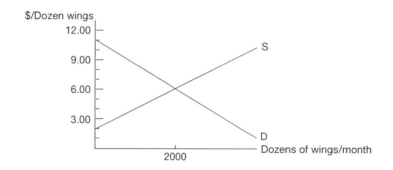

a. Calculate Rob's total revenue when he sells 2000 dozen wings per month. Show this on the graph.
b. Calculate the consumers' total expenditure on 2000 dozen wings at Rob's. Show this on the graph.
c. What are the units for the total revenue and total expenditure figures?
d. Show the mutual benefits for Rob and his customers when they exchange 2000 dozen wings. Indicate how much of this is consumers surplus and how much is rents for Rob.
e. Show Rob's alternative costs of providing this quantity of wings.

4. Down at Romeo Beach there are four suppliers of ice cream. Tooty's would be willing to sell 480 cones per day at $3.25 per cone and 310 at $2.25. Frooty's would be willing to sell 635 cones per day at $3.25 and 470 at $2.25. Rooty's would be willing to sell 350 cones per day at $3.25 and 260 at $2.25. Bob's would be willing to sell 27 cones per day at $3.25 and 11 at $2.25. Calculate the aggregate supply of ice cream cones at Romeo Beach at both prices. On one graph draw and label Tooty, Frooty, Rooty and Bob's individual supply curves and aggregate supply curve for ice cream cones.

5. Aria Highstrung makes exactly 12 custom made guitars per year. No more, or she would have to sacrifice quality; no less, or her finely tuned skills would wane. Her supply curve and the demand curve for her guitars are shown below. The supply curve S represents only the costs of production and indicates a price of $1400. This amount does not include the $250 transactions costs of ensuring Aria and her customers each fulfil their part of the contract. On the graph show how these transactions costs affect the price and quantity supplied. Price = _____ Quantity supplied = _____
Are there any lost benefits from trade? Explain.

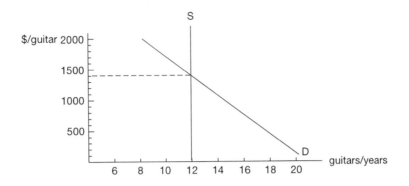

6. The following are the total value schedules for Marilyn and Joe. Each currently has combination D.

	Marilyn			Joe	
	$TV	Scones		$TV	Scones
A.	12.00	7		19.00	7
B.	11.10	8		15.00	8
C.	10.50	9		12.00	9
D.	10.00	10		10.00	10
E.	9.60	11		8.50	11
F.	9.30	12		7.85	12
G.	9.10	13		7.35	13

a. If Marilyn and Joe trade, do you expect Marilyn's marginal value of scones to increase or decrease?

_____

b. If trade was only possible through a middleman, what are the most scones they would exchange and the most money the middleman could make from brokering a deal?

Scones _____   Money _____

7. Use the graph below to answer the questions that follow.

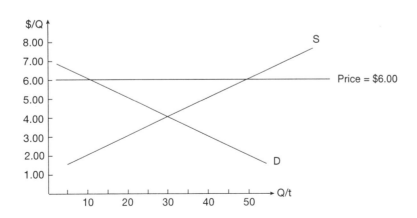

a. With the price externally set (i.e., not by the market) at $6.00 what quantity is a consumer willing to buy? _____ What quantity is the producer willing to supply? _____

b. What quantity of goods would be exchanged? _____

c. Calculate the lost gains from trade with the $6.00 price control. _____

d. With the removal of this price control, what would the optimal price and quantity be? _____

8. Big Jane Sorich owns 9 Jaguars in addition to some other cars. She is willing to part with some of her cars for a price according to the table below. Calculate Big Jane's supply schedule for her Jaguars and graph the resultant supply curve.

Market Price $'000's	Quantity Demanded	Supply Schedule
95	1	
90	2	
85	3	
80	4	
75	5	
70	6	
65	7	
60	8	
55	9	

9. Big Jim Gottbucks (Big Jane's husband) owns 8 Rolls Royces in addition to some other cars. He's willing to part with some of them according to his MV schedule below. Calculate Big Jim's marginal cost schedule for his Rolls and graph the curve.

Quantity	Marginal Value $'000's	Marginal Cost
1	140	
2	130	
3	110	
4	100	
5	85	
6	75	
7	65	
8	40	
9	30	

TRUE - FALSE QUESTIONS
Provide a one or two sentence explanation with your answer.

1. A supply curve represents the quantity of a good someone is willing to supply at a given price.

2.   A condition of Pareto efficiency is achieved when the (opportunity) cost of a good for suppliers is equal to the marginal value of that good for consumers.

3.   When price exceeds a consumer's marginal value for a good the consumer will buy the good.

4.   The mutual benefits of trade are represented or measured by the price at which a good is exchanged.

5.   Economies based on central command do not allow for the creation of wealth through unregulated trade, therefore they do not grow as fully as they would were unregulated trade to exist.

6.   In a pure exchange situation (i.e. with no production) there are no costs involved.

7.   Some trade is preferred to no trade between individuals.

8.   A producer will produce additional units of a good as long as marginal cost equals price.

9.   Money is an exchange medium representing the cost of other goods forgone during an exchange.

10.   An efficient economy ensures that the benefits from exchange are distributed evenly.

11.   When people trade, their marginal value for the good they have received falls.

12.   Between countries more trade is preferred to less trade by all people.

MULTIPLE CHOICE QUESTIONS
Choose the best answer.

1. A producer will choose to produce more of a good when:
a.   the cost of producing an additional unit of the good is greater than the consumer's marginal value for that good.
b.   marginal costs exceed the price of the good.
c.   the price of the good exceeds the cost of producing an additional unit of the good.
d.   prices increase.

2. Which of the following is not an explanation for the positive slope of the supply curve?
a.   higher prices induce producers to supply greater quantities.
b.   increasing costs are incurred as less efficient resources are used to produce additional output.
c.   the law of diminishing marginal product.
d.   consumer demand for goods steadily increases, inducing producers to supply steadily greater quanities.

3. At the trading post I observed a wealthy trapper and a poor trapper buying their winter's stock of powdered milk for $3.00/lb.
a.   The wealthy person's MV value for the milk is less than the poor person's, because $3.00 is nothing to a wealthy person.
b.   The wealthy person's MV for the milk is more than the poor person's, because they can buy anything they want yet they choose to buy milk.
c.   The wealthy person's MV for the milk is the same as the poor person's, because they are both choosing to buy the milk at the same price.
d.   The MV's of these two people for milk cannot be compared, because they have different incomes and preferences.

4. Why would a supplier and buyer exchange another unit of a good after they have already exchanged several units already?
a.   Because the buyers marginal value of the good still exceeds the sellers marginal value of the good.
b.   Because of the behavioral postulates.
c.   Because they can, without making either of them worse off.
d.   All of the above.

5. Which of the following is not a transactions cost associated with buying and selling fish?
a.   an inspector certifying the freshness of the fish.
b.   shipping the fish from the fishing boat to the store.
c.   the clerk weighing the fish before charging you.
d.   your comparison shopping among three stores to determine a fair price.

6. A supply curve with a steep slope implies that the producer,
a.   would increase the quantity supplied only slightly given a relatively large increase in price.
b.   would increase the quantity supplied greatly given a relatively large increase in price.
c.   would increase the quantity supplied only slightly given a relatively large decrease in price.
d.   would increase the quantity supplied greatly given a relatively large decrease in price.

7. Halting or preventing exchange from continuing up to the point of Pareto optimality implies which of the following:
a.   mutual benefits have been exhausted.
b.   diminishing marginal value.
c.   lost gains from trade.
d.   none of the above.

8. The possibility of trade
a.   exists only when individuals have surpluses of some goods.
b.   exists only when marginal values differ among traders.
c.   is hindered by middlemen who raise prices to cover their costs.
d.   causes people's marginal values to differ from each others.

9. The "rights" associated with owning any good
a.   are the uses of the good in fact controlled by the owner.
b.   are those that are legally guaranteed.
c.   depend heavily on the cooperation of other people.
d.   all of the above.
e.   a. and c. only.

10. In a situation where two people are trading their endowments, as greater quantities of a good are traded the supplier's or seller's marginal value for the good,
a.   increases
b.   decreases
c.   remains constant

11. At a point where a consumer's marginal value of a good is less than the seller's marginal value (alternative cost), any trade would imply that
a.   the good was being traded from someone who did not value the good to someone who did.
b.   mutual gains have not been exhausted.
c.   resources were being wasted.
d.   a and b.

12. An aggregate supply curve indicates
a.   the total quantity of a good supplied by all suppliers.
b.   the total amount of money required by all suppliers in an economy to produce a given quantity of goods.
c.   a summation of producer's costs for a given quantity of goods.
d.   the total quantities of a good that all suppliers are willing to supply at given prices.

13. There are three people, one seller and two buyers, who exchange a good. One day a new buyer appears and negotiates a new, higher price for the good with the seller. At the new price all three buyers and the seller continue to trade. Which of the following statements is true?
a.   The terms of trade under the new deal have worsened for the two original buyers and are acceptable for the new buyer and the seller.
b.   The terms of trade under the new deal have improved for all buyers and the seller, because they all still voluntarily enter into trades at that price.
c.   The terms of trade under the new deal have worsened for all three buyers, because the price of

the good is higher than before.
d.   The terms of trade under the new deal have only improved for the seller.

14. As the price of raspberries decreases a person possessing a stockpile of raspberries would:
a.   consume fewer raspberries himself and offer more for sale.
b.   consume a constant amount for himself and offer a constant amount for sale.
c.   consume a greater amount himself and offer fewer for sale.
d.   consume fewer himself and offer fewer for sale to others.

15. The area under Denise's supply curve of harmonicas is $75 at a quantity of 5. From this we know which of the following is true?
a.   Total revenues to Denise are $75 for the sale of her harmonicas.
b.   The price of harmonicas is $15 each.
c.   Denise values each harmonica at $15.
d.   Denise will sell all five harmonicas if she is paid at least $75.

16. The supply and demand curves can be drawn as smooth lines because,
a.   the numbers on the axes are really average rates of consumption or supply (quantity per unit of time).
b.   technically we can subdivide most physical goods into fractional amounts.
c.   it is a standard convention of economics that one draws a smooth line rather than the discrete points that make up a curve.
d.   none of the above.
e.   a and b.

17. Upon observing the buying habits of Whitaker Smallwood and his brother Rupert, we discover that Whitaker rarely ever buys any music to listen to, while Rupert buys music regularly. From these observations we can induce:
a.   that Whitaker dislikes music.
b.   that Rupert's MV for music is greater than Whitaker's.
c.   that Rupert is wealthier than Whitaker
d.   that Whitaker's MV for music seldom exceeds the price.
e.   both b and d are correct.

18. Since ancient times markets for trading goods have formed because,
a.   establishing markets is necessary for establishing civilization.
b.   they have been the surest way for political leaders to control and gather their own wealth from the people.
c.   they provide the least costly means for people to exchange goods and accrue the benefits from trade.
d.   people have always had surpluses of goods that they needed to trade away.

19. Which of the following conditions would promote haggling over the price of a good.

a.   when the good is commonly purchased and in reasonably large quantities.
b.   when the market is made up of numerous buyers and sellers of the good.
c.   when there are clearly defined and enforced property rights.
d.   none of the above.

e.   a and b.

20. If we observe two people engage in the exchange of money for a t-shirt at a price of $14.99, we know which of the following to be true:
a.   the buyer and seller's marginal values for the t-shirt are equal.
b.   the buyer's marginal value for the t-shirt is less than or equal to $14.99 and the seller's marginal value exceeds or is equal to $14.99.
c.   the buyer and seller's marginal values for the t-shirt both exceed or are equal to $14.99.
d.   the buyer's marginal value exceeds or is equal to $14.99 and the seller's marginal value is less than or equal to $14.99.

SHORT ANSWER QUESTIONS

1. It is said that "everyone has their price", meaning that anything can be bought for enough money. What does economic theory have to say about this?

2. What is the real cost of engaging in exchange for consumers and suppliers.

3. Realtors charge commissions of about 6 percent to "help" people buy and sell property. Is 6 percent too much to pay realtors? What do they provide that could be worth a 6 percent commission? Explain.

4. Many Indians own parcels of reservation lands. These individuals can rent the land, say to farmers, and they can prevent others from using the land without their permission, but they cannot individually sell the land to anyone outside of the tribe to make money. According to economic definitions, is this land the private property of the Indian owners? Explain why or why not.

5. Describe how two economists - husband and wife with a shared bank account - would exchange gifts on birthdays or other appropriate holidays, if they were going to remain true to economic principles.

6. Describe how money lowers transactions costs.

7. Evaluate the following criticism of middlemen.

> Their meer (sic) handling of Goods one to another, no more increases the wealth in the Province than persons at a fire increase the Water in a Pail by passing it through twenty or forty hands.

8. Explain how a wealthy person who has just bought 5 apples and a poor person who has just bought 2 apples can have the same marginal value for another apple.

ANSWERS TO REVIEW QUESTIONS

Answers to PROBLEMS AND EXERCISES

1. Total benefits are the difference between the marginal values of the two exchangers.
    1 pair of earrings: $35 - $5 = $30.
    2 pairs of earrings: $25 - $10 = $15.
    3 pairs of earrings: $15 - $15 = $0.

The total benefits would not change in response to the price change because Lupe and Inez' marginal values for the earrings remain as they are.

2.

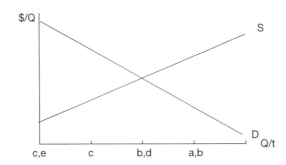

3. a. Total Revenue = Price x Quantity; $6.00/dozen x 2000 dozen/month = $12,000/month.
b. Total Expenditure = Price x Quantity; $6.00/dozen x 2000 dozen/month = $12,000/month.
c. $/month. When multiplying price x quantity remember that the units must come along too. Dozens cancel out during multiplication leaving $/months.
d. Total Benefits = the shaded area between the supply and demand curves up to the point of equilibrium (the intersection of the supply and demand curves). Using the formula for the area of a triangle, 1/2base x height, the total benefits are:

$$TB = 1/2(\$11 - \$2) \text{ x } 2000 \text{ dozen/month}$$
$$TB = \$9000/\text{month}$$

Consumer's surplus is the triangle above the price line and below the demand curve.
$$CS = 1/2(\$11 - \$6) \text{ x } 2000 \text{ dozen/month}$$
$$CS = \$5000/\text{month}$$

Rents are the triangle below the price line and above the supply curve.
$$Rent = 1/2(\$6 - \$2) \text{ x } 2000 \text{ dozen/month}$$
$$Rent = \$4000/\text{month}$$

e. Rob's alternative costs will be the area below the supply curve up to a quantity of 2000 dozen/month.
$$AC = [1/2(2000 \text{ doz./mo.}) \text{ x } (\$6 - \$2)] + [2000 \text{ doz./mo. x } \$2]$$

AC = $8,000/month

4. Aggregate supply of ice cream cones at Romeo Beach are as follows:

	$3.25	$2.25
Tooty	480	310
Frooty	635	470
Rooty	350	260
Bob	27	11
Total	1492	1051

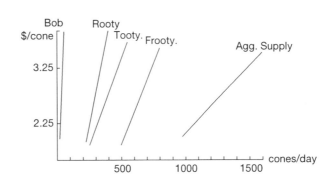

5. The price consumers would pay would be $1150 per guitar. The transactions costs have no effect on the quantity supplied in this case, because of Aria's insistence of making 12 guitars per year regardless of price. Because of her perfectly inelastic supply, she ends up absorbing the entire transaction cost, as would happen with a tax. Because quantity does not change, there are no lost gains from trade.

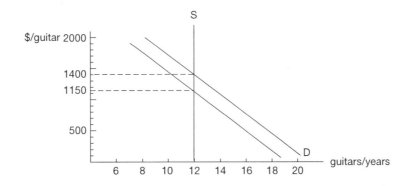

6. a. Increase. Marilyn trades scones to Joe. As she does so she has fewer scones. Marginal value increases as the quantity of scones she has decreases.

b. 2 scones and $1.05. Marilyn's marginal value for one less scone (9 scones) is $.50; Joe is willing to pay up to $1.50 to get an eleventh scone. Likewise Marilyn would accept anything more than $.60 for her ninth scone and Joe would pay up to $.65 to get a twelfth. After that Joe's MV for another scone ($.50) is less than Marilyn's MV ($.90) so trade would stop. Joe is willing to pay up to $2.15 and Marilyn is willing to accept $1.10 or more for the two scones. A middleman could charge Joe $2.15 and make him better off, while paying Marilyn $1.10, making her better off, leaving $2.15 - $1.10 = $1.05.

7. a. Consumers willing to buy 10 units; Supplier willing to supply 50 units.
b. They would exchange 10 units, since any more would make the consumer worse off.
c. The lost gains from trade due to the price control are:

1/2($6 -$2) x (30 - 10)
$40.00

d.   The optimal price and quantity, where all benefits would be exhausted in the absence of price controls, are $4.00 and 30 units.

8.	Price	Qd	Supply
	$95 K	1	8
	90	2	7
	85	3	6
	80	4	5
	75	5	4
	70	6	3
	65	7	2
	60	8	1
	55	9	0

If at a market price of $95,000 Big Jane demands only one of her cars, then she would be willing to part with the other 8 for some price less than $95,000. The rest of the table demonstrates that as price falls people will consume greater quantities of a good.

9.	Quantity	Marg. Value	Marg. Cost
	1	$140 K	40
	2	130	65
	3	110	75
	4	100	85
	5	85	100
	6	75	110
	7	65	130
	8	40	140
	9	30	

Big Jim values his eighth Rolls at $40,000. That is his minimum cost to sell it. He would sell the next for anything greater than $65,000 (his MV of his seventh car). Having sold seven of eight cars he would only sell his last car for $140 thousand or more. Big Jim and Big Jane's situation differ in that for Jane, a price is given that determines quantity demanded and supplied (Q = f(P)). With Jim, a quantity is given that determines marginal value and cost (P = f(Q)). The cost and value principles are the same.

Answers to TRUE - FALSE QUESTIONS

1. True. The causality of a supply curve runs from the set price to the variable quantity supplied. Compare this to the reverse case where the quantity is set, from which you can then determine the suppliers marginal cost.

2. True. At this level no further gains are available because beyond this point the supplier's costs will exceed the consumer's value for the good.

3. False. Consumers will only buy goods when their marginal value for the good is higher than the

price. That way they end up with benifits in excess of the price they have to pay.

4. False. The price is only the price for the good. The mutual benefits are some amount of value that the consumer has for the goods purchased (Consumer's Surplus) and similarly, a more measurable amount of rents gathered by the supplier through the exchange of the good.

5. True. Unregulated trade implies there are no barriers to achieving economic efficiency, at a level determined by the individual buyers and sellers, which by definition would be the maximum possible. In a command economy prices and output levels are determined by people who make their best guess as to what is optimal, which is far less successful.

6. False. There is a cost to every action, and to every good. That is the idea of opportunity costs. The cost of exchange is the foregone opportunity to consume the exchanged good yourself if you are the supplier, and the foregone opportunity to consume something else if you are the buyer.

7. True. If no trade existed, then enormous benefits would be unrealized. People would have to produce everything they consumed by themselves, making specialization difficult.

8. True. As long as the producer receives a price equal to his/her marginal cost of producing the good, which covers all opportunity costs, we assume that they will continue to produce and exchange the good.

9. True. Although you give a supplier money in exchange for a desired good, you are really giving up some quantity of other goods that could have been purchased with the money.

10. False. Economic efficiency has nothing to do with the distribution of benefits, except the amount of benefits there are to distribute. Distribution is an ethical, political, legal, or some other type of question. Economic efficiency means only that the benefits from trade have been fully exhausted.

11. True. According to the law of diminishing marginal value, the greater one's consumption of a good the lower one's marginal value for that good, holding all other things constant. As you trade for greater quantities of a good your marginal value for the good will fall.

12. False. In some situations third parties may be hurt by trade, even though it is to the benefit of others. Therefore, for these people, more trade is not preferred to less trade.

Answers to MULTIPLE CHOICE QUESTIONS

1. c	5. b	9. e	13. a	17. e
2. d	6. a	10. a	14. c	18. c
3. c	7. c	11. c	15. d	19. d
4. d	8. b	12. d	16. e	20. d

Answers to SHORT ANSWER QUESTIONS

1. For the most part economic theory would support this statement, except that there is no accounting for preferences. People generally prefer not to sell their children, their bodies, their love, and they do not regardless of price. If we hold preferences constant, however, then virtually everything is subject to exchange and suppliers will supply things when the price exceeds their marginal value of their product.

2. Consumers forego the use of some exchange medium, such as money, while suppliers forgo the use of the good they are supplying. They are similar in that in both cases the traders are forgoing their highest valued alternative use of their resources.

3. Any given realtor may not be worth 6 percent commission, but in general the commission "price" is established according to the market - the interaction of buyers and sellers of realty services. If 6 percent were too much, i.e. the realtors were making abnormally massive profits, then others would begin offering realtors services in competition, ultimately driving the commission down to the equilibrium level. Realtors, in general, reduce the cost of buying houses for the average person by at least the cost of the commission. Realtors provide a current list of available properties, and information on the quality, location, price, size, taxes, neighborhoods, etc. of the homes they list. Without them each buyer would have to gather this information. This would be very costly.

4. Indians do not have complete rights over this property as they cannot transfer or sell the rights of the land to another at a mutually agreed upon price. Economic property rights definitions present a continuum of ownership and use rights over different attributes of property. These range from incomplete "private" rights (such as in the case of Indian ownership of tribal land), to public or State lands.

5. They wouldn't. They know they cannot buy a gift that will satisfy their partner as much as a gift their partner buys for themselves. Moreover, since they share a bank account, giving cash is merely a decision on how much the person should spend on the gift -- in many relationships a joint budget decision. In the end the best way would be to simply give them a card and ask, "what did I get you".

6. Money lowers transactions costs by eliminating the time required to discover a double coincidence of wants -- the situation where a buyer of good A wants to pay with good B, so this buyer must find a seller who not only has good A, but is willing to accept good B for it. Additionally with a government sanctioned and produced uniform trading currency, the traders do not have to spend as much time trying to guarantee the quality of each good they are paying with - for example is that lump of gold pure, or how old are those three fish you're giving me.

7. The author erroneously focuses on the amount of water in one pail implying it is analogous to wealth in society. The proper focus is on the rate at which transactions occur due to the services of middlemen. Middlemen increase the rate of transactions throughout the economy which increases wealth in society. They don't directly create wealth, they assist others in creating wealth by reducing the costs of trading. In this way middlemen are very much like those hands passing the pails of water to put out a fire. With an efficient number of hands the rate at which water can be brought to the fire will increase. The hands do not increase the water in each pail, but they do increase the water available to put out the fire.

8. Since they both pay the same price and their marginal values both equal the price, then their marginal values must be equal. People choose to buy a good whenever their marginal value exceeds or is equal to the price. Because of the law of diminishing MV, the more they consume the lower their marginal value becomes. So, as they buy the good, the apples, each of their marginal value's diminishes until their marginal value converges toward the price. Over time they will always buy that good until their MV for the good equals the price, then they will stop. At this point they have enjoyed all of the benefits from consuming the good over time that make up consumers' surplus.

CHAPTER 5
Supply and Demand

PRINCIPAL GOALS

1.0 **Recognize the difference between a change in quantity demanded (or quantity supplied) and a change in demand (or supply). (Objectives 1.1, 1.2)**

2.0 **Learn how to analyze market shocks using the tools of supply and demand. (Objectives 2.1, 2.2, 2.3)**

3.0 **Understand and identify elasticity measurements. (Objective 3.1)**

4.0 **Understand the effect of taxes on markets. (Objectives 4.1, 4.2)**

OBJECTIVES
Answers to bold-faced questions appear at the end of the dialogue.

"Fat -- that's the enemy Ginny. Mark my words, ten years from now scientists will have traced most of the major health problems in this country to our diet."

"Then why are you stuffing chocolate chip cookies into your mouth?" Ginny asked.

"I have identified the enemy, I haven't defeated it."

"Didn't the paper recently report that they thought this fat-free food fad was self-defeating? They argued that a decline in the demand for fatty foods would lead to a fall in fatty food prices, but this price fall would then simply increase fatty food consumption. Do you think the journalist was an economist?"

"Only a bad one," replied Mo. "I think there's something wrong with their reasoning, but I can't quite put my finger on it. Do you see it?"

"No, but I think this is what the book of knowledge covers in the section on changes in demand versus changes in quantity demanded. With a little enlightenment I bet that we can figure out the journalist's mistake. But first let's get this vocabulary under control; there were a lot of new words in this chapter."

OBJECTIVE 1.1 Recognize definitions for the important new vocabulary.

Question 1. Match the term with its definition(s). Write out definitions for any undefined terms.

a. change in quantity demanded
b. change in demand
c. change in quantity supplied
d. change in supply
e. inferior good
f. normal good
g. complementary good
h. substitute good

i. income elasticity   j. cross price elasticity
k. income elastic   l. income inelastic

_____ a change in the quantity of a good that suppliers are willing to sell resulting from a change in any other factor contributing to the supplier's decision to supply the good, other than the price of the good.

_____ a measure of a change in consumption of one good in response to a change in a person's income.

_____ goods for which demand increases (an outward shift of the demand curve) as income increases.

_____ graphically, a movement from one point to another (either higher or lower) along the consumer's existing demand curve (read off the axes).

_____ goods that are used or consumed together.

_____ a new marginal value for any quantity, or at any price a new quantity demanded.

_____ a measure of the change in consumption of one good when the price of a second good changes.

_____ graphically, a movement of the entire supply curve (either decreasing quantity inward or increasing quantity outward).

_____ goods for which consumption decreases as income increases.

_____ a change in the quantity of a good that consumers are willing to buy resulting from a change in the price of the good.

_____ when a person increases their consumption of a good in response to an increase in their income, but the percentage increase in their consumption of the good is less than the percentage increase in their income, $0 \leq \eta \leq 1$.

_____ goods that are used or consumed as replacements or alternatives for each other.

_____ the percent change in quantity consumed due to a percent change in income.

_____ a change in the quantity of a good that consumers are willing to buy resulting from a change in any other factor contributing to the consumer's decision to consume/buy the good, other than the price of the good.

_____ when a person increases their consumption of a good in response to an increase in their income, but the percentage increase in their consumption of the good is greater than the percentage increase in their income, $\eta > 1$.

_____ a change in the quantity of a good that producers are willing to sell resulting from a change in the price of the good.

_____ the percent change in consumption of x per the percent change in the price of y.

OBJECTIVE 1.2 **Recognize the implications of, and correctly draw shifts of the demand and supply curves in response to, changes in various constraints.**

"Now, about these curves shifting. I think we need to know exactly when to do what with the curves. When do you see a change in the quantity demanded or quantity supplied and when do you see a change in demand or supply? When does a curve shift, and when is there just a movement along the existing curve?"

"Is that a question?"

"Yes it's a question", Mo said.

"According to the Book, Chapter 5, verse 5.1,

If any variable other than the price of this good changes, the demand curve itself *shifts*, that is, the whole demand curve moves."

"So you don't move the entire curve **EVER**, when the changing constraint is the price of the good. That makes sense, since the price of the good is measured along the vertical axis."

"Changing the price just moves you up or down the vertical axis, which is equivalent to moving up or down the existing curve," Ginny added.

"You only shift the entire curve when some other constraint changes," Mo said.

"Correct, such as?"

"Uh, income. And, uhhhh, income. Have I mentioned income? Where is that list he gave, chapter 1? Yes, page 19: income, prices of goods -- hey I thought..."

"I think he means prices of substitute or complementary goods," Ginny said. "And maybe the prices of inputs since they affect supply."

"Oh right", Mo said, then continued reading, "time, technology, laws and customs, the state of our health, our education, skills -- basically all the things that affect the demand or supply for the good. Uh-oh."

"What."

"You have that look like you're going to ask one of those, 'why is the sky blue' questions."

"Well no one has ever given me a satisfying answer to that one. Yours is easier: why do you think changes in all of these other things cause a shift in the curves while a change in price is just a movement along the curve?"

"Actually I can answer that," Mo said. "Although the supply and demand for a good depend on a number of different factors, when you plot them on a graph, you only have two axes. So you must choose two of the variables that can then "vary" along the axes. Since economists are interested in, and have behavioral postulates about, the quantity a consumer is willing to buy at various prices, the graphs generally have price on one axis and quantity on the other. All of these other variables have to be held constant along any particular curve, because only price and quantity are measured along the axes. When one of these other variable does change, it shifts the entire curve."

"So if we changed what was measured on the graph to, say, income on the vertical axis and quantity on the horizontal axis then a change in income would appear as a movement along the curve and a change in price would cause a shift in the curve?"

"That would follow," agreed Mo. "Let's try drawing an income-quantity graph with price changing, and compare that to the normal case of a price-quantity graph with income changing."

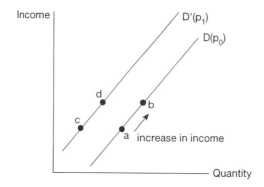

"Okay", Mo continued, "a change in income on an income-quantity graph should represent the different quantities buyers would demand at different incomes."

"Right, so you're just moving from one point to another on the same 'demand' curve, like from 'a' to 'b'," Ginny said.

"But if the price increases from p_0 to p_1 for example, your income doesn't change, but you want to buy less of the good. So that's a point closer to zero on the quantity axis, but at the same income right?"

"Yes, like a move from 'a' to 'c'. Increasing price at income level 'b' would result in a point like 'd'. If we join the points plotted at the higher price, we get a second 'demand' curve. So the change in price results in a shift of the entire curve."

"That works out", Mo said. For our usual price-quantity graph it would be the same only a change in price would be represented by the existing curve and a change in income would be the external factor causing a shift in the entire curve.

Question 2. Suppose you had plotted your demand curve for your favorite dessert (raspberry cheesecake) as a student, when your income was $800/month. Perhaps at $2.75/slice you buy one slice per week, and if there is a sale at $1.50/slice you buy two slices per week. Plot your demand curve below:

P   Qd/wk

2.75   1
1.50   2

Income = $800/month

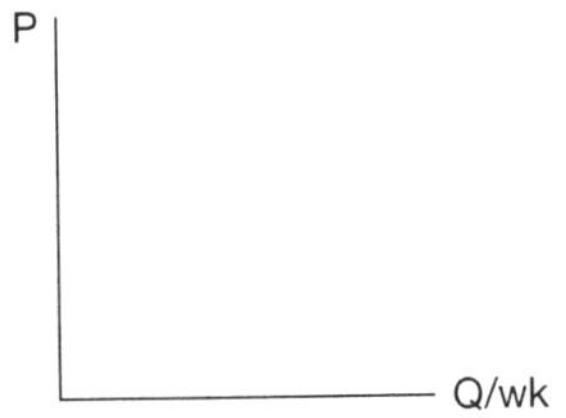

```
P |
  |
  |
  |
  |
  |
  |_____ Q/wk
```

Now suppose you graduate and get a job that pays $1,500 month. Chances are, at those same prices, you would buy more cheesecake. Perhaps now at $2.75/slice you would buy two slices per week, and at $1.50/slice you would buy three slices per week. Plot this new demand curve on the original graph.

P   Qd/wk   Income = $1500/month

2.75   2
1.50   3

If some other variable like income had been plotted along the vertical axis, the price of the good would have been held constant along that curve. We could have, for example, drawn a 'demand' curve for income changing from $800/month to $1,500/month, and plotted this against the quantity of cheesecake consumed per week. But because we only have two dimensions, the price of the good would have to be held constant along the curve. This time, a change in the price of the good would shift the curve. Below, draw (on the same graph) and compare the two 'demand' curves given when the price changes from $2.75 to $1.50.

Income   Qd/wk
----
800   1
1500   2

Price = $2.75

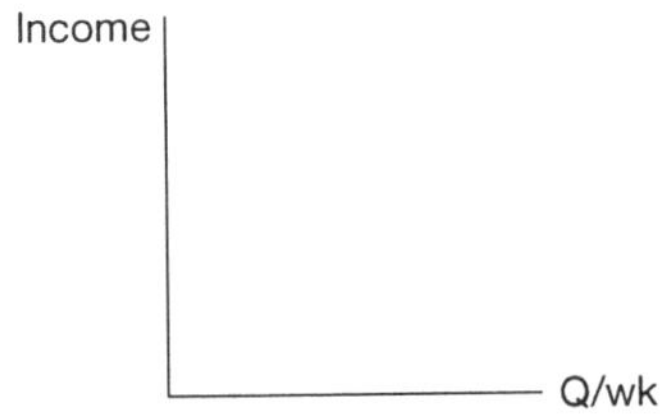

Income   Qd/wk
----
800   2
1500   3

```
Income |
       |
       |
       |
       |
       |
       |_____ Q/wk
```

Price = $1.50

Question 3. On a technology-quantity graph, graph the effects of an increase and decrease in technology on the quantity supplied (the supply curve) of an electronics manufacturer. Graph the effects of the same increase and decrease in technology on the company's supply curve on a price-quantity graph.

Question 4. Draw a demand curve on the price-quantity graph above. Illustrate with arrows the <u>change in supply</u> due to an increase in technology and the increase in the <u>quantity demanded</u>.

* * * * * * *

"So there's really no mystery in what shifts the curves, and what does not. It simply depends on what is on the axes, versus what is held constant when the curve is drawn," Ginny said. "But judging from the book the most common graph to work from will be the price-quantity graph."

"So have you figured out the journalist's mistake?" Mo asked.

"Well, I think he's confused a change in demand with a change in quantity demanded. A decrease in demand due to the health scare would reduce the price of fatty foods, that much is true. But the decreased price would not shift demand back up. The market is just at a new equilibrium at the lower price and quantity."

"How can you have all that insight and no food hang-ups Ginny?"

"The hard thing for me is that I always want to get the consumer and producer involved. It seems that some shocks to the market should affect both sides."

OBJECTIVE 2.1 **Chart the sequence of effects of a change in constraints on both supply and demand curves.**

"They do," replied Mo, "but one party is usually affected directly, this is the shift of the curve, and the other party is affected by the change in price that results from the curve shifting. For example, when they said that oat bran could reduce cancer, it increased the demand for oatbran. This increased the price of oatbran, which led to an increase in the <u>quantity supplied</u>, a movement along the supply curve."

"So when one of the factors being held constant along the supply or demand curve changes, that curve will shift, or change. This <u>change in</u> supply, for example, changes the equilibrium price and hence the <u>quantity demanded</u>, by the law of demand, and traces out a movement along the demand curve."

"Right, and a change in demand will change price and lead to a change in quantity supplied. It's through this mechanism that both parties respond to, or are affected by, changes in the market."

"So from our earlier graph, a change in consumers' income would not only lead to an increase in demand, but also to a change in the quantity supplied", Ginny said.

"Exactly", Mo replied. "Look at this graph. If you have an increase in consumers' income you get a shift in the demand curve, correct? When you increase demand like that, according to this graph the equilibrium point moves from A to B and the price rises from whatever, P_1 to P_2. So the effect of the change in demand on the producer is a change in quantity supplied from Q_1 to Q_2."

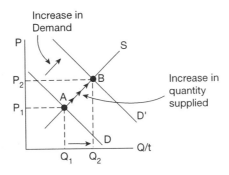

"Clearly there's an economics gene running in your family Mo. You better keep that in mind if you ever contemplate procreating."

"Too bad it was missing from the parent's of the journalist."

Question 5. Think through and list the sequence of effects for supply and demand curves, and prices and quantities of the following situations. Draw a graph depicting the changes; be careful labelling your axes.

a) The effect on the silk market of a disease that kills 50% of the silk worms in Asia.

P = _____

Q = _____

Chapter 5 - 8

b) Completely unexplainably people decide bell-bottom pants are the thing to have.

      P = _____

      Q = _____

c) The technological advance enables popcorn farmers to produce 25% more corn per acre this year.

      P = _____

      Q = _____

* * * * * * *

"So it's pretty important to get the sequence of effects in their proper order to correctly analyze a change in some constraint."

"I think so", Mo said. "The only thing left that I have in this section are substitutes and complements, and inferior and normal goods."

OBJECTIVE 2.2 Determine which goods are complements, substitutes, inferior, or normal from the way people consume them. Graph with supply and demand curves the effects of changes in income and price on these various types of goods.

"Well I did a fair amount of thinking about these after reading Silberberg," Ginny said. I think we have to be careful here. We shouldn't assume that certain goods are inferior or normal, or substitutes or complements. I mean on an exam if they ask about peanut butter and bread, we're pretty safe to say they are complements."

"Agreed," said Mo, "what's your point."

"My point is that in the real world we only know which goods are inferior or normal, or substitutes or complements, by observing how individuals consume these goods. When we see them consume less peanut butter as their income rises, then we know that peanut butter is an inferior good for them. If they eat less bread too, then we infer that bread and peanut butter are complements for those people."

"So what you're saying is that we shouldn't say this good is inferior, therefore the demand curve moves this way or that, but that the demand curve moved this way or that, therefore this good is inferior, normal or whatever."

"That's what I'm saying Mo."

"That's a good point, but we'll probably get questions from both directions."

"No doubt, but that doesn't mean we shouldn't really understand what's going on."

Question 6. Identify the type of goods (normal, inferior; substitute, complement) based on the behavior of the people in the following situations.

a. Clark graduated from college a year ago. He has been working at a software engineering firm for 9 months. While in school he was earning about $600 per month; He now makes about $3,000 per month after taxes. For dinner in college, Clark ate grilled cheese sandwiches twice a week, spaghetti three times a week and hamburgers twice a week. He now eats take-out pizza once a week, and spaghetti and hamburgers each three times a week. He used to drink approximately 15 beers a week. He now drinks 6-12 beers a week and 1 bottle of wine to accompany his spaghetti.

Indicate whether the income elasticity is < 0 (inferior), 0 - 1 (normal, income inelastic) or > 1 (normal, income elastic), for grilled cheese, spaghetti, hamburgers, pizza, beer and wine. Can you tell which are substitutes and which are complements?

b. For 37 years the Wilson's have eaten pot roast for Saturday night supper. Mr. Wilson began his career 38 years ago as a shipping clerk for Bauhaus Building Supply. He is currently Vice President of Marketing. Mrs. Wilson began work 18 years ago as a nurse at an elementary school.

Pot roast is a _____ good for the Wilson's. The income elasticity of demand is probably in the range of _____.

c. Officer Raven has been promoted for breaking a rare bird smuggling case. His promotion raised his income and prompted Mr. Gull, owner of the local donut shop and amateur ornithologist, to declare that Officer Raven could get his coffee for half price from now on. Officer Raven responded by having an extra cup of coffee each night, and an extra apple cruller donut.

What do we know about the income elasticity of demand for coffee? _____ What about the relationship between coffee and donuts?_____

OBJECTIVE 2.3 **Work through and accurately graph the sequence of effects in one market of**

a change in a related market.

"Now we're really getting into it, don't you think?", Ginny said. "We can analyze all kinds of things that happen in the world."

"Like what happens to the Fig Newton market when war breaks out in the Middle East", Mo said.

"What?"

"Isn't that where figs come from?"

"I guess so", Ginny said. "If the Fig Newton market is affected, what would happen to the Oreo or Mrs. Fields cookie markets?"

"Or the milk market?" Mo continued.

"Maybe it's Keebler and Nabisco that are behind all of the instability over there. You know most people think its over land and religious differences, but perhaps its all about cookies."

"I could appreciate that", Mo said, 'Fig Newtons are naturally low in fat. Maybe their share of the American cookie market is growing too quickly."

"Anyway, if war broke out in the Middle East cutting off supplies of figs, there would be a decrease in the supply of Fig Newtons, correct?"

"Correct, which means the whole supply curve would shift inward to the left because at every price, any price, there are fewer figs available. Let's draw as we go."

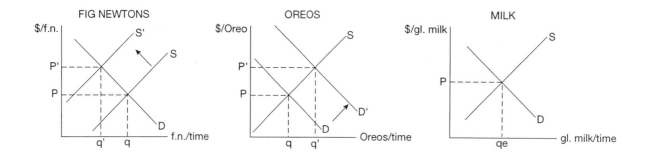

"So the upshot is that the price of Fig Newtons would increase and the quantity demanded by cookie lovers would decrease. Now what would happen to the Oreo market Mo?"

"I've got this all figured out", Mo said. "Oreos are a substitute for Fig Newtons. There would be an increase in demand for Oreos, again a change not due to any price change in Oreos. So the curve would shift outward to the right. As a result the quantity supplied would increase, but this would be accompanied by an increase in the price of Oreos."

"What about milk," said Ginny, "you can't have cookies without a glass of milk. But we've got a decrease in the supply of Fig Newtons and an increase in the quantity supplied of Oreos. Maybe the overall cookie market doesn't change that much?"

"I guess not, or at least we can't say that there would be any change one way or the other. Personally, I feel Oreos are better with milk than Fig Newtons so I would predict an increase in milk consumption with the shift to more Oreos. But that's just me."

"If we just isolated the Fig Newton effect though, we would predict that milk is a complementary good and therefore we would predict a decrease in demand for milk as there are fewer Fig Newtons available. Quantity supplied of milk would decrease and the price would also decrease."

"Adam suggested that before I start shifting curves around, I should think through the effects that some event will have on price and quantity. The result on my graph should match my intuition."

"Well your intuition about the cookie market is finely tuned Mo, but what if we're looking at iron ore?"

"The same principles apply. For example, if any good becomes illegal, what do you expect to happen to price and quantity?"

"I would expect price to rise and quantity to fall," reasoned Ginny.

"So would I, and that's all Adam means -- your common sense should act as a check for the results of what you're doing on the graph."

Question 7. Graph the effects of the described shock or change on the given related markets.

a. The introduction of Compact Disk technology on 1) record albums and 2) reference materials.

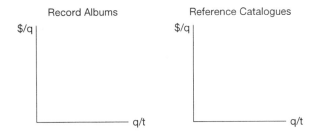

b. The arrival of home video on demand on 1) video movie rentals and 2) movie production by studios.

c. The effect on the synthetic fabric market of a disease that kills 50% of the silk worms in Asia.

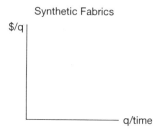

OBJECTIVE 3.1 Calculate income elasticity and cross-price elasticity <u>and</u> identify when goods are income elastic or inelastic.

"Should we continue with these elasticities, or is that stretching it?" Mo asked.

"Only if I have to endure more stupid puns," Ginny replied. "I think I understand what elasticities are about, but I'd like to calculate a few for practice."

"I knew you were going to say that, so I looked up a few from Adam's old quizzes and problem sets. Here's one on income elasticity.

> **Problem:** If Marcel's consumption of yogurt increased from 2 per week to 8 per week when his income increased from $300 per week to $400 per week, what is the income elasticity of yogurt? Is normal or inferior? Income elastic or inelastic?

"Well I'll just take those numbers and plug them into the formula $\Delta Q/\Delta M \times M/Q$," Ginny said. So $\Delta Q = 8 - 2 = 6$; $Q = 2$; $\Delta M = \$400 - \$300 = \$100$; and $M = \$300$. Put it together and I've got

$$\frac{6}{\$100} \cdot \frac{\$300}{2} = \frac{\$1800}{\$200} = 9.$$

Yogurt for Marcel is normal, because the sign is positive, and income elastic because it's greater than one."

"You're turning into a quant jock Ginny. I got the same answer using the formula comparing the percent change in consumption compared to the percent change in income right, $\Delta Q/Q$ divided by $\Delta M/M$."

"Okay, so $\Delta Q/Q$ is 6/2 = 3x100% = 300%. And $\Delta M/M$ is $100/$300 = .3x100% = 33%. Hey that's not so hard. Want to try cross-price elasticity Mo?"

"No, I think I've got the big picture here. It's just the same type of calculation but for the percent change in the price of some good and the percent change in the quantity of a second good. I was talking to Adam about these and he said that there is really an elasticity measurement for any of the factors that make up the demand function, or supply function."

"Demand function?", Ginny asked.

"Yeah, the demand or supply functions are basically the collection of all the variables that would have an effect on a person's demand for a good or a supplier's supply of a good. Like price, income, the prices of substitutes and complements, the cost of technology, all of the constraints really. The elasticity measure is the percent change in quantity demanded (or supplied) over the percent change in the variable."

"Hmmm", Ginny said cautiously, "so the percent change in supply due to a percent change in the cost of technology, for example, would be the technology elasticity of supply then."

"Yes, I think so, but he said for this course and most of economics people only use price elasticity of demand, ϵ, income elasticity, η, cross-price elasticity of demand, ϵ_{xy}, and price elasticity of supply, ϵ_s. You can see the pattern below:"

$$\epsilon = \frac{\% \Delta Q}{\% \Delta P} \qquad \eta = \frac{\% \Delta Q}{\% \Delta M} \qquad \epsilon_{xy} = \frac{\% \Delta Q_x}{\% \Delta P_y} \qquad \epsilon_s = \frac{\% \Delta Q_s}{\% \Delta P}$$

"I'm glad this is just an intro course," said Ginny.

Question 8. For the following problems determine if the goods are inferior or normal, or substitutes or complements by calculating the income or cross price elasticities (where necessary). If appropriate determine if they are elastic or inelastic.

a. The cross elasticity of good x per price of good y is -.37.

b. Deborah's income has fallen by 3% in the last year so she has decreased her consumption of cheesecake by 10%.

c. Hans noticed that the price of hot Italian sausage went up from $2.29 to $2.79 a pound. He decided to alter his recipe for tomato sauce and now buys only 1 lb. of sausage and 2 lbs. of hamburger.

Previously he bought 2 lbs. of sausage and 1 lb. of hamburger.

d. Thomas, received a pay increase from $1800 per month to $2400 per month. He noticed after some time that his consumption of Old Style beer decreased from 24 cans per month to 6.

* * * * * * *

"Do you want to discuss Silberberg's example about the economics of abortion?" asked Mo.

"I'd rather not just now."

"Oh, I'm sorry Ginny. Is this a sensitive subject for you?

"No, I just haven't read it yet. I skipped over it because I've been concentrating on getting this Chinese history paper due."

"You should have picked a country with a shorter history, like Canada. When's it due?"

"Monday."

"Are you close?"

"Within a couple of millennia. The problem is that I have to work Friday and Saturday night. It's going to be tight."

"Not to bum you out or anything, but you know we have our econ exam next week," Mo said.

"Next week! Oh man, am I hurting. I've got a presentation due in another class next week. Aaargh, what am I going to do?"

"Enrol in the time management seminar I'm thinking of putting on in the summer."

"You're too much Mo."

"For now let's just work through taxes since you've read that part. You should go back over the adoption application before the exam though."

"Right, I'll squeeze it in between the Ming and Qing dynasties."

"How many types of taxes are there anyway?" Mo asked.

"I think there are three types, per unit, ad valorem and lump sum, and they can be used for different situations; like a sales tax could be a per unit tax or an ad valorem tax", Ginny said. "I think we need to do be able to first identify the type of tax in each situation we're analyzing."

OBJECTIVE 4.1 **Recognize definitions for the important new vocabulary.**

Question 9. Match the term with its definition(s). Write out definitions for any undefined terms.

a. empirical
c. gross
e. tax
g. per unit tax

b. net
d. deadweight loss
f. ad valorem tax
h. lump sum tax

_____ a government imposed fee or charge that imposes a cost on those who produce or consume the targeted good or service.

_____ the lost gains from trade resulting from a level of output that is less than the economically efficient level.

_____ an imposed fee that is charged according to the value of the good produced or consumed.

_____ an amount of money, a cost or a price calculated *after* any amounts are removed for taxes, commissions, fees, etc.

_____ a government imposed fixed fee that is charged independent of the quantity consumed or produced.

_____ as determined by measurement and/or through observation. Not as determined by presumption, intuition or postulate.

_____ an imposed fee that is charged for each unit of a good produced or consumed.

_____ an amount of money, a cost or a price calculated *before* any amounts are removed for reasons such as taxes, commissions, or fees.

OBJECTIVE 4.2 **Think through and show on a graph the consequences of ad valorem, per unit, and lump-sum taxes on supply and demand behavior.**

"The other thing we have to know which taxes affect the supplier and which ones the consumer", Mo said.

"Well I was wondering about that," said Ginny. "It seems to me from the examples that Silberberg gives on pages 168-171, that it really doesn't matter who the tax is against and whether you're moving the supply curve or the demand curve, because, in the end, in terms of who pays the tax, the results don't change."

"Hmmm. Let's try it ourselves, because if that's true then we can always just show the effects of taxes on the supply curves, like Silberberg does for the most part. Let's draw a graph showing a $1.00 per pack cigarette tax imposed on consumers, and put a graph next to it with the equivalent tax on tobacco producers."

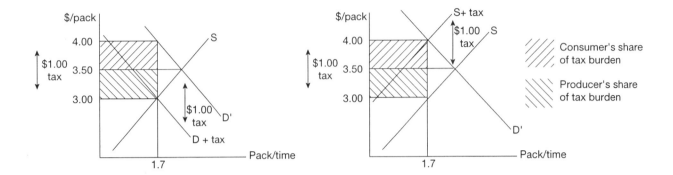

"The per pack tax on consumers," Ginny said, "would trace out a new lower demand curve that represented the quantity demanded at the after-tax price. We can show this as a shift in of the demand curve the distance of the tax -- $1.00. Correct?"

"Correct, and a change in the quantity supplied as a result", Mo added.

"Now to get the final price to the consumer for a pack with the tax we have to go vertically up from the new equilibrium quantity of 1.7 packs per day to the old demand curve, then over to the price axis."

"So it's $4.00 on our graph, and the price to suppliers is taken from the point where S and D' cross, which is $3.00."

"The price to consumers only rises from $3.50 before the tax to $4.00 with the tax," said Ginny. "So even though there is a buck tax per pack the price only goes up $.50 to consumers."

"Clearly the producers are paying the other $.50, because now they're only getting $3.00 per pack. Because they can both respond through quantity demanded or supplied to the price change, neither must absorb the entire tax burden."

"For the tax on tobacco producers it's exactly the same except the producer is now responsible for paying the tax money to the government."

"So the supply curve shifts inward by the same $1.00 amount and quantity demanded decreases to 1.7 packs from 2 packs per day", Mo said. "The prices end up the same with consumers paying $4.00 per pack as compared to $3.50 before, and the supplier only gets $3.00 per pack."

"Which means they end up splitting the cost of the tax exactly as before. Although the 50-50 is a coincidence here. In general, whoever can respond more, that is, has the greater elasticity, consumers or suppliers, will bear less of the tax."

"Well isn't that a handy bit of information to have", Mo said. "We can do our analysis on either set of curves and come out the same."

"Let's do a sample tax problem", Ginny said, "then that'll be about enough for me."

"Me too. Here's one about per unit and ad valorem taxes on apples from Washington and Idaho."

> **Problem:** Determine the net effect on the cost of high quality and low quality locally grown apples in Idaho from a $.10 per unit tax and a 50% ad valorem tax. Your final answer should be a statement of the alternative cost of high quality apples in terms of low quality apples. For example 1 HQ = 3 LQ. Determine this ratio for the pre-tax situation, and each post-tax case.

Apples		Idaho	$.10/unit	50%
High Quality	$.40			
Low Quality	$.20			
Alter. Cost				

"One high quality apple costs two low quality ones to begin with", Ginny said.

"And the price of one high quality apple with a 10 cent tax would be $.50 versus $.30 for the low quality apple", Mo said. "But under a 50% tax the high quality price would rise to $.60 and the low quality only to $.30."

"So the cost of a high quality apple under the 10 cent tax drops to 1.66 low quality apples but stays 1 HQ = 2 LQ with the ad valorem tax."

"So what does that mean?" Mo asked.

"It means that if you put a ten cent tax on apples in Idaho a larger proportion of high quality apples will be consumed than before the tax, because they become relatively cheaper. I guess people will eat fewer apples altogether because they become more expensive with the tax, but the proportionate decrease in high quality apples will be lower. With a 50 percent tax, however, people will eat fewer apples altogether because the price is higher than before the tax, but they will eat the same proportion of high quality apples as before the tax, because the relative price of a high quality to a low quality apple is the same."

"Aha", Mo said. "So we can alter people's apple eating behavior with one kind of tax or another."

"Do you want me to tax your cookie consumption, perhaps ten cents per chocolate chip?"

"I'd just switch into oatmeal raisin. But I was thinking about how this helped to explain why we only get the highest quality imports of Scottish shortbread. A transportation fee is like a tax, so it makes sense to export the highest quality product anyway -- the fee becomes a smaller propotion of the final price. This tax principle is the same as the 'Shipping the Good Apples Out" example in chapter three.

Question 10. Consider the effect of a 30 cent/gallon gasoline tax on the quantity demanded of supreme and regular unleaded gas when supreme costs $1.60 per gallon and regular unleaded costs $1.20. A larger change in quantity demanded is expected for <regular/supreme> gasoline.

Consider instead the effect of a 25% gasoline tax on the quantity demanded of supreme and regular unleaded gas when supreme costs $1.60 per gallon and regular unleaded costs $1.20. A larger change in quantity demanded is expected for <regular/supreme> gasoline.

Would you expect demand to be more elastic for regular or supreme? _____ Do supplier and consumer pay the same share of the tax for each type of gasoline? _____ Who pays a greater share for supreme gas? _____

Graph the unleaded gasoline market with a 30 cent/gallon tax. Indicate the areas representing the consumer's and the supplier's portions of the tax, and the lost gains from trade due to the tax.

$/gallons

gallons/t

ANSWERS TO DIALOGUE QUESTIONS

Question 1. Vocabulary: d, i, f, a, g, b, j, d, e, a, f or l, h, i, b, f or k, c, j.

Question 2.

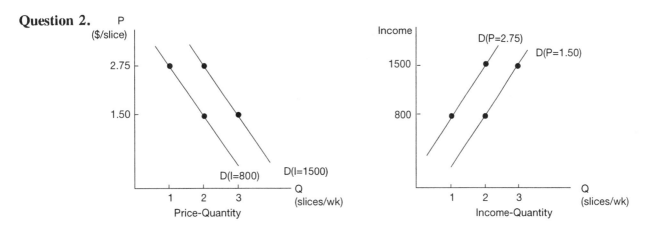

Question 3. Since technology T, is graphed on the vertical axis of the graph on the left an increase or decrease in technology can be shown on a single supply curve as a movement along the curve either outward (as measured on the quantity axis) for the increase in T or inward for the decrease in T. The change in T is considered endogenous, meaning a change from within what is defined in this graph (technology and quantity).

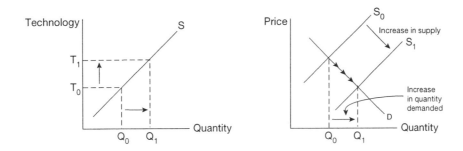

The graph on the right shows the effect on the company's supply curve of a change in technology when T is exogenous, meaning outside what is defined in the graph (in this case price and quantity). The increase in T would enable the company to produce a greater quantity of the good, S_1 on the horizontal axis. This is shown as a shift in the supply curve from S_0 outward to S_1. The same effect only in the opposite direction applies for a decrease in technology (unusual). Notice that for all of the effects of the change in technology on supply, the demand curve remains unchanged, though the quantity demanded increases and decreases. This change in quantity demanded is a result of the change in prices caused by the improved (or worsened) ability of the producer due to the technological change.

Question 4. See the right hand graph of question 3 above.

Question 5. a. decrease in worms - decrease in quantity of silk supplied - increase in price - decrease in quantity demanded.

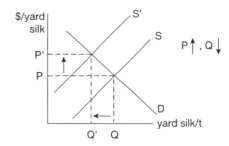

b. increase in demand for bell bottoms - increase in price (people willing to pay more) - increase in quantity supplied.

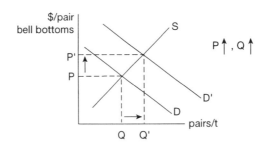

c. increase in supply of popcorn - decrease in price - increase in quantity demanded.

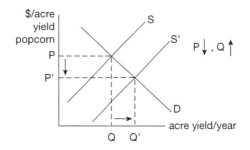

Question 6. a. I know I wouldn't want to live with Clark, but we know nothing about which goods are substitutes or complements, because no prices have changed, only income. For income:

Grilled Cheese	<0, inferior
Spaghetti	0, normal, income inelastic
Hamburgers	0 - 1, normal, income inelastic
Pizza	>1, normal, income elastic
Beer	<0, inferior
Wine	>1, normal, income elastic

b. Pot roast is a normal good for the Wilson's. Even though their income has increased over the years they have not substituted out of pot roast for a better cut of meat. Since their consumption of pot roast has remained constant this would still be a normal good with an income elasticity of 0.

c. We cannot isolate what causes the change in Officer Raven's behavior, since income increased at the same time as price decreased. Therefore we can say nothing about the income elasticity of demand for coffee. Coffee and donuts, however, are complements, as donut consumption changed in the same direction as coffee consumption.

Question 7. a. <u>Record Albums:</u> People have substituted out of record albums (vinyl) and into CD's: decrease in demand for record albums - decrease in quantity supplied of record albums - decrease in price. <u>Reference Catalogs:</u> CD technology will also lead librarians and the consumers of library materials to demand their reference catalogues in CD-ROM format, rather than as books: decrease in demand for reference catalogs - decrease in quantity supplied and decrease in price.

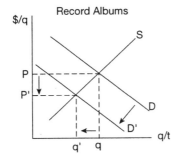
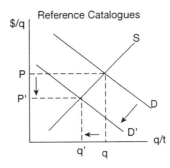

b. <u>Video Rentals:</u> As substitutes the anticipated response, though this is disputed depending on how the prices for video on demand end up, is a decrease in demand for video rentals - decrease in quantity supplied - decrease in price. <u>Movie Production:</u> Indeterminate response. The two are complementary, but we don't know what effect the change in technology (service) will have on the quantity of films produced. Potentially, there might be a small increase in demand for movies - increase in quantity supplied - increase in price.

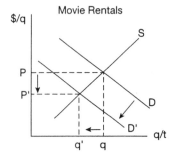
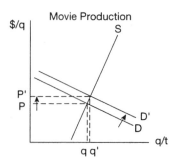

c. Synthetic fabric: Fewer silk worms - decrease in the supply of silk - increase in the price of silk - increase in demand for the substitute synthetic fabric - increase in price of synthetic - increase in quantity supplied of synthetic fabric.

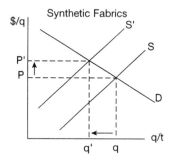

Question 8. a. Since the cross price elasticity is *minus* .37, goods x and y are complements, but not as strongly complementary as if the elasticity were -1.5 for example. The farther the cross elasticity measure from 0, the stronger the substitute or complementary relationship between the two goods.

b. Income elasticity = 10%/3% = 3.33. 3.33 indicates that the increase in consumption was greater than the increse in income, so Cheesecake to Deborah is income elastic. Cheesecake is also a normal good as the sign is positive on the elasticity measure.

c. Cross Price Elasticity of Hamburger = 100%/22% = 4.54. Positive sign indicates substitutes and at 4.54 Hans clearly considers the two to be highly substitutable.

Math:
%ΔQ of hamburger = 2 lbs. - 1 lb./1 lb. x 100 = 100%.
%ΔP of sausage = $2.79 - $2.29/$2.29 x 100 = $.50/$2.29 x 100 = .218 x 100 = 22%.

d) Income Elasticity = 33%/-75% = -2.27. Old Style beer is an inferior good to Thomas. Note that there is no elastic/inelastic distinction for inferior goods. They are just inferior.

Math:
%ΔM (income) = $2400 - $1800/$1800 x 100 = $600/$1800 x 100 = .333 x 100 = 33%.
%ΔQ = 6 - 24/24 x 100 = -18/24 x 100 = -.75 x 100 = -75%.

Question 9. Vocabulary: e, d, f, b, h, a, g, c.

Question 10. <u>$.30 per gallon tax:</u> A larger change in quantity demanded is expected for regular unleaded gasoline. There will be less of both purchased given the tax, but a per unit tax makes the relative price of Supreme cheaper compared to regular.

<u>25% tax:</u> Neither. The relative prices of Regular and Supreme do not change with an *ad valorem* tax therefore no substitution between these two markets is expected, only an absolute decrease in the quantity demanded of both.

I would expect demand for Supreme gasoline to be more elastic. No. For both types, who pays a greater share depends on the elasticity of demand relative to the elasticity of supply. But if the elasticity of demand for Supreme is greater than for regular, consumers of Supreme will substitute away more than consumers of Regular, so the supplier would pay more of the tax on Supreme than Regular.

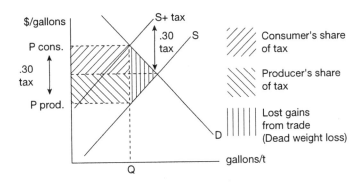

THE BIG PICTURE

With this chapter you begin to apply the model of supply and demand, as well as several economic tools of analysis and measurement. Of interest to economists is the effect, especially on price and quantity, of various shocks to markets. For example, what happens to the Fig Newton and Oreo cookie markets when the supply of figs is cut off by evil doings in the Middle East. You should feel comfortable with the patterns of movement in supply and demand, and price and quantity given changes in constraints such as income, prices of related goods, and taxes.

These patterns of change conform to the behavioral postulates. What you are studying is the formal system for measuring and describing these behavioral patterns. Never forget that economic analysis only encompasses positive questions, not normative ones. Therefore, all of the shifting of curves, moving along curves, classifying goods as substitutes, complements, normal or inferior, gains from exchange, deadweight loss, cross-price elasticities and the like is based on a scientific method, logical reasoning, and observation. In many respects the economic model is quite limited -- perhaps more than you realize (though less than you think!) at this point. But even with such limits, as you are beginning to see, it can be incredibly powerful as an explanatory model of human behavior.

Silberberg's example of the economics of adoption is a case in point. Is reducing the act of adopting a child to a simple exchange of "goods" palatable to you? Many people shrink at the thought. Of course adoption is an enormously complex subject that would fall under any number of academic disciplines, including sociology, psychology, history, and social work, but the point is that *any time there is an exchange, whether of inanimate or animate objects -- steel or children -- we can apply the analytical tools and principles affecting supply and demand.* In the process we can gain another perspective on some of society's most urgent and complicated issues.

Except for the price of the good, quantity demanded and quantity suppplied are functions of mostly different variables. Demand includes income, prices of related goods, etc. Supply has to do with technology and the costs of inputs in the production process. In both cases, when the graph you are working on has price on one axis and quantity on the other, the only variable that causes a movement along the same supply or demand curve as already exists is a change in the price of the good in question. Changes in any other variables in the function cause the entire curve to shift or move in one direction or the other.

REVIEW QUESTIONS

Answers to all review questions appear at the end of this chapter.

TIP: You must be prepared to look at the curves and what they represent from several different perspectives. Remember, the supply curve can be interpreted as a marginal cost curve if Q becomes the independent variable; likewise the demand curve and marginal value curve look the same but the causality between $/Q and Q go in different directions.

The price axis is generically $/Q, a money per physical unit measure (this is often simply P for price, MC for the cost of production, or MV for the marginal value of consumers). The quantity axis is just quantity produced or consumed. The quantity axis is a rate, Q/time, though we are often lazy and just write Q. Take some time to think about the units and labels on the axes.

PROBLEMS AND EXERCISES
Write your answer in the space(s) provided.

1. From the information below, draw a graph with the quantity of cappuccinos on the horizontal axis, and the price of cappuccinos on the vertical axis. Draw the demand curves when the price of a substitute, cafe mochas is $1.00/cup and $1.50/cup.

P Capp	Qd/wk Capp	Qd/wk Capp
2.50	3	4
1.50	5	6
	P Moch = $1.00	P Moch = $1.50

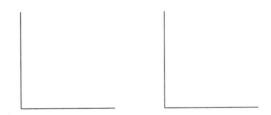

Now, on another graph, put the price of mochas on the vertical axis (still against the quantity of cappuccinos consumed) and draw the demand curve for cappuccinos when the price of cappuccinos is $1.50/cup and $2.50/cup.

2. The instability of the OPEC cartel in the 1980s led to an increase in the production of oil, and a subsequent fall in the price of gasoline. Using supply and demand diagrams, indicate the effect on price

and quantity in the market for:
a. Cars in general
b. Small cars relative to large cars

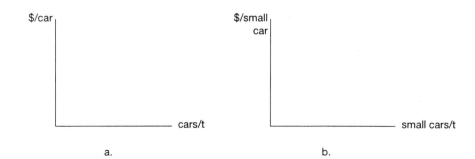

3. Some politicians have advocated taxing airline travel to raise revenues for compensating individuals who suffer noise pollution from living near major airports.
a. If a $25 tax was levied on every airline ticket sold, would you expect to see relatively more or less first class tickets sold, compared to regular class (that is, how would the proportion of first class to regular class change)? Assume no income effects. Explain.

b. From the information in Question 4, would producers or consumers bear the burden of the tax, why?

4. Consider the invention of a super-speed magnetic levitation train that could travel across the country just slightly slower than an airplane. Would the elasticity of demand for airline services increase or decrease with this invention, and why?

5. To reduce his overweight child's consumption of candy bars an economist plans to sell candy bars to the child at the market price plus a parental tax. To induce the child to cooperate, the parent offers to increase the child's allowance by an amount equivalent to their purchasing power before the tax. The child's acceptance of the deal includes an agreement not to buy candy bars elsewhere. Under this arrangement will the child's consumption of candy bars actually decrease? _____ Will the amount of "tax" the parent collects be as large as the increase in allowance? _____ Explain.

6. In the late 1980s reports indicated that technology, above average growing conditions, and a surge towards self-sufficiency had led to an increase in the world supply of grains.
a. One analyst remarked that the increase in supply would decrease the price. The reduced price, in

turn, will increase the demand, driving the price back up. Explain the error in this argument.

b. Show, using a separate supply and demand diagram for each market, the effects of the drop in the price of grains on the market for:
   i. Breakfast cereals made with grains;
   ii. All other non-grain food groups.

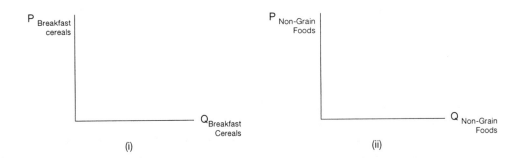

7. Assume that the (inverse) demand curve for cantalope is: P = 60 - 2Qd, where P is the price per pound (in cents) of cantalope and Qd is the quantity demanded per year (in millions of pounds). Assume also that the (inverse) supply curve for cantalope is: P = 2Qs, where 2Qs is the quantity supplied per year in millions of pounds.

a. What is the equilibrium price per pound of cantalope? _____   What is the equilibrium quantity of cantalope produced? _____
b. What are demand and supply elasticities at the equilibrium point? _____
c. Indicate whether each of the following will shift the demand curve for cantalope to the left, the right, or have no effect:
_____ 1) a report by health authorities that cantalope weakens bones;
_____ 2) an increase in the price of honeydew melons;
_____ 3) an increase in per capita income; and
_____ 4) an increase in the wages of workers producing cantalope.

8.   When the Federal Aviation Administration deregulated the airline industry, air travel prices fell dramatically. Suppose the price elasticity of demand for airline services in this price range has been estimated at .85.

a. Would you predict the total expenditure by consumers has increased, decreased, or remained constant since deregulation? Explain.

b. Would the number of customers per month using airtravel be larger or smaller 5 years from now, as compared to the average monthly use in the year immediately following the price fall? (Assume all other things constant such as the price of alternative methods of travel and technology.) Why?

c. Diagram the effect of airline deregulation on the P and Q of:
     i.   the market for train travel.
     ii. the market for plane mechanics.

           (i)   (ii)

9. Despite growing concern over social and environmental consequences, deforestation of rainforests continues worldwide. Although the cleared land is not suitable for growing many crops, the timber is valuable and in some cases the land can be used for cattle ranching.
a. Using supply and demand diagrams, illustrate the effect of cutting down the forests on these markets:
     i.   The worldwide timber market;
     ii. The market for protein sources other than beef (such as chicken or fish).

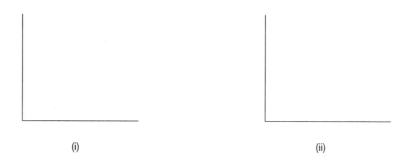

           (i)   (ii)

b. The Brazilian government is re-evaluating their policy on deforestation. Suppose they decided to impose a per unit tax on each tree cut. If the price elasticity of demand for timber is 1.82 in that price range, what effect will the price increase have on the before tax total expenditures by consumers?

c. Would you expect the rate of Brazilian timber consumption to be more or less six months after the tax price increase compared to the month immediately following the increase? Explain.

10. The market supply curve for gasoline is given by:

P ($/gal.)	3	4	5
Qs (gal./t)	0	2	4

a. Write down the equation for the supply curve.

b. If the market demand curve for gasoline has been estimated at Qd = 12 - P, find the equilibrium price and quantity. P = _____ Q = _____

c. What are the demand and supply elasticities at equilibrium?

ϵ_d = _____ ϵ_s = _____

d. If the government puts a per unit tax on consumers of $1, calculate the after tax price to consumers (Pd) and producers (Ps). Pd = _____ Ps = _____

e. Calculate total government revenue, the amount paid by consumers, the amount paid by producers, and the dead weight loss imposed by the tax. Illustrate these areas on a diagram.

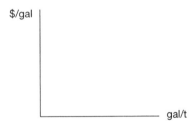

11. You have been hired as an economist by Gotham Cities Metro Transportation Department. You have estimated that:
a. the elasticity of demand for bus service is -0.4;
b. the cross price elasticity of demand for bus service with respect to the price of gasoline is 2.0;
c. the income elasticity of demand for bus service is -0.5.

Given these elasticity estimates, answer the following questions.
a. You believe that consumer incomes will rise 10% during the next year. What change in the quantity of bus rides demanded during the next year would you predict? Assume for simplicity that no change in the price of bus fares occurs as a result of a change in consumer incomes.

b. Do your elasticity estimates indicate that bus service is a normal good or an inferior good?

_____ Is bus service a substitute for, or a complement to, gasoline? _____

c. A new exise tax on gasoline raises the price of gasoline paid by consumers from $1.00 to $1.10 per gallon/litre. What change would this gasoline tax cause in the quantity of bus rides demanded?

12. Drug use in America received a great deal of attention in the 1980s. Refer to the diagrams below and choose which diagram BEST shows the effect on the drug market in the U.S. of:

a. Campaigns such as Nancy Reagan's "Just Say No" program.
b. U.S. helicopters in Bolivia to deter shipments of cocaine.
c. Above average weather conditions for growing marijuana crops in North, Central and South America.
d. Increased use of urine testing for drug use in the workplace.
e. A rising average income for U.S. residents.

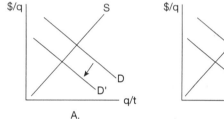 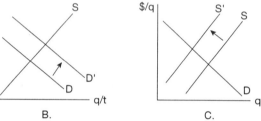 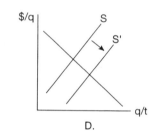

A.   B.   C.   D.

TRUE - FALSE QUESTIONS
Provide a one or two sentence explanation with your answer.

1.   If the price of tea rises due to a change in supply, the price of coffee is likely to rise as a result.

2.   An increased tax on gas won't reduce consumption. The higher price may at first reduce demand but the reduced demand will eventually bring the price down again, with consumption likely unchanged.

3.   An increase in the wages of farm workers will not reduce the supply of farm products, because the increased cost will be passed along to the consumer through higher prices.

4.   If both demand and supply increase, the equilibrium price must increase.

5.   The disappearance of anchovies off the coast of Peru in 1972 caused a scramble for protein-rich

substitutes, notably soybeans. Because soybeans were used in animal feed, this could eventually translate into higher cattle prices.

Refer to the graphs below showing the demand for bus rides by Mr. Smith and the supply by city metro.

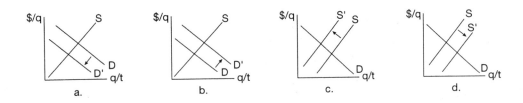

6.   Graph "a" illustrates the probable effect of a decrease in taxicab fares.

7.   Graph "a" illustrates the probable effect of an increase in the price of downtown parking spaces.

8.   Graphs "a" and "c" illustrate the probable effect of a strike by city metro bus drivers.

9.   Graphs "a" or "b" illustrate the probable effect of an increase in Mr. Smith's income.

10.   Graph "d" illustrates the probable effect of a unionization of bus mechanics.

11.   Graph "b" and "d" illustrate the probable effect of an eductional campaign for commuters to promote the environmental benefits of public transport.

Suppose the differential between full-serve and self-serve gasoline is 10 cents per gallon for the service.

12.   A fixed per gallon tax of $.25 that would increase the price of gasoline from $1.00 to $1.25 per gallon for self-serve, and $1.10 to $1.35 per gallon for full serve is expected to lead to a relatively greater proportion of self-serve gasoline to be sold.

13.   A fixed per gallon tax will lead to an absolutely smaller quantity sold of self-serve gas.

14.   An ad valorem tax of 25% is expected to lead to a relatively greater proportion of self-serve gasoline to be sold.

MULTIPLE CHOICE QUESTIONS
Choose the best answer.

1. A substantial decrease in the price of crude oil
a.   will increase the demand for coal.
b.   will increase the demand for oil.
c.   will increase the quantity supplied of oil.
d.   will increase the quantity demanded of oil.

2. The price of apples has increased by 33 percent. The Musselman family is consuming 10 percent more apples.
a.   Their demand for apples is price inelastic.
b.   Apples are a luxury good for the Musselman's.
c.   The increased price of apples must have increased the supply.
d.   The Musselman family is likely a supplier of apples.

3. Does an increase in the demand for Economics 200 for next semester increase the cost to some students intending to take the course?
a.   No, because tuition is not set at the equilibrium level.
b.   Yes, if the course is then taught in a larger room that is more expensive to heat.
c.   Yes, if the course must then be taken at a less satisfactory time.
d.   No, because tuition is fixed.

4. "As the price of coffee rose, consumer demand declined. In addition, the quantity demanded of tea rose, causing its price to rise." This statement:
a.   is essentially correct.
b.   contains one error: The quantity demanded, not the consumer demand (for coffee), declined.
c.   contains two errors: Demand, not quantity demanded, for tea increased, and the price of tea fell.
d.   contains two errors: Demand and quantity demanded are confused twice.

5. Which of the following would have no effect on the demand for television sets?
a.   an increase in the price of television sets.
b.   an increase in the incomes of consumers.
c.   an increase in the price of radios, a substitute good.
d.   a decrease in the price of movie tickets.
e.   all of the above affect the demand for tv sets.

6. The price of frozen vegetables fell, and the quantity sold also fell. Which event is consistent with this observation (all else equal)?
a.   trade barriers restricting exporting of frozen vegetables.
b.   trade barriers restricting importing of frozen vegetables.
c.   the price of agricultural land increased.
d.   the price of fresh vegetables fell.

7. If there is a decrease in the supply of a complement to bananas, then there will be a(n)
a.   decrease in the demand for bananas.
b.   decrease in the supply of bananas.
c.   increase in the demand for bananas.
d.   increase in the supply of bananas.
e.   increase in the equilibrium price of bananas.

These graphs show Safeway Grocery's supply and the Jones family's demand schedules for hamburger.

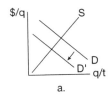 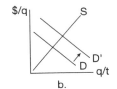 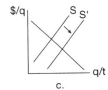 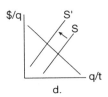

8. Which graph depicts the effect of an increase in the Jones' income?
a. A   b. B   c. A or B   d. C   e. A or C   f. none

9. Which graph depicts the effect of an increase in the wholesale price of beef?
a. A   b. B   c. C   d. D   e. none

10. Which graph depicts the effect of a reduction in the wages paid to Safeway butchers?
a. A   b. B   c. C   d. D   e. C or B

11. Which graph depicts the effect of a disease spoiling chicken and turkey meat.
a. A   b. B   c. C   d. D   e. C or B

12. Which graph depicts the effect of a butcher shop with fresh cuts opening up next door.
a. A   b. B   c. C   d. D   e. C or B

13. Some farm land can produce either corn or soybeans. If the demand for corn increases, then
a.   the demand for soybeans should increase.
b.   the demand for soybeans should decrease.
c.   the supply of soybeans should decrease.
d.   the supply of soybeans should increase.
e.   the market for soybeans should be largely unaffected.

14. If demand is relatively inelastic and supply elastic, then the burden of a tax on the good will be
a.   borne mostly by producers.
b.   shared equally by producers and consumers.
c.   borne mostly by the government.

d.   borne mostly by the poor.
e.   borne mostly by consumers.

15. If consumers suddenly increase their demand for beef, the supply curve will probably shift left for
a.   pig farmers, since pork is a substitute for beef.
b.   nobody, since the cattle market is a purely competitive one.
c.   potato farmers, since potatoes are usually consumed with beef.
d.   sheep ranchers, since they use the same land and labor as cattle ranchers.

16. Which of the following is likely to result in a shift in the supply curve for dresses?
a.   an increase in consumer prices.
b.   a reduction in tariffs that allow manufacturers to import cotton cloth at lower prices than before.
c.   an increase in dress prices.
d.   higher prices for skirts, pants and blouses.
e.   none of the above.

17. The price of coal fell and the quantity sold also fell. Which of the following events is consistent with this (all else equal)?
a.   the price of oil fell.
b.   large wage increases to coal miners.
c.   installation of more efficient coal mining equipment.
d.   consumer incomes rose.
e.   none of the above.

18. The price of fish rose and the quantity sold fell. Which of the following events is consistent with this (all else equal)?
a.   consumers developed a taste for fish.
b.   the price of meat rose.
c.   consumer incomes fell.
d.   the price of frozen fish for export increased.
e.   none of the above.

19. The supply curve for eggs will shift to the right if
a.   a virus kills millions of chickens.
b.   cholesterol is found to cause heart disease.
c.   chicken feed prices fall.
d.   the government taxes chicken coops.
e.   none of the above.

20. A good will tend to be more income elastic if
a.   it is a luxury.
b.   there are no close substitutes for it.
c.   it is a small part of the household budget.
d.   if it is addictive.
e.   none of the above.

21. Sam Stone owns a dairy farm that produces milk. He is also a milk drinker. If the price of milk rose for some reason, what would be the effect on the quantity consumed by Sam?

a. It increases.
b. It decreases.
c. It may increase or decrease.
d. It increases initially, then decreases a small amount.

22. If consumers spend more on apple juice after its price rises than they spent before, we know that the demand for apple juice
a. does not obey the law of demand.
b. is greater than the supply.
c. is inelastic.
d. has increased.
e. none of the above.

23. Which of the following would be most likely to cause a decrease in the demand for ski-lift tickets?
a. A holiday weekend.
b. Sales on ski equipment at major retail stores.
c. An increase in the price of ski-lift tickets.
d. Road construction on the mountain passes leading to ski resorts.
e. None of the above.

24. What would be the <u>dominant</u> effect on the market for male and female prostitution if the sale of services was legalized?
a. Supply increase, price increase, quantity increase.
b. Supply increase, price decrease, quantity increase.
c. Demand increase, price increase, quantity decrease.
d. Demand increase, price increase, quantity increase.
e. None of the above.

25. The elasticity of demand for prostitution services has been estimated at approximately .76 over its current price range. Based on this, after legalization one would expect
a. substitution by consumers into jogging and aerobics.
b. an increase in demand for prostitution services.
c. total revenues to decrease.
d. total expenditures to increase.
e. none of the above.

26. If prostitution was legalized, an obvious effect on the market for middleman services would be?
a. Supply increase, price decrease, quantity increase.
b. Supply decrease, price increase, quantity decrease.
c. Demand increase, price increase, quantity increase.
d. Demand decrease, price decrease, quantity decrease.
e. None of the above.

27. The demand for computers has risen dramatically at the same time as unit production costs have decreased. As a result of these developments we can expect,
a. a decrease in price and no predictable impact on output.
b. a definite decrease in price and increase in output.
c. an increase in output with no predictable change in price.

d.   no predictable changes in either price or output.

28. The price of coffee rose and the quantity sold fell. Which of the following events is consistent with this observation (all else equal)?
a.   Consumers developed a taste for coffee.
b.   The price of tea rose.
c.   The price of tea fell.
d.   The rental price of coffee growing land increased.
e.   None of the above.

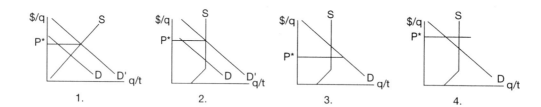

29. If there are empty seats at the university basketball game when the price per ticket is P*, then this situation can best be represented by which graph in the figure above?
a. 1   b. 2   c. 3   d. 4

30. The presence of scalpers at the Super Bowl (people selling tickets at a price above the quoted ticket price of P*) suggests that the market for stadium seats could be represented by which of the above graphs?
a. 1   b. 2   c. 3   d. 4

31. Which graph above best respresents the response of a profit-maximizing stadium owner to the home team making it into the playoffs?
a. 1   b. 2   c. 3   d. 4

32. The price of bagels rose 20 percent and bagel sales fell 35 percent. Cream cheese sales also fell 25 percent. From this information we can say all but which of the following?
a.   Demand for bagels is elastic.
b.   Bagels and cream cheese are complements.
c.   The demand for cream cheese is inelastic.
d.   Total expenditures by consumers on bagels decreased.
e.   we can say all of the above.

33. A simultaneous decrease in demand and supply will always result in
a.   a decrease in the equilibrium price.
b.   an increase in the equilibrium price.
c.   a decrease in the equilibrium quantity.
d.   an increase in the equilibrium quantity.

e.   a decrease in both price and quantity.

34. Lawyers must buy lump sum malpractice insurance. Insurance firms are considering raising their premiums by 20 percent. If this occurs, lawyers would most likely immediately pass on to their clients,
a.   all of this increased cost.
b.   a portion of this increased cost.
c.   an amount equal to their marginal revenue.
d.   none of this premium increase.

35. In the short-run, as a result of the higher premiums described above, one would expect the supply of legal services to
a.   be unaffected.
b.   depend on the location of each firm's average cost curve.
c.   increase because of increased prices of legal services.
d.   decrease because of increased marginal costs.

36. Suppose that instead of the increase in insurance premiums, the cost to lawyers of processing legal documents increases. The lawyers would be most likely to pass onto their clients,
a.   all of the increased cost.
b.   a portion of this increased cost.
c.   an amount equal to their marginal revenue.
d.   none of this fee increase.

Vegemite is a food product made from the waste yeast slurry from the beer brewing process, water, salt, and onion and celery flavoring. This is all vacuum concentrated into a spreadable paste. Nine out of ten households in Australia have a jar of Vegemite in the kitchen.

37. If the price of onion and celery flavoring increases, the effect on the vegemite market will be:
a.   price up, quantity down.
b.   price down, quantity down.
c.   price up, quantity up.
d.   price down, quantity up.

38. If the price of jam, a substitute for vegemite, decreases, the effect on the vegemite market will be:
a.   price up, quantity down.
b.   price down, quantity down.
c.   price up, quantity up.
d.   price down, quantity up.

39. If the price of Vegemite rises by 80%, and Australians decrease consumption from 5,000 to 4,000 metric tons annually, the price elasticity of demand over this price range would be estimated as:
a.   inelastic.
b.   elastic.
c.   unit elastic.
d.   insufficient information to conclude.

40. Assume in Australia there is good quality Vegemite that sells for $2.00 a jar and poor quality Vegemite that sells for $1.00 a jar. If it costs $4.00 per jar to ship vegemite to the United Sates, we

would expect, compared to Australia:
a.   more poor quality Vegemite in the United States.
b.   equal amounts of poor and good quality Vegemite in the United States.
c.   more good quality Vegemite in the United States.
d.   no good qualtiy Vegemite in the United States.

41. The answer for the previous question is based on
a.   the law of demand.
b.   the theory of comparative advantage.
c.   the law of absolute advantage.
d.   the postulate of diminishing marginal valuation.

42. Assume there is a drought in Australia that destroys the wheat crop. The result is a decrease in the supply of bread (and toast). The effect on the market for Vegemite is:
a.   price up, quantity down.
b.   price down, quantity down.
c.   price up, quantity up.
d.   price down, quantity up.

43. If the price of video games declines from $110 to $99 and consumer purchases increase by 15%, then we know:
a.   video games are a normal good.
b.   video games are a luxury item.
c.   the price elasticity of demand is elastic.
d.   the price elasticity of demand in inelastic.
e.   b and c.

SHORT ANSWER QUESTIONS

1. "Because the decrease in the demand for summer cottages caused by the recession pushed down the prices of cottages cottages, the supply of vacation cottages has fallen." Does this statement correctly use the language of supply and demand? If not, how would you correct it?

2. The Ottawa Citizen reported on October 11th that Canada's Environment Minister was not including any taxes in the government's new Green Plan. According to the paper, "...the minister doesn't think taxing fossil fuels will make people use them less."
    a. How does this statement agree or disagree with the laws of economics?
    b. What precisely must the Minister be assuming about the elasticity of demand for fossil fuels? Do you agree?
    c. If the Minister is correct, what effect would a price increase in fossil fuels have on the market for hydro power?

3. Evaluate the economic (NOT PERSONAL) reasoning of the following: "If the fact that fat contributes to cancer is heavily publicized, the demand for poutine (a popular item in central Canada made of french fries with gravy and cheese curd) will fall. The price of poutine, then, will also fall. But at the lower price people will buy more poutine, thus increasing rather than reducing the consumption of poutine."

ANSWERS TO REVIEW QUESTIONS

Answers to PROBLEMS AND EXERCISES

1.

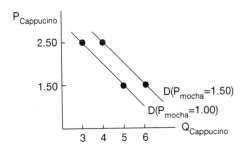 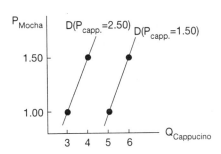

2. A fall in the price of gasoline would increase the demand for cars in general, but decrease the demand for small cars <u>relative</u> to large cars. Overall, the quantity of small cars consumed could still rise, just not as a percentage of total car sales.

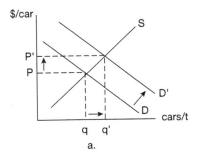 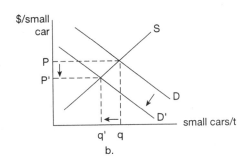

3. a. Relatively more first class tickets would sell, since the additional cost of first class becomes a relatively smaller proportion of the total ticket cost. Economy class becomes relatively more expensive.
b. Since the elasticity of demand is less than one, the consumers may bear the burden of the tax, although we we would need to know the elasticity of supply to be sure, Only if demand elasticity is less than supply elasticity will this be true.

4. The elasticity of demand for airline services would increase (become more elastic) because there would be a new substitute for airline travel.

5. The child's consumption of candy bars will decrease, becasue the relative price of these bars (relative to everything else the child buys) have gone up with the tax. The parent, therefore, will collect an amount in tax less than the increase in allowance.

6. a. The reduced price increases the quantity demanded, not the demand. There is nothing in the question to suggest a shift of the entire demand curve.

b. Supply would shift to the right for breakfast cereals made with grains; though some food groups are complementary to grains and would experience a demand increase, overall demand would shift to the left for non-grain food groups.

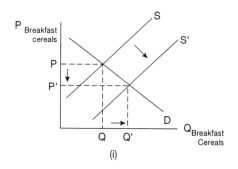

(i)

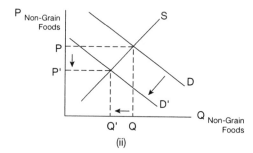

(ii)

7. a. Setting them equal, 60 - 2Q = 2Q, so Q = 15. Subbing back in to either equation, P = 30.
b. $\epsilon_d = -1$, $\epsilon_s = 1$
c. 1) the demand shifts to the left;
   2) the demand shifts to the right;
   3) the demand shifts to the right assuming cantaloupes are a normal good;
   4) no effect, this shifts the supply curve to the left.

8. a. I would predict the total expenditure by consumers has decreased because the elasticity is less than one. The % decrease in price will be greater than the corresponding % increase in quantity demanded.
b. The number of customers per month using airtravel would be larger 5 years from now, as more consumers substitute in to airtravel. This is the second law of demand.
c. i. the demand for train travel would decrease. P and Q would decrease.
   ii. the demand for plane mechanics would increase. P and Q would increase.

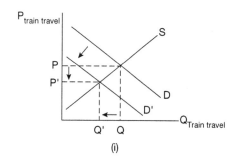

(i)

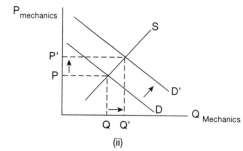

(ii)

9. a. i) The supply of timber worldwide would increase;
ii) With more ranching, the supply of cattle would increase, lowering beef prices. Consequently the

demand would decrease for protein alternatives.

b. Total expenditures would decrease.

c. The rate of Brazilian timber consumption would be less six months after the tax price increase because people will have had time to find substitutes in response to the price increase. This is the second law of demand again.

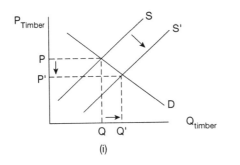 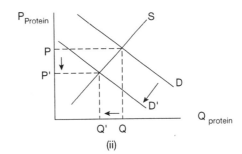

10. a. $P = 3 + .5Q$, so the supply curve is: $Qs = -6 + 2P$.
    b. $P = 6$, $Q = 6$ c. $\epsilon_d = -1$, $\epsilon_s = 2$
    d. $Pd = 6\frac{2}{3}$, $Ps = 5\frac{2}{3}$
    e. Total government revenue $= \$1 \times 5\frac{1}{3} = \$5\frac{1}{3}$, of which consumers pay $\$\frac{2}{3} \times 5\frac{1}{3} = \$32/9$ and producers pay $\$\frac{1}{3} \times 5\frac{1}{3} = \$16/9$. Dead weight loss is $.5[\$6\frac{2}{3} - \$5\frac{2}{3}) \times (6 - 5\frac{1}{3})] = \$\frac{1}{3}$.

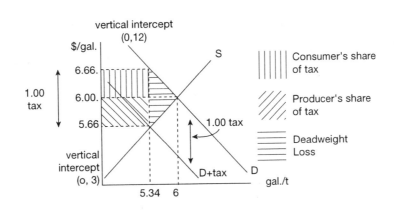

11. a. With a 10% rise in incomes, quantity consumed would fall by 5%.
    b. Bus rides are an inferior good since the income elasticity is negative, and a substitute for gasoline since the cross price elasticity is positive.
    c. A 10% increase in price would lead to a 4% decrease in quantity demanded.

12. a. A, demand decreases.
    b. C, supply decreases (shifts left).
    c. D, supply increases (shifts right).
    d. A, demand decreases.
    e. B, demand increases assuming a normal good.

Answers to TRUE - FALSE QUESTIONS

1. True. The demand for coffee (a substitute for tea) would rise, raising the price of coffee.

2. False. There will be a decrease in quantity demanded at the higher price with nothing indicated to shift the entire demand curve back to the right.

3. False. An increase in the wages of farm workers will raise costs and therefore reduce the supply of farm products. Because demand is not perfectly inelastic, some, but not all, of the increased cost will be passed along to the consumer through higher prices.

4. False. The equilibrium quantity must increase but the net effect on price depends on which shift dominates.

5. True. An increase in demand for soybeans will raise prices. The increased price of the soybean input will shift the supply curve for the output (cattle) to the left, raising prices in those markets also.

6. True. A decrease in taxicab fares would decrease the demand for substitutes such as bus rides.

7. False. An increase in the price of parking spaces is expected to increase the demand for bus rides.

8. False. Only graph c. A strike by city metro bus drivers would decrease supply, raise price, and decrease quantity demanded, not demand.

9. True. It depends on whether bus rides are a normal or inferior good.

10. False. Graph "c" illustrates the probable decrease in supply (shift left) from a unionization of bus mechanics if wages rise as a result.

11. False. Only graph "b" illustrates the probable effect of an educational campaign. The increase in demand would raise price, leading to an increase in quantity supplied, but no shift in supply.

12. False. Since the per unit tax makes the service relatively less expensive, a relatively greater proportion of full-serve gasoline is expected to be sold after the tax.

13. True. Since the tax raises the price of gasoline, though this cannot be shown unequivocably since it is relative prices that govern the law of demand.

14. False. An ad valorem tax doesn't change relative prices, and therefore is not expected to change pre-tax proportions of full-serve versus self-serve gasoline.

Answers to MULTIPLE CHOICE QUESTIONS

1. d	12. a	23. d	34. d
2. d	13. c	24. b	35. a
3. c	14. e	25. c	36. b
4. d	15. d	26. d	37. a
5. a	16. b	27. c	38. b

6. d	17. a	28. d	39. a
7. a	18. e	29. d	40. c
8. c	19. c	30. c	41. a
9. d	20. a	31. b	42. b
10. c	21. c	32. c	43. c
11. b	22. c	33. c	

Answers to SHORT ANSWER QUESTIONS

1. No, this statement incorrectly uses the language of supply and demand by confusing a change in quantity supplied due to a price change (caused by the decrease in demand) with a change in supply. The statement should read: "Because the decrease in the demand for summer cottages caused by the recession pushed down the prices of cottages, the quantity supplied of vacation cottages has fallen.

2. a. This statement contradicts the law of demand by suggesting that a price change from the tax hike will not lead to a change in quantity demanded.
b. The Minister must be assuming perfectly inelastic demand for fossil fuels. This is unlikely, and in fact we have observed people's consumption change as the price changes.
c. None, because there would be no substitution out of fossil fuels.

3. This is another example of confusing shifts in curves with movements along curves. If the demand falls there will be a new lower equilibrium price, period. The quantity consumed will not increase again until something shifts the demand curve to the right (such as an increase in the price of a substitute) or the supply curve to the right (such as a decrease in the price of potatoes).

CHAPTER 6
Cost and Production

PRINCIPAL GOALS

1.0 Understand how specialization (division of labor) and comparative advantage in an economy result in gains from trade. (Objectives 1.1, 1.2, 1.3, 1.4)

2.0 Recognize the relationship between the MC curve and the Supply curve. (Objectives 2.1, 2.2)

3.0 Understand the relationship between production and costs. (Objectives 3.1, 3.2, 3.3)

4.0 Identify the source of rents. (Objectives 4.1, 4.2, 4.3, 4.4)

5.0 Understand Pareto efficiency and transactions costs. (Objective 5.1)

OBJECTIVES
Answers to bold-faced questions appear at the end of the dialogue.

"Geez, Ginny, you look terrible."

"Thanks. You look great too."

"Sorry. I mean you just look tired. What did you do last night?"

"Karl convinced me to go hear this band called *Dialectical Materialism* with him after work. They were great, but I didn't get home until about 3:30."

"Why Ginny Hill, 3:30 and on a *school* night. And with a strange man", Mo said with mock concern.

"Karl is strange, isn't he?"

"Without a doubt. Do you want to go over this chapter or do you want to go back to bed?" Mo asked.

"If that isn't the most obnoxious question -- of course I want to go back to bed, but I'm here aren't I?"

"Charmingly so. So last night was a celebration because you think you aced the econ exam?"

"Okay, *that's* the most obnoxious question," snapped Ginny. No, I don't think I aced the exam, in fact, I think I screwed up several questions. Not only that, I had to skip the Ming Dynasty to finish my Chinese history paper on time. Anything else?"

"Steady, I just hope there's nothing more to this academic suicide than simple college colitis. Anyway, since you're of infirm mind and spirit I will spare you from having to think too much today. The first thing on the list is specialization and how that relates to comparative advantage and gains from trade."

"Okay," Ginny yawned.

"We have to master a building blocks first, like the production possibilities frontier. But perhaps we should warm you up with your favorite part Ginny -- the vocabulary."

OBJECTIVE 1.1 Recognize definitions for the important new vocabulary.

Question 1. Match the term with its definition(s). Write out definitions for any undefined terms.

a. specialization
c. multiplier effects
e. absolute advantage
g. marginal cost
i. average cost

b. division of labor
d. comparative advantage
f. production possibilities frontier
h. total cost
j. industry marginal cost

_____ The sum of the marginal costs of producing each unit of a good up to a specified quantity.

_____ Being able to produce the greatest quantity of a good, not considering the opportunity costs.

_____ a graphic representation of the maximum levels and combinations of production (of two goods or categories of goods) possible for an individual, firm or an entire economy given resource constraints.

_____ total cost divided by the quantity produced.

_____ the cost of producing an additional (one more) unit of a good.

_____ the devoting of workers' energies toward mastering the necessary knowledge and skills to perform only a subset of tasks required to produce a whole good.

_____ the advantage of being able to produce a good at the lowest relative cost.

_____ an aggregate measure summing the marginal costs of each firm in the industry.

_____ the tendency, encouraged by competitive markets, to employ resources for the specific and limited uses for which they are best suited in order to enhance their productivity for producing a desired good.

_____ the area under the marginal cost (supply) curve.

_____ a change experienced by one sector of a specialized economy as a consequence of a change occurring in another sector.

_____ the process of specialization for labor resources.

OBJECTIVE 1.2 Interpret a production possibilities frontier.

"So, do you understand what the production possibilities frontier is?" Mo asked.

"Yes, it's the line that represents how many coconuts and/or fish Crusoe and Friday can produce. They can produce anywhere on the line or inside the line, but they can't produce outside the line unless they, I don't know, learn some new way to catch fish or snag coconuts."

"The interesting thing about them though", Mo said, "is that at any point on the frontier the slope of the curve is an expression of the opportunity cost of producing one good or another."

"Where did you get that?" Ginny asked.

"Well, Silberberg mentions it in the book and I asked Adam -- as you move left to right along the frontier, for example, the cost of each additional coconut is the number of fish given up. So the slope at that point is the marginal cost of coconuts."

"I'll give you full credit for it anyway", Ginny said. "But let me see if I get this. The slope of the PPF is the cost. When Crusoe moves from A to B in figure 6-1 his slope is 3 fish - 2 fish = 1 fish, over 0 coconuts - 1 coconut = - 1 coconut. So the slope is 1/-1 = -1."

"Right, the cost of Crusoe producing one more coconut is one fish."

"So the point is...?"

"The main point is that through the production possibilities frontier and figuring out Crusoe's and Friday's opportunity cost of producing fish and coconuts you can determine who has the comparative advantage in producing what."

OBJECTIVE 1.3 Determine absolute and comparative advantages for two producers.

"A comparative advantage means they can produce the good for the least cost doesn't it?", Ginny asked.

"Yes, which is why the slope of the PPF being equal to the cost is so useful. You calculate the slope and boom you know Crusoe is the lower cost producer of fish and Friday is the lower cost producer of coconuts."

"Wait a minute", Ginny said. "You're going too fast. So you know that Crusoe has a slope of -1 and Friday has a slope of what?"

"Minus one-half."

"Okay, -1/2," Ginny said. "So with fish on the vertical axis the slope represents the marginal cost of acquiring another coconut. Because the slope tells us how many units of the vertical axis we must give up (rise, or fall as the case may be) to get another unit of the good on the horizontal axis."

"That's right. So Friday's marginal cost of coconuts is 1/2 fish, while Crusoe's marginal cost of cocunuts is 1 fish. Friday has the lower marginal cost of coconuts, so he should specialize in cocunuts. The marginal cost of fish will just be the inverse slopes."

"It's useful for me to talk through what the ratios mean," said Ginny, "1F/2C for Friday and 1F/1C for Crusoe. Friday must give up two coconuts for one fish, while Crusoe only has to give up one. So it only costs Crusoe one coconut to produce one more fish. It costs Friday two coconuts to produce one more fish. It costs Crusoe less to produce one more fish so he is the low-cost producer of fish."

"Which you could express as MC fish = 2 coconuts for Friday, and MC fish = 1 coconut for Crusoe. Since MC_{fish} (Friday) > MC_{fish} crusoe, Crusoe has the comparative advantage fishing."

"Yes, which I could certainly express in notation if someone had difficulty with the words," said Ginny.

Question 2. The Cleavers have a house cleaning business. Determine who is the low-cost producer, and therefore has the comparative advantage for cleaning bathrooms and vacuuming.

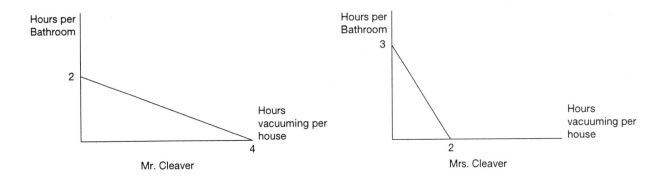

Question 3. a. On a good day while rafting down the Mississippi, Huck Finn can steal 2 pies or 3 sheets of cornbread. Tom Sawyer on the other hand can make off with 3 pies or 4 sheets of cornbread. Draw the PPFs for Huck and Tom below.

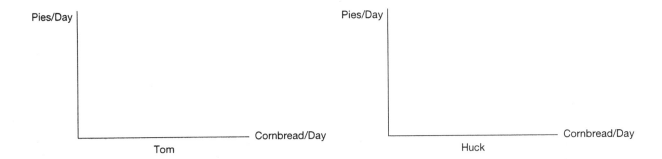

b. Draw a new PPF representing the total Finn-Sawyer economy.

Pies/Day

Cornbread/Day

c. If Huckleberry would eat 2 pies and 1 cornbread on a regular day and Tom would eat 1 pie and 4 cornbread, would they be able to keep themselves in pie and cornbread? _____

d. Tom was lying. He really only eats 1 pie and 1 cornbread. Working from their comparative advantages, if they wanted to feed themselves and possibly engage in some trade with people they met on the river, what is their joint economy likely to "produce" if they specialize? _____ What would Huck produce? _____ What about Tom? _____

* * * * * * *

"Are you finished Mo? Can I ask you a question?"

"Sure."

"Is there any real significance to having an absolute advantage versus a comparative advantage?"

"Beyond being able to produce for your own needs, it's important when there's an opportunity to specialize and trade. The more you can produce the more you can trade," answered Mo.

"I was thinking of a situation like World War II, when the U.S. and Canadian economies probably tried to produce, absolutely, the greatest quantity possible of certain goods necessary for the war."

"But even still they would specialize to the extent possible, although trade between countries was limited. It's just that the mix of output would change. Absolute advantage just means your PPF is farther out than someone else's, while comparative advantage determines its slope."

"Right, its slope. Hmmm", Ginny exhaled.

"Hmm? Is that an I understand hmm, or an I'm confused hmm?" Mo asked.

OBJECTIVE 1.4 **Be prepared to articulate why specialization is limited according to the extent of the market.**

"It's a kind of 'I just made a connection' hmm", Ginny said. "I was thinking about absolute and comparative advantage and the limits of specialization."

"What about them?"

"Well, I was just thinking about this Crusoe and Friday economy. It's not too realistic in a lot of ways."

"No kidding Ginny, it's worse than Gilligan's Island. How do they stay alive? If Crusoe can't cut himself more than three coconuts a day, I'm afraid he's a dead man. And Friday's supposed to be a native Caribbean right? And he can't catch more than four fish a day. What was he, a child accountant chained to a desk? How do you get to be an adult native of the Caribbean in those days and not know how to catch more than four fish a day?"

"I get your point Mo. But my point is why would he even catch four fish a day? He's alone except for Crusoe and together they won't eat more than four fish. Any more and it's a waste of time and fish. It's that extent of the market thing."

"Ah, I see what you're saying. Like the quote at the end of the chapter. The lone rancher never got to eat beef because they'd end up with too much meat; it would go to waste."

"Cattle, cattle everywhere and not a steak to eat," said Ginny. "Whether you have an absolute advantage or even a comparative advantage the degree to which you can specialize depends on the number of people out there -- the size of the market -- who are available and able to buy and trade for your product."

"That's a good point Ginny."

"I think I'm still a little confused though. If the PPF represents the marginal cost of producing fish or coconuts or whatever, then is it a marginal cost curve?"

"Oooh, good question," Mo said. "I don't think so, because first of all it's the slope of the PPF that represents the marginal cost of production -- not the PPF itself."

"Aha, you're right. Even though the slope is the opportunity cost in terms of the other good, the PPF is really just a representation of the maximum possible production."

"Besides, a marginal cost curve would be on a graph with price and quantity, not quantity and quantity like the PPF," said Mo.

"But we should be able to make a supply curve out of the PPF. Silberberg did in the book."

OBJECTIVE 2.1 Compare demand to marginal value and supply to marginal cost.

"That's true, and remember that MC and supply curves are pretty much the same thing. It's only a matter of whether you're asking what quantity they would supply at a given price -- that's a supply curve. Or what their incremental cost is at a given quantity."

"And that would be a marginal cost curve," Ginny said. "But the actual curve would be the same for both right?"

"From what I understand so far."

"That's exactly the same for the demand curve and the marginal value curve, remember?"

"Sure, if you start from the quantity axis and ask, at this quantity how much is this worth to you, or what is your marginal value for it, then you're interpreting the curve as a marginal value curve."

"Or you can start from the price axis and ask, at this price how many or what quantity will you demand. The vertical axis, $/Q, can represent either the price of the good, the marginal value of the good to the consumer, or the marginal cost to the producer."

"Okay," Mo said, "but now the trick is to covert a PPF into a supply curve."

OBJECTIVE 2.2 Derive a supply curve from a PPF.

"So that's just a matter of determining what quantity of the good a producer would supply at a given price. We need an example here. Do you see one in Adam's stuff?"

"Here's one with PPFs for New Zealand and Australia producing sheep and kiwi fruits."

"Another down-under stereotype," Ginny grumbled. "Sheep and kiwis. They produce more than that."

"It's just an example," Mo said.

> **Problem:** Construct a joint supply curve for sheep for New Zealand and Australia.

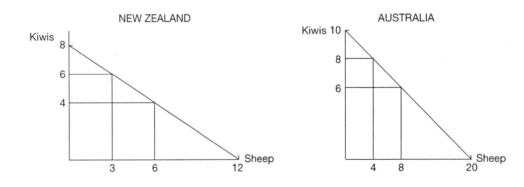

"Do you want to tackle the slope Ginny?"

"Okay, it's 6 - 4 kiwis over 3 - 6 sheep, which is 2 over -3 so -2/3 for New Zealand. And 8 - 6 kiwis over 4 - 8 sheep, which is 2 over -4 or -1/2 for Australia."

"So for New Zealand, MC sheep = 2/3 kiwi, and in Australia, MC sheep = 1/2 kiwi. Since 1/2 < 2/3, the Australians are the low-cost producers of sheep."

"Or from the perspective of the marginal cost per kiwi, New Zealand gives up 3 sheep for 2 additional kiwis, which is 1.5 sheep per kiwi. The Aussies give up 2 sheep per kiwi, so the New Zealanders are the low-cost producers of kiwis. Now what do we do?" said Ginny.

"Well we engage in a diabolically complicated series of calculations, computing the mean distance of the kiwi orchards from analagous sheep herds then extrapolate that onto the willingness of New Zealanders to part with marginal mutton. Adjusting everything for sub-equatorial factors and phenomena, such as toilet bowl water siphoning out in a counter-clockwise direction."

"Indubitably," Ginny replied. "And the answer is, the Australians will supply 20 sheep for a minimum price of 1/2 kiwi per sheep. So just like in the book the supply curve will be flat from 0 to 20 sheep at a price equivalent to 1/2 kiwi. If people want more than 20 sheep they're going to have to pay more to the New Zealanders, who are willing to supply 12 sheep for a price of 2/3 kiwi each."

"So the supply curve jumps up there at 20, like I've drawn below."

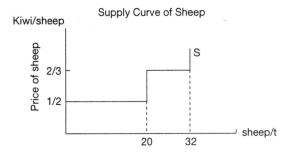

Question 4. Draw the combined Huck Finn and Tom Sawyer market supply curve for cornbread using the PPF's and information in Question 3 above. Think about how you label the graph axes.

* * * * * * *

"And again", Ginny said, "that can also be seen as the marginal cost curve."

"Absolutely", Mo replied.

"It becomes pretty clear from this that to produce anything there is a cost. Whether you think of it in terms of money or kiwi fruits."

OBJECTIVE 3.1 **Describe how production can involve a variety of costs, not all of which are included in producers' calculations.**

"I know. If you think back to chapter one when we learned about opportunity cost it wasn't so clear, but now the real cost of everything seems more obvious. One more sheep costs you two-thirds of a kiwi and you have to choose which you will produce because you can't have both."

"I think environmentalists have been trying to get people to realize this for years," Ginny said. Part of the cost of production is the loss of plants, animals, air, soil and water quality, maybe our atmosphere, and ultimately our own health. But I don't know that these environmental costs are part of the marginal costs in our examples."

"I don't know," said Mo. "Suppose you have to clearcut an acre of forest to graze sheep. It's not easy to know the full costs of that forestland. The rancher knows what he has to pay for the land, which must be at least the value of the timber. But it's unlikely that he has to pay for the marginal decrease in air quality or biodiversity resulting from cutting down the trees. Not to mention all the greenhouse "gas" in the form of methane from flatulating sheep."

"I think it's cow's gas that's the big problem Mo."

"Cattle, sheep, they all look alike. Anyway, we don't have good measures for those costs and besides, no individual owns those things so who would he pay?"

"How about splitting it between everyone who has to breathe slightly lower quality air as result?" suggested Ginny.

"Well it sounds good in theory, but I think its harder in practice because there aren't many markets for these public goods like air. I think this is the type of problem we study in Chapter nine."

"So the kiwi farmer makes his production decision taking into account his private costs, but not the social ones? According to what we've just learned, he's willing to take a price that's too low. Oh, let's not talk about it. I just get bummed out.

"Maybe you should become an environmental economist Ginny. It might be a little more effective than your current plans of chaining yourself to a tree."

"I don't know, maybe I should. If I don't flunk out first."

"Well to make sure that doesn't happen let's get back to my list of objectives."

OBJECTIVE 3.2 Calculate total cost and average cost from marginal costs.

"What I thought was important was that total cost and average cost can both be calculated from the marginal cost curve. It's really just a mathematical relationship," said Mo.

"What do you mean mathematical relationship?", Ginny asked apprehensively.

"Don't panic Ginny," Mo said. I just mean that total cost is equal to the sum of the marginal costs for each additional unit produced up to some given quantity."

"Geez you sound like the textbook Mo."

"In other words, for the linguistically challenged, suppose you want to produce twenty sheep. There is a marginal cost for producing the first sheep, the second sheep, the third and so on up to twenty right?"

"Right."

"Well if you add up all twenty of those separate marginal costs you have your total cost. Perhaps a visual description would help Ginny?"

"Thank you."

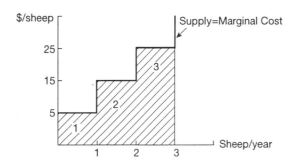

"The total cost is going to be this whole area between the marginal cost curve and the horizontal axis up to the quantity you produce. But if this were in a table of data all you would see is MC = 5, 15 and 25, for sheep 1, 2 and 3. So the total cost would be 5 + 15 + 25 which is 45."

"Thank you again", Ginny said. "But what about marginal cost, how do you figure that out?"

"You mean if you're not given the numbers?" Mo said. "Well, if you're given total cost you have to take the change in total cost divided by the change in quantity, $\Delta TC/\Delta Q$."

"So in our example here moving from 2 sheep to 3 sheep the change in total cost is \$45 - \$20, or \$25 and the change in quantity is 1. So the marginal cost of the third sheep is $25. It works!"

"Of course it works. Now for average cost its just the total cost divided by the quantity produced."

"I see, so as you tried to tell me before, there is a relationship among marginal, total and average costs that can be determined through the use of mathematics."

"That is indeed what I said."

Question 5. Calculate the marginal cost, total cost and average cost of producing 9 eggs from the following diagram.

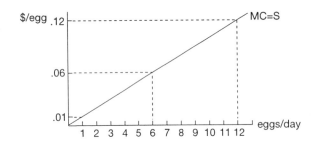

MC = _____

TC = _____

AC = _____

OBJECTIVE 3.3 Describe the relationship between aggregate supply curves and minimum total cost.

"This is a lot like everything else", Ginny said. "There are marginal, total and average everythings aren't there: values, revenues, products, what else?"

"Costs."

"Yes, costs. And this supply curve is really just the same as the supply curve we learned in chapters four and five."

"Pretty much," Mo said, "but don't you think he's really trying to point out that supply here is based on production and not just possession of some good for trade, like the oyster example?"

"Yes I do," said Ginny. "I also think he's trying to drive home that you can't have production without costs. So total cost is the minimum total cost to the producer, and by extension the minimum total opportunity cost to society, of producing that quantity of goods; whatever quantity that is."

"And if you create an aggregate supply curve you have a curve that represents society's total supply of and cost for producing that good."

"Very clever, or interesting", Ginny said, "that society's costs and the producers' costs are the same, don't you think?"

"Yes, but that way the producer's interests and society's interests become the same and the producer ends up doing what's best for society while doing what's best for himself or herself."

"Which means operating at the least cost and maximizing rents," Ginny said.

"This sounds like Adam's invisible hand."

"Your brother's hand is invisible Mo?"

"Adam Smith nimrod. People are just out there trying to do what's best for themselves. It just so happens that it turns out to be the best thing for society, economically speaking that is."

"If," corrected Ginny, "there are no social costs, like pollution, that aren't being ignored by producers, which of course would affect the producer's rents as well."

OBJECTIVE 4.1 Recognize definitions for the important new vocabulary.

Question 6. Match the term with its definition(s). Write out definitions for any undefined terms.

a. rents   b. quasi rents
c. fixed resources   d. sunk costs
e. increasing marginal costs at the extensive margin
f. monopoly power   g. economic or Pareto efficiency

_____ irretrievable investments in capital goods made by a firm.

_____ all benefits from exchange have been exhausted.

_____ the ability of a firm to restrict output and raise market price.

_____ as the quantity produced continues to increase lesser quality resources are used and the return from these resources is diminished.

_____ the part of a payment for a good or service, above and beyond the amount necessary to meet the producer's costs, but that only exists because the producer made the neccessary initial investment to develop the product in the first place.

_____ the situation where it is not possible to make any individual better off through trade without making someone else worse off.

_____ costs incurred by producers in the past to construct capital goods for production.

_____ being the only producer, defined by some geographic area or the uniqueness of the product, of a good or service.

_____ resources that cannot be altered to yield a greater quantity of output.

OBJECTIVE 4.2 **Calculate producers' surplus/rents; Explain the fundamental source of these rents.**

"So are you comfortable with rents?", Mo asked.

"No, I told you in chapter three that I paid too much for my dorm room considering the quality of my neighbors."

"Does this clever repartee mean you're coming out of your sleep-deprived fog Ginny?

"Rents are the seller's surplus, which in Chapter four was the difference between the price received by the seller and their marginal value for consuming the good themselves."

"But that was just for a pure exchange economy. Can you give me the new definition with production and costs?"

"It's the difference between the price received and the marginal cost of producing the good," replied Ginny. Basically it's that space between the marginal cost curve and the price line."

Question 7. A company produces 15,000 valves per month at a marginal cost of $1.80 per valve for the first 5000, $3.20 per valve for the second 5000 and $4.70 for the third 5000. The market price for valves is $4.70 each. Calculate this company's rents when producing 5000, 10,000 and 15,000 valves. Draw a graph depicting these rents.

Q valves	Rent
5,000	_____
10,000	_____
15,000	_____

* * * * * * *

"Okay, so we know at least that much", Mo said. "But I want to know about the source of rents that Silberberg talks about. What did you make of that?"

"I didn't quite get to that. Karl recommended an all black outfit for going to hear the band -- something that suggested suffering was his advice. This urban scene is a little new to me -- it took me a while to get the right look."

"Is that the look of an incredibly hip but unemployed college dropout? If so you might want to save the outfit for later use."

"Geez Mo, don't you ever relax?"

"Adam and I have been a little too busy trying to help Mom make ends meet. Evenings spent listening to musical expressions of our lost generation are a bit of a luxury. I'll just wait until they locate us, then I'll join back in."

"Well, you look lousy in black anyway."

"In the interests of time," Mo began, "what Silberberg said about the source of rents was that of all the producers producing, the producer with the lowest costs got the biggest rents. It had to do with rising marginal costs at the extensive margin."

OBJECTIVE 4.3 Determine the limits on levels of output due to the constraint of rising marginal costs (at the extensive margin) and diminishing marginal returns.

"Okay, rising marginal costs at the extensive margin," Ginny said. "What does that mean?"

"It means that the more you produce the more costly it is, because the resources you're using are getting worse and worse, or less productive."

"Can you give me an example?"

"Well, how about your life. Not to mention the fact that you're going to burn out from going to school, working and going out, but you're trying to produce A quality school work with D quality resources."

"What?"

"Your job, here at the university, is to produce school work right? Papers, tests, reading, knowledge?"

"In a certain way I suppose so," said Ginny.

"Well, for one class it's not so hard to produce A quality work right? Even when you're working and doing other stuff."

"Sure, depending on the course. I don't know if I could ever get an A in Calculus."

"Okay, but in general though you can do it, because you have sufficient resources to produce that quality of work, like time, energy, and intelligence. But when you try to increase your production by adding a second, third and fourth course it gets harder and harder to get all A's. Your resources for the second, third and fourth courses are not as good as for the first course, when you are fresh and *awake*."

"In other words, I can use my best hours in the morning for my first course, but a second course means I have to use some of those drowsy afternoon hours," Ginny said.

"Exactly", Mo said. "To produce more work of a certain quality you have to devote more or your resources, but the quality of those resources gets worse..."

"Diminishes."

"Yes, diminishes, because instead of studying when you're fresh and getting plenty of sleep, you're studying and doing papers in the middle of the night when you're burnt out after work and partying. Those are D quality resources."

"You're right," sighed Ginny. "But even at my freshest I can't do math as well as you."

"Not all producers have the same quality resources and the ones with the most productive resources get the most rents, because among all of the producers of their good, a producer with the most productive resources can produce the good at the lowest cost. I earn rents on mathematical output, but you earn them on conceptual reasoning."

"So all of these suppliers are producing their good up until the point where marginal cost equals price," said Ginny, "and the producers with the lowest marginal costs are getting the most rents because..."

"Because the gap between their costs and the price that consumers and producers arrive at through the market is the greatest. Think if you can produce sunglasses for $10.00 a pair and I can produce them for $15.00 a pair and they sell for $40.00 a pair, who makes the biggest rents? The producers who have less productive resources make smaller rents than the more productive producers."

Question 8. Answer the following questions using the four graphs below.

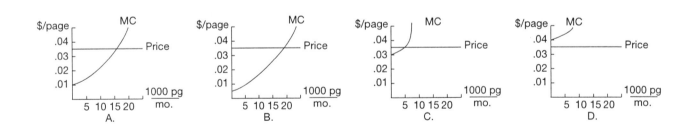

1. Rank the four print shops from lowest to highest marginal cost.

      1. _____   2. _____   3. _____   4. _____

2. Rank the four print shops from lowest to highest rents.

      1. _____   2. _____   3. _____   4. _____

3. Determine the quantity produced by each print shop at .01, .02, and .035 cents.

               A.   B.   C.   D.

.01
.02
.035

4. In the graph space below draw an aggregate supply curve for the four print shops.

$/page

1000 pages
per month.

5. Calculate total costs for the four print shops.
        A. _____   B. _____   C. _____   D. _____

6.   What minimum price is necessary to induce shop D to begin production?

    _____

7. a. If the price per copy falls from .035 cents to .02 cents, which shop(s) continue(s) producing? _____ Which cease(s) production? _____
    b. If the price per copy falls to .01 cents which shop(s) will continue producing? _____

OBJECTIVE 4.4 Describe Quasi rents.

"The other thing you, or we, need to remember is the difference between rents and quasi rents."

"Quasi rents? What are those?", Ginny asked.

"Silberberg describes them as the rents that pay the producer back for any investments they made before they actually produced the product. His example was the drug companies which invest millions in developing a drug and getting it approved by the government before they get to sell it to the public. After all of that work and investment the drug company has to produce the new drug and market it like any other product. What Silberberg is saying is that the price of the new drug covers the actual production costs *and* all of the research costs that went into developing the new drug."

"So what's the difference between a rent and a quasi rent?" asked Ginny.

"I guess a quasi rent shows up just like a regular rent, but it comes from owning a specialized capital good, rather than raw resource. In other words, you could earn rents from owning an oil field, but quasi-rents from owning a specialized rig designed and built to extract oil under particular conditions."

"So a quasi rent refers only to those cases where some investment has been made that specializes an input, essentially making it not easily replicable. That makes sense, because nonreplicable resources in general are the source of rents."

"Silberberg says that if the company was legally or otherwise prevented from getting these quasi rents then they wouldn't make the initial investment, and there wouldn't be a final product."

"Okay, so is that it for this chapter Mo? There's been a lot of material."

"Well, he also talks some more about economic, or Pareto efficiency."

"That's just where there are no more gains from exchange to be had isn't it?"

OBJECTIVE 5.1 **Define Pareto or economic efficiency as that quantity where MV = MC or that price where Qd = Qs.**

"Yes, but with production the point of economic efficiency occurs when, at the quantity exchanged, the consumer's marginal value equals the producer's marginal cost, and they'll both equal price."

"So it's where the marginal cost curve crosses the marginal value curve. Which makes sense," Ginny said, "because if they exchange any more then the cost of producing more of the good is greater than the amount the consumer would value the good, let alone pay for it."

"Exactly," Mo said. "Or equivalently it's where the demand and supply curves cross, or at that price where quantity demanded equals quantity supplied."

"So this must also be the point where the greatest benefits occur for society," said Ginny.

"I guess so, where the sum of consumers' surplus and producer's rents are as large as possible."

"Well," Ginny yawned again, "my MV for another tidbit of new economic knowledge is pretty small right now. I'm going to work through some of these problems as my penance for last night's frivolous behavior, then I think the invisible hand will lead me to my room for a restorative little power nap. Thanks for spotting me on this one Mo."

Question 9. a. From the table below determine the point where Pareto efficiency is achieved.

Q	$MV	$MC
1	60	10
2	40	15
3	20	20
4	0	25

b. Calculate the total benefits from exchange.

c. Calculate the value of the wasted resources if these producers were ordered to produce four units. Graph your results below.

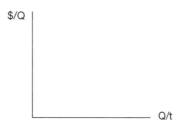

d. Try to find the point where Pareto efficiency is achieved in the case below. Why do you know it must exist?

Q	$MV	$MC
10	120	95
20	110	100
30	100	105
40	90	110

ANSWERS TO DIALOGUE QUESTIONS

Question 1. Vocabulary: h, e, f, i, j, g, b, d, j, a, h, c, b, h.

Question 2. Baths cleaned per house vacuumed:
Slope for Mr. Cleaver (Ward) 2 - 0/0 - 4 = -1/2.
Slope for Mrs. Cleaver (June) 3 - 0/0 - 2 = -3/2.

Ward	June
1 house = 2 bath	1 house = 2/3 bath
1 bath = 1/2 house	1 bath = 1.5 houses

Ward Cleaver's comparative advantage is cleaning the bathroom, while June's is vacuuming the house.

Question 3.
a.

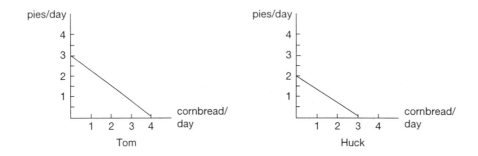

b.

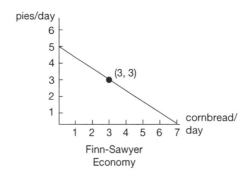

c. No, given that consumption they cannot feed themselves. Their joint consumption is beyond their PPF.

d. 1) Huck and Tom would produce 3 pies and 3 pans of cornbread.

2) Huck would specialize in cornbread and Tom in pies.

Question 4. Tom Sawyer would supply 4 pans of cornbread at 3/4 pie per pan and Huck Finn would supply 3 pans of cornbread at 2/3 pie per pan.

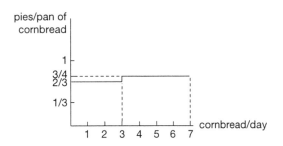

Question 5. Marginal cost of the 9th egg is $.09 cents. ($\Delta TC/\Delta Q$)
Total cost of 9 eggs is $.40 cents. 1/2 base x height: 4.5 x .09 = .405
Average cost of 9 eggs is $.045. (TC/Q)

Question 6. Vocabulary: d, g, e, h, f, b, g, d, h, c. Rents were not defined.
rents (production and exchange) - a payment in excess of what is necessary to call forth production of some good or service.

Question 7. To calculate rents you have to calculate the amount of money the producer makes on each valve beyond their costs of making that valve (or that quantity of valves).

• **5000 valves:** $4.70 - $1.80 (price received minus the marginal cost of the valves) = $2.90. $2.90 per valve profit times 5000 valves = $14,500.00.
• **10,000 valves:** $4.70 - $3.20 = $1.50. $1.50 x 5000 (only making this rent on valves 5001 to 10,000) = $7,500.00. Total rent for 10,000 valves is $14,500 + $7,500 = $22,000.00.
• **15,000 valves:** $4.70 - $4.70 = $0. $0 x 5000 = $0. Total rents on 15,000 valves = $22,000.00.

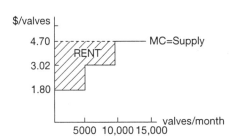

Question 8.
1. B, A, C, D
2. B, A, C, D
3.

	A	B	C	D
.01	0	5,000	0	0
.02	8,000	13,000	0	0
.035	15,000	20,000	5,000	0

4.

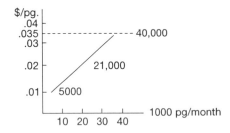

5. Assume the curves are straight lines, then calculate the areas beneath the marginal cost curves. For some of the print shops you must calculate both the area of a triangle and a rectangle depending on where the MC curve hits the vertical axis.

A: triangle with altitude 2.5 cents and base 15,000 copies, plus rectangle length 15,000 copies and width 1 cent.

7,500	15,000	
x.025	x .01	
$187.50	150.00	Total Cost = $337.50

B: triangle with altitude 3 cents and base 20,000 copies, plus rectangle length 20,000 copies and width .5 cent.

10,000	20,000	
x .03	x .005	
300.00	100.00	Total Cost = $400.00

C: triangle with altitude .5 cent and base 5000 copies, plus rectangle length 5,000 copies and width 3 cents.

2,500	5,000	
x.005	x .03	
12.50	$150.00	Total Cost = $162.50

D. zero, since there is no production at 3.5 cents per copy. It should be noted here that in order for the firm to stay open, they are still paying what are known as fixed costs. These were ignored for this question. You'll have more on this in Chapter 8.

6. A price greater than 4 cents per copy will induce copy shop D to begin operations.

7. A and B continue. C drops out at 2 cents.
   Only B will continue operating at 1 cent.

Question 9.
a. Pareto efficiency is achieved at a quantity of 3, where MC = MV.
b. If you graph these functions and calculate the area of consumers' surplus and producer's rents, the total benefits will equal $112.50. If you use the numbers in the columns, consumers' surplus is the difference between a price of $20 and MV for each Q, so CS = 40 + 20 = 60. Rents are the difference between a price of $20 and MC for each Q, so rents = 10 + 5 = 15, for a total of $75.

c. At Q = 4, MC = 25, but MV = 0. The value of the wasted resources is the area of the triangle where MC > MV, which is 1/2(25 - 0) = $12.5.

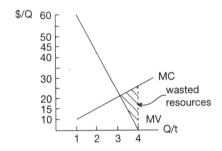

d. Because it is not clear from the numbers at which quantity MV = MC, the equilibrium point must be determined algebraically. The equation of the MV curve is $MV = 130 - Q. The equation of the MC curve is $MC = 90 + .5Q. Equilbrium Q, the point of Pareto eficiency, is at Q = 26.67.

THE BIG PICTURE

Before about 3000 B.C., only limited trade and exchange existed. People were unable to produce a surplus of food that would support extensive specialization and therefore widespread trade. Everyone had to spend their time producing the food, shelter, and protection necessary to sustain family and clan life. Eventually the Sumerians of the Tigris-Euphrates river valley (present day Iraq) where civilization first occurred, developed the mathematical, engineering and organizational knowledge and skills to produce irrigation channels which opened up a broader expanse of land for farming and led to larger communities. As this developed so too did the Sumerian economy with more extensive production and trade among the people and with outside groups. But their ability to engage in trade was still limited by the size of the populations (the extent of the market) supported on the resources of the surrounding river valleys, and the distance between communities. Wherever human civilization has flourished, the mechanism of exchange has been there. Exchange has encouraged people to specialize; only when you can trade the product of your specialized labor for the goods you need to survive can you engage in specialized activities.

Inherent in production are costs. The use of any resource to produce any good implies the opportunity cost of using that resource for something else. Chapter six emphasizes exchange like chapter four, but it introduces production and the transformation of resources into the pure exchange economy based on endowments. The market system of production and exchange leads to an efficient use of resources, as resources are bid away by those producers who will provide the highest valued goods to consumers and who will produce them at the least cost.

Chapter 6 begins an in-depth exploration of production and the theory of supply. This exploration doesn't conclude until Chapter 8. The material you've just gone over in Chapters 4 and, to a lesser degree, 5, also address supply but at the market level, explaining the basic motivations, and the interaction and changes in market supply and demand as various constraints change. Chapters 6 through 8 delve deeper, beyond the market level into the production decisions of individual firms, which altogether make up the market level phenomena explained in Chapters 4 and 5.

REVIEW QUESTIONS

Answers to all review questions appear at the end of this chapter.

PROBLEMS AND EXERCISES
Write your answer in the space(s) provided.

1. The PPF's below for computers and oatbran are drawn for a point in time for an economy.

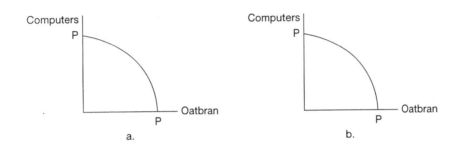

a. Suppose, due to relaxed immigration policies, more workers are supplied. Draw a new curve in (a) marked WW to reflect this change. (This is a qualitative question; quantities or magnitudes do not matter).
b. Assuming that PP is again the initial curve, draw a new curve CC in (b) reflecting a climate change resulting in a longer growing season.

2. Imagine a country with infinite forest land and labor. Two goods, furniture and food, are produced using these inputs only (using no tools, and seed is free and infinite). All workers are identical in their ability to produce furniture or food and land is homogeneous. There is no teamwork or assembly-line production.
a. On the graph below, think about what the production possibilities curve looks like.

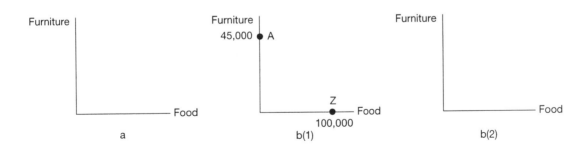

b. 1) Draw a new production possibilities curve that shows that land and labor are not infinite. Possible endpoints are given.

2) Draw a new production possibilities curve that shows that some workers are better food producers and some are better furniture producers.

c. Calculate from the curve in part b.1)

      1) How much furniture is produced if 50,000 kg. of food is produced? _____

      2) If 15,000 units of furniture are produced, how much food is produced? _____

3. Suppose Graciela is indifferent between the following bundles of iced tea and hard boiled eggs:

	Iced Tea (glasses)	Hard Boiled Eggs
A	2	8
B	3	6
C	4	5

Nigel is indifferent between the following bundles of iced tea and hard boiled eggs:

	Iced Tea (glasses)	Hard Boiled Eggs
D	3	9
E	4	5
F	5	2

a. Who places a higher marginal value on iced tea? _____

b. Who places a higher marginal value on eggs? _____

c. Begin them at bundles B and E and describe a mutually beneficial exchange.

4. If the average cost of producing 24 cans of spam is $.34 per can, and the average cost of producing 25 cans is $.33 per can, what is the marginal cost of producing the 24th can? _____

5. Bob and Doug trap for fur in remote Northern Ontario. They survive on fish and berries. If Bob spends his entire day fishing he can catch 2 fish. If he spends his day gathering berries he can gather one pound of berries. Doug can catch a maximum of 3 fish a day, or gather one and a half pounds of berries.

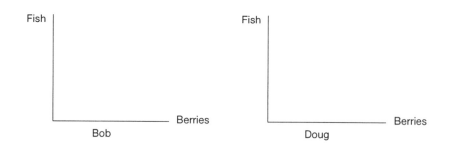

a. Draw their production possibility curves above.
b. Who has the absolute advantage in fishing? _____ In berry gathering? _____
c. Who has the comparative advantage in fishing? _____ In berry gathering? _____
d. Can these two immediately be made better off by trade? _____ Is there a reason for them to specialize?

e. Suppose Bob masters Doug's fishing techniques and increases his daily total to 3 fishes. What would be the mutually beneficial pattern of trade now?

f. Bob consumes 1 fish and two thirds of a pound of berries, and Doug consumes 2 fish and a half pound of berries. Including Bob's new fishing ability, if they trade according to comparative advantage, how much extra (after satisfying their original consumption levels) fish or berries can they produce and share on a full day's work? _____ fish, or _____ berries. Draw Bob and Doug's joint production possibility frontier showing the possible extra output.

TRUE - FALSE QUESTIONS
Provide a one or two sentence explanation with your answer.

1. A point inside a society's production possibilities frontier represents a production combination that is less than the maximum output for the society in question.

2. Specialization only works if exchange is possible.

3. A straight-line (linear) production possibilities curve implies that opportunity costs are zero.

4. Comparing any two points along a PPF there is always one that represents a more optimal level of production.

5. The gains from exchange for producers and consumers are greatest when total revenue or total expenditures is maximized.

6.   There is always a potential net gain when the amount a consumer is willing to pay for an additional unit of a good exceeds the amount at which someone is willing to sell that unit.

7.   A negatively sloped production possibilities curve implies that opportunity costs are positive.

8.   If all inputs were identical, there would be no reason to specialize.

9.   A PPF that is convex to the origin would not exhibit rising marginal costs or diminishing returns at the extensive margin.

10.   Rumor has it that Harrison Ford used to work construction. If Ford still has the competitive advantage in construction in the area, he would be expected to build everything himself.

MULTIPLE CHOICE QUESTIONS
Choose the best answer.

Brazil and Canada can both produce oil and wheat. If Brazil produces only oil, it can produce 1 million barrels a year. If it produces only wheat, it can produce 300 thousand bushels of wheat. Canada can produce two million barrels of oil per year with all its resources, or 700 thousand bushels of wheat if it only produces wheat. Use this information to answer questions one and two.

1. Brazil and Canada's marginal cost of producing one million barrels of oil is respectively:
a.   300,000 bushels of wheat and 700,000 bushels of wheat.
b.   300,000 bushels of wheat and 350,000 bushels of wheat.
c.   100,000 bushels of wheat and 200,000 bushels of wheat.
d.   100,000 bushels of wheat and 150,000 bushels of wheat.

2. Who has the comparative advantage in oil and wheat production?
a.   Brazil has the comparative advantage in both.
b.   Canada has the comparative advantage in both.
c.   Brazil in oil, Canada in wheat.
d.   Canada in oil, Brazil in wheat.

3. Which of the following would most likely cause the production possibilities curve to shift to the right?
a.   employing unemployed labor.
b.   shifting labor from one good to another.
c.   a bubonic plague epidemic.
d.   a shift in social priorities.
e.   none of the above.

4. Which of the following is NOT illustrated by a production possibilities boundary?
a.   Scarcity.
b.   Opportunity cost.

c.   Necessity for choice.
d.   Absolute prices of the goods.

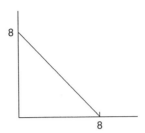

5. The production possibility frontier shown above is most likely for
a.   missiles and milk.
b.   wood and cattle.
c.   peaches and plums.
d.   fish and wine.
e.   none of the above.

Joe and Ernie own coffee shops in the same district. Their respective production capabilities are given below as the maximum possible outputs/hour given resources and technology.

	Joe		Ernie	
Brewing coffee	40	0	10	0
Baking bagels	0	40	0	30

6. From this information we know that:
a.   Joe has an absolute advantage in coffee only.
b.   Joe has an absolute advantage in bagels only.
c.   Ernie has an absolute advantage in coffee and bagels.
d.   Ernie has an absolute advantage in coffee only.
e.   none of the above.

7. We also know that:
a.   Joe has the comparative advantage in coffee and bagel production.
b.   Ernie has the comparative advantage in coffee and bagel production.
c.   Joe has the comparative advantage in coffee production.
d.   Ernie has the comparative advantage in coffee production.
e.   none of the above.

8. Mutually beneficial trade could occur with terms of trade:
a.   Joe buys 1 coffee for 2 bagels.
b.   Joe buys 1 coffee for 1/2 bagel.
c.   Joe buys 1 bagel for 2 coffees.
d.   Joe buys 1 bagel for 1/2 coffee.

e.   none of the above.

9.   According to the law of comparative advantage, a nation or individual, should buy those economic goods for which it
a.   has an absolute advantage.
b.   has a comparative advantage.
c.   is a low opportunity cost producer.
d.   is a high opportunity cost producer.

Use the following information to answer questions 10 and 11. The U.S. and Japan produce two goods, rice and semi-conductors. Their production possibility curves are given below.

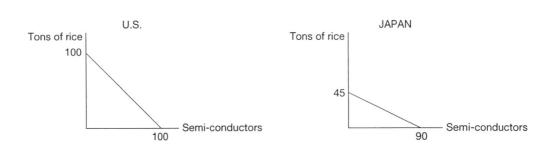

10.   The U.S. and Japan's respective marginal cost of producing rice is:
a.   one semi-conductor and one-half semi-conductor
b.   one semi-conductor and 2 semi-conductors
c.   100 semi-conductors and one-half semi-conductor
d.   100 semi-conductors and 45 semi-conductors

11.   Who has the comparative advantage in rice and semi-conductor production?
a.   The U.S. has the comparative advantage in both.
b.   Japan has the comparative advantage in both.
c.   The U.S. in rice and Japan in semiconductors.
d.   The U.S. in semiconductors and Japan in rice.

12.   As a general rule, technological progress
a.   reduces the slope of the production possibilities frontier, making it shallower.
b.   increases the slope of the production possibilities frontier, making it steeper.
c.   shifts the production possibilities frontier outward, away from the origin.
d.   shifts the production possibilities frontier inward, toward the origin.
e.   makes the production possibilities frontier more bowed out.

13.   When a firm or economy is operating efficiently, it is operating
a.   outside its production possibilities frontier.
b.   inside its production possibilities frontier.
c.   anywhere along its production possibilities frontier.

d.   at the intersection of the production possibilities frontier with the vertical axis.

e.   at the intersection of the production possibilities frontier with the horizontal axis.

14. The more efficiently an economy is producing at a given time, the

a.   farther its production possibilities frontier at that time will be from the origin.

b.   steeper will be its production possibilities frontier.

c.   flatter will be its production possibilities frontier.

d.   thicker will be its production possibilities frontier.

e.   closer the point representing its output will be to the production possibilities frontier.

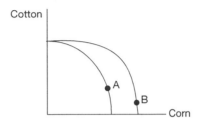

15. In the figure above, the shift of production from A to B can be explained in part by all but which of the following:

a.   an advance in biochemistry that raises corn yields per unit of land and labor inputs.

b.   society's preferences have shifted in favor of cotton.

c.   previously unemployed corn workers were finally put to work.

d.   corn farmers invested heavily in new harvesting equipment.

Two cities, Toronto and Kansas City, have resources to produce two goods, baseball teams and roller derby teams. Using their production possibility curves below, answer questions 16 and 17.

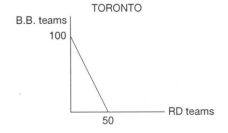 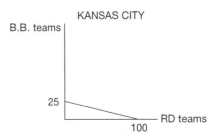

16. Who has the comparative advantage in baseball and derby production?

a.   Toronto has the comparative advantage in both.

b.   Kansas City has the comparative advantage in both.

c.   Toronto and Kansas City have the comparative advantage in baseball and roller derby production respectively.

d.   Kansas City and Toronto have the comparative advantage in baseball and derby production respectively.

17. The range of terms of trade that is beneficial to both cities is:

a.   Toronto buys 1RD for < 2BB, and Kansas City buys 1BB for < 4RD.

b.   Toronto sells 1RD for < 2BB, and Kansas City sells 1BB for < 4RD.

c.   Toronto buys 2RD for < 1BB, and Kansas City buys 4BB for < 1RD.

d.   Toronto sells 1RD for < 4BB, and Kansas City sells 1BB for < 2RD.

SHORT ANSWER QUESTIONS

1. Most developing countries do not have a comparative advantage in the development and application of new technologies. Given that national economies tend to specialize, would economic theory suggest that it is highly likely that underdeveloped countries will always be the low-skilled, low-income sector of the international economy?

2. In professional sports, when rookies are first drafted there is some uncertainty as to how they will fare in the big leagues. Imagine a player who ends up a superstar, playing well above his draft price. Who gains the rent from this player's abilities if the player can't be traded? Who gains the rents once the player is a free agent?

3. Most people would admit that many products available to consumers in North America are not necessary for survival (how many pairs of shoes, tapes/CD's or nose earrings does one person need to own?). Some would argue that we spend most of our money on commercial goods that is of little real value. Isn't economic theory suggesting that in competitive markets the exchange of these goods is <u>efficient</u> and that society is deriving <u>benefits</u> from this trade. But wouldn't it be more efficient, and wouldn't society receive greater benefits, if we devoted these resources to better health care, education (like free university educations), research and development, etc.?

4. One frequently hears phrases these days warning of how the U.S. is losing its competitive advantage in certain industries. Is this a reasonable arguement for protectionism?

ANSWERS TO REVIEW QUESTIONS

Answers to PROBLEMS AND EXERCISES

1.

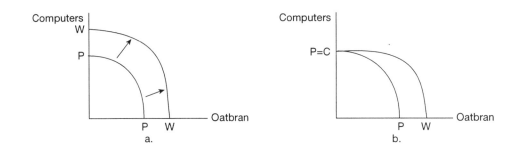

a. There would be an increase in the production posibilities of both computers and oatbran (curve WW).

b. Only the horizontal axis would increase with the longer growing season as computers do not use land as an input (curve CC).

2.

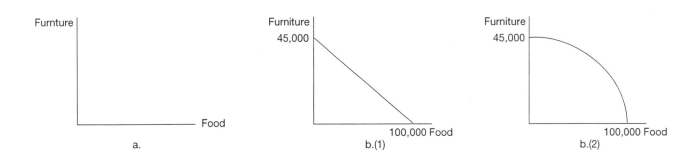

a. With infinite resources there would be no downward sloping curve, because one output does not have to be produced at the expense of the other. The production possibilities could not be bounded and shown on the graph. They are infinite.

b. 1) If resources are not infinite, but not specialized, the PPF will be downward sloping but linear. That is, the cost of trading one output for another (reflected by the slope of the PPF) is constant if inputs have no comparative advantage producing one input over another.

   2) With heterogeneous inputs, the curve will be concave to the origin (bowed out). As the economy tries to produce more and more of one output, resources without a comparative advantage in this output will have to be used, increasing the cost of each additional unit.

c. 1) 22,500
    2) 66,667

3. Calculating MV's of tea and eggs:

Graciela

	Iced Tea (glasses)	MV tea	Hard Boiled Eggs	MV eggs
A	2		8	
B	3	2 eggs	6	½ tea
C	4	1 egg	5	1 tea

Nigel

	Iced Tea (glasses)	MV tea	Hard Boiled Eggs	MV eggs
D	3		9	
E	4	4 eggs	5	¼ tea
F	5	3 eggs	2	⅓ tea

a. Nigel places a higher marginal value on iced tea.
b. Graciela places a higher marginal value on eggs.
c. Nigel could trade Graciela 2.5 eggs for 1 glass of iced tea. Nigel would be willing to pay 3 eggs for his 5th glass, so he is .5 eggs better off, and Graciela would be willing to accept 2 eggs so she is better off.

4. $.09. The change in total cost is $8.16 to $8.25.

5.

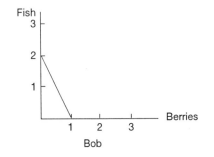 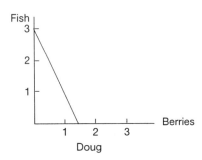

a. Their PPF's are as above.
b. Doug has the absolute advantage in both.
c. There is no comparative advantage in either activity because their opportunity costs are the same.
d. There is no benefit to them trading immediately, but their could be if specializing allows them to expand their production of one of the goods beyond current limits.
e. Output would be greatest if Bob fished and Doug gathered berries.
f. To get their previous total of 3 fish and 7/6 lb. berries (2/3 + 1/2), Bob would specialize in fishing. Since he could catch all 3 fish, that leaves Doug to gather the berries. But Doug can gather the 7/6 lb. of berries and have time left to gather 1/3 of a pound more (for a total of 1 1/2 lbs) or to catch 2/3 fish. The PPF for the Bob and Doug economy would look like:

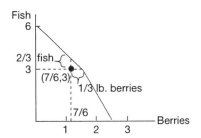

Answers to TRUE - FALSE QUESTIONS

1. True. This indicates that the society is not using all their resources to their potential.

2. True. Without trade, individuals or countries are forced to produce everything they wish to consume.

3. False. A linear PPF implies that opportunity costs are constant, but positive.

4. False. Any point along the PPF is efficient. Where that society chooses to produce depends on aggregate preferences.

5. False. Gains from exchange are greatest when the sum of consumers' and producers' surplus (or rent) are maximized.

6. True. This difference between marginal value and marginal cost is the basis for exchange.

7. True. The negative slope indicates that you cannot obtain more of one output, without giving up some of the other.

8. False. Specialization could still increase output through economies of scale, learning by doing, etc.

9. True. Rather, it would suggest falling marginal costs as the economy moved to producing one or the other output exclusively.

10. False. He may have the competitive or absolute advantage, but his comparative advantage lies in movies. The cost of his time (for construction) is what he could be earning in a film.

Answers to MULTIPLE CHOICE QUESTIONS

1. a	6. e	11. c	16. c
2. d	7. c	12. c	17. a
3. a	8. d	13. c	
4. d	9. d	14. e	
5. c	10. b	15. b	

Answers to SHORT ANSWER QUESTIONS

1. Yes, at least in the short run. In the long run, through investments, the discovery or appearance of new resources (natural resources, extraordinary individuals, etc.), or a change in trading partners' preferences or production possibilities, comparative advantage could change.

2. The team owner will gain the rookie's rents as long as the player is locked into a contract. Once he becomes a free agent, his trading price will reflect his talent and the rookie will gain his rents.

3. No. We presume individual's in society are maximizing their well-being, subject to the constraints they face; otherwise they would behave differently. Economic efficiency is an objective notion based on society's marginal valuations and costs. If we observe an individual buying one more nose ring rather than a similar priced unit of health care, we must presume that they value the nose ring more (per $), and therefore this purchase produces the greatest benefit. Our concern is not with why people value nose rings, or a belief that they should value health care more. Exceptions for determining society's benefit as a whole arise with public goods and externalities (when individuals do not capture the full benefit or pay the full cost of their actions), discussed in Chapter 9.

4. No. Countries don't have competitive advantages or disadvantages, firms do. Further, the gains from trade are based on comparative, not competitive advantage. Even if a company had the competitive (or absolute) advantage in the production of several outputs, it is their opportunity cost of producing outputs that determines comparative advantage and trade patterns. In other words, you still do not produce yourself what you can buy more cheaply (in terms of the resources you have to give up).

CHAPTER 7
THE LAW OF DIMINISHING RETURNS

PRINCIPAL GOALS

1.0 Understand the nature of production as a physical relationship among resources or inputs. (Objectives 1.1, 1.2, 1.3, 1.4)

2.0 Distinguish between diminishing returns at the intensive and extensive margin, and understand the source of rents. (Objectives 2.1, 2.2)

3.0 Understand how firms seek to maximize profits considering the physical possibilities of different input combinations and the cost of each input. (Objectives 3.1, 3.2)

4.0 Understand how different institutional (legal) rules over property rights affect the quantity and use of inputs hired for production (i.e. resource allocation). (Objectives 4.1, 4.2)

OBJECTIVES
Answers to bold-faced questions appear at the end of the dialogue.

"Did you see our midterm grades were finally posted Mo? Two weeks after the torture. Clearly these clever teaching assistants have never taken a psych course and don't understand the value of immediate feedback."

"Does this mean that you should have had your head patted right away?"

"No. My exam was the moral equivalent of a mess on the rug. I should have had my nose rubbed in it. I suppose you got a milkbone."

"Maybe a small treat."

"Well I'm not out of it yet," said Ginny. Unfortunately it seems to me like we went to another level in this chapter."

"Sort of," said Mo. "Actually I felt like chapter six was explaining a lot of the same things as chapter four, but with the costs of production thrown in. And now this chapter is telling us even more about production and costs."

"That's what I mean. We've gone from just looking at the surface changes in economic activity -- you know a change in demand versus a change in quantity demanded -- to being inside the decision to add another unit of capital to increase profits."

"Keep in mind Ginny that all of this, at least chapters 4, 6 and 7, are about supply, not demand. And supply does have several levels, because before you put your product on the market you have to consider both production -- the physical combinations of inputs possible -- and the costs of those different inputs."

"Whereas for demand, you're already dealing with the final product and just looking at consumption choices based on output prices."

"That's right," said Mo, "although both producers and consumers are trying to maximize: consumers their well-being through what they purchase, and producers their profits through what they sell. Part of the difference between the two is simply that the consumer's behavior is governed by the diminishing marginal value they personally experience. The producer may experience rising marginal costs, but its not a personal thing, it's just a production issue."

"I suppose the fact that they come together to exchange, for their mutual benefit, doesn't mean there should be identical explanations for their behavior."

"And remember, most people play both roles depending on whether they're buying or selling," added Mo, "I'm a producer maximizing profit when I'm running the CD exchange, but a consumer when I go to the store for groceries."

"I'll try to keep the big picture in mind," said Ginny, "right after we deal with the multitudinous new words in this chapter."

OBJECTIVE 1.1 Recognize definitions for the important new vocabulary.

Question 1. Match the term with its definition(s). Write out definitions for any undefined terms.

a. factors of production/inputs	b. outputs
c. variable inputs	d. fixed inputs
e. durable goods	f. capital
g. production function	h. factor demand
i. wage/rental rate of factor inputs	

_____ goods that last for more than one production period, such as tractors, refrigerators, robotic production machines, etc.

_____ a mathematical expression of the relationship between the type and quantity of inputs and the amount of output that they can produce.

_____ the product of the production process.

_____ the cost to the producer of hiring factor inputs.

_____ inputs whose quantity cannot be changed in the short-run, only in the long-run.

_____ the value marginal product function relating input wages to the quantity of inputs demanded.

_____ those things that are combined in a production process to create goods for consumption.

_____ land, labor or capital (machinery).

_____ inputs whose quantity can be changed in the short-run.

_____ goods which are produced specifically to be inputs in the production of other goods.

OBJECTIVE 1.2 Describe the physical relationship within production expressed as a production function.

"So underlying cost is the physical combination of inputs to produce the output," said Mo. "That's what the production function is describing."

"I wanted to ask you about that. When we have these equations -- these functions -- that are supposed to represent something real, like production, are they always in the form $Y = f(L,K)$?"

"That's their general form. Basically they're mathematical symbols describing a relationship between, or among, dependent and independent variables. This one says that the amount of output, Y, is a function of the amount of labor, L, and capital, K, that are used in the production process."

"That's what Silberberg wrote", Ginny said, "but the f means function of, or is dependent on?"

"Yes, but you could use any letter to symbolize the same thing. Y, the level of output, is the dependent variable -- meaning that output levels are dependent on all the variables listed in the parentheses. And in these equations the variable on the left-hand side of the equal sign is always the dependent variable."

"Well I'll be. A regular convention of mathematics right here in front of me. That would have passed me by without my noticing."

"Oh but there's more Ginny. The variables on the right-hand side of the equal sign would then be the...?"

"Independent variables?"

"That's right. Don Pardo tell her what she's won."

"No no, not the home version of this game, I'll take the years supply of Kit Kats. Seriously, that makes sense to me because production is dependent on putting a farmer, L, on a tractor, K, to till, plant seed, cultivate and harvest a crop of wheat, Y."

"In some cases, we'll know the relationship more specifically, like $Y = 1K + 1L$, which would say to harvest one field of wheat, Y, you always use one tractor and one driver. But to keep things general, the form $Y = f(K, L)$ is often used."

"One thing though", Ginny said. "How do materials like seed and fertilizer fit into this production function. Are they capital like a tractor?"

"I think so. Seeds and fertilizer are goods produced to be inputs into the production of other goods, namely wheat or corn or whatever you want to grow."

Question 2. Create functions for the following dependent variables. Include only the most important factors as independent variables.

| dependent | independent | function |

a. weight gain
b. a good pizza
c. a good relationship
d. good music

OBJECTIVE 1.3 Recognize definitions for the important new vocabulary.

Question 3. Match the term with its definition(s). Write out definitions for any undefined terms.

a. marginal product   b. total product
c. average product   d. value marginal product
e. diminishing marginal product (the law of)
f. intensive margin (diminishing returns at the)
g. returns to scale

_____ price x marginal product.

_____ The additional output produced by an input, multiplied by the price at which that extra output is sold.

_____ the case where a diminishing marginal product occurs as a result of more *intensive* use of an existing factor of production (i.e., applying greater amounts of one or more inputs to a fixed amount of another factor input already in use).

_____ the change in output due to adding another unit of land, labor or capital to a production process.

_____ After some point, as units of a variable input are continuously added to other fixed factor inputs in production, the marginal product of the variable input will become smaller.

_____ total product divided by the number or amount of the specified input used to produce that total.

_____ the sum of the marginal products.

OBJECTIVE 1.4 Describe the relationship among marginal product, total product and average product.

"All of these marginal, average and total products are just like marginal, average and total value, or costs, or any other of the other marginal, average and total things we've been studying", Mo said. "These are just measures of output. It's pretty straight forward."

"It is but it's important to remember that when you measure the marginal product of some input by the change in output, everything is held constant except the addition of one more unit of that input. So remember to hold things constant with marginal product."

"Okay," Mo said. "And like marginal and total value and cost, if you add up all of the marginal products you get total product. But I wanted to show you -- which maybe you knew already but -- if marginal product is positive then total product has increased. If it's negative then total product has decreased."

"Let me think about this for a second. If marginal product is positive, like plus 10, then total product is increasing. Of course, by 10; as long as you're adding positive numbers to total product it will increase. Even when marginal product is falling, as long as it is positive total product must be increasing."

"Right, and when marginal product is greater than average product, average product must be increasing, or, of course, if it is less than average product, then average product is being pulled down. Here, let's look at Silberberg's table 7-1 on page 225.

Table 7-1

(1) Number of laborers	(2) Total Product	(3) Marginal Product	(4) Average Product
1	3	3	3.00
2	8	5	4.00
3	15	7	5.00
4	21	6	5.25
5	26	5	5.20
6	30	4	5.00
7	33	3	4.71
8	35	2	4.38
9	36	1	4.00
10	36	0	3.60
11	35	-1	3.18

With only one laborer marginal product is three, and of course the same as total and average product," continued Mo. "The second worker increases output by five. Five is greater than the average product of three, so average product increases. Keep going."

"Okay, the third worker increases output by seven which is greater than the average product of four, so according to your rule the average product must increase and it does to five. Let's look ahead here. The fifth worker has a marginal product of five, which is *less* than the average product of 5.25, so average product should decrease -- AND IT DOES -- incredible."

"Yeah, yeah. You'll thank me later Ginny. In a table it's pretty easy to see which numbers are greater than which, but look at this graph."

"I see what you mean," Ginny said. "Marginal product and average product are rising and falling, but their relationship isn't completely obvious from the graph."

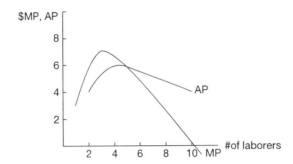

"The key is that you have to look at the quantity axis first then read up to the curves and over to the y-axis (vertical axis) where the product numbers are. So at two laborers, for example, it's clear that the marginal product curve is higher up the y-axis than the average product curve."

"Yes, and it's also clear that the average product is still increasing or rising at that quantity."

"Right, but when we go to five laborers marginal product is just below the average product, (5 versus 5.20), which is where the average product begins to fall."

OBJECTIVE 2.1 Determine how continuously adding a variable input to a productive process when one input is fixed, eventually yields a diminishing marginal product and diminishing marginal returns at the intensive margin.

"You can also see the point after three laborers where marginal product begins to fall," Ginny said. "The total product curve still goes up, but its not climbing as steeply as before. And look at how the marginal product curve begins falling then too."

"I dare say that's your diminishing marginal product in graphical form," Mo said.

"And this is all based on the fact that at least one input is being held fixed while we add others?"

"Yes. I think that's the key to this whole idea of the *intensive margin*. Everything has a limit on how much it can produce or how fast it can work. For a while you may get an increasing amount of output as additional workers let you specialize, but eventually if you've only got the one factory or the one acre of farmland or a fixed amount of machinery, they're going to start getting in each other's way. And if you just keep hiring workers, things might get so crowded that output actually begins to fall."

"But no one would hire workers until total product started to fall would they?"

"No, but workers are still hired after marginal product has begun falling. Even if the MP of the eighth worker falls to 2, like in Table 7-1, if their wage is less than what you can sell the two outputs for, it still makes sense to hire them."

"Farming is a really good example then," Ginny said, "because if you've only got a thousand acres, then you've only got a thousand acres. If farmers want to increase output, then they usually have to farm the same piece of land more intensively by adding more labor, more fetilizer, or more machinery. But the land can only absorb so much fertilizer, or hold so many laborers or machines."

Question 4. a. Determine your own marginal, total and average comprehension (number of pages comprehended) of Silberberg's textbook as you add additional hours of effort to your fixed brain capacity. Assume your first hour is when you are freshest. Fill in the table below. At what point does your marginal comprehension begin to diminish? _____ When does it reach zero? _____ Is it ever negative? After how many hours would you stop studying? _____

Hours	Marginal Comprehension	Total Comprehension	Average Comprehension
1			
2			
3			
4			
5			
6			
7			
8			
9			
10			

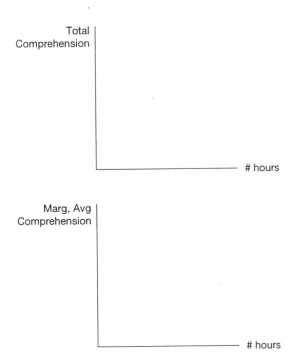

b. In the space above, graph your marginal (MCmp), and average comprehension (ACmp) curves on one graph, and your total comprehension (TCmp) curves on another graph above it (lining up the horizontal axes with hours of study). Indicate on <u>both</u> graphs where the marginal product (comprehension) curve is negative, and where this curve indicates diminishing marginal comprehension.

* * * * * * *

"Farming more intensively?" Mo said. "That's what returns *'on the intensive margin'* actually means isn't it? I've been trying to figure out the difference between the intensive and the extensive margin."

OBJECTIVE 2.2 **Compare diminishing marginal returns at the extensive and intensive margins.**

"On the intensive margin, you use inputs that are of equal efficiency, but they are applied to a fixed amount of other inputs already in production, and they end up leading to a diminishing marginal product. On the extensive margin you bring resources or inputs to bear that are less efficient so you end up with a diminishing marginal product. So on the extensive margin are the new inputs fixed in quantity or quality?"

"Not necessarily," said Ginny. "Say we're talking about a two-hundred acre farm, but the farmer only works 100 acres. On the extensive margin, if the second hundred acres is farmed the additional output from the second hundred acres will be less than the first for the same amount of labor and machinery."

"But your example assumes that the quality of the second hundred acre plot is lower."

"That's the whole idea. If the quality was higher Mo, it would have been used first."

"Okay. So the surest way to observe diminishing returns on the extensive margin is to apply the same labor and machinery to the old and new land -- then you would just get the effect of the land productivity on output."

"Yes. Input quality and variability are the difference between the extensive and intensive margins. On the intensive at least one variable is fixed and the others are assumed to be of equal quality; on the extensive margin there are no fixed inputs and they are assumed to be of varying quality. It's really a matter of timing," said Ginny.

"Timing?"

"Sure, think about the linen industry and some woman who runs a clothing factory. Suppose demand is rising and increasing the price for linen. What can this woman do? In the short-run all she can do is maybe add more labor to her current factory (which for simplicity economists assume are of equal quality to the other labor). She can run the place 24-hours a day, but at some point hiring more people will result in a diminishing marginal product -- diminishing returns at the intensive margin. Over the long-run, however, she could expand into another, perhaps lower quality workspace. In addition, other less productive factories that are only profitable at the new, higher price may open up. This is dimishing returns at the extensive margin."

"I see."

"Now, how about letting me ask you a question?" Ginny asked. "What is the source of rents?"

"I had to re-read this section to figure out that it's related to productivity for both the extensive and intensive margins," Mo said. "This is a different spin from Silberberg's and David Ricardo's explanation on page 228, but what they're saying is that rents are the difference between the price of the good and the marginal cost of producing the good. The bigger the gap between the price and the marginal cost, the bigger the rent right?"

"Right."

"Well the size of the gap then is determined by where the market sets the price and how much your costs are. At any price there are going to be several firms producing whose costs are determined by how productive their inputs are. So, for example, on the extensive margin if you've got one coal mine where the marginal cost of producing a ton of coal is $5.00 and at a second mine the marginal cost is $10.00, then we know that the rents are bigger at the first mine than at the second. The source of the rents is the higher productivity, and therefore the lower costs at the first mine."

"Does it matter what the price is?"

"Only that whatever the price of a ton of coal is in this example, it's high enough to get the coal producer to use both mines. And the gap between the price and the marginal cost of a ton of coal at the better mine must be bigger than the gap at the less efficient mine by at least $5.00 a ton, because that's the gap between the marginal costs at the two different mines."

"So the source of the rents is actually the gap between price and marginal cost."

"No, not exactly," Mo said. "The gap measures what rents are. The source of the size of the gap is how relatively productive your inputs are, which is what Silberberg and Ricardo are saying."

"I can see that. What about the intensive margin?"

"Well it's the same principle, but you just have to think a little differently. As an example, suppose that we're adding workers at the same wage."

"That's actually true in many cases."

"Okay, so again it's the marginal cost of producing the good versus the price of the good," said Mo. If you pay each worker $50 a day and the marginal product of the second worker is higher than the first, then your marginal cost for the additional output falls. If you add a third worker, but this worker yields a smaller marginal product, then your marginal cost rises."

"Meaning you're paying more for each additional unit of output. But what's the source of the difference in the rents?"

"The source of the rents is again the difference in productivity between the inputs added. But now its not because the quality of your inputs varies, but rather because each variable input's productivity is affected by some other input being fixed."

OBJECTIVE 3.1 **Demonstrate and express in an equation how a firm with one variable input, to maximize profit, will hire that input (factor of production) to the point where the value of its marginal product equals its cost.**

"Along the same lines," Ginny said, "I'd like to go over how firms know how many workers to hire and machines to buy to get them to the right level of output in the first place?"

"That's explained by the equation on page 231."

"You mean $p \ x \ MP = w$? It seems to me that it should have a 'greater than or equal to' sign instead of just an equal sign to show that you hire inputs up to that point but not beyond it."

"I suppose it could, but if output could be divided into infinitesimally small portions rent would be exhausted by hiring workers until the value of the last product just equalled the wage."

"What kind of questions do you think they might ask on this?"

"I just happened to look one up", Mo said.

> **Problem:** Which of the following candy-makers would hire an additional worker to produce Ever-lasting Gobstoppers if the worker's marginal product was as given and the price of a Gobstopper was $.35?

	A	B	C	D
Marginal Product (per hour)	18	20	16	18
Wage (per hour)	$6.50	$7.00	$5.50	$7.00

"Okay so for A we calculate p x MP = w; which is $.35 x 18 = $6.40."

"No it's not", Mo said. "$.35 x 18 is only $6.30."

"Details. What's important is that it's less than $6.50. Therefore in the interest of profit maximization this worker gets the boot."

"For B, $.35 x 20 is $7.00. Seven dollars equals seven dollars, so this worker gets hired."

"Even if they just break even like that?", Ginny asked.

"Sure, because with that worker the company just reaches the point where they have gotten all possible rents. Almost like the last Gobstopper the factory produces with this new worker *just* exhausts benefits."

"So there are rents being earned on the marginal product of this last worker up to the very end."

"What about C and D Ginny?"

"$.35 x $.16 is $5.60, greater than the $5.50 wage, so this worker is employed. For D, $.35 x 18 is $6.40..."

"$6.30"

"Just trying to annoy you. $6.30, which is less than the $7.00 wage so this worker gets the pink slip."

Question 5. Determine the optimal number of sled-dogs Django Biedermaier would harness for a journey to the North Pole given the data in the following table. (Hint: Find the "wage" of the dogs). Django would harness _____ dogs.

North Pole Expedition				
(1)	(2)	(3)	(4)	(5)
Number of Dogs	Value of Marginal Miles	Value of Total Miles	Value of Average Miles	Total Dog Costs
4	$0	$0	$0	$200
5	170.00	170.00	34.00	250
6	51.00	221.00	36.83	300
7	51.00	272.00	38.85	350
8	68.00	340.00	42.50	400
9	68.00	408.00	45.33	450
10	85.00	493.00	49.30	500
11	51.00	544.00	49.45	550
12	34.00	578.00	48.16	600
13	17.00	595.00	45.77	650

* * * * * * *

"Could we just keep going and do the 'more than one variable factor' situation too?" Mo asked.

"That's alright with me, I didn't quite get the part where he said 'By division, these two relations imply $pMP_l/w_l = pMP_k/w_k$'."

OBJECTIVE 3.2 Demonstrate and express in an equation how a firm with more than one

variable input, to maximize profit, will hire inputs (factors of production) to the point where the MP per wage ratio of all factor inputs are equal.

"All he's done is divided the top equation by the bottom equation and cross multiplied the w_l and pMP_k," explained Mo.

"A clever little manipulation. Is it legal?"

"Sure, because I could always rewrite the two equations with p alone on the left hand side of each, $p = w_l/MP_l$, and $p = w_k/MP_k$. Then I can set them equal to one another because p obviously equals p. That is, the price of my output is the same regardless of which input contributed marginally to producing it."

"Okay so then you'd have $w_l/MP_l = w_k/MP_k$. What do you do next."

"That's it," Mo said. "Oh. Then I can invert these to get them to look like the ones in the book and multiply both sides by p if I want the p back. An equality doesn't change as long as I do the same thing to both sides. But don't you think what it means is even more important than the mathematical manipulations -- Hmmm?"

"What it means is relatively easy I think, compared to why it works that way. What it means is getting the most bang for your buck. So if the contribution in output per dollar cost of each input isn't equal, you can do better by hiring more or less of one of the inputs. In economics lingo, to minimize costs 'the ratio of the marginal product of each factor to its wage must be the same for all factors.'"

Question 6. Chin and Jiggles want you to advise them on whether to buy another ice cream machine, or hire another worker for their dessert shop. A machine costs $6,000 to rent for the year, and a worker costs $12,000. The respective marginal productivities are $MP_l = 3$, and $MP_k = 1$. They are currently operating with 8 units of labor and 2 units of capital. What would you advise?

OBJECTIVE 4.1 Recognize definitions for the important new vocabulary.

Question 7. Match the term with its definition(s). Write out definitions for any undefined terms.

a. private property
c. socialist cooperative
e. residual claimant

b. common property (open access)
d. over use (of resources)

_____ the organized group can exclude others in the larger society from using and deriving income from the property.

_____ a condition that implies the total output of society would be higher, resulting in further gains from trade, if utilization of the property was reduced.

_____ a system where the rights to use, and derive income from property do not legally or socially reside with any individual or firm, but with all members of the social group.

_____ the person who claims or is responsible for any residual (excess) profits or costs associated with producing a good.

_____ a system where the rights to use and derive income from, (but not necessarily individually sell) property reside with a collective of individuals.

_____ noone has the right to exclude another from using the property.

_____ a system where the rights to exclusive use, to derive income from, and to transfer property may according to law and social practice be held by a private individual or firm.

OBJECTIVE 4.2 Recreate the resource allocation decision under common property, private property, and social cooperative property rights systems.

"How about this property rights and the allocation of resources section?" Ginny asked. "I thought it was really interesting."

"Me too. How different types of ownership result in different levels of production and employment of resources. I'd never really thought about that. It's pretty straightforward don't you think?"

"Not too bad. But I wanted to make sure that when he's talking about which system is economically efficient he's not talking about which is the best or most equitable system -- like how the Navajo should organize themselves. He's talking about our definition of economic efficiency, the exhaustion of mutual benefits."

"Absolutely," Mo said. "It's just a question of maximizing the value of the resources. The three systems each lead to different number of workers and output, but only one level, and hence one property rights system, attains economic efficiency. But you'll note that this depends on assuming that the costs of instituting, running, and enforcing the different systems are the same."

"Which is obviously not the case," Ginny said. "With open access, or common property, you don't have to spend any money enforcing your right, because there are no rights."

"So to get a maximum *net* value of the resources you have to factor in the costs, but it's still true that private rights will maximize the *gross* value of the resources."

"Alright then, the only other thing for me is to work through a problem or two to make sure I understand the effects of the three property rights systems and can identify the levels of production and number of workers hired under each of them."

"Okay," Mo said. "But first I want to show you my chart to remember people's incentives under the different property rights systems."

Private Property	VMP = W
Socialist Cooperative	Max VAP
Common Property (open access)	VAP = W

"That's useful Mo. So the first one is the incentive under a private property system to..."

"To hire inputs until the value of the marginal product (VMP) equals the wage of the input. This occurs because the owner gets to claim the profit, but also has to bear the full costs. So he's not going to waste resources by paying wages to someone or something that doesn't deliver at least an equal amount in return."

"Right, and under the socialist cooperative you've got the incentive to maximize the value of the average product -- VAP?"

"Yes, because they have the ability to control the number of workers or other inputs hired, so their incentive is to do what's best for themselves, which is maximize their *share* of the output. So they want the biggest average product possible."

"And then finally under the common property open access system the incentive is for everyone to use the resource until they can earn more doing something else. Which means until the value of their average product equals their wage."

Question 8. As sheepherders are added to a given section of land, the daily value of total output (VTP) and marginal product (VMP) and average product (VAP) are as indicated below.

No. of Herders	$ VTP	$ VMP	$ VAP
1	7.00	7.00	7.00
2	13.00	6.00	6.50
3	18.00	5.00	6.00
4	22.00	4.00	5.50
5	25.00	3.00	5.00
6	27.00	2.00	4.50
7	28.00	1.00	4.00
8	28.00	0.00	3.50

Suppose the herders can earn $4.00/day in non-agricultural jobs in a village nearby. Fill out below how many sheepherders will work the land if it is privately owned, common property, or a socialist cooperative. Calculate and compare the differences in rent and the loss in net social benefits in each case.

	Private	Common	Co-op
No. of herders			
Rent			
Net social loss			

ANSWERS TO DIALOGUE QUESTIONS

Question 1. Vocabulary: e, g, b, i, d, h, a, a, c, f.

Question 2.

Dependent	Independent	Function
a. Weight Gain	Caloric Intake, Exercise, Genetics, Age	$WG = f(CI, E, G, A)$
b. Good Pizza	Thickness & dryness of crust, quantity & spices of sauce, quantity & quality of cheese, quality & number of other ingredients.	$GP = f(T_c, D_c, Q_s, S_s, Q_c, Ql_c, Ql_i, N_i)$
c. Good Relationship	Love, Consideration, Physical Attraction, Communication	$GR = f(L, Cn, PA, Cm)$
d. Good Music	Emotion, Intuition, Inspiration, Melody, Beat, Rythum, Practice	$GM = f(E, I, Isp, M, B, R, P)$

Question 3. Vocabulary: d, d, f or e, a, e or f, c, b.

<u>Returns to Scale</u> is missing: a measure of whether a change in factor inputs of a certain proportion result in an equal, greater or lesser proportional change in output. Returns to scale can be increasing, decreasing or constant.

Question 4.

Hours	Marginal Comprehension	Total Comprehension	Average Comprehension
1	20	20	20.0
2	15	35	17.5
3	10	45	15.0
4	5	50	12.5
5	3	53	10.6
6	2	55	9.2
7	1	56	8.0
8	0	56	7.0
9	0	56	6.2
10	0	56	5.6

a. In my case marginal comprehension immediately begins to diminish, decreasing by 5 pages when a second hour of study is added. My marginal comprehension reaches 0 at 8 hours. It never becomes negative, because I cannot read negative pages per hour.

b. Placing the graphs one above the other allows you to line up the quantity of hours, then see at what quantities things happen on the MCmp, ACmp and TCmp curves.

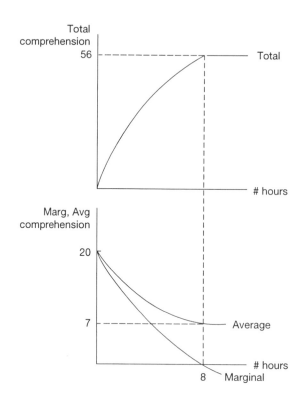

Question 5. Django will run 11 dogs, because at 11 dogs the value of marginal miles is greater than or equal to the "wage" or marginal cost of dogs, found by calculating the change in total dog costs.

Question 6. The $MP_l/w_l = MP_k/w_k$ is equal to:

$$\frac{3}{12,000} > \frac{1}{6,000}$$

$$.00025 > .00016$$

Since the marginal product of labor per dollar cost is greater than of capital, you should add more labor.

Question 7. Vocabulary: c, d, b, e, c, b, a.

Question 8.

	Private	Common	Socialist Coop.
No. of Herders	4 herders	7 herders	1 herder
Rent	$6.00	$0	$3.00
Net Loss	$0	$6.00	$3.00

Common property loss: the difference between the value of marginal product and the opportunity cost of $4 for the 5th, 6th, & 7th workers. This $1 + 2 + 3 is lost to society when these workers are added. Socialist coop. loss: the $2 + 1 difference between the value of marginal product and the opportunity cost of $4 for the 2nd and 3rd workers that is not earned because the number of herders is only 1.

THE BIG PICTURE

Suppose you get this great idea for a product. Maybe some kind of cloth thing that you can play with in a group or individually -- sort of a combination frisbee/hackey sack. You want to make a million of these toys and sell them all and get rich. But first you must produce it.

To do this you must determine the necessary inputs, and the possible combinations of those inputs that produce various output levels (there is more than one way to skin a cat). The combination you choose will depend on the relative wages of these inputs. To hire these inputs, beginning with labor, you must enter the market to bid away workers from other firms. To get these workers your firm must pay them a wage that at once outbids other firms and at least covers the workers' opportunity costs for their time spent working at your firm. You must also enter into markets for capital, including possibly a bank loan for start-up money. In your case, maybe you just need some material, sewing machines, a room somewhere, and some other small supplies. All of these inputs you are hiring will be combined to create this product.

Not surprisingly, all of these inputs have a cost. Physical production of goods always implies costs, which we can manipulate or consider in terms of the cost per cloth toy produced (average cost) or the cost of producing one more cloth toy (marginal cost). When you sell this product to the consumer, the price must be at least equal to the marginal cost of producing the little cloth wonders, or you will be paying more out in wages than you are receiving as revenue. If this toy is truly unique you can probably get away with setting the price reasonably high (in fact you'd have a monopoly, but more on this in chapter 11). If lots of other firms had the same great idea, your production levels won't even affect prices. The price will be determined through the market where buyers and sellers meet to exchange the toy as described in chapters four and five.

This chapter describes, theoretically, to what level and in what proportions your firm should hire labor and capital from the various input markets in order to maximize your profits, or rents, given the market price you face. This decision is made in conformance with the principles of diminishing returns at the extensive and intensive margins. Given the firm's set of capital-labor combinations to choose from, the relative cost of these (and other inputs) is the crucial factor in making a profit-maximizing decision.

REVIEW QUESTIONS

Answers to all review questions appear at the end of this chapter.

PROBLEMS AND EXERCISES
Write your answer in the space(s) provided.

1. Determine the optimal quantity of factor input Y this producer should employ given the information in the graph below.

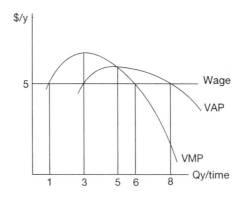

2. The following table gives the total units of output produced by different numbers of workers.

No. of Workers:	1	2	3	4	5	6	7	8
Output/day :	3	11	21	30	36	41	43	44

Assume only labor is required to produce this product. If labor costs $11 per unit, how many units of labor per day will a profit maximizing firm purchase if output sells for a price of $6.00?

3. Consider a lake where the number of fish caught varies with the number of people fishing as follows:

#fisherpeople:	1	2	3	4	5	6	7	8	9	10
Total fish (TP) caught per day:	13	25	36	46	55	63	70	76	81	85

Assume that all fish caught can be sold for $10 each; all fisherpersons can earn $100 per day in their next best alternative; and that there is no depletion of the stock of fish in the lake for any level of fishing.
a. Calculate the MP and AP schedules for fisherpeople.
b. How many people will be fishing if the lake is:
    1) a cooperative able to restrict entry?
    2) common property with no entry restrictions?
    3) private property?
c. Explain why MP, not AP, measures society's gain when someone decides to go fishing in this lake.

4. Draw quick sketch graphs of marginal, average or total product curves depicting the following situations (don't forget to label the axes):

   a. Total product when marginal product is negative.

   b. Average product when marginal product is constant.

   c. Marginal product when total product is constant.

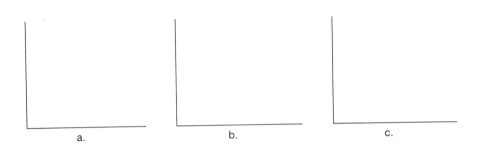

a.   b.   c.

5. Consider the following table of data collected by engineers of a major company. It represents the relationship between inputs and outputs.

CAPITAL

		0	1	2	3	4	5	6
	0	0	0	0	0	0	0	0
L	1	0	1.0	1.41	1.73	2.0	2.24	2.45
A	2	0	1.41	2.00	2.45	2.83	3.16	3.46
B	3	0	1.73	2.45	3.00	3.46	3.87	4.24
O	4	0	2.0	2.82	3.46	4.0	4.47	4.89
R	5	0	2.24	3.16	3.87	4.47	5.00	5.48
	6	0	2.45	3.46	4.24	4.89	5.48	6.00

a. Does this production function exhibit increasing, decreasing, or constant returns to scale (i.e. if you double your inputs do you get more, less, or a constant rate of return)?

b. Does this production function exhibit rising, constant, or decreasing marginal product of labor?

6. Production with one variable input.

a. From the table below, find the AP and MP of labor. Note that the numbers in this table refer to physical quantities rather than monetary values.

Land		1	1	1	1	1	1	1	1	1
Labor	0	1	2	3	4	5	6	7	8	
TP		0	2	5	9	12	14	15	15	14

b. Plot the TP of labor on one graph and the AP and MP of labor on another graph directly below it (these graphs should have quantity of labor on the horizontal axis).

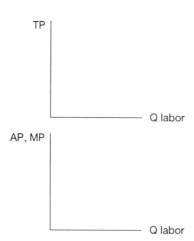

c. What is the relationship between
  1) MP and the maximum point of AP of labor?
  2) MP and the maximum point of TP of labor?

d. In terms of "labor" and "land", what does the law of diminishing returns state?

e. Determine where the law of diminishing returns starts operating.

TRUE - FALSE QUESTIONS
Provide a one or two sentence explanation with your answer.

1.   If total product is decreasing, marginal product must be negative.

2.   The production function relates the cost of producing output to the cost of inputs.

3.   The marginal product of a factor of production is independent of the attributes possessed by that

factor, it is only dependent on the quantity of other inputs used with that factor.

4.   If total product is rising (increasing), marginal product must be rising (increasing).

5.   The rents to a firm increase any time an input whose marginal value product exceeds its wage is added to production.

6.   If average product is falling, marginal product must be below average product.

7.   Diminishing marginal returns is only a short run phenomenon.

8.   A system of private property rights always maximizes the gross value of resources.

9.   A system of property rights that induces workers to direct their energies into labor that is valued less by consumers than other available work would be an economically efficient system.

10.   If AP is rising, then MP must also be rising.

11.   If AP is falling, then MP must be less than AP.

12.   If the TP of labor is increasing at a decreasing rate, both the AP and MP of labor are positive and decreasing.

13.   The marginal product of a factor of production is always defined in terms of changes in that factor when the amount of other factors is fixed.

MULTIPLE CHOICE QUESTIONS
Choose the best answer.

1. A negative marginal product
a.   is associated with negative average product.
b.   may be consistent with rising or falling total product.
c.   is consistent with a falling total product.
d.   indicates that total product is increasing at a decreasing rate.
e.   all of the above.

2. When the value of a firm's marginal product of capital is less than the cost of hiring additional units

of capital the firm will,
a.   hire additional capital.
b.   hire additional labor.
c.   hire neither.
d.   stop hiring additional capital.

Below is a schedule relating the marginal product of labor (measured in units of output per day) to the number of units of labor hired each day. Use this data for questions 3 through 7.

L	1	2	3	4	5	6	7
MPL	100	80	60	40	20	10	-10

3. How many units of labor must be hired each day before the total daily output is 280?
a. 4   b. 3   c. 7   d. 5

4. The maximum total daily output if labor is hired one unit at a time is:
a. 240   b. 100   c. 300   d. 310

5. Would a firm ever hire a seventh unit of labor?
a. yes   b. no   c. yes, if the wage was low enough.

6.   What would the wage have to be to hire six and one-half units of labor? (Assume the marginal product schedule is linear).
a. $100   b. $ 0   c. $ 10   d. labor would have to pay you.

7. What is the average product of 5 units of labor?
a. 300 units   b. 60   c. 20   d. 5

8. If a firm were able to calculate that their $pMP_l/w_l = pMP_k/w_k$ was 3:2 (3 for labor, 2 for capital), the firm would,
a. increase labor.   b. increase capital.   c. decrease labor.   d. increase both.

9. When marginal product exceeds average product, AP is
a. increasing.   b. decreasing.   c. constant.   d. increasing or decreasing.

10. With no ownership of a particular resource, the incentive for people is to:
a.   use the resource only to the degree that some few users, who were the initial users, get the maximum benefit per person.
b.   preserve the resource for future generations.
c.   use the resource until their benefit from it falls below some other use of their time.
d.   destroy the resource.

11. Wages are
a.   The price of hiring factors of production.
b.   the opportunity cost to society of employing factors of production in any particular use.
c.   a form of income to a worker.
d.   all of the above.

Use the following information to answer questions 12 through 14.

The U.S. Food and Drug Administration has recently classified a drug which could possibly cure AIDS as an "orphan" drug. An orphan drug is any drug which is developed for an illness or condition affecting less than 200,000 people.

In order to encourage research and development for drugs with small potential markets, the FDA grants manufacturers exclusive selling rights and provides simpler regulatory review, thus "orphan" status provides a certain level of incentive to the drug manufacturers.

12. FDA measures supporting the manufacture of "orphan" drugs,
a.   cause drug manufacturers to reduce production to the socially efficient level.
b.   cause drug manufacturers to increase production to the socially efficient level.
c.   cause drug manufacturers to produce too few drugs from a socially efficient viewpoint.
d.   cause drug manufacturers to produce too many drugs from a socially efficient viewpoint.

13. At the quantity of drugs which would be produced in the absence of the "Orphan Drug Act", which are true?
a.   Social marginal benefits are greater than private marginal costs.
b.   Private marginal benefits are equal to private marginal costs.
c.   Private marginal benefits are greater than social marginal benefits.
d.   a and b are true.

14. Given your answers to the previous two questions, how should the government, hence society, allocate its public moneys for drug research and development?
a.   Provide equal amounts to a selected number of drug research and development efforts.
b.   Provide as much money as neccessary for those efforts that they know will result in life-saving drugs.
c.   Provide money in such a way that the resultant benefits per dollar spent are equal among all the funded research efforts.
d.   Provide money according to the recommendations of the private drug manufacturers.

15. If a firm's MP of labor is 22 units per hour, the price of the good is $.60 and the wage of labor is $10 per hour,
a.   the firm would hire additional labor.
b.   the firm is not maximizing profit.
c.   the firm has not yet experienced diminishing marginal product.
d.   all of the above.
e.   a and b only.

16. Assuming a firm has employed factors of production to the point where $MP_l/w_l = MP_k/w_k$, and is maximizing profit, if the wage of labor decreases the firm will:
a.   let go labor.
b.   do nothing because they are at the profit maximizing levels of factors of production.
c.   hire more capital.
d.   hire more labor.

17. At the point in time when adding an additional worker results in marginal output valued less by

society than the wage of the worker, we know that
a.   Society's marginal benefits exceed their marginal costs.
b.   society often values things that aren't really worthwhile.
c.   the worker could lower their wage to achieve a more highly valued result.
d.   the worker could produce a more highly valued output by working somewhere else.

Use the following table and information to answer questions 18 through 20. As workers are added at a farm, the daily total output (TP) is as below:

No. of Workers:	1	2	3	4	5	6	7	8	9	10
Total Output :	2	6	18	28	34	39	42	44	45	43

Assume workers can earn $5 in their alternative employment.

18. How many workers will work on this farm if the land is common property?
    a. 1   b. 4   c. 6   d. 9

19. How many workers will work on this farm if it is privately owned?
    a. 1   b. 4   c. 6   d. 9

20. How many workers will work on this farm if it is a coop with entry restrictions?
    a. 1   b. 4   c. 6   d. 9

SHORT ANSWER QUESTIONS

1. Explain why marginal output eventually diminishes when inputs of the same quality are added to some fixed resource within a firm.

2. Explain why the following is a misinterpretation of diminishing returns: "Too many cooks spoil the soup."

3. Suppose that a firm employs only capital (K) and labor (L) in its production process. The price of a unit of capital is $10 per day and the price of a unit of labor per day is $24. If the marginal product of labor is twice the marginal product of capital, should the firm employ more workers, employ more capital, or continue to use its current mix of capital and labor? Briefly explain your reasoning.

4. We often hear about the demise of the family farm in North America. Small family farms are having to sell out to huge agri-businesses, because they can't operate profitably. How would an economist view this process of the steady transfer of land from small family farms to large corporate farms. (Hint: What does the transfer of resources imply about the ability of small farmers to produce rents from their lands?)

5. Explain why the maximization of net benefits for any individual or group requires the equalization of additional net benefits from every input and at every margin.

6. It would perhaps seem a reasonable strategy for a firm to try to achieve an output level where the average product (the output per worker) is as high as possible. If you were senior vice-president in charge of something or other at this firm, would you support this strategy? Explain why you would or would not.

ANSWERS TO REVIEW QUESTIONS

Answers to EXERCISES AND PROBLEMS

1. The firm would hire 6 units of factor Y where its wage equalled its value marginal product (VMP).

2. Profit maximization occurs where P = MC (note that setting wage = p x MP, where p x MP = VMP, can be rewritten as wage/MP = p. Also, since MC = wage/MP, it follows that p = MC). To find MC, first find labor's MP by taking the change in output for each worker hired, then divide the wage of $11 by the MP:

Output/day:	3	11	21	30	36	41	43	44
MP:	3	8	10	9	6	5	2	1
$MC = $11/MP:	3.7	1.4	1.1	1.2	1.8	2.2	5.5	11

At output price = $6.00, 7 workers would be hired, with the MC of the 7th worker equal to $5.50.

3. a.

#F:	1	2	3	4	5	6	7	8	9	10
MP:	13	12	11	10	9	8	7	6	5	4
AP:	13	12.5	12	11.5	11	10.5	10	9.5	9	8.5

b. 1) a cooperative will maximize AP so there will be 1 person fishing.
   2) common property decisions are based on $AP = wage, so 7 people would be fishing.
   3) a private owner would set $MP = wage = $100, so 4 people would be fishing.

c. MP, not AP, measures society's gain when someone decides to go fishing because MP takes into account that individual's effect on the other people already fishing.

4. a. Total product is falling when marginal product is negative.
   b. If marginal product is constant, then MP must equal AP. If each increment does not change, then the average must not change and must equal the increment.
   c. If total product is constant, MP is zero (each additional worker adds nothing). AP would continuously decline as the same total is divided by an increasing number of workers.

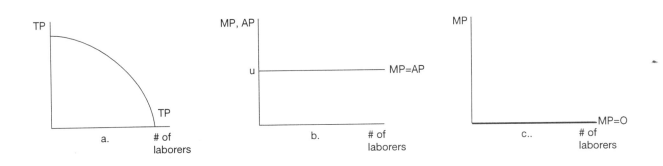

5. a. Constant returns to scale. 1 L and 1 K produce 1 output. Doubling inputs to 2 L and 2 K doubles output to 2 units. Doubling again; 4 L and 4 K produce 4 output.

    b. For marginal product of labor, L increases while K is held constant (this is a short run phenomenon). Look, for example, at the second column. Holding K = 1, labor's total product is 1.0, 1.41, 1.73, 2.0, 2.24, 2.45. The marginal product of labor (MP), therefore, is 1.0, .41, .32, .27, .24, .21. So MP of labor is decreasing.

6. a. AP = TP/Labor, MP = ΔTP/ΔLabor

L:	0	1	2	3	4	5	6	7	8
AP:	-	2	2.5	3	3	2.8	2.5	2.1	1.75
MP:	-	2	3	4	3	2	1	0	-1

b.

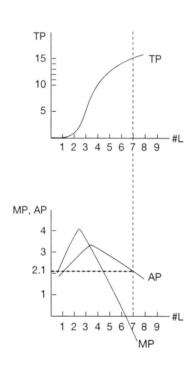

  c. 1) MP cuts AP at AP's maximum.
    2) MP equals 0 at the maximum of TP.
d. Increasing labor, while holding land constant, will eventually result in units of output increasing at a decreasing rate.
e. The law of diminishing returns begins here after the third, or with the fourth, worker.

Answers to TRUE - FALSE QUESTIONS

1. True. Each additional variable input, such as labor, is now somehow reducing total output.

2. False. The production function relates the <u>quantity</u> of inputs to the <u>quantity</u> of outputs. It measures real values only, and says nothing about costs or nominal values.

3. False. Productivity depends on the inherent attributes of the factor, whether it is a complement or substitute to other factors used in production, and the quantity of those other factors used.

4. False. MP must only be positive for total product to rise. MP may be positive and increasing (2, 4, 7), or positive and decreasing (10, 7, 3). This will determine if TP increases at an increasing or decreasing rate.

5. True. Any input that produces a quantity of goods that, when sold, bring in more money than it cost to produce them, will add to the rents of the firm.

6. True. A decreasing average implies that the incremental unit is below the average, pulling it down.

7. True. Diminishing marginal returns arises because at least one input is fixed. In the long run all inputs are variable.

8. True. The incentive in a private property rights regime is for the owner of resources to maximize rents, hence the resource's gross value. Does a system of private property rights always maximize the *net* value of resources? No, the difference between the gross and the net is the cost to individuals and society of maintaining one property rights system compared to another.

9. False. It is economically <u>inefficient</u>. Greater benefits would result from a system that induced workers to engage in labor that is the highest valued alternative of consumers.

10. False. MP can be rising or falling. The crucial point is that MP is above (greater than) AP.

11. True. The direction of AP is affected by the location of MP (greater or less than AP).

12. False. If the TP of labor is increasing at a decreasing rate, the MP of labor must be positive and decreasing and the AP must be positive, but AP can be rising or falling depending on whether it has reached its maximum or not. Try drawing this one out.

13. True. One cannot identify the marginal product of a unit of capital, for example, if both capital and labor are changing at the same time.

Answers to MULTIPLE CHOICE QUESTIONS

1.	c	6.	b	11.	d	16.	d
2.	d	7.	b	12.	b	17.	d
3.	a	8.	a	13.	d	18.	d
4.	d	9.	a	14.	c	19.	c
5.	b	10.	c	15.	e	20.	b

Answers to SHORT ANSWER QUESTIONS

1. Marginal output diminishes because additional inputs are eventually crowded out after a certain point; and thus under utilized. For example, suppose there is a house on fire. With the available neighbors and their buckets, you quickly decide to set up a bucket brigade and put the fire out with water from the house's pool. A little organization and you're soon moving 15 buckets every minute. Others arrive, with buckets, and the increase in buckets per minute is stupendous, 18, 25, 35 buckets a minute.

Soon the pool is surrounded by people dipping buckets and passing them down the lines and you're moving 48 buckets a minute. The people keep coming, however, shoving their way up to the pool and making it a little difficult to dip and pass because there is only so much pool edge. The buckets per minute increases but not by as much; only up to 50. Now the whole neighborhood is there but not all can reach the pool because the bucket-dippers are cheek-to-jowl against the edge of the pool, dipping and trying to turn around to pass. As they turn to pass they are clanging their buckets, knocking them out of each other's hands, and the number of buckets per minute is starting to decline.

In some cases the fixed input or resource has a size limit (like the pool) or a limit to what it can sustain (like the amount of water in the pool). For example farm land can be worked with more machinery or labor, but the soil has a limit to how intensively it can be farmed.

2. The law of diminishing returns is really about total product increasing at a decreasing rate, not total product decreasing. No firm would operate where the marginal input decreased output.

3. The marginal product of labor is twice that of capital, but the price of labor is more than twice as much, so $MP_l/w_l < pMP_k/w_k$. The firm should therefore hire more capital.

4. In private property rights systems, factors of production are bought and sold according to their value for producing certain goods and rents for the owner. The large corporate farms buy the land because they believe they can earn a rent from it. They offer a price which reflects their perception of the value of the land under their control. If the larger, more efficient, corporate farm offers the current owner an amount greater than he/she can derive from their rights of ownership to the land, the small family farmer will sell; it is in their interest to do so.

The land as a productive resource has been transferred from a less efficient producer to a more efficient producer. The corporate farm will produce greater rents and a larger social benefit. Positive economics offers little, if anything, in terms of a judgement about the desirability of this transfer for society, or the social value of the family farm.

5. If the net benefit per dollar spent for each input was not equal, this implies that the same quantity of output could be produced at a lower cost.

6. Striving for an output level with as high an average product as possible ignores incremental costs and benefits. For example, suppose you produced the following hourly output schedule from hiring:

#L	TP	AP	MP
1	4	4	4
2	10	5	6
3	18	6	8
4	20	5	2

If you were trying to maximize average product you would hire 3 workers, but not the 4th. But suppose output sold for $1 and each worker cost only $1 per hour. The fourth worker's value is $2 per hour; their MP times the price of output. Stopping at four workers would not maximize profit.

CHAPTER 8
Supply In Competitive Markets

PRINCIPAL GOALS

1.0   Understand the characteristics of the competitive market model and why firms are price takers in this type of market. (Objectives 1.1, 1.2)

2.0   Recognize how certain production and cost principles apply to all firms, regardless of whether they are price takers or price makers. (Objectives 2.1, 2.2, 2.3)

3.0   Understand profit maximization and the decisions competitive price taking firms make in the short and long run. (Objectives 3.1, 3.2, 3.3)

4.0   Understand the allocative consequences of price controls. (Objectives 4.1, 4.2, 4.3)

OBJECTIVES
Answers to bold-faced questions appear at the end of the dialogue.

"Pyro Pete almost burnt down our house again last night. I can't believe mom hasn't turfed him yet," said Mo.

"What happened?"

"He says he was just trying to contact his deceased aunt Minnie; apparently special seance candles are necessary to bring back the dead."

"So why is your mom being so compassionate?" Ginny asked.

"She claims it has nothing to do with compassion, just paying the bills. The boarding house business is pretty competitive, and if she kicks out Pyro she just has to replace him."

"Maybe she could rent the room to his aunt Minnie. I bet she's quiet."

OBJECTIVE 1.1 List the characteristics of a competitive market.

"And easy on the utility bill," added Mo. "Though I'm not sure how we would collect rent?"

"It could be tough, she might have even better excuses than Pete."

"Maybe, but you know those ghosts, they're soooo easy to see through."

"Oh that was bad Mo. Now when you say it's competitive do you mean it's part of the competitive model we're studying?" asked Ginny.

"Absolutely, because lots of other people rent out rooms in the area, the rooms are more or less similar in all the houses, the tenants can move around easily, and there's good price information for comparisons. I also suspect there are lots more people ready to rent out their extra rooms if the rental rate gets high enough to make the inconvenience worth their while. It's a pretty easy business to enter if you already own a home with extra rooms."

"So basically your Mom doesn't have too much power, given that there are so many other options. She probably can't even really control the rate she charges."

"No, it's really set by the market; total demand by all the renters and supply by all the boarding houses. If Mom tries to raise her price above the going level, the tenants will all move to a neighboring house."

"She's a price taker."

"She's been called worse," said Mo. "Her biggest worry, though, is that some city councillors are proposing rent controls. Maybe she should open a diner like Jim."

"I don't know, I think the diner business is just as competitive."

"Sure it is. There's lots of other fast food joints, and they all sell about the same thing -- though Jim's meatloaf is uniquely bad. It's probably not a perfectly competitive market, but just think about how Jim sets his prices based on what everyone else in the business and the neighborhood is doing."

Question 1. Describe the general characteristics of the competitive model. What sort of demand curve do individual firms face for their product in such a model?

OBJECTIVE 1.2 Recognize definitions for the important new vocabulary.

Question 2. Match the term with its definition(s). Write out definitions for any undefined terms.

a. price takers	b. perfectly competitive markets
c. price makers	d. variable cost
e. fixed cost	f. long run supply curve
g. short run marginal cost	

_____ firms which are large enough, in terms of production levels, to affect the market price of the good with their own production decisions.

_____ a supply curve indicating levels of supply or output that will be produced at given prices when all factors of production can be varied.

_____ an input cost which does not vary over some time period.

_____ firms within perfectly competitive markets.

_____ a cost that is "fixed" by contract or some other means, so that the firm must pay this cost regardless of production decisions, profit levels, or other factors outside of bankruptcy.

_____ markets in which the number of firms is large enough to make it virtually impossible for an individual firm to affect market prices through its output decisions.

_____ The marginal cost curve of a firm when, by definition, the firm can only vary one input (or at least one input is fixed).

_____ an input cost which varies over some time period as the input varies.

OBJECTIVE 2.1 **Express the relationship between diminishing marginal product and rising marginal costs algebraically and graphically.**

"So does the fact that Jim is part of an almost perfectly competitive market, mean that he faces a rising marginal cost curve at the Diner?"

"He probably does," Mo said, "but not because he's in a competitive industry. It's because of diminishing marginal product which is a production phenomenon that can occur regardless of the market environment in which you operate."

"So anybody can have rising marginal costs?"

"Absolutely, I think the market structure just affects how much they produce, given their marginal costs."

"Now we're getting down to it," Ginny said. "Rising marginal costs are a function of diminishing marginal product, regardless of the market."

"Yes just like the equation on page 256, MC = w/MP. Diminishing marginal product results in rising marginal costs when wages are held constant."

"Because as marginal product gets smaller the denominator gets smaller, but wages in the numerator stay the same so that's like 10/10 = 1, 10/5 = 2, and 10/1 = 10. Marginal cost increases."

"You got it. Does diminishing marginal product occur at the Diner?" asked Mo.

"For sure. Think about our output as the number of meals served. If Jim started getting more business he could hire more cooks and servers. At first output might increase, because people could specialize -- some cooks doing just prep, some just salads, for example, and on the floor some servers would just seat people and serve drinks or bus tables, and others could concentrate on taking orders and serving meals. Right now, one cook prepares the entire order for a table and one server does all the other jobs."

"But if you add all of those new people, then keep adding more, ultimately their incremental contribution will fall," said Mo. "There will be no more room to specialize and they'll start to get in each other's way, since the size of the kitchen and dining room, and the kitchen equipment is fixed. Does Jim pay everyone the same wage?"

"Well, no. Wait staff is different from cooks and dishwashers, but all wait staff are paid the same wage and cooks are all paid the same," said Ginny.

"So within job categories everyone gets the same wage, and the additional output contributed by each new worker would be positive, but ultimately falling. That means that the incremental cost of each meal served must rise and Jim faces a rising marginal cost curve."

Question 3. Benny bakes burger buns for Jim's Diner and other joints around town serving similar fare. Benny pays his help $300/week. Their output per week is given below:

Labor	1	2	3	4	5	6
Output (TP of labor)	100	300	700	1000	1200	1300

Calculate Benny's marginal cost curve for burger bun baking. Where does diminishing marginal product of labor begin? _____

OBJECTIVE 2.2 Identify fixed versus variable costs.

"What about Jim's costs other than labor? Like ketchup, ground beef, heating, rent, and those stupid tartan berets he makes us wear? Do these things affect his marginal costs?" asked Ginny.

"Some do. Silberberg says that fixed costs don't affect marginal costs. So any costs that don't vary with your output, which in this case is the number of meals, will not affect Jim's marginal costs."

"Which means that the cost of ketchup and ground beef are variable costs, like the cooks and servers, because the more meals you want to serve the more of these variable inputs you need. Rent is obviously a fixed cost, because Jim has to pay it every month regardless of the volume of business. Heating and those ridiculous tams are a bit trickier."

"I think heating would still be a fixed cost, since Jim has to pay to heat the Diner during winter business hours regardless of the number of meals being served," said Mo. "What's a tam?"

"Those awful hats we have to wear. Those must be a variable cost, because the more meals, the more servers, the more berets. Unfortunately Jim's costs don't include how much we hate wearing them."

"He thinks they're sporting. Remember Ginny, he gets his fashion direction from the golf course."

"That's true, he voluntarily wears plaids. Anyway, so his rent and heating costs don't affect his incremental, marginal costs of serving another meal. That makes sense."

Question 4. a. Determine Jim's monthly marginal costs of producing meatloaf from this cost data.

Qmtlf/month	TFC ($)	TVC ($)	MC ($)
0	500	0	
10	500	6	
20	500	8	
30	500	9	
40	500	10.5	
50	500	14	
60	500	21	

b. Suppose Jim's rent increases by $50/month. Calculate marginal costs at the higher rent.

* * * * * * *

"Fixed costs are costs though," said Mo, "they must affect something."

"Jim always talks about how heating bills and rent eat into his profits," offered Ginny.

OBJECTIVE 2.3 **Distinguish between economic and accounting profit.**

"Of course! Total revenue minus total cost equals profit," said Mo. So if his fixed costs increase then his total costs increase which cuts into his profits."

"The same would be true for his variable costs wouldn't it? Either way it cuts into his profits."

"Do you think Jim makes much money?" Mo asked. "My only way of knowing is his clothing; and his taste in clothing is so bad I can't tell whether or not that stuff is expensive."

"He *says* the diner has always shown a profit. But he spends so much time there ordering supplies, making schedules, paying the bills, watching his loyal employees. I don't know if it's really profit."

"I know! Does he pay himself a salary? According to Silberberg his accounting profit might be high -- you know just according to the actual wages and payments he makes and the revenue he brings in -- but his economic profit, taking into account the opportunity cost of his labor time, might be quite low."

OBJECTIVE 3.1 **Recreate the steps for a profit-maximizing firm in a competitive market.**

"It could be. You know this business about making a profit is funny. Somehow I just can't imagine Jim actually calculating his marginal cost to figure out how to maximize profits."

"I doubt he actually sketches out some curve, but I bet if hiring one more cook costs him more than the additional revenue from the lunches he prepares, he wouldn't do it," said Mo. "Besides, if he isn't implicitly making those kind of decisions I think he would have gone out of business a long time ago."

"That makes sense. But if firms operate where P = MC, how does anyone make any profit?"

"Price just equals marginal cost on the last unit. He makes profits on earlier units. In a competitive market, price is constant for every unit. But remember that MC is rising, so for all those units where

MC is below P, he is making money. He just stops producing when marginal cost rises up to the price."

"And profit at that quantity is determined by subtracting total cost from total revenue," said Ginny.

"Or he could take the difference between price and average cost times the number of meals he makes."
If you expand Q(P - AC), you get PxQ - QxAC, which is TR - TC. It's the same answer either way."

Question 5. a. Calculate the profit maximizing or loss minimizing quantity of lunches for Jim to serve monthly from the information below. TFC include heating and rent, TVC include labor, ingredients and the stupid caps, and Q refers to the monthly quantity of meals served. The average lunch price is $2.25.

Q/mth	TFC ($)	TVC ($)
0	500	0
100	500	170
200	500	200
300	500	280
400	500	370
500	500	530
600	500	880

b. Calculate Jim's monthly accounting profit at that quantity.

* * * * * * *

"So how do we figure out economic profit Mo? We need to figure out the cost of Jim's time."

"What's the best wage he could be earning elsewhere?" asked Mo.

"Well, he claims he could be playing on the tour if he didn't have to spend so much time managing us."

"You mean the pro golf tour? Give me a break. More likely he'd be serving up meatloaf in the snackshop of some city club. I would guess his foregone take home wages are $18,000 a year, tops."

"O.K., that's $1,500 a month, which would kind of be a fixed cost because he spends almost the same time doing administrative stuff no matter how many meals we're serving. But that's not quite true. Hiring and monitoring vary with servers and cooks, and servers and cooks vary with meal output."

"Let's just treat it as a fixed overhead cost for now," Mo said. "At Jim's profit maximizing level of, say 500 lunches per month, his fixed costs become $2,000. Adding those to variable costs of $530 results in total costs of $2,530. Total revenue is $2.25 times 500 lunches, $1,125."

"Sounds grim. That's a loss of $1,405, which would be the difference between a price of $2.25 and average cost of $5.06 on 500 lunches. How can he afford to live?"

"I don't know, he's still going home with $95 in his pocket, but he must have a trust fund somewhere. It's only his economic profit, taking into account the opportunity cost of his foregone wages, that puts him in a loss position."

"So does this mean we overestimated his ability to earn money elsewhere?" asked Ginny. "As I've suspected, the opportunity cost of Jim's time is zero?"

"Maybe it's the flexibility of the job, being his own boss, and the joy of seeing a tartan clad workcrew is worth the lower income to him," said Mo. "We didn't put anything into our calculation to account for job satisfaction. What I wonder is why he doesn't shut down in the summer, when business is slow?"

OBJECTIVE 3.2 Determine a firm's shutdown point.

"He wouldn't have to pay my wages if he shut down, but he'd still have to pay rent and he would still have to pay to maintain the property and do some administrative jobs. His fixed costs don't change."

"So he only gets rid of variable costs, and if he's closed he doesn't earn any revenue. It must be that the $2.25 per lunch is greater than the average variable costs of producing it."

"That's what the text was saying: if price is above AVC the firm will produce, but if it's below AVC the firm will shutdown, at least temporarily. That's why the supply curve of a firm is its marginal cost curve, *above average variable cost*, because if it's below AVC then the firm doesn't supply anything."

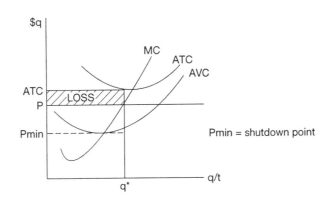

"Suppose a Diner, or any business, kept losing money though. That would mean that price was below average total cost, but it could be above average variable cost. Don't you think that firm would want to shut down permanently?" Mo asked.

"I think it would depend on what they thought costs and prices would be in the future. Jim, for example, thinks he has a continuous supply of cheap labor because of the University. And this $2.25 lunch price is only temporary, he says, to compete with the fast food burger chain that just opened down the street. He figures once people try the Diner they'll come back and be willing to pay a little more."

"He may be right," said Mo. "That burger joint has changed hands a lot. It's pretty easy to change ownership there if you keep it a burger place, since the basic building, kitchen, tables, and chairs are pretty generic. A new owner can just hang their sign."

"That's true, but most of the stuff in the Diner wouldn't have much resale value. Jim has JDD embossed, embroidered, and emblazoned on everything possible. So even with temporary losses he might be inclined to hang on a little longer waiting for a better market."

"Why two D's?"

"The full name is Jim's Divine Diner. The Divine got lost somewhere in the meatloaf."

OBJECTIVE 3.3 Describe the dynamics of the competitive model.

"Silberberg is back to intensive and extensive margins again. We read about this in Chapter six and seven. I'm pretty comfortable with it."

"Me too," Ginny said, "although here I think he's trying to get at the dynamics, the way things change, in the competitive model. The basic supply and demand graphs are pretty static, I mean, they're drawn for a point in time. But obviously the market and our economy is a lot more fluid than that."

"I agree, he's drawn short run and long run supply curves on one graph, which we haven't seen before."

"As I understand it, with an increase in demand, in the short run firms try to increase output by just adding more variable inputs, usually labor. But in the short run, by definition, at least one input is fixed. So they experience diminishing marginal returns at the intensive margin as the marginal product of these workers adds to output, but at a decreasing rate."

"In the long run, two things happen. First, firms already producing will have the opportunity to adjust all of their inputs to a new mix that minimizes costs for the new level of output."

"Which means setting the ratios of the marginal products over the wages of each input equal, so that the quantity of output per dollar cost is the same for the last worker hired as the last piece of capital used."

"The second thing that happens is that firms with less productive resources that weren't profitable before, may become profitable now that the increase in demand raised the market price. So they start producing with these less productive inputs, leading to diminishing returns on the extensive margin."

Question 6. Graph and describe in words the response in a competitive market to a decrease in demand.

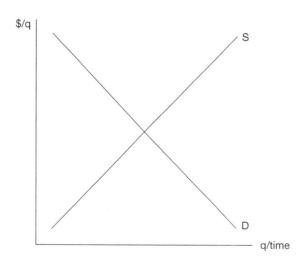

OBJECTIVE 4.1 **Recognize definitions for the important new vocabulary.**

Question 7. Match the term with its definition(s). Write out definitions for any undefined terms.

a. price control
c. price floor
e. shortage

b. price ceiling
d. market clearing price
f. surplus

_____ this condition exists with a price control above the market clearing price.

_____ a price control that limits the minimum price at which a good can be legally sold.

_____ the quantity demanded exceeds the quantity supplied.

_____ the price at which the quantity supplied equals the quantity demanded.

_____ a price control that limits the maximum price at which a good can be legally sold.

_____ the quantity supplied exceeds the quantity demanded.

_____ a legal measure, usually imposed by governments, that limits the extent to which the price of a good can increase, decrease or otherwise change from a determined level.

_____ this condition exists with a price control below the market clearing price.

_____ equilibrium price.

OBJECTIVE 4.2 **Diagram a market with a price ceiling leading to a shortage.**

"So what's this about possible rent controls that your Mom is dreading. Sounds like a great idea to me, coming from a renter's perspective of course."

"Well it may sound great Ginny, but I suspect that you may not benefit as much as you think."

"How so? Wouldn't my rent be lower?"

"Perhaps, if you could find an apartment. And even if you do you may end up spending more per month than you would without the controls."

"Is this just like the gasoline example?" asked Ginny.

"Exactly the same idea. Suppose the market clearing price for rooms is around $200/month. At that price, 15,000 rooms rent out. Now, suppose the city decides that $200 is too much for poorer people to pay, and they slap on a rent control of $125/month. What do you suppose happens?"

"Well, if I were your Mom I'm not so sure I would go through the hassle for $125 a month. I might just quit renting rooms. For sure I wouldn't spend much time or money maintaining the rooms."

"OK, so there's a decrease in the quantity of rooms supplied, and a decrease in the quality of some of those remaining. That's on the supply side. What about your response as a renter?" asked Mo.

"If I already lived there and the landlord didn't shut down I sure wouldn't move. But if I was thinking about getting my own place but couldn't quite afford it at $200/month, now I'd try to move."

"Alright, now there's an increase in quantity demanded because of the low price, but less mobility in tenants lucky enough to be in one of these rooms when rent control takes effect."

"I get your point Mo. An increase in quantity demanded but a decrease in quantity supplied. That's a shortage. Let's try drawing that."

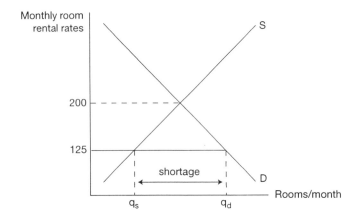

"Normally the quantity supplied, qs, equals the quantity demanded, qd," said Mo, "and we just write qe. But now qs is less than qd at the controlled price. The difference between them, that horizontal distance, is the shortage of rental rooms."

"It's the horizontal distance, not an area?"

"Yes, because the shortage is a quantity, which is measured along the horizontal axis. An area on this graph would represent a value, because it would be price times quantity."

"Curious that it's called a price ceiling when it's below the equilibrium price," Ginny said. "It looks like a floor. It must be that the price control acts as a ceiling, not letting the price rise to equilibrium. Market forces are pushing up from below, such that without the price control the price would rise."

"Now how do think rooms will be allocated if there's all this excess demand?"

"People like your Mom could charge a monthly fee to rent the key to the room, or charge $125 for the room but $100 to rent the furniture. I could end up spending more than $200 anyway."

"I think so. Also my Mom might discriminate more among renters -- no pyromaniacs for example. Others might discriminate against people with kids, or students, or based on gender or ethnicity."

"That seems unfair," said Ginny.

"Sure, but if you have all this excess demand discrimination becomes a luxury that those so inclined will now indulge in. Without the rent controls, rooms were simply allocated based on ability to pay."

"So the very people the controls were designed to help may be worse off. That sounds like a lot of my friends who can't find work because of minimum wage laws."

OBJECTIVE 4.3 **Diagram a market with a price floor leading to a surplus.**

"I think the minimum wage case is exactly the same," said Mo, "except that now the price on the vertical axis, in this case a wage, is held above equilibrium."

"So it's a price <u>floor</u>", Ginny said, "because the pressure is for prices to fall; but they can't fall below the floor."

"Let's draw this case. Hourly wages will be on the vertical axis."

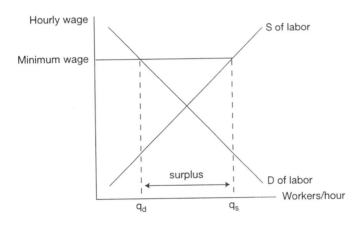

"The high hourly wage cuts the demand for labor at qd," said Ginny, "making firms want to cut back employees where possible."

"But the high wage cuts labor supply at qs, inducing all those workers who were just at the margin before, to enter the labor force."

"You mean like students who were deciding between work and summer courses or graduate school?"

"Sure, or spouses who were staying at home with kids, people who were thinking of retiring, and so on."

"So, all these people enter the labor force at the same time that employers are trying to reduce their workforce. That's where the surplus of labor comes from."

"And how do you suppose those few jobs are allocated now? asked Mo."

"To those willing to work part time and without benefits, or those that the employer knows."

"Or those who speak the language, "look" like the employer, or have facial hair."

"Facial hair? You mean men rather than women?"

"Precisely," Mo said. "And employers would also favor people with experience, which is what hurts our friends. We're expected to have experience before we've had any work experiences. But I don't know, with a surplus of labor, doesn't it make sense to choose those with experience, since you have to pay them all the same wage?"

"I suppose so," said Ginny. "But some people must be better off, for example those who keep their jobs and now earn more money."

"Sure, it's like the tenants who get the rent controlled rooms.   But I think the important thing to recognize is that if prices are controlled, the goods or services will be allocated through other means. Side payments, waiting lines, discrimination, violence, patronage, lotteries, etcetera, are all alternative methods of allocation. And the method of allocation may not be desirable and end up hurting the very groups the controls were intended to help."

"So what you're saying is that if these rent controls go through, poor Pyro will be on the street."

"As quick as it takes to light a match, and his aunt Minnie with him."

Question 8. Tickets to the 1994 World Cup soccer games in the U.S. were sold out immediately. Rumor was that scalpers were offering tickets at twice their original selling price. Diagram this situation, and label the shortage/surplus of tickets.

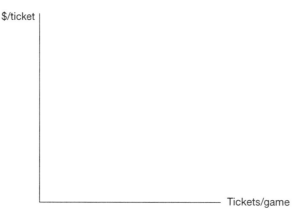

Question 9. What forms of allocation do you often observe for concert tickets? (Does anyone remember the 1972 Rolling Stones tour?)

ANSWERS TO DIALOGUE QUESTIONS

Question 1. A competitive market (often referred to as a perfectly competitive market) is made up of firms that are price takers, called so because their output decisions are too small to affect the market price of the good. Thus, they have to *take the price* determined in the market by demand and the sum of all the firms' supply. Generally this occurs in markets with a large number of firms selling a homogeneous product. Individual firms face a horizontal, perfectly elastic demand curve. Entry and exit is assumed costless so the marginal firm must earn zero economic profit for a long run equilibrium.

Question 2. Vocabulary: c, f, e, a, e, b, g, d.

Question 3. The easiest way to calculate Benny's marginal cost curve is to first calculate the MP of labor, and then use the formula: MC = wage/MP, knowing that the wage is $300. The MP is the change in output for each additional worker, $\Delta Q / \Delta \#L$:

Labor	1	2	3	4	5	6
Output	100	300	700	1000	1200	1300
MP	100	200	400	300	200	100
$MC	3	1.5	.75	1	1.5	3

Diminishing marginal product of labor begins after the third worker, or with the fourth worker, where MP begins to fall and MC begins to rise.

Question 4. Jim's monthly marginal costs of producing meatloaf are the change in total costs divided by the change in output. Since $\Delta TFC = 0$ by definition, $\Delta TC / \Delta Q = \Delta TVC / \Delta Q = MC$.

Q	0	10	20	30	40	50	60
MC($)		.6	.2	.1	.15	.35	.70

The $10 increase in fixed costs does not change the marginal cost schedule.

Question 5. The profit maximizing level occurs where $P \geq MC$. Marginal costs should therefore be calculated.

Q/mth	TFC	TVC	TC	MC ($)	AC ($)	Profit
		(. . . $ . . .)				
0	500	0	500			
100	500	170	670	1.7	6.70	-445
200	500	200	700	.3	3.50	-250
300	500	280	780	.8	2.60	-105
400	500	370	870	.9	2.175	30
500	500	530	1030	1.6	2.06	95
600	500	880	1380	3.5	2.30	-30

The profit maximizing quantity occurs at about 500 lunches per month. Profit was determined by first calculating TC (TFC + TVC), then AC (TC/Q), subtracting AC from the price of $2.25 and then multiplying that difference by 500. TR - TC also works.

Question 6. A decrease in market demand lowers price and induces each firm to reduce their quantity supplied, indicated by a movement along their short run supply curve (SRS) in the diagram below. In the short run, this is accomplished by laying off variable inputs, usually labor. In the long run, these firms will have time to adjust all of their inputs to a new optimal mix for producing the reduced quantity. As well, the marginal firms (those with the least productive inputs) will leave the industry if price falls below their AVC's. These two adjustments continue until the market reaches a new equilibrium at the intersection of demand (D') and the long run supply curve (LRS).

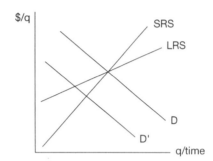

Question 7. Vocabulary: f, c, e, d, b, f, a, e, d.

Question 8. Tickets to the World Cup soccer games must have been priced below equilibrium, creating a shortage given by the horizontal distance qs - qd. The shape of the supply curve indicates fixed capacity at some point.

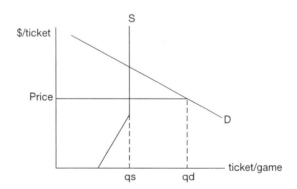

Question 9. Concert tickets are often allocated by waiting in line. Individuals with a low time cost may buy blocks of tickets and resell them at higher prices (scalping). Actually, we don't remember the '72 Stones tour either, but the story goes that fans in Vancouver rioted and vandalized property because so many did not get tickets after waiting overnight. In response, the Stones began allocating tickets by lottery.

THE BIG PICTURE

As we mentioned in The Big Picture of Chapter 6, Silberberg's presentation of the theory of supply culminates in this chapter. This seems like a good time for a retrospective, to see where all this fits in terms of the economic paradigm and the direction of the book. A lot of material has been covered, and we hope a glance back will help you to feel good about your progress. You are now potential *masters* of supply and demand; having essentially worked over the whole of the competitive model.

So what, you may be wondering, is the overarching point of all of this? The point is that economics is about explaining changes in human behavior -- in consumption, production and exchange, and in different market settings. Chapter 1 provided a brief description of the economic paradigm complete with supply and demand. You should go back and re-read this and see how much you've learned. Chapter 1 provided the overall framework of economic analysis without too much distinction between individual firms and markets. Chapter 2 laid the foundation of behavioral postulates upon which the structure of economic analysis is based. Basically the postulates are irrefutable statements about the way people behave facing scarcity, and the choices they make as constraints change. Chapter 3 explored the law of demand: the operational statement of Chapter two's behavioral postulates. The theory of demand applies to all market models, competitive or not.

Chapter 4 introduced the fundamental activity of exchange, which involves both suppliers and consumers, and presented some explanations for how and why we get involved with exchange. Chapter 5 built on Chapter 4 with a more complete explanation of exchange but at the market level and within the competitive model. Against this background Chapters 6 and 7 begin an in depth analysis of supply. Silberberg's analysis, while remaining in the competitive model, moves from the market level to the level of an individual firm: the nitty gritty of individual choices about production and supply.

This concludes in Chapter 8, where we gain full view of the competitive model at the firm level. This view is of individual firms who must accept the price as determined by the larger market. Individual firms strive to combine resources to maximize rents, which includes producing an output at the least cost. Rents accrue when marginal costs are below the market price. This understanding complements and supports the view we had in Chapter 5, where we saw the competitive model, but at the market level.

REVIEW QUESTIONS

Answers to all review questions appear at the end of this chapter.

PROBLEMS AND EXERCISES
Write your answer in the space(s) provided.

1. Assume that you are currently employed at a job paying $24,000 a year. Your older brother has offered you a job paying $30,000 a year, but you want to start your own business. What is the opportunity cost of your labor to use in calculating the economic profit from your new business?
_____

2. Suppose that the MP of the fifth cook you hire to prepare food for your catering business is 50 appetizers per day. If each cook is paid $250 per day, and labor is the only variable input, what is the marginal cost associated with the output of this cook? _____

3. Below is the marginal product schedule of B.C. tree planters in trees per day. L is the number of planters hired.

L :   1   2   3   4   5   6   7   8   9   10
MPL: 100   90   80   70   60   50   40   30   20   10

a. _____ planters must be hired each day before the total daily output is 450.
b. If planters are paid $120 per unit per day, the marginal cost at an output level between 450 and 490 units per day is _____.
c. If this firm gets $4.10 from the provincial government for every tree planted, a profit maximizing firm will hire _____ planters.

4. This problem illustrates the relationship between production and cost. There is one variable input, labor, and one fixed input, land. Information on output (Q) is below. The wage rate is $10 per laborer and $20 per acre of land.
a. Complete the table below

Land	Labor	Q	MP(L)	FC	VC	AFC	AVC	ATC	MC
1	0	0							
1	1	10							
1	2	25							
1	3	35							
1	4	40							

b. Describe the relationship between the MP of labor and MC.

5. The market demand curve for Wiley's western wieners at the Stampede snackshop has been estimated at Qd = 20 - P, while the market supply curve is Qs = 14 + 2P.
a. Find the equilibrium price and quantity for wieners.

b. If the price is set by law at $1.00, diagram the wiener market showing the quantity supplied and the quantity demanded under the price control, and the resulting surplus or shortage.

$/wieners |

wieners/t

6. Suppose that you quit your $25,000 a year job as a school teacher to begin private lambada dance lessons. At the end of the first year, your accounting books show the following:

Payment on $20,000 loan for start-up costs	$3,000
Insurance	$6,000
Advertising	$1,000
Gravol, breath mints, and other office supplies	$3,500
Tapes of pulsating music	$1,500

Your total billings the first year are $40,000.

a. Your accounting profit, which only considers the explicit costs of payments to factors of production you don't own, is _____ .

b. Your economic profit, which considers all costs, is _____ .

c. If, instead of lambada teaching, you could earn $27,000 a year touring with the Carmen Miranda memorial dance troupe, would your accounting profit be affected? _____ Your economic profit? _____

d. If, instead of borrowing $20,000, you had $20,000 of your own savings to use, would your accounting profit be affected? _____ Your economic profit? _____

e. From c., an interest rate of _____ on your loan would allow you to just break even.

7. In 1993, as the Toronto Blue Jays were racing toward their second World Series victory, many Jays fans were frustrated getting tickets to the Skydome. Everywhere more tickets were wanted than were available.
a. What is this situation called by economists? _____
b. What other methods of ticket allocation might you predict in these circumstances?

8. Fill in the table below using the following information:
   a. AFC for 6 units of output is 2.
   b. AVC for 4 units of outpt is 2.50.
   c. TVC is increased by 4 when the 5th unit of output is added.
   d. AC of 6 units of output is .30 more than for 5 units of output.
   e. AFC + AVC for 2 units of output is 10.
   f. MC is 1 for a change in output from w to 3 units.
   g. It costs 6 more to produce 1 unit of output than to remain shutdown.

Q	TC	MC	AC	AFC	TVC	AVC
0						
1						
2						
3						
4						
5						
6						

9. The following table gives the total peach output on an Ottawa valley orchard resulting from the use of one through eight peach pickers per day.

Pickers	Total Peaches
1	6
2	13
3	22
4	28
5	32
6	34
7	35
8	34

Only labor is required to pick peaches. If labor costs $90 per day and peaches sell for $15.00 per bushel, how many pickers per day will a profit-maximizing orchard owner hire? _____ (Hint: calculate a marginal product and marginal cost column).

10. Assume there are ten identical firms in a market. Fixed costs are zero and each firm operates at a constant MC = $10.00. The market demand for their product is linear with vertical and horizontal intercepts of 30.
a. If this market is competitive, the market price will be _____ and _____ units will be produced.
b. Total consumer surplus will be _____.
c. If the government puts a $5 per unit tax on the producers, price will be _____ and the quantity exchanged will now be _____.

d. The _____ bears the entire burden of the tax in this case because the _____ curve is perfectly elastic.

11. Urin Urout Ltd. is a new firm in the competitive business of testing for drug use. Their cost and output schedule are given below:

Output : 0	1	2	3	4	5
Total Cost ($): 5	12	17	20	25	31

a. What is U.U.'s fixed cost of operation? _____
b. What is the average variable cost of producing 2 units? _____
c. Assume labor is the only variable input. With which output does diminishing marginal returns from labor begin? _____
d. If the price is constant at $5.25 per unit, how many units would the firm produce to maximize profits?

_____
e. What are U.U.'s profits or losses at this point? _____
f. If U.U. is losing money (they may or may not be in this case), should they shutdown temporarily? _____ What additional information would be needed to make a decision about selling the company in the long run?

12. Assume that the supply curve for oranges is Q = 40, and the demand schedule is given by the following:

P	30	15	0
Qd	40	60	80

a. What is the equation of the demand curve?

b. What is the equilbrium price and quantity?

c. If the government puts a price control of 45 cents in the market, how big is the resulting surplus or shortage?

d. Diagram this market with the 45 cent price control.

TRUE - FALSE QUESTIONS
Provide a one or two sentence explanation with your answer.

1. A rising marginal cost CAUSES the marginal product to fall.

2. The market demand curve for a perfectly competitive firm is horizontal.

3. If marginal cost (MC) is rising, average cost (AC) is less than MC.

4. The larger the output of a firm, the smaller the fixed costs of the firm.

5. Shut down point occurs when price is less than average variable cost.

6. Diminishing marginal product only occurs in competitive markets.

7. If AVC is rising, MC is greater than AVC.

8. A firm that cannot earn enough revenue at any rate of output to pay its fixed costs, should temporarily shut down.

9. If diminishing marginal returns from labor have begun, short run marginal cost is rising.

10. In the short run, as a firm's output expands, average fixed costs fall.

11. A price ceiling holds the price above equilibrium.

12. A firm's cost curves include their opportunity costs.

MULTIPLE CHOICE QUESTIONS
Choose the best answer.

1. The marginal cost curve must be
a. rising at all output levels.
b. rising when total cost is rising.
c. less than average fixed cost when the average cost curve is rising.
d. greater than average total cost when the average cost curve is rising.

e.   falling when the average total cost curve lies below the marginal cost curve.

2. For a firm in a perfectly competitive market, a technological advance would cause
a.   the MC curve to shift left.
b.   the MR curve to shift left.
c.   AFC to increase.
d.   the demand curve to become flatter.
e.   none of the above.

3. A firm in a perfectly competitive market believes it can
a.   not influence the price of the product.
b.   obtain a higher price if it advertises.
c.   obtain a higher price if it improves its product.
d.   sell more units if it offers the product at a lower price.
e.   both b and c above.

4. A competitor in a perfectly competitive market will temporarily shut down in the short run whenever
a.   price is less than average total cost.
b.   price is less than average fixed cost.
c.   price is less than average variable cost.
d.   marginal revenue is less than marginal cost.
e.   average revenue is less than average total cost.

5. If consumers suddenly increase their demand for beef, the average total cost curve would probably shift upward for
a.   potato farmers, since potatoes are usually consumed with beef.
b.   sheep ranchers, since they use the same land and labor as cattle ranchers.
c.   pig farmers, if consumers consider pork a substitute for beef.
d.   chicken farmers, since most cattle ranchers also raise chickens.
e.   none of the above.

6. If the total cost of producing 8 units is $53, and the marginal cost of producing the ninth unit is $10,
a.   the total cost of 7 units is $43.
b.   the average total cost of 9 units is $10.
c.   there are no fixed costs.
d.   the average total cost of 9 units is $7.

7. The short run supply curve for a perfectly competitive firm is the
a.   MC curve at or above the AVC curve.
b.   MR curve at or above the ATC curve.
c.   ATC curve at or above the minimum.
d.   ATC curve at or above the minimum of MC.

8. Perfect competition is characterized by
a.   P < MC.
b.   differentiated products.
c.   downward sloping market demand curve.
d.   both b and c.

9. Price ceilings are likely to
a.   result in the accumulation of surpluses.
b.   increase the volume of transactions as we move along the demand curve.
c.   increase production as consumers respond to higher consumer demand at the low ceiling price.
d.   result in the development of black markets.
e.   none of the above.

10. If the quantity of sandals is fixed by law below the market clearing price,
a.   a surplus of sandals will result.
b.   sandal inventories at shoe stores will increase.
c.   sandal sellers will spend more on advertising.
d.   the quantity of sandals purchased will be less than the quantity desired at that price.
e.   none of the above.

11. The imposition of an above equilibrium wage rate will cause employment to fall off more when the demand for labor is,
a. greater than the supply.   b. elastic.   c. less than the supply.   d. inelastic.

12. If the total cost rises as the level of output produced increases, then
a.   marginal cost must be rising.
b.   average cost must be rising.
c.   diminishing marginal returns must have set in.
d.   none of the above.

13. If the total cost of producing 7 units is $56, and the marginal cost of the 8th unit is $16, then
a.   there are no fixed costs.
b.   the average cost of the 8th unit is $9.
c.   the total cost of 8 units is $70.
d.   the marginal cost of the 7th unit is $4.

14. If, at the prevailing price, less of a good is desired than is available for sale,
a.   the price is below equilibrium.
b.   the price is at equilibrium.
c.   the price must fall.
d.   the price system cannot allocate the good efficiently.
e.   inflation of the price level will result.

15. The supply curve for product X is a vertical line. If the government establishes a floor $1 above the market clearing price, the surplus of product X will be greatest if the price elasticity of demand in that range is (in absolute value):
a. 3.00   b. 1.25   c. 1.00   d. .25

16. A firm's average total cost per month equals $3 x Q, where Q is the number of units of output produced per month. The total cost of the third unit of output produced per month is
a. $3   b. $9   c. $15   d. $27

Suppose your are hired to predict the effects of two different agricultural policies the government is proposing. The first, graph (i) is a price floor on wheat. The alternative, graph (ii) is a subsidy or deficiency payment for farmers, given by the shaded area.

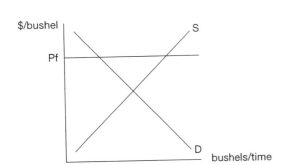

(i)

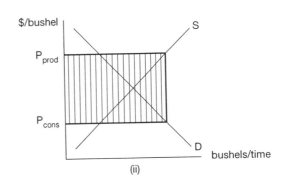

(ii)

17. The effect on the price consumers pay and producers receive under each policy is:
a.   under (i), consumers pay and producers receive a higher price.
b.   under (i), consumers pay a higher price and producers receive a lower price.
c.   under (ii), consumers pay and producers receive a higher price.
d.   under (ii), consumers pay a higher price and producers receive a lower price.

18. Which policy results in too many resources being used to produce wheat?
a.   (i) only because wheat must be stored.
b.   (ii) only.
c.   (i) and (ii).
d.   (i) only because there are lost gains from trade.

19. What effect will an increased demand for housing in King county have on the cost of growing strawberries in the county?
a.   No effect, since you cannot grow strawberries on land on which new housing has been constructed.
b.   The cost will fall because only the best land will now be used for growing strawberries.
c.   The cost will rise because strawberry patches will acquire more value as housing sites.
d.   The cost will not change but the price of strawberries will rise because of an increase in the prices of a substitute.

20. Suppose that marginal cost starts out below average cost and then reaches a point where it is above average cost. Which of the following is true concerning average cost?
a.   Average cost increases and then decreases.
b.   Average cost decreases and then increases.
c.   Average cost continuously decreases.
d.   Average cost continuously increases.
e.   Average cost will always decrease.

21. Firm X's average total cost per month equals $5 x Q, where Q is the number of units of output produced per month. The marginal cost of the third unit of output produced per month is
a. $5   b. $15   c. $25   d. $35

Use the following diagram to answer questions 22 to 24.

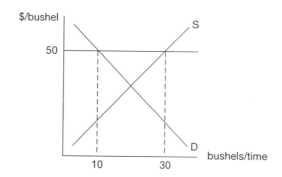

22. If the current price of coffee was $50 bushel,
a.   producers would want to supply more coffee than consumers would wish to buy.
b.   producers would want to supply less coffee than consumers would wish to buy.
c.   equilibrium could be reached if demand decreased.
d.   the price of coffee would have to rise in order to bring about equilibrium.
e.   a and c are true.

23. Suppose that the price was cotrolled at $50 through a price floor and the government told producers to supply the quantity they desired at that price. The result is
a.   a surplus of 10 bushels.
b.   a surplus of 20 bushels.
c.   a shortage of 10 bushels.
d.   a shortage of 20 bushels.

24. At a price floor of $50, if 30 bushels are produced, which of the following is true?
a.   There is excess demand.
b.   There will be queues for coffee.
c.   Coffee rationing will occur.
d.   The cost of producing the 30th bushel exceeds our marginal valuation of it.

25. The dramatic drop in oil prices has increased the demand for automobiles. This would probably increase average total costs for
a.   the airline industry, since flying is a substitute for driving.
b.   the tire industry, since automobiles require tires.
c.   the suspension bridge industry, since bridge builders use the same steel and other metal inputs as the auto industry.
d.   no one, since the auto industry is a unique industry.

26. If the number of firms in a competitive industry is decreasing, one would expect price to be
a. greater than MC.
b. less than MC.
c. greater than AC.
d. less than AC.

27. The figure below displays the cost curves of a firm in a perfectly competitive market. Profits at a price of 10 would be
a. 5 per unit.   b. 400.   c. 6 per unit.   d. 450.   e. cannot be determined.

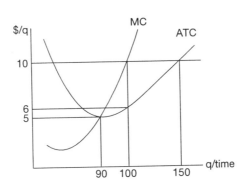

28. For the firm depicted in the figure above, the long-run price and quantity will be
a. P=5, Q=90   b. P=6, Q=100   c. P=10, Q=150   d. cannot be determined

29. In the long-run, the firm depicted in the figure above will leave the industry if the price falls below
a. 10   b. 6   c. 5   d. cannot be determined

30. There is something wrong with the graph below because:

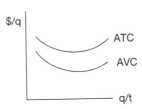

a. AFC are rising.
b. AVC > ATC.
c. marginal cost is rising.
d. none of the above.

SHORT ANSWER QUESTIONS

1. The text explains that firms in competitive markets are price takers, so the market price effectively becomes the demand curve they face (rather than the market demand curve). Try to draw a diagram for a price taking firm in a competitive industry next to the market diagram where the price is set.

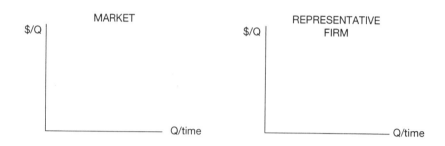

2. People often talk about the auto industry, for example, as being very competitive. Would you characterise GM, Chrysler, and Ford, as being price takers? Why or why not? How would you reconcile your observations?

3. Assume that the textiles industry is perfectly competitive. Explain how each of the following events would affect the textiles industry in the short-run and in the long-run, and where diminishing returns at the intensive and extensive margin are experienced. Use a graph to help explain your answer.
   a. The market demand for textiles increases.
   b. The wage rate of laborers in textiles plants rises. Assume that labor is a variable input in the short-run.

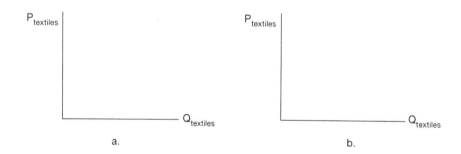

4. Many economics professors could be earning higher salaries working in the private sector rather than teaching at universities. Assuming their costs are comparable in either job (although universities tend to have pretty lax dress codes), does this mean we are all earning negative economic profit? How can we afford our pocket protectors?

5. How long can a firm earning zero economic profit stay in business?

6. Suppose along the same street there was a small shop selling magazines, and a small shop printing their own magazine. The first shop contains magazines, shelves, a front desk and a cash register. The second shop contains printing dyes, a printing press, and plates. If both companies were losing the same

amount of money, which do you think would be more likely to try and sell their business, and which might try to hang on longer? Why?

7. Many farm sector lobbyists have argued that agriculture needs special supports and price controls to aid its members because it is such a competitive industry. Why would being a firm in a competitive industry necessitate price support?

8. Most economists would agree that some price supports and controls in agriculture have led to resource misallocations, and a transfer of wealth to large farm operations rather than "family farms". In addition, to the extent that these controls lead to food prices higher than they otherwise would be, many farm support policies are regressive since the poor tend to spend a larger portion of their income on food. Why do you suppose these policies endure?

ANSWERS TO REVIEW QUESTIONS

Answers to PROBLEMS AND EXERCISES

1. $30,000 because that is your highest foregone wage.

2. Using MC = w/MP produces MC = $250/50 = $5.

3. a. 6. This is found by adding up MP's.
   b. MC = $120/40 = $3.
   c. MC is equal to or just less than price at 8 workers.

4. a. Use the formulas

Land	Labor	Q	MP(L)	FC	VC	AFC	AVC	ATC	MC
1	0	0	0	20	0	-	-	-	-
1	1	10	10	20	10	2	1	3	1
1	2	25	15	20	20	.8	.8	1.6	.67
1	3	35	10	20	30	.57	.86	1.4	1
1	4	40	5	20	40	.5	1.4	1.9	2

   b. MP rises and then falls, MC falls and then rises as MP begins to fall. They are inversely related.

5. a. In equilibrium, Qd = Qs, so they can be set equal to solve for price: 20 - P = 14 + 2P, 6 = 3P, P = 2. Substitute this into either equation for quantity, Qd = 20 - (2) = 18, or Qs = 14 + 2(2) = 18.

   b. Since $1.00 is below the equilibrium price of $2.00, a shortage will result. Qd no longers equals Qs so each equation must be solved separately. To find the shortage, plug the price control of $1.00 into the demand curve (for Qd at $1.00) and the supply curve (for Qs at $1.00). Qd = 20 - 1 = 19, and Qs = 14 + 2(1) = 16. The shortage is the difference between Qd and Qs, which is 3.

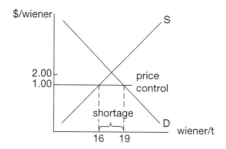

6. a. Accounting profit: $40,000 - ($3,000 + $6,000 + $1,000 + $3,500 + $1,500) = $25,000.

   b. Economic profit, considering your foregone salary, (that is, paying yourself a wage) is: $40,000 - ($3,000 + $6,000 + $1,000 + $3,500 + $1,500 + $25,000) = $0.

c. No, accounting profit would be unaffected, but yes, economic profit would fall by $2,000 when the increased value of your time was factored in.

d. No, and no, since the $20,000 has already been accounted for.

e. Paying $3,000 on $20,000 implies a current interest rate of 15%. If that was rate was 5%, the payment would fall to $1,000, and economic profit (in c.) would be $0.

7. a. A situation of excess demand is called a shortage.
   b. Allocation by waiting in line, scalping and black market sales, patronage, and perhaps violence could be expected.

8.

Q	TC	MC	AC	AFC	TVC	AVC
0	12	-	-	-	0	6
1	18	6	18	12	6	4
2	20	2	10	6	8	4
3	21	1	7	4	9	3
4	22	1	5.5	3	10	2.5
5	26	4	5.2	2.4	14	2.8
6	33	7	5.5	2	21	3.5

9.

Pickers	TP Peaches	MP	$MC = w/MP$
1	6	6	15
2	13	7	12.86
3	22	9	10
4	28	6	15
5	32	4	22.5
6	34	2	45
7	35	1	90
8	35	0	∞

4 pickers would be hired. Note that P = MC at both 1 and 4 pickers, but a firm would never stop hiring when MC was falling.

10. a. If this market is competitive, price will equal MC, so P = $10, and Q = 20.
   b. Consumer surplus will be ½[($30-$10)*20] = $200
   c. A $5 per will increase price to $15, and reduce quantity to 15.
   d. consumer, supply

11.

Output:	0	1	2	3	4	5
TC ($):	5	12	17	20	25	31

MC ($):   7   5   3   5   6

a. Fixed costs occur even when output is zero, so $5.
b. AVC = TVC/Q = (TC - FC)/Q = (17 - 5)/2 = $6.
c. DMR's begins when MC begins to rise, so after the third output, or with the fourth.
d. At a price of $5.25 per unit, the firm would produce 4 units to maximize profit. (Note, they would not produce 2 units where MC is falling).
e. At 4 units, TC = $25, and TR = $21, so the firm is losing $5.00.
f. The shutdown decision requires information on AVC. At four units AVC equals $5, ($25 - $5)/5. Since price > AVC, the firm should continue to produce because it must pay its FC regardless, but without production, it earns no revenues. Making a decision about shutting down completely, or selling, requires information about price and cost expectations, and the resale value of the capital assets (FC).

12. a. The demand curve can be found by noting that the horizontal intercept is 80 (the value of Q when P = 0), and the inverse slope is ΔQ/ΔP = 20/15 = 4/3. So we can write: Q = 80 - (4/3)P. Alternatively, extend the table leftward to where Q = 0. This occurs at P = 60, the vertical intercept. The slope is ΔP/ΔQ = 3/4, so we can write: P = 60 - (3/4)Qd. Note that these two equations are identical. With P on the left hand side it is called an inverse demand curve. With Qd on the left hand side it is called demand curve.

b. Equilibrium price and quantities are found by setting demand and supply equal (or through substitution -- it depends on how you prefer to solve simultaneous equations) and solving for P and Q. Q, by virtue of the supply curve that is a vertical line at 40, is fixed at 40. Demand cuts this line at: 80 - (4/3)P = 40, so P = 30.

c. A price control of 45 cents lead to Qd = 80 - (4/3)45 = 20. With Qs fixed at 40, the surplus is 40 - 20 = 20.

d. The diagram is below.

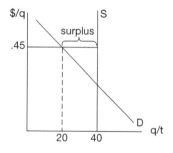

Answers to TRUE - FALSE QUESTIONS

1. False. A falling marginal product causes marginal cost to rise.

2. False. The market demand curve is downward sloping. The individual firm faces a perfectly elastic

demand curve at the market price.

3. False. If AC is rising, MC must be greater than AC to pull it up. It is the <u>direction</u> that AC's are moving and the <u>location</u> of MC that is important.

4. False. Although larger firms may have larger fixed costs, there is no necessary relationship between the size of a firm's output and their fixed costs.

5. True. Since FC must be paid regardless of whether the firm produces or not, as long as a firm can cover their variable costs they should continue to produce to earn the revenue.

6. False. The production process of all firms is subject to diminishing marginal product regardless of whether they are price takers are price makers.

7. True. MC must be pulling AVC up.

8. False. Even if the firm shuts down its FC must be paid, but by shutting down they earn no revenue.

9. True. Diminishing marginal returns from labor will increase the cost of each additional unit of output (MC).

10. True. As TFC are spread over a larger output, AFC's fall.

11. False. A price ceiling holds the price below equilibrium, it prevents the price from rising.

12. True. Cost curves should reflect the true cost of all resources, which is their value in their highest foresaken alternative.

Answers to MULTIPLE CHOICE QUESTIONS

1. d	7. a	13. b	19. c	25. c
2. e	8. c	14. c	20. b	26. d
3. a	9. d	15. a	21. c	27. b
4. c	10. d	16. d	22. a	28. d
5. b	11. b	17. a	23. b	29. d
6. d	12. d	18. c	24. d	30. a

Answers to SHORT ANSWER QUESTIONS

1. The market diagram is the usual supply and demand diagram we have been using. The market price is the demand curve faced by the individual firm, which then produces where its MC = price. In this case, economic profit is zero (which is normal for the marginal firm) because P = ATC at q*.

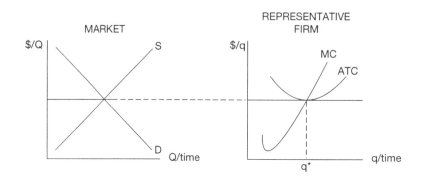

2. Most people would not characterise these car companies as being price takers, because their decisions <u>do</u> affect the market price. This example indicates the importance of the model of competitive markets, versus the process of competition. Competitive behavior between firms exists in the competitive market model, but also in other market models that you will study in chapter 12. The distinguishing feature of the competitive model is not that competitive behaviour exists, but that firms are price takers.

3. a. An increase in the market demand for textiles would increase the market price, and induce firms to increase their quantity supplied, moving up the short run supply curve (SRS). In the short run when at least one input is fixed, this is accomplished by increasing their variable inputs. (leading to diminishing returns at the intensive margin). In the long run, all inputs will be varied to cost minimize at the new output level, and new firms will enter as the higher price allows them to be profitable (the long run supply curve, LRS). This is diminishing returns at the extensive margin.

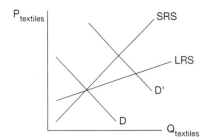

b. An increase in wage rates will shift the market supply curve to the left. Firms will decrease their quantity supplied by laying off their variable input in the short run, and varying all inputs to cost minimize in the long run. Some marginal firms, those earning the least rents before the cost increase, will exit the industry.

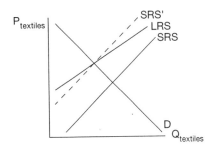

4. We may be earning zero economic profit unless you assign some value to the nonsalary benefits of the two jobs. In that case, the total benefit of teaching may exceed the higher salary from the private sector. Simple economic profit calculations often ignore nonmonetary factors, not because they are unimportant, but because they are difficult to assign a value to. Either way, we are still taking home an accounting income sufficient to keep us outfitted in pocket protectors.

5. Indefinitely. Zero economic profit means that all the resources used by that firm could not be earning a greater return anywhere else (i.e. the value of their next best alternative has already been taken into account).

6. There are two factors that suggest the magazine printing company would try to hang on longer. First, they have more firm and business specific capital, so the resale value of their assets would be lower. Second, it is unlikely that the magazine market as a whole would change very rapidly, so the retailer's fortunes are unlikely to change. For the magazine producer, however, their market could improve dramatically if their magazine suddenly "takes off" for some reason.

7. It doesn't. In fact, well functioning competitive markets are one of the last places price supports will improve resource allocation.

8. Rent seeking by rural lobbyists and the politics of winning seats in rural ridings. Also, once these policies are in place, especially quotas and subsidies, they can be very costly to dismantle.

CHAPTER 9
Property Rights and Transaction Costs

PRINCIPAL GOALS

1.0   Understand the meaning of property rights and transaction costs. (Objectives 1.1, 1.2)

2.0   Understand the implications for our model of recognizing that transaction costs are not zero. (Objectives 2.1, 2.2, 2.3, 2.4, 2.5)

3.0   Appreciate game theory as a tool for studying property rights problems. (Objective 3.1)

OBJECTIVES
Answers to bold-faced questions appear at the end of the dialogue.

"Mo, you won't believe who I ran into this weekend at the Jazz Festival on the peninsula."

"Dizzy Gillespie?"

"I wish, but that's impossible. Unfortunately he's dead Mo. I ran into Silberberg."

"Whoop-de-doo, so he listens to jazz."

"Not just listens Mo, he was playing at the festival."

"Playing? In a band? Silberberg's a musician?

"He plays the banjo. I told him I couldn't believe he was into music."

"What did he say?"

"He said, 'Do you think I was born middle-aged, teaching economics?'"

"Did you answer truthfully?" asked Mo.

"Of course not. But it gave me a lift in an otherwise upsetting two days. The shoreline is really polluted in spots by what I suspect is illegal dumping of waste. I can't believe companies can get away with that."

"It sounds like a classic example of poorly defined property rights."

OBJECTIVE 1.1 Define property rights and transaction costs.

"The legal property rights are defined." said Ginny, "Companies aren't supposed to use the ocean as a dump. The problem is enforcement."

"So it's the economic property rights that are incomplete?"

"I think so, since Chapter 9 talks about how these property rights are different. Legal rights specify the value of your property in principle, but economic rights determine that value in practice."
"But Silberberg defines property rights as 'one's ability to exercise a choice freely.' That's a bit obscure, don't you think?"

"Sort of. I find it useful to think about the right to use some property in any manner I choose, including selling it, earning income from it, and keeping others away from it," said Ginny.

"But the companies haven't been excluded from the ocean," pointed out Mo.

"No, in this case, the transaction costs of 'establishing and maintaining property rights' as he says -- of enforcing the rights of residents to pollution free water, is obviously too high."

"Since you're already speaking in definitions, why don't we do some keywords?

OBJECTIVE 1.2 Recognize definitions for the important new vocabulary.

Question 1. Match the term with its definition(s). Write out definitions for any undefined terms.

a. property rights	b. transactions costs
c. resource allocation	d. private cost
e. social cost	f. externalities
g. contracts	h. share contract
i. piece rate contract	j. fixed rent contract
k. wage contract	l. public goods
m. free rider	n. game theory
o. zero sum (game)	p. signaling
q. liability	r. joint consumption

_____ the legally or otherwise recognized "rules" which govern who is entitled to the benefits from exchange and production of resources and goods.

_____ the difference in costs between social cost and private cost.

_____ an agreement in which one party agrees to pay the other party a share of the value of the output in exchange for the rights to use the others resources.

_____ costs associated with production and resource use, which are internalized and recognized by the producer of the good.

_____ simultaneous or non-rival consumption of a single good or service by more than one person.

_____ a mathematical framework representing the situation in which two or more individuals compete for payoffs which depend on their own actions and those of their rivals.

_____ the complete, actual cost of producing a good or using a resource.

_____ an agreement in which one party agrees to pay the other party for their time spent producing a good or service.

_____ the costs of exchange that are associated with determining and ensuring exactly the nature and quality of what is being transacted.

_____ costs associated with production and resource use, which are not internalized by the producer of a good or owner of resources.

_____ one's ability to exercise a choice freely.

_____ being responsible for the costs and damage that occur in transactions and with production or resource use.

_____ a mutually agreed upon set of rules or conditions governing the exchange or transfer of rights and liabilities associated with the production and use of goods or resources.

_____ the costs of establishing and maintaining property rights.

_____ an agreement in which one party agrees to pay the other party a set, prearranged amount, that is not tied to output levels, in exchange for the use of some resource or good.

_____ goods which are consumed jointly by many people at one time, but one person's use of the good does not diminish another's use of the good.

_____ how resources end up being distributed among competing users.

_____ strategic situations where there are no mutual benefits to be gained, only exclusive gain at the expense of others.

_____ a production agreement in which one party agrees to pay the other party for each unit of a good produced.

_____ the act of one party in a potential exchange conveying to the other party some information about the service or good being exchanged through a proxy or signal.

_____ someone who would not pay for a good or service when they could not be excluded from using the good or service.

* * * * * * *

"So tell me Ginny, how do these transaction costs differ from production costs? You're obviously in your environment here."

"Ignoring your lame pun, I do enjoy this stuff. It's amazing how clearly I can think when there are no numbers involved. Transaction costs are those costs incurred before, during, or after an exchange by someone making sure that what they think they are buying or selling is in fact what they are exchanging. Like taking the time to read consumer report magazines or having a mechanic inspect a used car before you buy it."

"So these costs don't add value to the product, like production would?"

"That's right. Transaction costs change the value of the exchange. Think about a family that contracts to have an outdoor deck built. Paying labor to apply a second coat of sealant to the deck is a production cost. It adds value to the deck. But since sealant is clear, it's difficult to know when you come home at the end of the day if that second coat has been applied. So any time and resources spent by the family making sure that the second coat of sealant was applied, are transaction costs."

"Well suppose they just hired a supervisor," said Mo, "whose job it was to monitor the workers to make sure the second coat was applied. Is that a transaction cost, and does that mean that a lot of management salaries are really transaction costs, not production costs? Doesn't supervision increase the value of the product?"

"Not generally beyond what was contracted for. The family was already paying for a deck that had two coats of sealant. So I would say that the component of a manager's salary that is for monitoring and ensuring that terms of a contract are *met*, rather than adding value, could be considered a transaction cost rather than a production cost."

"So who supervises the manager? Isn't this an endless cycle of transaction costs?"

"It could be, unless the person paying for the deck seals it themselves. But clearly that's not their comparative advantage or they wouldn't have hired someone in the first place. It would be interesting to look at the ways people try to minimize these transaction costs with contracts or other incentives."

Question 2. Classify the following as transaction costs or production costs:

Counting your money after exchanging pesos for dollars at the border _____
Adding compost to your garden _____
Squeezing fruit at the market _____
Buying a guard dog _____
Buying a sheep herding dog _____
Interviewing babysitters _____

OBJECTIVE 2.1 Explain how property rights and transaction costs fit into our model, i.e. what changes and what does not.

"So how does our model handle all this?" asked Mo. "Is chapter 9 essentially introducing a new model?"

"Not at all. We're still working within the same theoretical framework because actions are still based on the same behavioral postulates: more is preferred to less, diminishing marginal value, and so on."

"If the axioms of behaviour are the same, we should end up with the same underlying demand curve."

"True," said Ginny, "its only the assumptions that change. And not the assumptions about consumers or producers *per se*, but about their *exchange*. Our model generates an equilibrium price and quantity that maximize gains from exchange. But that outcome depends on assuming that the cost of things like enforcing and instituting dumping rights and the rights to twice sealed decks were zero."

"So this chapter is about how the predictions from our model will change when we consider these transaction costs that prevent property rights from being perfectly defined."

"Basically. But let's go in steps here, because beginning with the wandering cattle example, Silberberg is actually changing two assumptions in our model, although the second is really a consequence of the first. First, that transaction costs are zero, and second that private costs are the same as social costs, that is, the producer considers all "external" costs in their decision-making. Now we are looking at our model when transaction costs and marginal external costs are positive. But let's do these changes one at a time."

"O.K.," Mo said, "let's change only the zero transaction cost assumption first. Now we recognize that it is costly for people to enforce their rights in an exchange, and you say that we will see some interesting contracts and activities arise to minimize those costs."

"That's right. These contracts mean that people will allocate resources differently than in the zero transaction cost case. Gains from trade are still exhausted, but they will be less than in the zero transaction cost case. If workers did not have to be monitored to ensure the second coat of sealant was applied, maximum gains from exchange on the deck construction would be split between the contractors and the family. With monitoring and enforcing costs, some of those gains would go to a supervisor, or maybe to no one, if, for example, the buyer decides to personally stand guard."

"Which depends on the value of that person's time versus the cost of hiring a supervisor."

"Right. The second assumption Silberberg changed is whether marginal external production costs or benefits exist or not. These are costs or benefits that "spillover" onto third parties not involved in the exchange. External costs and benefits follow from transaction costs being positive, because they arise from incomplete property rights."

"I understand negative externalities, like contaminated waste water from a pulp and paper mill," said Mo. "The mill doesn't take into account the cost of the pollution on other parties that use the river, like fishermen and swimmers, not to mention the fish. But give me an example of a positive external benefit?"

"Education and training produce external benefits. Even as we speak we're building this human capital that will have positive spillover effects for the community we live in."

"I'm going to enrich my neighbor by knowing the Coase theorem? Explaining to him how we can make a contract governing the amount of trash his kids can throw in my yard? He'd be snoozing before I was half way through."

"I think the theory is that the more education, the higher the average income, the greater the tax base, the more public services, the less crime, and so on," replied Ginny.

"So these benefits should be considered as part of the market demand or value curve, like marginal external costs are really part of the marginal cost curve. We could write: MCs = MCp + MEC (marginal social cost equals marginal private cost plus marginal external cost), MBs = MBp + MEB (marginal social benefit equals marginal private benefit plus marginal external benefit), and when MEC = 0 and MEB = 0, MCs = MCp and MBs = MBp."

"We could write that -- if we wanted to. Previously when we assumed these externalities were zero, private costs and social costs were equal, and private benefits and social benefits were equal. MC was simply called marginal cost, with no distinction made for public or private. But now MCs and MCp differ, which *can* have implications for how resources are allocated."

Question 3. Dry cleaners in Mexico City are responsible for emitting over 7,500 tons of VOC (volatile organic compounds) into the air each year. Suppose a single cleaner's private marginal costs are P = .10 + Q, where Q is pounds of clothing cleaned per day. Further, suppose that the cost of the VOC emission has been estimated at $.25 per pound of clothing. Draw the MCp and MCs curves for this typical cleaner. Indicate the MEC and equation for MCs.

What if, due to some compounding effect, the MEC increased with each pound of clothing according to: MEC = $.25Q? Draw the new MCs curve.

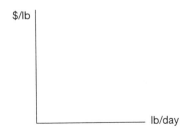

Draw a market where the MEB declines with consumption. Can you think of an example?

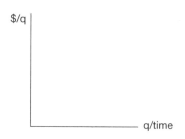

* * * * * * * *

"But I thought," said Mo, "that the whole point of the wandering cattle example, and the Coase theorem, was that as long as property rights were given to someone and the two could contract or reach some agreement, an efficient allocation of resources was still possible."

"That's true, in which case externalities don't really matter since they only arose from the incomplete property rights."

"And if property rights, or liability, aren't assigned at all?"

"Anarchy, I guess. Either the farmer would shoot all the wandering cattle, or the rancher would set fire to the crops."

"What about when externalities are not present, but transaction costs are so high that they exceed the potential gains from exchange?" asked Mo.

"Well I think it depends on the case. First of all, if you're just talking about some open access land where there's no congestion because it has little value, like some hinterland in Northern Canada, then transaction costs are uninteresting. I'm talking about the case where transaction costs impede exchange, which presumes that exchange would occur in their absence.

"Which wouldn't happen for goods that aren't scarce, because there's nothing of value to exchange."

"Right. So we're talking about scarce goods where gains from exchange are possible. Now there are still a few possibilities. First, transaction costs could simply prevent exchange. No trade, no wealth."

"What's another possibility?"

"Public goods, which I want to talk about later on. But basically exclusion costs may be so high that the good would never be provided privately because it would be too hard to charge for its use. So instead, it's provided publicly and paid for through taxes."

"But there is open access to these public goods, like parks, so won't there be congestion?"

"Sometimes, but then by definition there's congestion, and we're back to the case with the MEC > 0."

"And congestion means they've crowded onto the land, possibly until the value of their average product equals their foregone wage and all rent has been dissipated," added Mo, "which is just the common property problem Silberberg described back in Chapter 7. Is there some way we can work through a single example that illustrates each of these cases?"

"Sure, but let's do it with reference to this chart Adam gave me showing what our model predicts when the assumptions about transaction costs and externalities change."

"Adam gave you that? When did you see Adam Ginny?"

"I ran into him at the University music store. He was in the Scottish folk music section."

"Adam was in a *music* store? And he just happened to be carrying a chart on property rights? What's next? He'll suddenly discover a taste for meatloaf and turn up at the Diner with some thoughts on the nature of the firm?"

"Well if Silberberg is a banjo player, Adam can be a closet bagpipe buff. Don't be so hard on your brother. He helped me determine in each case if an efficient allocation of resources was possible."

"He was also providing a living example of signaling that Silberberg talks about in this chapter. Anyway, what definition of efficiency did you use?"

"Well basically that social marginal cost equalled social marginal benefit on the last unit exchanged. But Adam suggested that I refer to efficiency as "first-best" when I'm talking about the zero transaction cost case where mutual gains are maximized, and "second-best" for the positive transaction cost case where mutual gains are still exhausted but not as large as with zero transaction costs."

Adam's Chart on Resource Allocation

	MEC/MEB = 0	MEC/MEB > 0
TC = 0 (property rights complete)	Efficient (first-best)	Efficient (first-best)
0 < TC < gains from exchange (property rights incomplete)	Efficient (second-best)	Efficient (second-best)
0 < TC > gains from exchange (open access)	-no scarcity -no congestion	Inefficient -congestion

Here are some notes I made explaining the chart.

Row 1: TC = 0

Resource allocation is our standard Pe, Qe with gains from exchange maximized, and shared between the buyer and the seller (consumer surplus plus producer rent). If TC = 0, external costs and benefits wouldn't arise.

Row 2: 0 < TC < gains from exchange

Here transaction costs are positive, but they don't exceed the potential gains from exchange, so some contract will be formed.

Property rights are incomplete because of the positive transaction costs of assigning and enforcing those rights.

Resource allocation will be *different* than with zero transaction costs, and total gains from trade will be smaller, but the incentive will be to somehow contract around these transaction costs to realize the potential gains. This will lead to a second-best, but efficient outcome, even with external costs.

Gains from trade will be exhausted, but will be smaller compared to the base case of TC = 0.

Row 3: 0 < TC > gains from exchange (scarce goods)

Transaction costs are positive and exceed potential gains from exchange, so no contract will emerge.

Resource allocation will be *different* than with zero transaction costs, but the allocation can still be efficient if there are no external costs (no congestion). An example is the provision of some public goods. If external costs or benefits exist with open access, inefficient resource allocation will occur.

* * * * * * *

"That was actually helpful Ginny. Now I have a great example: 23,000 miles above earth is what's called the geostationary orbit. That's where you want your broadcasting and telecommunication satellites because in that orbit, their distance from earth never changes. Thirty years ago there were basically no rules, or property rights over the geostationary orbit. But it was also really only the U.S. and the U.S.S.R. putting satellites up there anyway, and there was lots of room."

"Fortunately thirty years ago geostationary orbit wasn't a scarce good because the Americans and Soviets weren't negotiating much. But since there was no congestion it didn't matter. On Adam's chart we're in Row 3, Column 1."

"But, as more countries started launching their own satellites, the geostationary orbit started getting crowded," said Mo. Satellites have to be several degrees apart, or they interfere with the signal of neighboring satellites."

"Which would be an external cost, and means MEC > 0. So now we're in a case like Row 3, Column 2."

"That's right. Well clearly, this wasn't an ideal solution. So the International Telecommunications Union decided to set up some rules in the radio regulations governing occupation of geostationary orbit."

"These rules, then, are the assignment of property rights."

"Yes! So this system, in principle is supposed to lead to an efficient allocation of the geostationary orbit." For example, it defines a category of "acceptable interference" that exists with a coordination agreement between the two satellite owners."

"So has it worked?" asked Ginny.

"Well, not yet in the opinion of most. There are some oddities with how slots are reserved, for example, that let the Kingdom of Tonga claim several prime slots when they had no satellites. Now they're trying to sell those slots to countries that may actually launch a satellite."

"Well so what? The division of the gains may not seem too fair, but at least exchange is occurring and the satellites won't be floating on top of each other so no signals are clear. As long as property rights are assigned resource allocation can be efficient."

"Well the legal rights are assigned, but the problem is that there is nobody to ultimately enforce international law. So I think some countries are going to ignore Tonga's legal orbital rights for their "paper satellites" and simply launch their own satellites into the slots."

"That's the same problem with international environmental agreements that deal with global issues like greenhouse gases."

Question 4. Answer the questions below based on the information given.

CASE 1: A homeowner grows raspberries in their backyard and sells a carton to the neighbor across the street. The buyer spends 30 cents worth of resources ensuring the berries have good color, smell and texture, and that the ones at the bottom are the same as the ones at the top. The raspberry grower's private marginal costs are 80 cents, and the neighbor's private marginal benefit is $2.00.

a. What is being exchanged here? That is what rights are being exchanged?

b. What are the transaction costs? _____ How large are the potential gains from trade here? _____ Would you expect an exchange to occur? _____

c. Suppose another neighbor didn't trust the raspberry grower, and wanted to inspect each raspberry at a cost of $1.30 in resources. Will an exchange occur? _____ Why or why not?

CASE 2: The berry growers backyard attracts insects which impede the right of their next-door neighbor to enjoy their backyards. Their next-door neighbor is forced to buy netting for their deck, which works out to about 40 cents per carton of raspberries.

d. What rights might be exchanged here? _____
e. What kind of cost is the 40 cents? _____
f. What are the true costs of growing a carton of raspberries? _____
g. Indicate whether the resource allocation will be efficient, or if too many or too few resources will be devoted to raspberry growing under the following four scenarios:

1) The raspberry grower has the right to grow whatever he wants in his backyard. There are no

transaction costs between him and his neighbor negotiating a contract.

2) The neighbor has the right to a pest-free deck. There are no transaction costs between him and his neighbor negotiating a contract.

3) The raspberry grower has the right to grow whatever he wants in his backyard. Hostility between the neighbors means that transaction costs are too high to negotiate a contract.

4) The neighbor has the right to a pest-free deck. Hostility between the neighbors means that transaction costs are too high to negotiate a contract.

OBJECTIVE 2.2 **Identify whether the other transaction cost problems in Chapter 9 lead to an efficient (first-best or second best) or inefficient allocation of resources.**

"Have you read the other property rights problems in Chapter nine?" asked Ginny.

"I have. I think the wandering cattle example is like the case of inefficient resource allocation when external costs are positive and the rancher and farmer can't negotiate a contract. Row 3, column 2 in your chart."

"But with a contract they could move to a second-best allocation of resources in row two, despite positive transaction costs and the marginal external cost."

"What about the marriage example? From the numbers in Table 9-2 the efficient result emerges regardless of whether the couple lives in a fault or no-fault state, as long as transaction costs are zero -- the Coase theorem. Since mutual gains are greatest when they are married, this is the efficient result."

"But transaction costs are not really zero," said Ginny. "In many cases, especially for women traditionally, their property rights are incomplete. Her contributions to the joint wealth of the marriage, such as putting her husband through school, raising children, or specializing in in-home work, have less value outside the marriage in the broader marketplace."

"I know, so with transaction costs her property rights are incomplete and she may or may not be able to compensate him. If she can, and they stay married, then clearly she has rights to at least $40 of her married wealth.

"Where did you get that number from?" Ginny asked.

"Because she only needs $10.01 to pay him, to make him better off staying married."

"I see. And if they end up divorcing, her rights must really be worth less than $40, that is, the transaction costs must exceed the mutual gains from marriage."

"But now I'm confused Ginny. I thought if potential gains from trade were greater than the transaction costs, a contract would be formed that led to the efficient solution. The joint gains from marriage are $100, and the transaction cost sufficient to prevent the marriage from lasting is only $10.01. $10.01 is a lot less than $100."

"But the gains from being in a marriage versus being divorced are only $10. It's not the absolute gains from marriage that are the issue, but the net gains, the gains relative to the next best alternative."

"So just the difference in the gains between being married and divorced. This situation is a little different because we have two all-or-nothing type outcomes to compare," said Mo.

"It's also a little different because I felt sort of sick for a couple of pages, and there wasn't even any math. I don't know, there's just something distasteful about this whole example."

"Was it the idea of a woman having to pay her husband to stay in the marriage, or the idea that she didn't have enough wealth to do it? A real life lesson for us Ginny -- three things we have to remember should we ever fall in love: contract, contract, contract."

OBJECTIVE 2.3 In words, graphically, and algebraically express the relationship between marginal and average.

"What about highway congestion?" continued Ginny. "Clearly that's an example of an externality arising from incomplete property rights. I think this is like the Chapter 7 example (Table 7-2) of the workers crowding onto the farm, plus a lot of MATH."

"It's also analogous to the private and social marginal cost relationship with the wandering cattle. I think the most important thing to come out of the math is equation 9-1: $MC(n+1) = AC(n+1) + n[AC(n+1) - AC(n)]$, and how it clearly shows the relationship between marginal and average cost."

"Clear as mud."

"Just plug in some numbers," said Mo. "Suppose n is car number 49. Then the equation just says that the marginal cost of the 50th car on the freeway, is the average driving time of the 50th car, plus how much they add to the average driving time of the 49 other cars, which is the difference between the average driving time with 50 cars on the freeway, and the average driving time with only 49 cars."

Question 5. Graph the average and marginal travel times in Table 9-3. What do you notice about the relationship between the AC and MC curves?

What does the vertical distance between these two curves represent for each car?

* * * * * * *

"I see, and it's this second component that the driver of the 50th car ignores. He or she only considers their average cost of driving the freeway versus their alternative routes. But their true cost when there's congestion must include how much they slow down everyone else. This second expression, the amount of driving time they impose on everyone else, is like the marginal external cost."

Question 6. There is a pedestrian tunnel network running under Carleton University that allows students to move between classes indoors. (Built because of the winters, but open all year round). The tunnel between the dorms and the student union building gets very congested sometimes, because it is a more direct route than above ground where you must walk around several buildings. The above ground route takes approximately 7 minutes. Travel time in minutes through the tunnel is given below:

Number of students	Average time	Total time	Marginal time
1	3.5	3.5	3.5
2	3.5	7.0	3.5
...			
6	3.5	21.0	3.5
7	4.0	28.0	7.0
8	4.5	___	___
9	5.0	___	___
10	5.5	___	___
11	6.0	___	___
12	6.5	___	___
13	7.0	___	___
14	7.5	___	___
15	8.0	___	___

a. Fill in the table.

b. With open access in the tunnels, how many students will take this underground route? _____

c. Is this efficient? Explain.

d. What is the efficient number of students to use the tunnel? _____

e. If students value their time at $.50 per minute, what toll could the University charge to achieve this level of use? _____

f. Graph your results (exclude total travel time).

g. Calculate the net benefits from moving to the efficient level of student traffic through the tunnels.

_____

OBJECTIVE 2.4 Distinguish the problem of congestion from the problem of exclusion with public goods.

"Next on the menu -- public goods."

"Do you suppose meatloaf is a public good?"

"Joint consumption isn't the same thing as no one wanting to consume it," said Ginny. If we're talking about goods with value, scarce goods, it means one person's consumption doesn't interfere with another person's consumption."

"Since these goods are defined as having no congestion, there can't be an externality. But I'm not clear about what this really has to do with property rights and exchange."

"According to Silberberg, 'jointness of consumption' is the attribute that makes public goods distinctive, not the property rights. It's just that public goods often suffer from high exclusion costs, which is a property rights issue. Like the geostationary orbit, and the ocean."

"So regardless of whether people can be excluded or not, if consumption is nonrival, it's a public good," said Mo. "If consumption is rival, regardless of excludability, the good is private, not public."

"The excludability will affect property rights though. If the costs of excluding are sufficiently high, chances are the State will retain property rights. Like parks with uninterrupted stretches of hiking trails. Since exclusion is difficult, a private company would have a hard time collecting enough money to make it worth their while to keep the land as a park.

"Or rights may simply be unassigned, like the ocean outside of the 200 mile zone," said Mo.

"I've often heard the ocean called a public good, and I agree that sailing your boat when there's miles between you and the next person implies no congestion. But what about going through the Panama canal? Or dumping waste that pollutes shorelines?"

"You're right, I think only certain parts and uses of the ocean are truly public. The Panama canal isn't a public good because it's congested. Furthermore, it doesn't even suffer from excludability problems. A toll for entry is charged, and rights are clearly defined and transferable. There's a treaty allowing for the gradual takeover by Panama and withdrawal of U.S. troops -- a transfer of rights."

"But when it comes to the dumping," continued Ginny, "that part or use of the ocean is no longer a public good. The companies and you can't both use that area for what you want without interfering with each other."

"So why aren't rights clearly assigned?"

"Suppose," said Ginny, "a charge of $100 per gallon of goop companies dump in the ocean would cover any cleanup costs. Now suppose there are 10 companies on the Olympic Peninsula, averaging 5 gallons of waste per week. In a zero transaction cost world that right would be worth about $5000 a week. Would you pay $5,000 for the right to collect the per gallon fee from these companies each week?"

"Not a chance, as a thinking business person. There's no way I could prevent the companies from illegally dumping. I hardly think they would come to me first to pay their $100 per gallon."

"You could patrol the waterways continuously," suggested Ginny.

"Paying two people $10 bucks an hour plus gas and boat rental for 24 hours seven days a week would probably cost me more than $5000."

"That's exactly the point Mo. The costs of enforcing your "private" rights over the ocean would be too high. With such high transaction costs, no market for trading these rights exists. So what often happens is the state maintains ownership over the property, or they set regulations, which also assigns rights."

"But state or public ownership here is due to the excludability problem, not because it's a public good."

"Correct, because as we just argued, in many cases it is not."

Question 7. Which of the following are public goods? Explain why or why not.

The legal system
Interstate highways
FM radio frequencies
Central Park in New York
Protection under the Constitution
Views of Mt. Rainier (Washington, USA)
Cable channels
Champs Elysees in Paris

OBJECTIVE 2.5 **Vertically sum demand curves, and explain why this is the appropriate method of determining aggregate demand for public goods.**

"Do you understand," asked Mo, "why it doesn't make sense to sum demand curves horizontally for public goods?"

"Sure, because summing horizontally is saying at some price, how much total quantity. But with public goods, once some quantity is provided, everyone can simultaneously consume it. I understand why we *don't* add up horizontally, across quantities; but not why we add up vertically."

"Because that's the only other choice? Why don't we try one of Adam's old questions on this."

> **Problem:** The town of Carlsbad in the Czech Republic lies above a spring whose water many Czech people believe has restorative powers. Each day residents of Carlsbad "take the cure" by drinking from the endlessly flowing spring wells along main street. There are two groups of spring water drinkers, the elderly and sick (e) who consider the water medicine, and the young (y) who believe they are immortal but just want to ensure it. Their respective monthly demand curves are: $Q_e = 5 - P$, and $Q_y = 6 - 2P$.
>
> a. Draw their individual demand curves.
> b. Draw in their market demand curve for this public good.
> c. What is the algebraic expression of the market demand curve for Q < 5? _____
> For Q > 5? _____
> d. If the price of spring maintenance is zero, what is the efficient amount of spring water for the city to provide? _____
> e. If price of spring maintenance is $5.00 per month, how much water should the city provide?
> _____
> f. What drinking fee can they charge each group? _____, _____

"O.K.," suggested Mo, "the first thing I think we should do is rewrite their demand curves with P on the left hand side -- as inverse demand curves. It's easiest to graph with them in that form anyway."

"So that means just rewriting them as $P = 5 - Q_e$, and $P = 3 - .5Q_y$."

"Now when we draw them, we know 5 will be the vertical intercept for the elderly, with a slope of -1, and 3 will be the vertical intercept for the young, with a slope of -.5."

"And the market demand is the vertical sum, so 8 for the vertical intercept. How do I get the slope?"

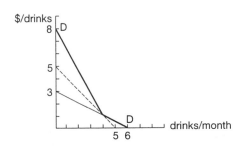

"Well two ways. Notice that at Q = 5, the elderly are satiated; they don't want any more water even at a price of 0. So the market demand curve becomes the same as the young's demand curve for all quantities greater than Q = 5. So you can just draw the market demand curve beginning at P = 8, down to where it hits the young demand curve at Q = 5, and then continue down to the horizontal intercept on the young's demand curve."

"What's my other choice."

"Similar, but solve algebraically for market demand. For Q < 50, (inverse) demand is P = (5-Qe) + (3-.5Q) = 8 -1.5Q. For Q > 50 it is just the young's demand curve: P = 3-.5Q."

"O.K. I've drawn that in. It seems to mean that if MC is zero, as much water as anyone wants should be provided. That would be 6 units," said Ginny.

"Which is the same thing as setting MC = 0, which would be a line along the horizontal intercept."

"And if MC = 5.00, we should sub that into the market demand curve to find the optimal level of water?"

"Right, 5 = 8 - 1.5Q, so Q = 2 per month."

"How do we find out how much each group would be willing to pay," asked Ginny.

"I think we just go back to their individual demand curves to find their marginal value for 2 units. In that case, the elderly would pay P = 5 - 2 = \$3, and the young would pay P = 3 - .5(2) = \$2."

"And \$3 + \$2 = \$5 = MC, which makes sense."

OBJECTIVE 3.1 **Work through a payoff matrix to find the outcomes under different assumptions about transaction costs.**

"OK, what about the prisoner's dilemma," asked Mo.

"I think this differs from the previous cases. The wandering cattle and divorce story were examples of how transaction costs could lead to a different allocation of resources than in a zero transaction cost world, and how contracts arose to try to minimize those costs. Likewise with the theory of the firm, but it gives us some specific examples of different contracts such as sharecropping to reduce resource exploitation, or piece-rate contracts to avoid shirking."

"And public goods are a distinct type of good, that happen to often be associated with the property rights problem of not being able to exclude others."

"Right. But the prisoner's dilemma isn't another example of a property rights problem," said Ginny. "Rather, it's a framework for understanding other examples -- specifically, for understanding how we can end up at a solution other than the one that yields the highest mutual gains."

"You mean, why as individuals we sometimes end up not doing what is in our best interest? Like cutting off our nose to spite our face?"

"Only sort of, because we're not trying to spite anything. We're trying to maximize our well-being, it's just that in the presence of some transaction costs we don't get to the first-best solution."

Question 8. Slick and Dick are partners in a private eye company. Every time they take on a case, they know that they can solve the most crimes each month if they pursue separate leads, and then meet back to share their information. Since each is by themselves, however, there is a great temptation to stop at the local pub while their partner skulks down dark back alleys. The payoff matrix below shows the revenue to their company from the number of crimes they solve each month, and the value of their pleasure sitting at the pub.

		Slick	
		Pursue leads	Pub
Dick	Pursue leads	100,100	-25,120
	Pub	140,-20	0,0

a. If Slick and Dick can costlessly monitor each other, what outcome will result?

b. Is this the efficient solution? Explain.

c. If each person tries to do what is in their own best interest, considering the action of the other, what will be the outcome?

d. Since mutual gains are greatest when each does their job, what type of contract might Slick and Dick arrange?

* * * * * * *

"So, you think Adam was signaling?" asked Ginny.

"No question. He was trying to give you some information that he would find excruciatingly difficult to give you in a straightforward way."

"That information being?"

"Playing stupid doesn't wash right now Ginny. You just explained an entire property rights chapter to me."

"Your brother's actually a nice guy Mo, but I worry about what choosing to become an Economics major signals about his personality."

"Well he'd certainly understand if you wanted to sign a prenuptial agreement."

"Would he understand if I turned into a raving environmentalist?"

"Sure, if you're raving rationally. We've just talked about how incomplete property rights can lead to too much pollution."

"But here's my problem Mo. I think that even when property rights can be assigned and enforced, and we can establish markets like transferable emission permits for air pollution, that we may not have an efficient allocation of resources."

"Blasphemy! You're disagreeing with the Coase theorem? I don't think Adam could live with that if it counters our basic postulates of behavior. Better to ask him to personally take a vow of poverty than to suspend his belief in the model's axioms of behavior."

"I'm not disagreeing with the Coase theorem -- because I don't think transactions costs are zero. I think that we undervalue environmental resources because of information costs -- scientifically, we don't know enough about the true costs of say, driving a species to extinction."

"That's because there's not enough spotted owls sitting in Congress."

"Or people representing future generations. We need those *Back to the Future* time machines. Too bad Michael J. Fox is Canadian and can't run for office."

"He's not really from the future Ginny."

"No kidding Mo."

ANSWERS TO DIALOGUE QUESTIONS

Question 1. Vocabulary: a, f, h, d, r, n, e, k, b, f, a, q, g, b, j, l, c, o, i, p, m.

Question 2.   Recounting your money: transaction cost
          Adding compost to your garden: production cost
          Squeezing fruit at the market: transaction cost
                Buying a guard dog: transaction cost
          Buying a sheep herding dog: production cost
          Interviewing babysitters: transaction cost

Question 3.

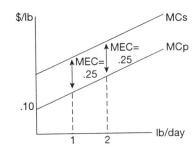 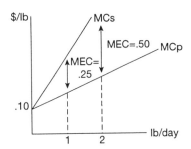

With MCp, P = .10 + Q, and MEC = .25   With MCp, P = .10 + Q, and MEC = $.25Q

MEB declines with consumption below. An example might be listening to your neighbor (who plays well) practice the violin.

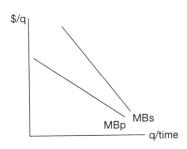

Question 4.
a. The market is for the exchange of private rights to consume, or otherwise, the carton of raspberries.
b. The transaction costs are 30 cents. The potential gains from trade are $2.00 - $.80 = $1.20 so yes,

an exchange is expected.
c. No exchange will occur.
d. The market is exchanging the right to grow berries (an activity) and to enjoy the backyard.
e. The 40 cents is a marginal external cost.
f. True costs of growing a carton of raspberries are $1.20.
g. 1) The resulting resource allocation will be efficient.
   2) The resulting resource allocation will be efficient.
   3) The resulting resource allocation will be inefficient with too many resources devoted to growing raspberries.
   4) The resulting resource allocation will be inefficient with too few resources devoted to growing raspberries.

Question 5. When AC is horizontal, MC must also be horizontal, and AC = MC. As AC begins to rise, MC must be above it (rise faster) to continue pulling up the average.

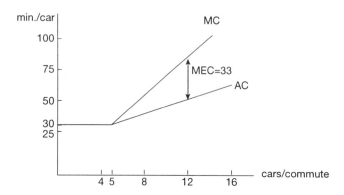

The vertical distance between these two curves represents the MEC (marginal external cost) for each car. For example, for the 12th car, the MEC is $33 ($84-$51).

Question 6.
a. Number of students	Average time	Total time	Marginal time
1	3.5	3.5	3.5
2	3.5	7.0	3.5
...			
6	3.5	21.0	3.5
7	4.0	28.0	7.0
8	4.5	36.0	8.0
9	5.0	45.0	9.0
10	5.5	55.0	10.0
11	6.0	66.0	11.0
12	6.5	78.0	12.0
13	7.0	91.0	13.0
14	7.5	105.0	14.0
15	8.0	120.0	15.0

b. With open access, 13 students will take the tunnel.

c. This is not efficient because their marginal cost exceeds the time it takes to use the alternative route.

d. It is efficient for 7 students to use the tunnel.

e. A $3.00 toll would achieve this level of use.

f. The graph looks like:

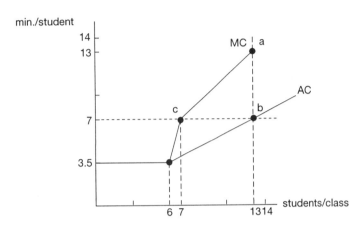

g. The net benefits from moving to the efficient level of tunnel traffic are triangle abc, where MC > P, 1/2[(13-7)(13-7)]= $18.

Question 7. Views of Mt. Rainier and protection under the constitution are almost always a public good. Cable channels and radio frequencies are not. The legal system, interstate highways, Central Park in New York, and the Champs Elysees in Paris are probably not public goods by day, when there is congestion, but are by night.

Question 8.

a. Both will pursue leads for a payoff of 100,100.

b. This is the efficient solution because mutual gains are greatest, which is the outcome that must prevail with zero transaction costs.

c. If each person tries to do what is in their individual best interest they will both go to the pub.

d. They might hire someone to monitor them, carry walkie talkies, etc.

THE BIG PICTURE

The perfectly competitive model of the previous chapters operates under the assumption that property rights are perfectly defined because transactions costs are zero. Everybody knows everything about what is being exchanged. This is done because these assumptions permit a more theoretically precise explanation for consumer and producer behavior. Given complete information and facing all of the private and social costs of production, a producer will hire inputs as the theory predicts and produce a quantity exactly up to the point where the price he gets for his product is equal to the marginal costs of producing it. The consumer understands exactly what she is buying and gets full rights to the goods she purchases; there is no waste associated with gathering information about the good or the producer.

In Chapter 9, Silberberg drops the assumptions of zero transactions costs and perfectly defined property rights to reveal scenarios in which we seldom get complete rights over the good exchanged or act in complete confidence as to the quality and nature of the good. The same behavioral axioms and analytical methods apply as in the previous chapters, but we might anticipate different responses in several ways, for example, the quantity of inputs hired by producers, the quantity of output supplied by producers, and the quantity demanded by consumers, among others. These different responses, in response to maximizing behavior facing positive transactions costs, leads to a different allocation of resources than in the case where property rights are perfectly defined. It is nature of these differences that is of interest in Chapter 9.

The study of individual and firm behavior under this new set of assumptions regarding property rights and transaction costs is an emerging field of inquiry within economics. This inquiry occurs within the basic economic paradigm but offers a new perspective beyond the traditional analysis to look at the exchange of rights over a good, rather than the exchange of the good itself. This approach is important for addressing a range of questions and issues that are not well handled by the zero transaction cost model.

REVIEW QUESTIONS

Answers to all review questions appear at the end of this chapter.

PROBLEMS AND EXERCISES
Write your answer in the space(s) provided.

1. Fred Flintstone raises brontosauria on his ranch in Bedrock. Barney Rubble owns a rockaberry farm next door. Fred's brontos are forever crashing the fence dividing his and Barney's property, to snack on Barney's prize rockaberries. Barney is furious. He needs the best rockaberries to win the Blue Ribbon bake-off. Column 2 indicates the marginal cost of maintaining each additional bronto.

No.of brontos	Marginal Private Cost	Marginal Crop Damage	Marginal Social Cost
1	$200	$100	_____
2	$250	$100	_____
3	$300	$100	_____
4	$350	$100	_____
5	$400	$100	_____
6	$450	$100	_____
7	$500	$100	_____
8	$550	$100	_____
9	$600	$100	_____
10	$650	$100	_____

a. Fill in the marginal social cost for each bronto.
b. Assume the market price for brontos is $500. How many brontos will Fred produce if:
    1) he is not liable for damages to Barney's rockaberries? _____
    2) he is liable for all damages? _____
c. Draw a graph indicating the MCp, MCs, and the level of output in each case.

d. If Fred is not liable, but he and Barney are able to negotiate a contract, how many brontos will Fred raise? _____
e. Is this the pareto efficient amount? _____

f. What theorem does this result illustrate? _____

g. If Fred was not liable, what price range could Barney offer to prevent Fred from producing beyond a pareto efficient level? _____

2. Amy owns a cafe/bookstore. Which of the following are transaction costs in Amy's business:

_____ hourly wages for her staff
_____ glass windows so customers can see the food being prepared fresh
_____ food stuff from wholesalers
_____ a timeclock to track staff hours
_____ books from publishers
_____ daily fee for 6:00 am delivery of the morning newspapers
_____ mirrors to monitor her staff and the customers

3.   Determine the most appropriate method by which the following activities should be paid - sharecropping, piece-rate, hourly wage or salary. Briefly explain your reasoning.

a. blueberry pickers

b. fir-tree planters

c. Gene Silberberg, Economics professor

d. Macdonald Jr., farmer on his father's farm land

e. Dr. Quincy, medical doctor

f. a wordprocessor operator

g. assembly line workers at a GM plant

h. Joe Carter, professional baseball player

i. Management Consultant at an accounting firm

4. Mrs. Rachel Lynde washes her clothes in the brook just upstream from the Cuthbert property. The Cuthberts tried to convince Mrs. Lynde that this practice was contaminating their water supply. Lynde argued that the brook was on her property, and therefore, she could do what she liked. The Cuthberts thought the brook was on their property, and did not feel their neighbour had any right to dirty it.

a. Is the brook a public good? Explain why/why not.

b. Do the Cuthberts and Mrs. Lynde each hold private legal property rights to the section of brook on their land? Do they also hold economic property rights? Discuss.

c. What rights (specifically) are incomplete? _____
Hint** This situation could not have been addressed even if the property deeds had clearly stated on whose property the brook was located.

5. With no traffic congestion, Burnaby commuters take 20 minutes via the Lougheed Highway to get to work in downtown Vancouver. With congestion, it takes longer. By side streets would take 60 minutes to get downtown.

a. Fill in the blanks in the following table. tt is travel time.

No.of cars	Average tt (mins)	total tt (mins)	marginal tt (mins)
1	20	20	20
2	20	40	20
.	.	.	.
.	.	.	.
7	20	140	20
8	24	___	___
9	28	___	___
10	32	___	___
11	36	___	___
12	40	___	___
13	44	___	___
14	48	___	___
15...	52	___	___

b. What is the impact of the 8th car on the highway? _____ the 9th? _____ the 10th? _____.
c. Explain how the equation for MC on page 20 (equation 9-1), indicates the difference between marginal cost and average cost?

d. At what point is the average commute on the highway the same as on the side streets? _____
e. Is it efficient (socially) for the 10th driver to take Lougheed highway to work? Why or why not?

f. What is the economically efficient level of highway use in this case? _____
g. Why does highway congestion occur in the first place? What might be some possible solutions to alleviating highway congestion?

6. (Refer to problem 5) Assume all the drivers in the previous problem made $12.00 per hour or $0.20 per minute. Suppose the highway is privately owned.
a. The toll that would result in the efficient number of drivers taking the highway is, _____.
b. How much will the owner collect in total tolls? _____

7. The Cuthbert's cows escaped trampling Mrs. Lynde's rose garden and every flower bed between Green Gables and Avonlea. The marginal and average cost curves for raising cattle are below (you can

think of marginal cost as representing social marginal cost, and average cost as private marginal cost.)

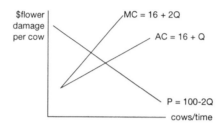

a. Compared to Question 1, what is different about the marginal external cost here?

b. If the town of Avonlea has no recourse when the cows destroy their flowers, how many cows will the Cuthberts raise? _____
c. What is the marginal external cost of this many cows? _____
d. Is this Pareto efficient? Why/why not?

e. If the town can bribe the Cuthberts to raise fewer cows, what price range must the bribe be in to reduce the number of cows by one? (Note that price is also not constant here, but rather must be determined using the demand curve) _____
f. How many cows will end up being raised? _____
g. What is the total net gain from the reduction in cows? _____

8. Anne values the public park near Green Gables at P = 10 - Q. Mrs. Lynde's value of that same park is P = 15 - Q. Anne and Mrs. Lynde can jointly consume the park without interfering with each other.

a. The park is a _____ good.
b. Below, draw in Anne and Mrs. Lynde's (inverse) demand curves for this park. Now draw in the aggregate demand curve for these two.

c. What is the algebraic expression of this aggregate demand curve for Q < 10? for Q > 10?

d. If the marginal cost of providing the park is zero, what is the optimal amount of park to provide?

_____

9. Suppose Matthew and Marilla Cuthbert have decided to spruce up the park and take over park maintenance. They estimate their marginal costs at a constant $9 per month.
a. What is the optimal amount of park to provide now? _____
b. If Matthew and Marilla decided to charge a monthly entrance fee to the park, how much could they charge Anne? _____   Mrs. Rachel Lynde? _____

10. Matthew and Marilla Cuthbert love to play "Hide and Seek". Marilla hides upstairs or downstairs, and Matthew can look upstairs or downstairs, but not both places. If Matthew finds Marilla downstairs he gets one scoop of ice cream, but if he finds her upstairs he gets four scoops of ice cream. If Matthew finds Marilla she gets no ice cream, if he doesn't find her she gets two scoops and he gets nothing.
a. Construct the "payoff matrix" for this game.

		Marilla	
		Downstairs	Upstairs
Matthew	Downstairs	____,____	____,____
	Upstairs	____,____	____,____

b. Is there an "equilibrium" strategy that dominates as the likely outcome if each player is trying to make themselves as well off as possible, given the action of the other? Explain.

c. Is there a strategy that maximizes mutual benefits? If so, which one is it? _____

d. With zero transactions costs, which outcome would be realized? _____ Why?

11. Hank hired 10 farm hands during the haying season. The value of total output produced by the 10 workers was $800; and the total labour costs per worker was $50. What is Hank's total share of output?

TRUE - FALSE QUESTIONS
Provide a one or two sentence explanation with your answer.

1. Positive transaction costs change the behavioral postulates of our model.

2. Our model will predict a different resource allocation with positive transaction costs than with zero transaction costs.

3. As long as transaction costs are positive, property rights can never be complete.

4. The Coase theorem states that with zero transaction costs, the distribution of the gains from trade

will be the same, regardless of the assignment of liability.

5.   If the marginal external pollution costs of a pulp and paper plant exceed the marginal private gains at the quantity produced, then the marginal social cost is less than the market price.

6.   The Coase Theorem implies that if Fred and Barney cannot negotiate a mutually beneficial agreement, Fred will produce brontos at the output level where marginal social cost equals market price.

7.   Tom owns a strawberry farm and an apple orchard. Regardless of the season, he pays his employees on a piece-rate basis. This type of contract is the most effective way of paying his farm hands.

8.   Transaction costs affect the size, the degree of specialization of firms, and the type of contracts employers write with their employees.

9.   An inability to exclude "free riders" and jointness of consumption characterize a public good.

10.   If the cost of enforcing your legal property right is too high (exceeds the value of that right), you do not hold economic property rights over that asset.

MULTIPLE CHOICE QUESTIONS
Choose the best answer.

1. If Old MacDonald employs 100 farmhands on his 100 acre establishment, and Farmer Brown employs 20 helpers on his farm of 20 acres, one would expect to see
a.   a higher incidence of sharecropping on Old MacDonald's farm.
b.   Farmer Brown more likely to pay his help an hourly wage.
c.   Equal amounts of sharecropping on both farms.
d.   a higher incidence of sharecropping on Farmer Brown's farm.
e.   a and b

2. The Coase Theorem states:
a.   if two parties are unable to negotiate a mutually beneficial contract, then MSC=P.
b.   if an individual or firm whose production processes imposes social costs on others was not liable for those costs, a pareto efficient level of production is still possible.
c.   farmers should always be conscious of the costs of production imposed on their neighbours.
d.   resources will be allocated efficiently between two parties and the income of each party will remain unchanged.

3. Piece-rate contracts:
a.   are the most efficient method of paying employees in the agricultural sector.
b.   discourage employees from shirking.

c. work only if output is easily measured.
d. c and d.
e. all of the above.

4. A public good is one which
a. is jointly consumed.
b. is often state provided.
c. the consumption of the particular good does not detract from the ability of another person to use or consume the good.
d. the exclusion of nonpayers of the good is often impossible.
e. all of the above.

5. The efficient production level of a public good is:
a. where the marginal cost of production equals the market price of the good or the consumer's marginal value of that good.
b. where marginal cost equals the horizontal sum of the consumers' marginal values.
c. where marginal cost equals the vertical sum of the consumers' marginal values.
d. where the public good is sold on a per unit or fee for service basis.

6. The Coase theorem says that
a. With perfectly defined property rights, the gains from trade are maximized.
b. With zero transaction costs, the gains from trade are maximized.
c. With positive transaction costs, the gains from trade are not exhausted.
d. a and b
e. b and c

7. Externalities occur when
a. economic property rights are complete
b. resources are underallocated to goods with negative spillover effects
c. individuals base their decisions on marginal costs
d. individuals base their decisions on average costs

8. The economically efficient amount of pollution is
a. zero.
b. where private marginal cost equals private marginal benefit.
c. probably higher than what we have now.
d. positive.

9. Public goods are often provided by the State because
a. they provide benefits to a large group of people.
b. it is difficult to exclude nonpayers.
c. their real value is less than their cost.
d. none of the above.

The Campbell and MacDonald clans feuded in Western Scotland for years. Each spent valuable resources guarding their barley fields and property to deter raids by the other. These resources would otherwise have been devoted to brewing scotch whiskey (brewed from barley). They often contemplated a truce. Their payoff in gallons of whiskey from cheating, and not cheating on the truce is given below:

		MacDonald's	
		Cheat	Don't cheat
Campbells	Cheat	12,10	23,5
	Don't cheat	5,19	16,15

Refer to the payoff matrix to answer questions 10 through 14.

10. With zero transaction costs, the outcome will be:
a. Both will cheat.
b. The MacDonald's will cheat, the Campbell's will not.
c. The Campbell's will cheat, the MacDonald's will not.
d. Neither will cheat.

11. With positive transaction costs, and each maximizing their position given the action of the other, the outcome will be:
a. Both will cheat.
b. The MacDonald's will cheat, the Campbell's will not.
c. The Campbell's will cheat, the MacDonald's will not.
d. Neither will cheat.

12. The difference between the cheat/cheat and the don't cheat/don't cheat outcome is that:
a. gains from trade are not exhausted in the cheating outcome.
b. efficiency only occurs with the non-cheating solution.
c. mutual gains are smaller in the cheating outcome.
d. a and c.

13. The cheat/cheat outcome would result regardless of transaction costs, if its minimum payoff was:
a. 17,15   b. 17,16   c. 18,15   d. 19,16

14. The difference between the clans appears to be:
a. the Campbell's are more honest than the MacDonald's.
b. the MacDonald's are better whiskey brewers.
c. the Macdonald's have more to gain, on net, from a truce.
d. we can deduce none of the above from a payoff matrix.

15. We would expect a firm that was not going to engage in opportunistic behaviour to be more likely to advertise if it was selling
a. posters and prints.
b. lifetime memberships to a fitness club.
c. razorblades.
d. haircuts.

16. Brand names are more likely for products
a. whose attributes are difficult for consumers to measure.
b. whose quality is homogenous.
c. that are sold in small markets.
d. a and b.

17. Contracts and regulations
a.   are types of transaction costs.
b.   are types of production costs.
c.   always reduce wealth.
d.   assign property rights.

18. Most parts of Banff National Park are a public good because
a.   non payers cannot be excluded.
b.   it is owned by the Canadian government.
c.   one person's use of it doesn't interfer with another's.
d.   all of the above.

SHORT ANSWER QUESTIONS

1. Stora Forest Industry, of Sweden, operates a subsidiary pulp and paper mill in Point Tupper, Nova Scotia. The company has threatened to move its operations if the provincial government does not subsidize the cost of refitting the plant so that it complies with federal and provincial pollution emission standards. From an economic point of view, why has the company been able to pollute the environment? How could a clearer delineation of property rights alleviate the situation?

2. The electromagnetic frequency (the airwaves or the radio spectrum) are often called a public good and licenses are issued for its use, often free of charge. Do you agree that the specturm is a public good? Why or why not? Do you think this may have changed since the first radio message was sent in 1905.

3. Explain how the Coase theorem altered the previous economic analysis of "externalities"?

4. Elissa was working on a short-term contract in Beijing for AT&T. She knew crafts were cheaper in China than at home, and wanted to purchase some handwoven tablecloths for her friends. What are the advantages and disadvantages of paying the craftsperson an hourly wage or on a piece-rate basis?

5. The Sunflower Cafe, in Circle, Alaska, makes its muffins out of soy milk. The only soy milk wholesaler in the North is in Anchorage, over 1000 km away. The price plus delivery must be negotiatied. It is based on the wholesaler's claim regarding their costs for the soy milk, the trip conditions, etc. Before each delivery the Cafe owner gathers as much information as possible about weather, fuel costs, soybean prices etc., to be in a decent bargaining position. If you owned the Sunflower Cafe, is there any incentive to try to merge with the soymilk wholesaler? Why or why not? Can you suggest any other possibilities?

ANSWERS TO REVIEW QUESTIONS

Answers to PROBLEMS AND EXERCISES

1. a. Marginal Social Cost equals Marginal Private Cost plus the Marginal Crop Damage (the external cost) of $100.

No.of brontos	Marginal Private Cost	Marginal Social Cost	Private Rent (P - MPC)
1	$200	$300	$300
2	$250	$350	$250
3	$300	$400	$200
4	$350	$450	$150
5	$400	$500	$100
6	$450	$550	$50
7	$500	$600	$0
8	$550	$650	
9	$600	$700	
10	$650	$750	

b. 1) If the market price for brontos is $500 Fred will produce 7 (where P = MCp) if he is not liable for damages.

   2) He will produce 5 (where P = MCs) if he is liable for all damages.

c. The graph looks as below:

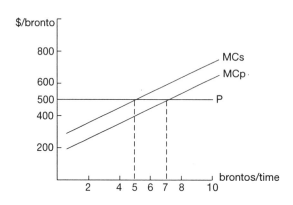

d. If Fred is not liable, but he and Barney are able to negotiate a contract, he will raise 5 brontos.

e. Yes, this the pareto efficient amount.

f. This result illustrates the Coase theorem.

g. If Fred was not liable, Barney would have to pay Fred something greater than $50 (Fred's rent) to not raise the 6th cow, and any amount greater than $0 to not raise the second. Barney's maximum price would be $100, the marginal external cost per bronto. The Coase Theorem predicts that because the loser loses more than the gainer gains, only 5 brontos will end up produced and the position of at least one of the groups will be improved.

2. The transaction costs, those having to do with ensuring the rights exchanged are those contracted for by both parties, are: glass windows so customers can see the food being prepared fresh, a timeclock to track staff hours, and mirrors to monitor her new staff.

3. I would choose the following methods to pay the activities listed: - sharecropping, piece-rate, hourly wage or salary.

a. blueberry pickers: hourly wage because blueberries are fragile.
b. fir-tree planters: piece-rate because fir trees are not and speed does not create much of a problem.
c. Gene Silberberg, Economics professor: salary, because his output is heterogenous and not easily counted.
d. Macdonald Jr., farmer on Old Macdonald's land: maybe sharecropping, but it would depend on the crop, if the son might under report the crop, and if the son would eventually inherit the land (so he would not exploit the soil).
e. Dr. Quincy, medical doctor: hourly wage because you don't want her to rush.
f. a wordprocessor operator: maybe piece-rate because quality is easily discernible and easy to fix.
g. assembly line workers at a GM plant: probably hourly
h. Joe Carter, professional baseball player: salary, because his output is varied and not easy to count, though he could be paid piece-rate bonuses for different components of it like home runs or RBI's.
i. Management Consultant: hourly or salary, depending on if they were being paid for overtime or not.

4. a. The brook is not a public good because their use interferes with each other.
b. No, economic property rights are incomplete. This situation could exist despite property deeds clearly stating whose property the brook was located on.
c. Specifically, the right to exclude others seem to be too costly to enforce.

5. a.

No. of cars	Average tt (mins)	total tt (mins)	marginal tt (mins)
1	20	20	20
2	20	40	20
3	20	60	20
4	20	80	20
5	20	100	20
6	20	120	20
7	20	140	20
8	24	192	52
9	28	252	60
10	32	320	68
11	36	-	-
12	40	-	-
13	44	-	-
14	48	-	-
15	52	-	-

b. Marg. cost is the 8th car's impact: (7x4)+24=52, for the 9th MC is 60, and for the 10th MC is 68.
c. The difference between average cost and marginal cost is the addition to other traveler's commute

time that MC considers: $n[AC_{n+1} - AC_n]$.

d. At 17 cars the average commute on the Lougheed highway would be the same as on the side streets.

e. No, it is not efficient for the 10th driver to take Lougheed highway to work because their marginal cost (which considers their effect on others) is greater than the marginal cost of the side street.

f. 9 cars, where MC equals the alternative (60 min.) is the economically efficient level of highway use.

g. Highway congestion occurs because individuals are not forced to pay for the true cost of their highway use. This is a common property problem -- property rights are poorly assigned.

h. Possible solutions to alleviating highway congestion are assigning private rights to the highway, in which case a toll will be charged, or have the State charge some type of toll.

6. a. The toll that would result in the efficient number of drivers is the value of the difference between AC and MC for the 9th driver, which is 32 minutes at $.20 per minute, or $6.40.

  b. $6.40 * 9 = $57.60.

7. a. Instead of being constant, the MEC rises with the number of cows. This suggests that as the number of cows rises, the flower-destroying behavior of each cow gets worse.

b. If the town of Avonlea has no recourse, the Cuthberts will raise 28 cows, the Q where Demand equals AC [100 - 2Q = 16 + Q].

c. The marginal external cost of this number of cows is the difference between MC and AC, $MC = 16 + 2(28) = 72, and $AC = 16 + (28) = 44, so $28.

d. This is not Pareto efficient, because MC does not equal P.

e. A bribe would have to be some amount between the MEC of $28 to the town and the Cuthbert's profit on the 28th cow which is $0. For the 28th cow, the profit would be price minus AC, or $44 [P = 100 - 2(28)] minus $44 [AC = 16 + 28].

f. The gap between AC and MC implies that with zero transactions costs, a mutually beneficial bribe will exist between the number of cows where AC = P, and the number of cows raised where MC = P. The town will be able to make it worth the Cuthbert's while to reduce the cows to 21, where MC = P.

g. The total net gain is the triangle where MC exceeded MV (demand), 1/2[MEC * (Qp - Qs)], 1/2[$28 * (28-21)] = $98.

8. a. public

b. The aggregate demand curve is the vertical sum of the individual curves. The vertical intercept is 25. At Q = 10, Anne does not want any more park (even if P = 0), so the aggregate demand curve past this point is simply Mrs. Lynde's demand curve.

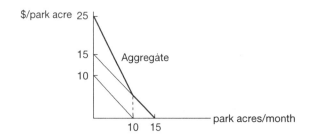

c. For Q < 10, the aggregate demand curve is P = (10 - Q) + (15 - Q) = 25 - 2Q. For Q > 10 it is just Mrs. Lynde's demand curve, P = 15 - Q.
d. If MC = 0, the optimal amount of park to provide is 15 units, where Aggregate demand equals 0.

9. a. If MC = 9, the optimal Q is 25 - 2Q = 9, Q = 8.
   b. Now use their individual demand curves: at Q = 8, Anne is willing to pay $P = $10 - 8 = $2, and Mrs. Rachel Lynde will pay $P = $15 - 8 = $7.

10. a. Construct the "payoff matrix" for this game.

		Downstairs	Marilla Upstairs
Matthew	Downstairs	1,0	0,2
	Upstairs	0,2	4,0

b. No, because reading across Matthew going downstairs first: if Marilla chooses downstairs, Matthew is better off downstairs; if she chooses upstairs, he is better off upstairs. Now read across Matthew going upstairs for each action of Marilla: if she goes downstairs he is better off downstairs, if she goes upstairs he is better off upstairs. So his best strategy varies with what she does, and the same is true for her.
c. Both parties upstairs would maximize mutual benefits.
d. With zero transactions costs this would be the outcome if they have agreed to somehow share the ice cream, because Matthew would be better off with half than any of his alternatives, and Marilla would be no worse off.

11. Hank's total share of output is 37.5% (800 - 500/800).

Answers to TRUE - FALSE QUESTIONS

1. False. Positive transaction costs change the constraints or assumptions of our model, not the behavioral postulates.

2. True. By definition if transactions costs are positive, contracting between parties is not costless. Therefore maximizing subject to transaction costs will produce a different distribution of resources than in maximizing behavior when transaction costs are zero.

3. True. Only with zero transaction costs are property rights complete.

4. False. The Coase theorem states that with zero transaction costs gains from trade will be maximized, regardless of the liability assignment, but the assignment of rights will affect how those gains are shared.

5. False. "... where the marginal damage exceeds the marginal private gains, occurs when and only when, the marginal social cost function... exceeds the market price..." (p. 9-6).

6. False. Fred will produce where marginal private cost=price.

7. False. Payments would end up varying considerably over the year, and zero outside of harvest season. Also you may be encouraging too rapid picking of delicate strawberries in their high season.

8. True. Transactions costs affect a firm's contracts with their customers, input suppliers, and workers.

9. False. The inability to enforce exclusion is a question not of jointness of consumption, but of enforcing property rights.

10. True. Your ability to derive the full value of those rights is diminished.

Answers to MULTIPLE CHOICE QUESTIONS

1. e	5. c	9. b	13. a	17. d
2. b	6. d	10. d	14. c	18. c
3. d	7. d	11. a	15. b	
4. e	8. d	12. c	16. a	

Answers to SHORT ANSWER QUESTIONS

1. Prior to setting the standards, property rights over the waterways were not assigned, leading to the common property result where Stora Forest did not consider the cost of their actions on others. A clearer delineation of property rights with standards and regulations establishes liability, so that Stora will have to recognize the external costs they are creating. Enforcement, however, may continue to be a problem.

2. The spectrum is actually quite crowded, with significant competition for frequency rights. It is not, therefore, a public good. With fewer uses of the spectrum in 1905 it may have been a public good.

3. The Coase theorem showed that an efficient allocation of resources could occur, even in the presence of "externalities", if property rights were perfectly defined, i.e. if transaction costs were zero. This result highlighted that externalities were property rights problems, and that a more complete assignment of rights is one method of moving toward a more efficient allocation of resoures.

4. The problem with piece-rate is ensuring quality: that the craftsperson did not rush the work or "cut corners". On the other hand, with an hourly wage the craftsperson might shirk by working too slowly. Since it would be difficult to monitor, they could even do other tasks that I ended up being charged for. Not knowing how long it should take to handweave a tablecloth increases the disadvantage of the hourly wage. On net, if I were Elissa my choice would depend on the cost of variable quality versus not being able to monitor the work.

5. Yes, there is an incentive to merge. If I owned the cafe I would want to secure a soymilk supply in some manner that prevented me from being "held hostage" by the supplier and having to incur the costs of gathering information each time to buoy up my negotiating position (and the costs of negotiating). Other possibilities include signing a long term fixed price contract, or becoming your own supplier by dealing directly with the wholesaler's supplier.

CHAPTER 10
Interest Rates and Capital Values

PRINCIPAL GOALS

1.0　Understand why people attempt to smooth their consumption over time. (Objectives 1.1, 1.2, 1.3)

2.0　Understand why there is an interest rate. (Objective 2.1)

3.0　Understand the relationship between inflation and the interest rate. (Objectives 3.1, 3.2, 3.3)

4.0　Understand how the interest rate affects the present and future values of money. (Objectives 4.1, 4.2, 4.3, 4.4)

OBJECTIVES
Answers to bold-faced questions appear at the end of the dialogue.

"So are you ready for another of our 'Sessions on Silberberg, an informative exploration into the principles of microeconomics'?" Ginny asked.

"Ready as I'll ever be for this week's topic, 'Interest Rates and Capital Values'. We need theme music."

"Before we start Mo, there's something I want to tell you."
"What?"
"Well, I..."
"Ginny, what? You're not...?"
"Not what?"
"I don't know, going out with Adam," Mo said.
"What? No! What I wanted to tell you was that I'm quitting school."

"WHAT!"

"Shhhh. Yes I'm quitting school at the end of the semester."
"Why?"

"Well," Ginny said, "I've thought about it a lot and I want to do something real...for the environment. I'm just getting more and more disgusted by all the pollution and somebody has to do something, so why not me? I've found this group that organizes people to adopt watersheds to try to clean them up and maintain them. They need an office person to help coordinate everything."

"Hmm. That sounds pretty interesting, but why do you need to drop out to do that?"

"They really need someone full time. And as it is I'm going to have to keep working at the Diner, because this organization doesn't have very much money. I would also be in charge of fund raising for my own salary. I don't know, I mean school is great, and education is important, but it's just so far removed from everything. I want to do something real and the job is there *now*."

"That's fine for the next year or two Ginny, but what about ten years from now, or twenty, or thirty? Investing just a couple of years more *now* in your education opens up way more possibilities for doing more in the long run. Didn't you read chapter 10?"

"Sure, but I didn't think it had much to do with my decision."

"It's completely relevant to your decision," Mo said, "let's go through it again. Since you did read it I presume that at least you're going to finish out the semester?"

"I am. I thought about dropping out right away, but there's not that much more to go. Besides, after carrying you this far in econ, I'm not going to leave you to fend for yourself now."

"You carrying me? I can see you need a dose of reality as well as common sense."

OBJECTIVE 1.1 Recognize definitions for the important new vocabulary.

Question 1. Match the term with its definition(s). Write out definitions for any undefined terms.

a. present consumption   b. future consumption
c. consumption over time   d. utility maximization
e. borrowing/lending   f. capital markets
g. principal   h. interest
i. compound interest   j. simple interest

_____ markets in which the borrowing and lending of money takes place.

_____ interest that is paid or received on the principal and any previous interest payments.

_____ the notion that people adjust their consumption levels, making tradeoffs between future and present consumption, so that the benefits of consumption are maximized.

_____ the premium charged or paid for earlier availability of money.

_____ anticipated consumption and its value in the future.

_____ the price charged or paid for the use of another's money in a given time period.

_____ interest that is paid or received on only the original principal year after year.

_____ the consumption and value of goods or money that occurs or exists today, in the present.

_____ the nominal amount of a loan (i.e. the amount that is actually loaned or borrowed).

OBJECTIVE 1.2 **List the factors that lead people to trade future for present consumption in order to even out their consumption over time.**

"I really liked this chapter," Mo said.

"Of course you did, it was all calculations."

"Not all. What about this idea of smoothing out consumption over time, between future and present."

"It's the law of demand," Ginny said. "The law of demand says that as price increases consumers will consume less of a good. It's also the law of diminishing marginal values -- the more you consume a good the lower your marginal value for that good becomes."

"Okay, but what's the good here?"

"Consumption. The more you consume the lower your marginal value for consumption. The catch is that it's across time rather than just in the present."

"That's exactly what it is," Mo said. "Up to now we've been looking at current consumption of real goods, what quantity at what price. This time factor is a little disorienting."

"We're still looking at what quantity and what price, but the price is now foregone consumption, either now or later. You have to choose now whether you want to spend all of your income or save some of it for later. If you consume a quantity of 80 percent of your income now the price is the foregone value of consuming that 80 percent at some point in the future, because you spent it. It's gone."

"But the explanation of our behavior is that we smooth out consumption over time?"

"That's right," Ginny said, "because of diminishing marginal values and the law of demand. If you have lots of income now and you consume more now, then your marginal value for more 'consumption' now will be low. You won't be willing to pay the price for any more, and the price is future consumption."

"So, for example, if I have no income now and no consumption, then my marginal value, or what I am willing to pay, for some consumption now is quite high. I'd be willing to pay, or give up, some part of my future income and consumption for more consumption now."

"Yes," Ginny said. "And making that kind of decision leads people to even out their consumption over time. Take me for an example, I'm poor now, but I anticipate earning a decent income in the future. So my marginal value of consumption is high now, but I expect it to be lower in the future when I'm richer. I'd trade some of that future...Heck I am trading it. I've got student loans, so I'm directly borrowing from my future self to consume college and Ramen noodles now."

"And your future riches will come from working at the Diner and this watershed group?"

"This won't be forever Mo, and we're not talking about my career choices."

"I'll leave that alone for now. Your point is that rather than consuming next to nothing now and waiting for the wealth of the future, we are willing and apparently quite able to transfer some of that future consumption to the present. So we are smoothing out our consumption over time and we can explain that with the law of diminishing marginal value and the law of demand."

OBJECTIVE 1.3 Describe the marginal value and marginal cost curve in a market where present consumption is traded for future consumption.

"So the only other thing really," Ginny said, "is that this willingness to trade present for future consumption actually takes place in the market, through borrowing and lending -- like we both did with our student loans; though I wasn't really thinking like this when I signed the loan papers."

"That's kind of interesting to think about isn't it? People who lend their money have a low marginal value for consumption now and people who borrow money have a high marginal value now. And it all channels through the markets for money, just like the market for shoes or anything else."

"Wouldn't the marginal value and marginal cost curves work just the same way as they always do? You know diminishing marginal value as quantity increases and rising marginal costs as quantity increases."

"Yes, like this," Mo said drawing out the supply and demand curve. "Only the axes would have quantity of present consumption on the horizontal axis and quantity of future consumption on the vertical, where the quantity of future consumption is the price of consuming additional units of present consumption."

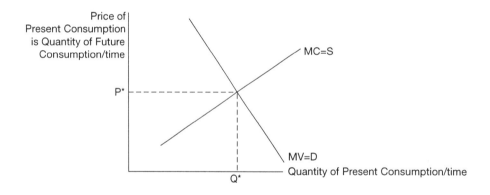

"Both axes could use dollars for their units though, couldn't they? I mean you'd measure both present and future consumption in terms of dollars, so that what you've really got is a value of present consumption and the price of consuming it in terms of the value of future consumption foregone."

OBJECTIVE 2.1 List at least two reasons (other than inflation) why interest is charged on borrowing and lending funds.

"So we've got people borrowing and lending, or at least wanting to, as they try to smooth out their consumption over time; let's talk interest rates," Mo said.

"Right. Interest rates. The price you pay to get funds sooner rather than later. What interests me is the idea that there is the desire in the first place to have their income now rather than in the future."

"Well that makes sense. They want it now because then they have options. They can spend it or save it, but they don't have choices if they don't have it yet. Which is why there is a competition for available funds, making borrowers willing to pay the price, the interest rate, to get these funds."

"But having options is not the only reason for interest rates. Silberberg said that some people also believe that individuals have a positive time preference, which sounds a lot like hedonism to me," Ginny said.

"Hedonism?"

"Yes, that your actions are motivated by the immediate pursuit of pleasure. A positive time preference means that all else constant, you simply value current consumption more than future consumption."

"Is that hedonism or just playing the odds? Who knows if you'll be around in the future," said Mo.

"I suppose. There's also the case of income growing over time. If you anticipate that your income will grow in the future, then you would be less willing to part with your money today. The borrowers who want your money today would have to offer you some inducement to give up your money. That feeds into the overall competition for scarce funds in the present that you were just talking about."

"I guess there is also the case, like Silberberg described, where you can increase your future income by investing in capital goods today. That would place a greater demand on currently available funds driving up the price. And the lender would be stupid not to charge some price for using his money to help someone else make even more money. What about inflation?" Mo asked.

"Inflation is part of the interest rate, but not a fundamental reason why interest exists in the first place."

OBJECTIVE 3.1 Recognize definitions for the important new vocabulary.

Question 2. Match the term with its definition(s). Write out definitions for any undefined terms.

a. real (interest rate)   b. nominal (interest rate)
c. asset   d. liability
e. wealth   f. capitalized value
g. exogenous   h. endogenous
i. bonds   j. stocks
k. equity   l. dividends
m. historical cost   n. liquidity

_____ developing or originating from without, or externally.

_____ a term used to imply the ease with which the value of an asset can be converted into some usable form, such as cash.

_____ the present value of a stream of future payments (income) from some asset.

_____ the interest rate that is listed daily and recorded on contracts by borrowers and lenders.

_____ shares of ownership sold by a corporation to fund some part of the operations of the company.

_____ a resource that generates income.

_____ the cost of an asset at the time it was purchased.

_____ the *net* value of a person's entire stock of capital or assets.

_____ a share of a corporations profits paid to someone who has purchased the corporation's stock.

_____ the nominal interest rate minus the anticipated rate of inflation.

_____ developing or originating from within, or internally.

_____ a debt owed because of previous borrowing.

_____ a means for corporations and governments to borrow money by promising to pay investors the principal plus some level of interest in the future in exchange for the use of their money now.

_____ the owned portion of a corporation, home or some other asset.

OBJECTIVE 3.2 Distinguish between real interest rates and nominal interest rates.

"I guess inflation is more involved with the difference between real and nominal interest rates," Mo said. "Think of the equation for the interest rate, $i = r +$ anticipated rate of inflation."

"Where r is the real rate, meaning its the real price of the earlier availability of funds," said Ginny.

"So the real rate will always be there, because of all the reasons for having an interest rate we just talked about, though it can increase and decrease with the circumstances."

"Right, but the nominal rate that is actually charged by lenders, has to take into account inflation."

OBJECTIVE 3.3 Identify the components of the nominal interest rate.

"So the nominal rate starts with the real rate, adds inflation and then a risk premium," said Mo.

"Did you see in the book that the real rate has been estimated to be between 0 and 2 percent at times?"

"Wow, that means on a 6 percent loan...the inflation rate is now 2 to 3 percent, so, well I guess that's not so bad. 1 to 2 percent for the riskiness of the loan."

"It could be higher though," Ginny said. "If the real rate were only 1 percent and inflation were right at 2 percent, then the risk premium is 3 percent."

"Who knows what the actual numbers are, and I presume they change. Speaking of which, did you see in the paper how the province of Ontario's credit rating has fallen from AAA to AA or something?"

"No what is this?"

"There are these organizations that rate companies and governments on how risky their bonds are based on their finances. A AAA rating means there is very low risk. If they are a disaster waiting to happen, then they get, I don't know, a C rating or something. Anyway Ontario's got such a huge debt that I guess this rating organization felt Ontario was a more risky investment, so they downgraded them."

"So the Ontario government might have to pay a higher interest rate on their bonds to get people to invest in them, eh?

"Maybe, eh?"

Question 3. Calculate the interest rate, if you were the banker, that Bob Jones and Leonardo Savant would have to pay to pursue their dreams in the following two cases. Bob wants to start his own accounting firm, Leonardo wants to make a movie embodying the meaning of the poetry of Allen Ginsberg. What risk premium would you assign to each of them?

Bob Jones: Age 35, married, MBA Harvard University. 10 years experience in accounting firm.

Leonardo Savant: Age 21, single, in his second year of film studies at UCLA.

Case 1: Real rate of interest (r) = 2%   Case 2: r = 2%
         Anticipated inflation (g) = 3%   g = 6%

* * * * * * *

"Well," Ginny said, "I guess that only leaves all of the math problems: present value, future value, annuities, perpetuities, anxieties."

"They're not that bad. Sometimes you're such a baby about doing a few calculations."

"I just don't think that way. You know when they say 'this equation *clearly* shows blah, blah, blah? Well it's never clear to me. In these problems I didn't know whether I was in the present taking the future value or the future taking a present value, or which formula was most appropriate for what case."

"I'll bet you can do them though, you just need a method or a structured way to think about them."

"I don't know, but let's give it a go."

OBJECTIVE 4.1 Recognize definitions for the important new vocabulary.

Question 4. Match the term with its definition(s). Write out definitions for any undefined terms.

a. present value   b. future value

c. annuity   d. perpetuity
e. stock (of resources)   f. flow (of services)

_____ a series of payments occurring at regular intervals (e.g. annually) for a fixed period of time.

_____ the calculation of what some future good or sum of money is worth today.

_____ the use or output gained from a unit of stock.

_____ a series of payments occurring at regular intervals for the indefinite future.

_____ the asset used to generate a flow of services or goods.

_____ the calculation of the value of some present good or sum of money at some point in the future, i.e. what it will be worth.

_____ an annuity that lasts forever.

OBJECTIVE 4.2 Gather together the relevant formulas for determining present and future values of money, annuities, stocks and flows, etc.

"Okay," Mo said, "the first thing you need to do is see how many formulas you're afraid of. So list them out right here." And Ginny did.

1. Future Value $FV = P(1 + i)^n$

2. Present Value $PV = \dfrac{FV}{(1 + i)^n}$

3. Present Value of Annuities $PV_A = \dfrac{A}{i}\left[1 - \dfrac{1}{(1 + i)^n}\right]$

4. Present Value of Perpetuities $PV_P = \dfrac{A}{i}$

"What about the one for the value of the corporation, $PV = E/i$?" Ginny asked.

"That's just the same as the perpetuity formula except instead of the A for an annual fixed payment, it's an E for the earnings of the company, which are a stream just like the annual payments of a perpetuity."

"Okay, so there are only four of them but the applications are limitless I'm sure. Look how many examples Silberberg had."

"Actually there are only three formulas. The first and second are the same, just written with a different variable on the left hand side of the equation. The P in equation 1 is the same as the PV in equation 2."

OBJECTIVE 4.3 **Describe the intent of the calculation in each formula.**

"Allright there are only three."

"The key to doing these," Mo said, "is understanding what the formulas can do for you. So two things: first, be clear about *when*, or for what time period -- present or future -- you are calculating the value of the money. And second, *how* you are paying or receiving the money or the value of the good."

"Keep going."

"Well first of all you start with two main possibilities, either you're calculating the value of money or some good now or in the future. And second you're deciding whether the amount you are calculating, either now or in the future, is a one-time amount or a stream of amounts."

"Okay."

"Okay? That's it. For each case you have to decide which combination of these things are relevant for you to calculate the necessary value or amount. Focus on the point in time of the calculation."

Question 5. Fill in the following table indicating when you are calculating the value or amount and whether it is a one-time payment or a stream of payments for each formula.

Formula	Calculating for When?	One-time/Stream
$FV = P(1 + i)^n$		
$PV = \dfrac{FV}{(1 + i)^n}$		
$PV_A = \dfrac{A}{i}\left[1 - \dfrac{1}{(1 + i)^n}\right]$		
$PV_P = \dfrac{A}{i}$		

OBJECTIVE 4.4 **Decide which formula to use and how to use them in the right situations.**

"Now as a good friend I've got to tell you that there is sort of a trick to using the annuity and perpetuity formulas," Mo said. "It's not really a trick. It's just understanding how to use the formulas, depending on what information is known. Remember that example Silberberg gives about borrowing $10,000 and making 4 equal payments in the future at 10 percent interest to pay off the loan? Well, the solution is to start by understanding that the present value is 10,000 and you must figure out what the A is in the annuity formula. So you need to rework the formula."

"Diabolical. No wonder I couldn't follow that one."

Question 6. In the remaining spaces of the table in Question 6, reconfigure the present value formulas for annuities and perpetuities solving for A, the amount of the annual payment (i.e., manipulate the formula so that A is by itself on the left hand side of the equation); complete the rest of the table by answering when the value is being calculated and what kind of payments they are, one-time or a stream.

$$* \ * \ * \ * \ * \ * \ *$$

"So do you want to practice a couple?"

"If you don't mind. It would help me a lot."

"Sure. Let's start with an easy one.

> **Problem:** How much would you have to pay me now, for me to give you $500 in one year with a 6 percent interest rate?"

"So I want to calculate an amount now that is a one-time payment. So that would be the present value formula -- I think. $PV = FV/(1 + i)^n$. So,

$$PV = \frac{\$500}{(1 + .06)^1} \qquad \qquad PV = \$471.70$$

"Which means that I would have to give you $471.70 now, it would earn interest at 6 percent, and you would give me $500 in one year," said Ginny.

"Or conversely, you would demand $500 from me in one year, if you gave me $471.70 now with the interest rate at 6 percent."

"Not bad," Ginny said. "Let's do one like Silberberg's examples, like the student loan one."

> **Problem:** You are heading into university and you have to pay tuition and fees at the end of the year. You've arranged to borrow $5000 at 5 percent interest at the end of each of the next four years. You have to repay the loan according to a schedule of 5 equal payments beginning 6 years from now. How much will you have to pay per year?

"Okay. Here we go. So -- what do I do Mo? Don't tell me. Okay both the loan and the repayment are streams of payments occuring in the future. I'm borrowing $5000 times 4 years, then I have to pay back some amount times 5 years. The question is when am I calculating all of these amounts?"

"Try to think about it from the bank's point of view," Mo said. "They're the ones lending you the money, so they're the ones who will be doing the calculating. What do they want?"

"They want to calculate how much they are loaning me over these four years then make sure I pay it back in such a way that they are making money," Ginny said.

"That's right. So when are they calculating how much they are loaning you?"

"Now, when I sign the loan papers. So I want to calculate the present value of the four future $5000 loan payments at 5 percent.

$$PV_A = \frac{\$5000}{.05} \left[1 - \frac{1}{(1 + .05)^4}\right] \qquad PV_A = \$17,729.33$$

"So they are lending you $20,000 in total, which has a present value of about $17,730, because those payments come in the future. That's step one," Mo said. "Now what are you going to do?"

"I'm going to figure out how much I have to pay the bank, or better yet, how much the bank wants to collect from me."

"Now you're talking. But before you start just remember that with student loans the banks don't charge students interest during the years they're in school. They only begin charging interest once you've graduated or whenever the loan agreement says you will start making repayments."

"Right, so the bank is treating this loan as if it didn't really happen until the fifth year, then it says, okay, we loaned you $17,729.33, pay up. And to ensure that they make money, they want to calculate how much $17,729.33 would be in total, five years in the future at 5 percent interest."

"Exactly, then after they know how much the total will be in five years they just have to figure out how to make that into five equal payments."

"I am all over this now," Ginny said.

"I think I've created a monster."

"So the future value of $17,729.33 -- I'm just going to lop off the $.33, so it's just $17,729."

$$FV = \$17,729(1 + .05)^5 \qquad FV = \$22,627$$

"And then to figure out the annual payment it's,

$$A = \frac{PVA}{1 - \frac{1}{(1 + i)^n}} * i \qquad A = \frac{\$22,627}{1 - \frac{1}{(1 + .05)^5}} * .05$$

$$A = \$5226.36$$

"I would have to pay back the equivalent of $5226.36 each year, for five years. Whew, what a problem. Was it good for you Mo?

"It was great Ginny. I've got one more for you. Try calculating the present value of your education in terms of how many acres of old growth you can save as an environmental economist versus your short term contribution from dropping out now to run this office."

"I'll think about it Mo."

Question 7. A traveling salesman comes to your door and offers you a revolutionary device that will give you roughly two free gallons of gas on every tankful you buy. What's more this device will "NEVER" wear out. "It's guaranteed to last a lifetime." "How much is it," you ask. He deflects the question asking you how much you're willing to pay for this "remarkable" device. What is your answer? (Note ** Assume 12 gallons per tank and an average price of about US$2.00/gallon of gas over your lifetime.)

ANSWERS TO DIALOGUE QUESTIONS

Question 1. Vocabulary: f, i, c, h, b, h, j, a, g.

Missing definitions:

borrowing/lending - these terms imply not only the borrowing and lending you immediately think of like banks lending money to people wanting to buy houses, but also the acts of individuals loaning their money (their savings) to a bank, or to governments or companies when they invest in stocks and bonds.

utility maximization - the act of behaving and making decisions that lead to the greatest well-being for oneself. This notion does not preclude the possibility that an individual's perception of the best outcome for themselves is also one that is also or only best for another individual, or his/her family, community, or nation.

Question 2. Vocabulary: g, n, f, b, j, c, m, e, l, a, h, d, i, k.

Question 3. Just to make it interesting we're ranking Bob and Leonardo's risk premiums as 2% and 10% respectively. Frankly, we feel that in the real world Leonardo would be politely shown the door at any respectable bank. Their respective interest rates:

Case 1
   Bob = 2% + 3% + 2% = 7%
Leonardo = 2% + 3% + 10% = 15%

Case 2
   Bob = 2% + 6% + 2% = 10%
Leonardo = 2% + 6% + 10% = 18%

Question 4. Vocabulary: c, a, f, d, e, b, d.

Question 5 and 6.

Formula	Calculating for When?	One-time/Stream
$FV = P(1 + i)^n$	Future	One-time
$PV = \dfrac{FV}{(1 + i)^n}$	Now	One-time
$PV_A = \dfrac{A}{i}\left[1 - \dfrac{1}{(1 + i)^n}\right]$	Now	Stream
$PV_P = \dfrac{A}{i}$	Now	Stream
$A = \dfrac{PV_A}{1 - \dfrac{1}{(1 + i)^n}} * i$	Future	Stream
$A = i(PV_P)$	Future	Stream

Question 7. To answer this question you must use the present value of a perpetuity formula. Therefore you need to estimate the annual savings of this device for you over your lifetime given the probable interest rate you will face. My solution follows:

Annual savings: I fill up just under once a week or about 42 times per year. At 12 gallons per tank, after every 6 fill-ups one would receive 12 "free" gallons or one tank. Thus after 42 fill-ups I would have saved the equivalent of 7 "free" tank fulls of gas, so I'm saving 7 x 12 = 84 gallons, or $168.00 per year with this device. Estimating an average interest rate of about 9 per cent over my lifetime and using the perpetuity formula,

$$PV_p = \frac{A}{i}$$

$$PV_p = \frac{\$168}{.09} = \$1866.66$$

I would be willing to pay up to $1866.66 for this device.

THE BIG PICTURE

The important or unique thing about Chapter 10 (aside from calculations of present and future value which you will use the rest of your life if you ever have any money to invest or you need to do cost-benefit analysis at work[1]) is that it brings into consideration the dynamic element of time into the analysis of consumer behavior. In all of the other chapters the analysis of locating the equilibrium price and quantity is focused on a point in time, as if we took a photograph of the market and determined where P and Q were in that photograph. If we wanted to check on this market later, when conditions had changed, we would take another still photograph and look again. Chapter 10 provides an extension of this basic model by including time. Thus, instead of looking across goods in a single time period you are looking more generally at income -- the ability to consume goods -- across time.

It is difficult to capture time in a static diagram. Sometimes we use two diagrams, one present and one future. Or we can use a single diagram with time on one of the axes, showing the tradeoff of present and future consumption.

You can rest easy, however, that this extension of the basic model you've learned is firmly within the same theoretical framework you've learned so far. The postulates of behavior still apply, the law of demand and diminishing marginal value still guide people's behavior across time. It is just a different perspective on the same consumer behavior. In fact Chapters 9 and 10 have both presented different perspectives on the basic economic paradigm. Chapter 9 showed how things change when the assumption of perfect information between buyer and seller during the exchange of a good is dropped. In that case the importance of the exchange of rights to the good is emphasized. In Chapter 10 the static assumption is dropped and our attention is drawn to the general consumption patterns of individuals over time.

---

[1] Cost-Benefit analysis is based on the fact that economic actions, among others, have costs and benefits to individuals, companies, governments, or society in general. Before pursuing a course of action (off-shore oil development, raising property taxes, lowering the speed limit, opening up a new store location, investing savings in stocks versus paying off your home mortgage, etc.) the costs and benefits of that action can be calculated using present value formulas and compared to other alternatives.

REVIEW QUESTIONS

Answers to all review questions appear at the end of this chapter.

PROBLEMS AND EXERCISES
Write your answer in the space(s) provided.

1. If you deposited $1000 in the bank on your 20th birthday at 5% interest, how much would be in the account on your 65th birthday, assuming simple interest? _____ How much would be in the account assuming compound interest? _____ How much would be in the account at 7% compound interest? _____ Discuss the reasons for the differences between the three amounts.

2. You have won a New Year's Eve cash prize. You are offered two different methods of payment:
     1) $1000 immediately   2) $1400 one year from now)

What option will you choose if the annual rate of interest is:
a) 10% _____   b) 50% _____

3. You, wake up and find yourself to be 68 years old. You have invested your retirement savings, a sum of $100,000, in an annuity that will pay you equal increments annually for 10 years. The payments are such that at the end of the 10 years the last payment will reduce the fund to zero. What is the amount that you will be paid annually when the interest rate is 12%. _____

If prior to investing your savings the interest rate falls from 12% to 9%, what would the difference be in your annual payments (from the 12% rate) coming from the annuity? _____

4.   This question is adapted from Robert Paul Thomas, **Microeconomic Applications: Understanding the American Economy. Wadsworth Publishing: Belmont CA. pp. 169-173.)**
Are professional athletes' salaries as big as they seem? For example this "reported" $12.55 million, 5 year contract calls for salary payments of $1.2 million per year for 5 years; a cash signing bonus to be paid immediately and a deferred bonus to be received in 10 years; also a deferred salary of $500,000 per year, beginning in 10 years to be paid for 10 years; and a new car. Determine for yourself how much this contract is worth to the player and how much it costs the franchise if the nominal interest rate is 6%.

	Payments	Actual Value
Salary ($1.2 mill x 5 yrs.)	$6,000,000	
Cash signing bonus	500,000	
Deferred bonus (in 10 years)	1,000,000	
Deferred salary (begin in 10 years:		
$500,000 x 10 yrs.)	5,000,000	
New BMW	50,000	
Total (Total for contract)	$12,550,000	

5. Some months after befriending an elderly man, he tells you that he's moving to New Zealand to spend his last days. As a gesture of thanks for your friendship, he wants to give you some money. He doesn't have a great deal but he can either give you $1200 a year for life or $15,000 now. You stammer, you blush, you tell him "No, I couldn't even think of it." All the while, however, you are trying like crazy to remember Silberberg's economics course, because you *know* the formula you need to figure this out is in his textbook. "Oh," you think, "why didn't I study harder???" Which option do you choose? Explain your answer showing calculations and any assumptions you are making.

6. For $1,600.00 a firm promises to blow insulation into your home's wall spaces and attic. They claim that this will lower your heating bill 25%. Currently you estimate your average monthly heating bill at $60.00, or $720.00 per year. The current nominal interest rate is 7%. Your current plan is to stay in the house for at least 5 years but you'll be gone by 10 years. Assuming their 25% claim is true, should you allocate your resources to do it? Explain your answer by showing your calculations.

7. a. If the national savings rate decreased what effect would this have on the interest rates. Show the effect graphically below. Be sure to label the graph's axes.
b. What effect would an increase in the productivity of capital have on the interest rates. Show the effect graphically next to part a's below. Be sure to label the graph's axes.

a. Change in Savings   b. Change in Productivity

TRUE - FALSE QUESTIONS
Provide a one or two sentence explanation with your answer.

1.   Income now is preferable to the same income in the future.

2.   The present value of some future amount of money represents the price (in the present) of that future amount.

3.   A relatively high interest rate indicates that consumption in the future is more highly valued than consumption in the present.

4.   If enough individuals wished to shift consumption from the present to the future, then the interest rate would be negative.

5.   It is possible to have a positive accounting profit and zero economic profit.

6.   People who save money are expressing their preference for future consumption over present consumption.

7.   The interest rate is solely determined by the government, the banks and other lending institutions.

8.   Economic analysis takes future income to be exogenous, that is individuals can do nothing to affect the levels of future income which would become available to them.

9.   Interest rates are affected by society's investment in capital goods.

10.   With 3% inflation, a nominal interest rate of 6% is the same as a real interest rate of 9%.

11.   If the real rate of interest is 2% and the actual inflation rate is 2%, then the market interest rate, before adjustment for the risk premium, would be 4%.

MULTIPLE CHOICE QUESTIONS
Choose the best answer.

1. Someone owes you $100. They offer several alternatives for paying you back. Which should you choose for the greatest present value at an interest rate of 10%?
a. $100 cash now.
b. $100 cash one year from now.
c. $110 two years from now.
d. $90 now, and a $10 signing bonus three years from now

2. You owe someone $100. He offers you several alternative methods for paying off the debt. Which should you choose? The interest rate is 10%.

a. $100 cash now.

b. $108 one year from now.

c. $131 three years from now.

d.   insufficient information to determine present value.

3. The present value of a durable good can be determined only when you know:

a.   how long it will last through time.

b.   the rate of interest.

c.   the size of the annual income stream generated by the good.

d.   all of the above.

4. If the rate of interest rises from 10% to 14%, the present value of $280, paid annually and forever,

a.   declines by $800.00.

b.   declines by $11.20.

c.   increases by $11.20.

d.   increases by $39.20.

5.   An economist would expect that a rise in the price of labor in 1938 (just before World War II) reflected:

a.   an increase in the supply of labor, because price increases as supply increases.

b.   a fall in the demand for labor as expectations of war mounted.

c.   the present value of expected higher food and other costs for workers.

d.   the present value of expected higher future earnings from labor (no expectations of war).

6. A corporate bond has a coupon attached promising to pay $100 interest each year of the bond's life. It matures in 5 years, at which time it pays out a nominal value of $1,000. If the market interest rate is 8%, the present value of the bond is:

a. $399   b. $749.10   c. $1,080   d. $682

7. Suppose you believe you could make an annual yield of 10% per year investing in the stock market. This is the highest yield of any investment (except possibly owning gold) of which you know. You now own 100 ounces of gold. This gold could be sold for $250 per ounce. Your opportunity cost for holding your gold (without selling) is:

a. $250/year

b. $2,500/year

c. $10,000/year

d. $1,000/year

8. If the nominal rate of interest is 15% and the expected rate of inflation is 10%, then the expected real rate of interest is (assume zero risk):

a. -5%   b. 5%   c. 10%   d. 15%

9. If inflation were always anticipated correctly, which group would still not be protected aainst losses from inflation?

a.   recipients of immediately indexed transfer payments.

b.   workers with cost of living clauses in their contracts.

c.   creditors with long-term loans outstanding.

d.   they are all protected.

10. If inflation were to halt unexpectedly (that is, actual inflation is less than expected inflation), which of the following groups would be worse off?
a.   recipients of immediately indexed transfer payments.
b.   homeowners with fixed mortgages.
c.   credit institutions who had financed long-term loans.
d.   they are all worse off.

11. The interest rate is:
a.   the price that must be paid in order to induce people to supply their income to others.
b.   the price set in the market for transferring future income to the present.
c.   the price that people who wish to consume more now are willing to pay others for supplying their money.
d.   all of the above.

12. The interest rate is positive because,
a.   people prefer present consumption over future consumption.
b.   people prefer future consumption over present consumption.
c.   the government wants to promote economic growth.
d.   it is costly to store wealth.

13. The present value of a future sum increases,
a.   the higher the interest rate and the greater the time.
b.   the lower the interest rate and the greater the time.
c.   the higher the interest rate and the shorter the time.
d.   the lower the interest rate and the shorter the time.

14. The future value of a present sum decreases,
a.   the higher the interest rate and the greater the time.
b   the lower the interest rate and the greater the time.
c.   the higher the interest rate and the shorter the time.
d.   the lower the interest rate and the shorter the time.

15. The value of capital (human or physical)
a.   is the future value of the price calculated according to the life-span of the capital.
b.   is the present value of the income it produces throughout its life.
c.   is the future value of the income it produces throughout its life.
d.   cannot be determined.

16. Adonis Goodlooks the daytime soap actor is without any other abilities. If he weren't acting he would be performing as a male stripper earning a small fraction of his actual salary. The difference in Adonis' actual salary from his next best alternative is an excellent example of
a.   the concept of opportunity costs.
b.   the concept of marginal value.
c.   the concept of economic rents.
d.   all of the above.
e.   a and c only.

17. If the anticipated inflation rate is 3% and the risk premium for a certain type of loan is 2%, but the nominal rate of interest is 7%, the remaining 2% represents,
a.   the premium for earlier availability of funds.
b.   the real interest rate.
c.   the productivity of capital.
d.   all of the above.
e.   a and b.

18. The rate of interest fully adjusted for any changes in the purchasing power of the currency borrowed or lended is the
a.   prime rate of interest.
b.   discount rate of interest.
c.   nominal rate of interest.
d.   real rate of interest.

19. If the current rate of inflation is 5%, but expectations are for the rate to decrease to 3%, lenders would,
a.   keep interest rates where they are until the change occurred, then adjust their rates.
b.   make no changes and make fatter profits as the inflation rate fell.
c.   incorporate the anticipated rate of inflation into their interest rates.

20. An unanticipated deflation will be of the greatest concern to which of the following:
a.   a firm with a high debt to equity ratio.
b.   a firm with a low debt to equity ratio.
c.   a firm that has borrowed by issuing stocks.
d.   a firm that has borrowed by issuing bonds.

SHORT ANSWER QUESTIONS

1. Explain why you would not loan out your money without charging interest.

2. Why is the interest paid on a savings account so much less than the interest charged on a bank loan? Consider that you are loaning the bank money when you deposit money in a savings account, and the bank is loaning you money when you take out a loan for school, a car or a house, so why isn't the interest rate the same in both cases?

3. A negative interest rate is difficult to envision. What conditions would have to exist in society for a negative interest rate to appear, and why do these conditions generally not exist?

4. What would happen to the marginal cost of lending (the interest rate), if there was significant future growth anticipated for the economy? What would happen if there was no growth anticipated? Explain why.

ANSWERS TO REVIEW QUESTIONS

Answers to PROBLEMS AND EXERCISES

1. 5% Simple Interest: $FV = P + n(p * i)$
    $FV = \$1000 + 45(\$1000 * .05)$
    $FV = \$3250.00$

5% Compound Interest: $FV = P(1 + i)^n$
    $FV = \$1000(1 + .05)^{45}$
    $FV = \$8985.00$

7% Compound Interest: $FV = \$1000(1 + .07)^{45}$
    $FV = \$21,000.00$

With simple interest, interest calculations are only made on the original principal and do not include the accumulating interest, so you are just adding $50.00 per year ($1000*.05) to the principal. With compound interest at 5% on the other hand, the interest calculation includes the accumulating interest with the principal. The interest payments and principal are compounded (joined together), so the effective principal increases as the interest amount is added to it each year; what begins as $1000 x 5%, increases after the first year to $1050 x 5%, then $1102.50 x 5%, and so on. The difference between 5% and 7% can also be attributed to "compounding". What begins as a meagre two percent difference in interest rates is being multiplied through each year as the sums increase. Over 45 years the difference is, as you can see, quite large.

2. a. **10%** The value of $1000 in 1 year at 10% interest is, $FV = \$1000(1 + .1)^1 = \$1000(1.1) = \$1100$. Conversely, the value today of $1400 to be received one year from now is, $PV = \$1400/(1 + .1)^1 = \$1272.73$. Clearly you should take option 2).

b. **50%** The value of $1000 in 1 year at 50% interest is, $FV = \$1000(1 + .5)^1 = \$1000(1.5) = \$1500$. The value today of $1400 to be received one year from now is, $PV = \$1400/(1 + .5)^1 = \$933.33$. With a 50% interest rate you should take payment option 1), because you would be $100 better off ($1500 vs. $1400 one year from now).

3. **12%** $A = \dfrac{\$100,000}{\left[1 - \dfrac{1}{(1 + .12)^{10}}\right]} * .12$ $A = \$17,698.42$

9% $A = \dfrac{\$100,000}{1 - \dfrac{1}{(1 + .09)^{10}}} * .09$ $A = \$15,582.00$

The difference in annuity payment is $2,116.41.

4. The actual value of the contract in present value terms is listed below in the column to the right of the math calculations; quite different than the nominal terms of the contract. The salary is a $1.2 million annuity for 5 years; the deferred bonus is a simple present value calculation; the deferred salary requires

that you first determine the value of the $500,000 for 10 years annuity, then calculate the present value of that amount as you bring it from 10 years in the future to the present; the signing bonus and the car are already in present value since they are paid immediately.

Salary: a $1.2 million annuity

$$PV_A = \frac{1.2 \text{ mill.}}{.06} \left[1 - \frac{1}{(1 + .06)^5} \right]$$

$$PV_A = \$5,054,835.66$$

Deferred bonus

$$PV = \frac{\$1,000,000}{(1 + .06)^{10}}$$

$$PV = \$558,394.78$$

Deferred Salary

a) $$PV_A = \frac{\$500,000}{.06} \left(1 - \frac{1}{(1 + .06)^{10}} \right)$$

$$PV_A = \$3,680,043.53$$

b) $$PV = \frac{3,680,043.53}{(1 + .06)^{10}}$$

$$PV = \$2,054,917.08$$

Actual Value (in PV terms)	
Salary	$5,054,835.66
Cash Signing Bonus	$ 500,000.00
Deferred Bonus	$ 558,394.78
Deferred Salary	$2,054,917.08
Car	$ 50,000.00
TOTAL VALUE	$8,218,147.52

5. My assumption is to anticipate an 8% interest rate over the course of my life. The $1200.00 per year is a perpetuity for all practical purposes.

$$PV_P = \frac{\$1200}{.08} = \$15,000$$

Given an 8% interest rate it would appear that the options are identical. The lower the anticipated interest rate the more attractive the annual payment; the higher the anticipated interest rate the more attractive is the one-time immediate gift.

6. 25% savings would equal $15.00 x 12 months = $180.00 per year. The present value of annuities of $180.00 per year for 5 years and 10 years (assuming no change in your heating costs) are calculated below. On a straight monetary calculation it is not worth it to go with this offer. You're spending $1,600 to save between $738.03 and $1264.24.

$$PV_A = \frac{\$180}{.07} \left(1 - \frac{1}{(1 + .07)^5} \right)$$

$$PV_A = \$738.03$$

$$PV_A = \frac{\$180}{.07} \left(1 - \frac{1}{(1 + .07)^{10}} \right)$$

$$PV_A = \$1264.24$$

7. Change in savings and change in productivity

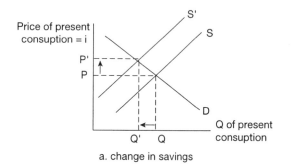

a. change in savings

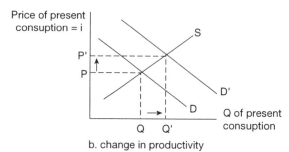

b. change in productivity

Answers to TRUE - FALSE QUESTIONS

1. True. You can't spend what you do not have; but you can always choose not to spend now what you have now. So you are no worse off for having the income now rather than in the future.

2. True. To ensure that you would receive some amount in the future, you would have to pay (i.e., invest) in some kind of interest bearing account or stocks today. That amount, or price, is the present value of the amount you want to receive in the future.

3. False. A relatively high interest rate means that the cost of present consumption has increased. This means people are willing to pay more (a higher interest rate) for present consumption in terms of future consumption foregone.

4. True. This is difficult to envision, but if all people valued future consumption more highly than present consumption, then they would compete with one another to trade their present income for future income. Those wanting future income would be willing to pay some amount, an interest rate, to receive present income in the future. This would be a negative interest rate, because instead of receiving extra money for providing their money to others for use in the present, they would be paying others to take their money in the present and giving it to them in the future.

5. True. Accounting profit comes from subtracting a firm's explicit costs (i.e., payment to factors it doesn't own like wages, interest payments on loans, rental payments for buildings or machinery, etc.) from total revenue. Many firms have positive accounting profits. Economic profit, on the other hand, is total revenue minus <u>total</u> costs, which are the opportunity costs of all resources used by the firm, including those owned such as your own capital or labor. Firms in competitive markets have zero economic profit.

6. True. Savings imply foregone present consumption.

7. False. The interest rate is fundamentally determined by the market of suppliers and demanders of money, or more accurately of present consumption. As with most markets, this leads to the establishment of a market clearing (equilibrium) price and quantity. The equilibrium price for units of present

consumption (i.e., money) is the interest rate. The government and the banks, although having some discretion, must for the most part respond to the market.

8. False. Economic analysis includes investment in capital goods, which increase the marginal product of other inputs in production, so that larger incomes can be produced in the future. Examples of such capital investments include, college educations or technical training, buying machinery for production, and research and development spending.

9. True. On a practical level, the interest rate is a product of the interaction of consumer's willingness to trade off present consumption for future consumption, and society's willingness and ability to do so. Society's ability to trade present for future consumption is described graphically by the production possibilities frontier (PPF) for that society. Investment in capital goods is a rational effort to expand the PPF outward, increasing future income beyond the level of current income. Increasing the PPF through investing greater amounts in capital goods, however, increases the marginal cost of foregoing present consumption. This in turn forces interests rates higher. The interest rate must be sufficiently high to induce consumers to forego present consumption for a future return.

10. False. The nominal rate, or actual quoted rate, includes an adjustment for the inflation rate. The real rate is the nominal rate minus the inflation rate -- in this case the real rate is 3%.

11. False. The nominal (market) rate incorporates the anticipated rate of inflation not the actual rate. The market rate would only be 4% if the *anticipated* future rate of inflation was also 2%.

Answers to MULTIPLE CHOICE QUESTIONS

1. a	6. c	11. d	16. e
2. b	7. b	12. a	17. d
3. d	8. b	13. d	18. d
4. a	9. d	14. d	19. c
5. d	10. b	15. b	20. b

Answers to SHORT ANSWER QUESTIONS

1. Since having income now is preferred to having it in the future, all people will desire to transfer at least some future income to the present. Interestingly, there is no future income in reality (it's not available until the future), only our present income. Therefore there is an excess demand for the available, present income. Those who wish to obtain more of the available pool of present income (i.e. more than they have) are willing to pay a premium for the availability of that money; indeed they are forced to pay a premium because others are also bidding for the scarce money.

If you momentarily find yourself willing and able to loan someone some money (i.e. postpone your present consumption), then to do so without charging interest is to postpone your present consumption without compensation, which goes against the fundamental preference to have income now over in the future. Additionally the effect of inflation will ensure that you, in fact, will have a diminished purchasing power in the future compared to the present if you do not charge an interest rate on your loaned money that is at least equal to the rate of inflation.

2. Part of the answer is the risk involved for each party. When you lend the bank money, your deposit

is guaranteed by the government (up to a certain amount) and there are numerous requirements on banks regarding how much of it they can use and what they can do with it. Moreover, most banks are long-standing institutions with public records of their worth and default history. Because of this security there is a very low risk premium paid by banks to individuals. When the bank lends you money however, there are far fewer guarantees and assurances that you will actually pay the money back, therefore a higher risk premium is assigned to these loans.

Another part of the answer lies in the alternative uses that are available for your money when you hold it versus your money when the bank holds it. The banks are middlemen providing the service of bringing money to investors, they are willing to pay you a price for your money, but they will charge a higher price when they loan it out again. This is possible because of the difference in marginal values people have for money. You might want to engage in money-lending to investors yourself, but the costs are high; it's easier to lend it to a middleman for a modest, but secure, price, then let them worry about finding and dealing with investors.

3. A large majority of people would have to value future income and consumption more than present income and consumption. Moreover, present income could not be stored costlessly until it was desired in the future. For a negative interest rate to exist, people could not have the option of simply storing their present income until the future. If this could be done, then no one would pay to receive present income in the future. These conditions do not exist in society because it is possible to store wealth virtually free (one only has to worry about theft). More importantly though, the vast majority of people do not value future income more than present income. Observation informs us that people attempt to even out the flow of income over time so that a more or less even pattern of consumption can occur. It is also the case that because more is preferred to less we would always prefer to receive our income now, then decide if, when, and how we want to consume it.

4. The marginal cost of lending would be high if people anticipate a high rate of growth in the economy and low if there is no growth anticipated. When people anticipate growth then they anticipate that their own standard of living will increase also, meaning their future consumption will increase from current levels. As people internalize this their willingness to give up present income will decrease, or in other words their marginal value for present income will increase. With a high marginal value for present income, lenders will demand and borrowers will have to pay a higher cost for their funds.

Conversely, if no growth is anticipated then there are no expectations for future consumption to be any higher than present consumption levels. Therefore the marginal cost of lending will be lower.

CHAPTER 11
MONOPOLY

PRINCIPAL GOALS

1.0 Understand the difference between price-taking firms and price-searching firms. (Objectives 1.1, 1.2, 1.3)

2.0 Understand the basic mechanics of monopoly pricing and how it differs from pricing in perfectly competitive markets. (Objectives 2.1, 2.2, 2.3)

3.0 Understand the effect of monopoly behavior on output and input factor markets. (Objectives 3.1, 3.2)

4.0 Recognize and understand the methods of the various types of price discrimination schemes. (Objective 4.1)

OBJECTIVES
Answers to bold-faced questions appear at the end of the dialogue.

"Hey Ginny, get a load of this. It's a review of Jim's Diner in the Seattle Weekly."

"No way! This has got to be related to the meatloaf."

"You're right. The reviewer says that Jim's Diner recently won the best meatloaf category in *Seattle's Best* food contest -- you didn't tell me. This food critic says he decided to go check it out for himself."

"And -- what did he think of it?" Ginny asked. "I hope I didn't wait on him."

"He liked it. He said people who live and work in the neighborhood are lucky to have an 'institution' like Jim's so close by."

"Oh please. This is getting WAY out of hand," Ginny said. "Jim thinks he's some kind of food genius because of that contest. He told me he wants to patent his recipe for meatloaf. I didn't know how to tell him, but it's not even his meatloaf. Karl makes it."

"You mean it's not even Jim's recipe?"

"Are you kidding? Jim had this recipe from some ancient Scottish aunt. Karl is *supposed* to be using it, but he took one look at the recipe and said he wouldn't feed that to his dog Lenin."

"So dour Karl made the prize-winning meatloaf." Mo said. "Did he win any other prizes for the boss?"

"No. Well he got second in soup and fourth in waffles," Ginny said. "What's amazing is that the place has been so busy since that contest. Maybe it will get even busier with the review."

"Jim must be loving this."

"No kidding. He's been in a good mood all week long. This review will have him singing verses of Robbie Burns. You can't patent a recipe for meatloaf can you?"

"I think it would be a copyright," Mo said, "and I don't think it would do him any good anyway. How would you protect your rights or collect any fines from violators. He'd be smarter to just keep it a secret. Right now he has a monoploy on that meatloaf."

"I knew you would figure out a way to make some connection between this and economics."

"Well, it's true," Mo said. "Nobody else in the neighborhood even serves meatloaf, except at home maybe; and for the next year, until they hold the best meatloaf contest again, nobody but Jim has the best meatloaf in Seattle. I'd say that's a monopoly."

"You're right. Is that your first objective for this chapter?"

"No, it's vocabulary as usual."

OBJECTIVE 1.1 Recognize definitions for the important new vocabulary.

Question 1. Match the term with its definition(s). Write out definitions for any undefined terms.

a. price searchers	b. monopoly
c. oligopoly	d. contestable markets
e. barriers to entry	f. patents
g. copyrights	h. decreasing cost industries
i. price discrimination	j. first degree price discrimination

_____ selling a unique product or in a unique geographic location, thus making the seller the only seller in the market.

_____ industries in which there are very high fixed costs relative to marginal costs and to the size of the market.

_____ firms whose decisions on output quantities affect the market price of the good.

_____ a price searching firm that is the only seller in the market for its particular good(s).

_____ a legal document granting the holder exclusive (monopoly) rights to produce, use, sell or profit from an invention, process, etc. for a specified number of years.

_____ a price searching firm, which is one of only a few firms in the market for its particular good(s).

_____ those conditions which would deter or prevent new firms from entering and competing in a given market.

_____ industries for which long-run average cost is continuously falling over the relevant range of output for the market.

_____ a seller for whom the entire market demand curve is the demand curve they face.

_____ natural monopolies.

_____ pricing schemes by which some consumers pay a different amount than other consumers for the identical product or service.

_____ markets into which competing firms can enter easily, offering similar products at similar prices.

_____ a legal status granting the bearer exclusive rights to publish, produce or sell the rights to various forms of literary, dramatic or visual arts, or commercial works (e.g. computer software, training manuals), or to use commercial labels, logos, etc., for a specified number of years.

* * * * * * *

"There weren't really very many new words in this chapter," Ginny said.

"No not really, but I have to admit, I had to go back and look up some of the old words that I wasn't quite sure of, like the elasticities. I always have to figure out what elastic and inelastic means."

"Can I ask you a question about one of these vocabulary words?" Ginny asked.

"Sure."

"It's these decreasing cost industries. I think I'm missing something. Silberberg shows that one firm can supply the good for a lower cost than two or more firms; and I understand that for some industry like electricity the start-up costs are very high and it just makes more sense to have one comapany put up power lines in your neighborhood rather than competing firms putting up two and three sets of power lines, but is that it? Is that all we're supposed to understand about this?"

"I think these are just a special case of monopoly that we should be able to recognize and describe," said Mo. I asked Adam about these too."

"What did he say?"

"Just that it's most efficient to only have one firm producing all the output, but that if you give a firm monopoly rights and they behave like a monopolist, you'll end up with a reduced level of output anyway. You want a single firm, but you want them to behave like a competitive one, that is, a larger output and lower price. So governments almost always regulate these firms to make sure they produce a greater quantity than they would as a monopolist."

"So that's it?"

"Yes, well...they're called decreasing cost industries because the supplier is always producing in the decreasing portion of their average cost curve. They can never produce a quantity great enough to get their average cost to its lowest point, because the market isn't big enough relative to their high start-up costs."

"Which is why, as Silberberg describes, it is most efficient for a single firm to supply the good. Okay, I feel better."

OBJECTIVE 1.2 Describe the characteristics of demand and supply in the two models you know so far: perfect competition (price takers) and monopoly (price searchers).

"So I understand producers in the monopoly model to be behaving quite differently from perfectly competitive firms," said Mo.

"The *consequences* of their behavior are different," said Ginny, "but both profit maximize." "It's really all just supply and demand."

"Oh really?"

"Sure. Just compare the two," said Ginny. "First, think about an individual firm in a perfectly competitive market, they don't really face a demand curve. They face only the market price for the good they produce. So it's like the demand curve is really horizontal at that price level."

"Because each firm is too small to affect the market price through their output decisions."

"Right. So they produce up to the point where their marginal cost equals the market price. But the demand curve for the market is still downward sloping. And the market supply curve is just the sum of each firm's marginal cost curve, above average variable cost."

"I need to draw these out for comparison," said Mo.

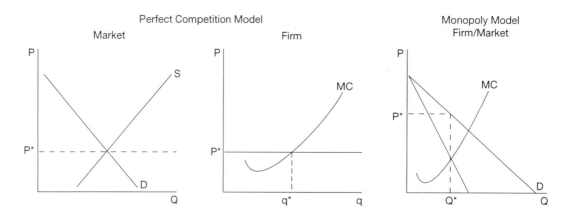

"In the perfectly competitive model, the firm and market diagrams are different," Ginny continued. But for the monopolist, since they're the only firm, the firm and the market are the same. The monopolist faces the whole downward sloping market demand curve as their demand curve. And they determine the price by controlling quantity of output, which moves them up and down the demand curve."

"It's interesting that the monopolist's marginal cost curve is the same as the perfectly competitive firm's."

"The only difference at the firm level then," Ginny said, "is on the demand side. Demand is the same at the market level. Costs are the same at the firm level, and only differ at the market level because the monopolist's marginal cost curve can't be interpreted as a supply curve."

"Which is because they don't "take" some market price and respond with a quantity (i.e. $Q = f(P)$). But you're right Ginny, it's all just demand and supply."

"Just trying to work with what I know Mo. Can we go back for a minute to why these monopolies exist in the first place or why the conditions exist in the market that support monopolies?"

OBJECTIVE 1.3 List the reasons why monopolies exist.

"Of course. What's the problem."

"Oh, no problem really," siad Ginny. I just want some more specifics. For example, how many kinds of decreasing cost industries are there?"

"I don't know, not many: electricity, sewer and water, there used to be the phone company, cable TV, maybe some others. The passenger trains --

"Okay, but not many, though they are important sectors of the economy. So there are a few examples there, how about from patents and copyrights?"

"There must be a lot of those," Mo said, "but it's difficult to determine when monopoly conditions exist, and it really depends on how you define the market. Like Silberberg described with "Kleenex" tissue; that company has the name but there are lots of other tissues out there. There are probably very few pure monopolists if you consider the worldwide market. But I think most firms have some control over the price, because they have some kind of monopolistic conditions in their favor, like convenience or location or some slight variation on their product which makes it somewhat unique."

"So ownership of some unique resource, like diamond mines, decreasing cost industries, government licenses, and patents and copyright all give rise to monopoly power," said Ginny.

"I think the key is to just remember that for a monopoly to exist there has to be some barrier to entry for other firms, preventing them from coming in and taking away profits from the monopolist."

Question 2. List your own examples of monopoly markets for each of the various categories below. Hint: Do not necessarily think big when trying to think of monopolies. Even a small firm may be a monopolist, depending on how you define the market.

Government licenses:

Patents/Copyrights:

Decreasing cost industries:

Exclusive ownership of resources:

* * * * * * *

"Okay that's great but I think we should get into pricing decisions, because that's where you can really see the difference between the monopolist and the perfectly competitive firm," said Mo.

OBJECTIVE 2.1 Identify and explain the significance of important points on a graph depicting the pricing strategy for monopolists.

"I can't believe I'm requesting this," said Ginny, "but before we get into all of these differences, I'd like to start with a graph so that I know what is what and where is where."

"The brainwashing continues. Soon you'll be requesting equations."

"I have my limits," Ginny said. "But we're still working with price on the vertical axis and quantity on the horizontal right? And there is the market demand curve, the monopolists marginal cost curve, and the marginal revenue curve, the one that cuts down below the demand curve."

"And from those three curves," Mo said, "we should be able to determine the quantity, price, total revenue, consumer surplus, everything; just like for the perfectly competitive market."

"Well wait a minute. We need the average cost curve to figure out rents, but let's just do price and quantity first," Ginny said.

"Okay, so the rule is that where marginal revenue equals marginal cost, rents or profits are greatest. And that's true for both models."

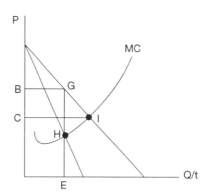

"Correct. So that would be point H, or quantity E, on this graph for a monopolist."

"Now," Mo continued, "the trick is to get the price the monopolist would charge by going from point H up to the demand curve to G then over to the price axis to price B. That's what the monopolist would charge for quantity E of this good."

"And the price is B because that is the consumer's marginal value for E units of the good."

"B is for monopoly, but in perfect competition C would be the price wouldn't it?"

"Yes, because that comes from point I where all the benefits from trade have been exhausted."

"Not only that but C would be the established market price and I would be the point where marginal revenue equals marginal cost for each firm, demand equals supply for the market."

"Wait, explain that," Ginny said.

"We just graphed that -- the horizontal demand curve for the firm in the perfectly competitive market. That's the distinguishing characteristic of the competitive market isn't it? That the equilibrium point is where P = MC = MR. The sum of these firms' marginal cost curves (above AVC) is the supply curve. So if you interpret MC as a supply curve for the perfectly competitive market, then D = S at price C."

"Hey, you've really got this stuff down Mo. And you're right, we did just do that. I just forgot that marginal revenue and demand are the same for price taking firms."

"Oh, you know that's why this monopoly model is so interesting, because the firm has choice. It can move to various levels on the demand curve and to various price levels by increasing or decreasing output."

Question 3. Following are cost and revenue tables for a monopolist. Complete the missing information in the table and determine the monopolist's output quantity and what price is charged.

Quantity _____ Price _____

Q_d	P	TR	MR	AC	TC	MC
0	10			4		
1	9			4		
2	8			4		
3	7			4		
4	6			4		
5	5			4		
6	4			4		
7	3			4		
8	2			4		
9	1			4		
10	0			4		

* * * * * * *

"Okay I'm getting this, but now, why is marginal revenue *below* price for the monopolist?" Ginny asked.

OBJECTIVE 2.2 **Explain and show graphically why marginal revenue is always less than price when the demand curve is downward sloping.**

"I had to ask Adam about that too," Mo said. "As always he drew me a graph, but it cleared things up. The big thing is that unlike in the perfectly competitive model where P = MC = MR on the last unit produced and where all benefits from trade are exhausted, in the monopoly model P is greater than MC and MR. This increases rents, but also implies deadweight loss."

"You mean all of the benefits from trade are not exhausted."

"Exactly. But that is a little bit off the point right now. Here's the graph, well graphs, Adam drew me showing why P > MR, which you know means P is not equal to MC."

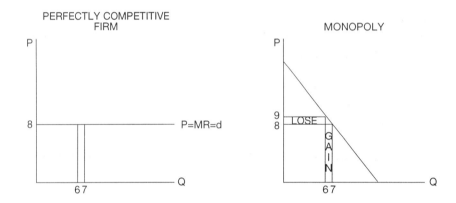

"He said that in the perfectly competitive model, with the flat demand curve equal to price, if the producer chooses to produce an additional unit of the good -- like from 6 to 7 units -- it doesn't change the price or the marginal revenue the producer receives."

"Sure. So the marginal revenue on the seventh unit is $8, just like it was on the sixth."

"Right, but for the monopolist who faces a downward sloping demand curve, if they decide next month to produce a seventh unit then the price falls; like here from $9 to $8. So marginal revenue on the seventh unit can't be $9, equal to the price."

"I see from your graph that although they gain revenue of one unit times $8 like the perfect competitor, the monopolist also loses $1 on each of the first six units they sell."

"That's right," Mo said. "And Adam says that's because monopolists, at least for this example, can't price discriminate perfectly -- meaning they can't charge different prices from one unit to the next. So if they choose to produce that seventh unit then the price falls on all units, not just the last one."

"Then to figure out the marginal revenue on the seventh unit, you have to calculate the total revenue for six units at $9 then TR for seven units at $8 and the difference is your marginal revenue. Which according to my calculations would be..."

"Two dollars, $56 - $54."

"I was getting there," Ginny groused.

"But you know Silberberg showed us another way which is MR = P_1 - ($\Delta P * Q_0$)."

"That would be,"

$$MR = \$8 - (\$1 * 6)$$
$$MR = \$2$$

"Hey it works."

"Of course. You're just taking the gain of $8 and subtracting the loss of $1 each on the other 6 units."

"Okay," Ginny said, "but do I understand correctly that marginal revenue will always be less than price when the demand curve is downward sloping, because of this idea that you always lose a little bit off of your total revenue because the price drops on all units sold."

"Yes, but the whole reason is really because the demand curve is downward sloping. Oh! That reminds me of another point about monopoly pricing, which I again asked Adam about. And that is why monopolists always price the product so that consumers are in the elastic portion of the demand curve."

OBJECTIVE 2.3 **Explain and show graphically why a monopolist prices in the elastic portion of the market demand curve.**

"Wait, I can explain that," Ginny said. "Profit is equal to total revenue minus total cost, right? Total revenues are greatest when, on a straight line demand curve, elasticity is equal to one -- or as Silberberg calls it, unity. And that is at the mid-point of the demand curve."

"But profits are greatest where marginal revenue equals marginal cost, not maximum total revenue. And the rule is that monopolists price in the elastic portion not at unity."

"Now just hold your horses, give me a chance here," Ginny said. "It really helps to have a diagram."

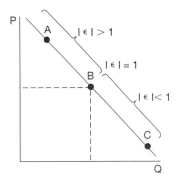

"Okay, there *are* two things going on here," Ginny continued. "The first is that on a linear demand curve elasticity, ϵ, equals one at the mid-point, B, of the line. Above B the demand is elastic and below B it is inelastic. And using the total revenue rule, if you decrease price from A, total revenue increases."

"Of course you can also prove that by putting in numbers and calculating price times quantity at each of the points on the curve. If you measure total revenue up and down the curve, like at points A and C, it gets larger as you move toward the mid-point, and is the largest when you're at the mid-point."

"The second thing though," said Ginny, "is that profit is largest when marginal revenue equals marginal cost. Clearly no one will produce where marginal revenue is negative, because they'll lose money."

"Well, not only that but if you have any costs at all, so MC > 0 which is the normal case, then your marginal revenue has to be more than just zero."

"Right, and if you look at the graph here marginal revenue is only positive up to the mid-point of the demand curve. Why you might ask? Because marginal revenue becomes negative when total revenue begins to get smaller or decrease, which it does below the mid-point in the inelastic portion of the demand curve. See how if you draw a straight line down from the mid-point B, you hit the intersection of the MR curve and the horizontal axis? At that point MR = 0, below it on the demand curve, MR < 0."

"Don't gloat," Mo said, "just hurry up and finish your explanation, or are you finished?"

"Almost, since most monopolists will have positive marginal costs, to produce where MR = MC implies a quantity that falls in the elastic portion of the consumer's demand curve."

"You know, you've come a long way with economics and the graphs. That was great Ginny."

"Well thanks, but let's not congratulate ourselves too much here. That makes me nervous."

"Okay, let's talk about efficiency..."

OBJECTIVE 3.1 **Identify and calculate the deadweight loss, consumer surplus and rents that occur under the basic monopoly model.**

"I think it's pretty straight-forward," Mo continued. "Silberberg says in the book, 'Monopoly is one of a variety of legal or economic institutions that can cause the economy to move away from a Pareto efficient point, where all gains from exchange are exhausted.'"

"Right, so we know that a monopoly is not as efficient as the perfectly competitive situation, but for practical reasons I think we need to be able to figure out, or calculate, the difference between the monopoly and the competitive models, and I think we should be able to show these things on a graph."

"I agree, we need to measure the loss in total welfare between the two models. I think this problem will give us what we need."

Problem:

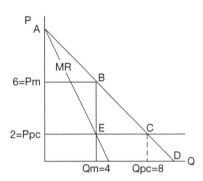

"Now if this were in the perfectly competitive model quantity Q_{pc} would be produced at a price of P_{pc}, and the line $P_{pc}C$ would be the marginal cost curve and the average cost curve."

"What?" Ginny said. "I'm lost already. Didn't we just decide that the perfect competitor faces a flat demand curve? Why isn't the demand curve flat and the marginal cost curve rising like in all the other examples we do with perfect competition?"

"I just used a horizontal, constant MC to make it easier, because if MC is constant, it also equals AC. And the demand curve is the market demand curve. We can't measure consumer's surplus in the perfectly competitive model without the market demand curve. You knew that, didn't you?"

"No."

"Well now you do. And to compare the perfectly competitive market to the monopoly market you should use the same market demand curve, as if all of the individual firms in the perfectly competitive market were bought out and operated by one giant monopolist. In both cases it's the same market demand curve. ANYWAY, with $P_{pc}C$ being the average cost curve we can calculate rents as (P - AC)Q right."

"Or total revenue minus total cost, but that's the same thing."

"But in the perfectly competitive market P - AC = 0 (2 - 2 = 0)," Mo said, "since it's the same line. So rents for the PC market are 0. Consumer surplus is the whole area ACP_{pc}. And there is no deadweight loss."

"Because all gains from exchange have been exhausted at quantity Q_{pc}."

"You can calculate the consumer's surplus right? So we don't need to do that."

"Sure, that's just 1/2 base time height for that triangle."

"Right. For the monopoly market, we are at quantity Q_m and price P_m -- where marginal revenue equals marginal cost -- so rents to the monopolist are the area P_mBEP_{pc} or by the numbers it's (6 - 2)4 = 16."

"That leaves these two triangle areas AP_mB and BEC," Ginny said.

"AP$_m$B is consumer's surplus and BEC is deadweight loss."

"That's a pretty significant deadweight loss: 2 x 4 is 8. That's $8 out of the total $32 possible."

"What amazes me," Mo said, "is how much of the consumers surplus the monopolist takes: $16 of $32."

"So the consumer loses half of their surplus to the monopolist and then half again of the half that's left is deadweight loss. At least in this example. That's outrageous."

"But remember it doesn't really matter economically whether the producer or the consumer gets it..."

"Sure that's easy for you to say, you're a monopoly CD exchange operator."

"Now check this problem out," Mo said. "I was looking through Adam's old exams and found this one."

> **Problem:** Calculate consumers surplus, rents and deadweight loss in the following example. Label all curves and areas, showing quantities and prices produced, as well as rents, CS, and deadweight loss.

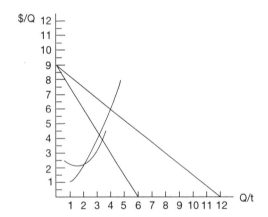

"That is quite a graph," Ginny said.

"Just remember that the marginal cost curve cuts through the average cost curve at its lowest point."

"That's right. So this is really not that hard at all. The monopolist would produce where MC = MR, which would be at 3 units and what looks to be a price of $6.75."

"And consumer's surplus is, as before, the area between the demand curve and a line at the $6.75 price."

"Which we have to calculate. So one-half base times height for the area is ½[3*($9-$6.75) = $3.375. We need rents and deadweight loss now."

"Well," Mo said, "rents are going to be (P - AC)Q. So ($6.75-$3)*3, is $11.25."

"How did you get that AC?" Ginny asked. "Is that from the point where the AC curve crosses the quantity line where MC = MR?"

"Yes, the line that goes straight up from a quantity of 3, up through MC = MR to the demand curve. Where AC crosses that line then you read over to the vertical axis. That horizontal line at $3 then becomes the bottom edge of the producer's surplus area."

"You know this is kind of a trick question. We can't really calculate the deadweight loss here, because the MC and AC curves are curved. Wouldn't we need calculus to do this accurately?"

"I think so," Mo said, "but we can get an approximation by pretending they're straight. Deadweight loss would be ½[($6.75-$4.50)*1]. That's $2.25, showing that simple monopoly pricing reduces economic efficiency, because monopolists don't produce enough to exhaust all the gains from trade."

Question 4. Using the data in **Question 3** above, graph (all on one graph) the demand, marginal revenue, average cost, and marginal cost curves the monopolist faces, then answer the questions below.

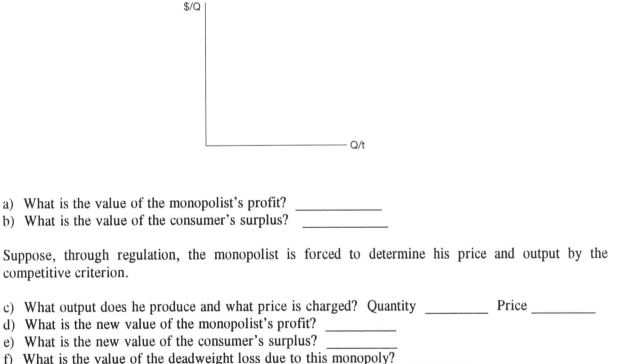

a) What is the value of the monopolist's profit? _____
b) What is the value of the consumer's surplus? _____

Suppose, through regulation, the monopolist is forced to determine his price and output by the competitive criterion.

c) What output does he produce and what price is charged? Quantity _____ Price _____
d) What is the new value of the monopolist's profit? _____
e) What is the new value of the consumer's surplus? _____
f) What is the value of the deadweight loss due to this monopoly? _____

OBJECTIVE 3.2 **Identify and calculate any possible inefficiencies in the use of inputs, resulting from monopoly behavior.**

"That's output though," Ginny said, "on the input side -- the factors of production -- the monopolist may be a price taker just like any firm."

"That's true. Like any firm they use inputs until the value of the additional output they get from the additional input equals the cost of hiring that input."

"Say no more. I'd like to talk about price discrimination, but that's about it for me."

OBJECTIVE 4.1 List and describe monopoly price discrimination schemes.

"Price discrimination schemes -- I counted three different schemes," Mo said. "Is that what you got?"

"I think so. There is perfect or first degree price discrimination. Then there was dividing the market into two groups, the more elastic and less elastic. And then finally, where you charge a certain price for the right to use some fixed part of the product, and a different price for the variable component of the product. That's the polaroid camera and film or IBM computers and computer cards example."

"Right, three different schemes. I thought the first degree price discrimination was interesting because if you look at it on a graph you can see how the monopolist could capture all of the benefits from trade. I mean there would be no deadweight loss, though consumer's surplus would also be zero."

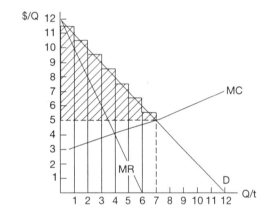

"So in this case the price on the first unit is something between $11 and $12, between $10 and $11 for the second unit, between $9 and $10 for the third, and so on until the quantity where their marginal cost crosses the demand curve."

"Yes, but another way to think of it," Mo said, "is the monopolist sets the price equal to the consumer's marginal value for each unit until their marginal cost equals the consumer's marginal value on the last unit produced."

"The upshot of it is that consumer's surplus is zero on each unit, because the monopolist has taken it all."

"You say that like it's a horrible thing, but from an efficiency standpoint it doesn't make any difference which party gets the benefit as long as someone gets it. Society loses most with regular monopoly pricing that leaves all that deadweight loss. Nobody gets those benefits."

"You're right monopolist Mo."

"Did you understand the second type, where the consumers are divided?"

"Yes, that was pretty straight-forward. You just have to be in an industry where you can divide up your customers into those who cannot substitute out of your product easily, even though you raise the price on them, and those who can. If you can do that then you can try this two prices approach."

"The main thing is that the firm, when it divides the market, is facing two different demand curves. This is like the third pricing scheme where although there is a single demand curve for computer services, it can be divided into a demand for the computer and another for the punch cards; or a demand for the Polaroid camera and another for the film; or one for the razor and another for the razor blades; or..."

"Okay, I get the point. So the monopolist would charge a relatively low price on the fixed component, the camera, and a higher price on the variable part, the film?"

"Right. They charge a low enough price to sell the camera to a lot of people. Those who place a higher value on the camera package are generally those who want to take more pictures. So they charge a higher price for the component of the package that varies with use: the film."

"So the monopolist ends up achieving largely the same thing as if they had charged the heavy camera users more for the camera than the light users. They will ultimately get the heavy users to pay more for the overall use of the product through the price of film rather than the price of the camera."

Question 5. Show graphically a type 2 price discrimination scheme.

TYPE 2 PRICE DISCRIMINATION

"Well I'm off to serve the hoardes who want to experience Seattle's best meatloaf. I guess Jim is trying to earn some rents before Karl sells the recipe, he's already raised the price and shrunk the serving size."

"Now that's a public service."

ANSWERS TO DIALOGUE QUESTIONS

Question 1. Vocabulary: b, h, a, b, f, c, e, h, b, h, i, d, g.

first degree price discrimination - a pricing scheme in which the seller charges consumers a price that is equal to the consumer's marginal value for each unit of the good.

Question 2. Although we can't think of all of the examples you will have, here are some possible answers.

Government/Official License: Cable companies who receive service area rights, food or other service companies at national parks, or airports or on university campuses, which often arrange multi-year contracts for being the sole provider of services.

Patents/Copyright: 3M's patent on "Post-it" notes, the use of Disney characters, the Apple logo.

Decreasing Cost Industry: All public utilities (water, sewer, natural gas for home heating, electricity).

Exclusive Ownership of Resource (including location): DeBeers Diamonds (they have controlled the distribution of diamonds through special agreements with the world's diamond producers since the 1930's), the only gas station in a small town.

Question 3. Quantity = 3   Price = 7

Q_d	P	TR	MR	AC	TC	MC
0	10	0	0	4	0	4
1	9	9	9	4	4	4
2	8	16	7	4	8	4
3	7	21	5	4	12	4
4	6	24	3	4	16	4
5	5	25	1	4	20	4
6	4	24	-1	4	24	4
7	3	21	-3	4	28	4
8	2	16	-5	4	32	4
9	1	9	-7	4	36	4
10	0	0	-9	4	40	4

Remember that if AC is constant, then AC = MC

Question 4. The slope of the MR curve is twice that of the demand curve, therefore the MR curve intersects the quantity axis at exactly half the quantity that the demand curve intersects at. Twice the slope appears as a line that is twice as steep. Using the data in the table to plot the MR curve is somewhat confusing until you realize that MR, and all marginal measures are measurements of change between points. Between Q=4 and Q=5 the change in TR, MR, equals 1. Between Q=5 and Q=6, MR is -1, so between Q=4 and Q=6, MR crosses the horizontal axis at $0. In fact it crosses the axis exactly at Q=5 though the table would lead you to believe MR=1 at Q=5.

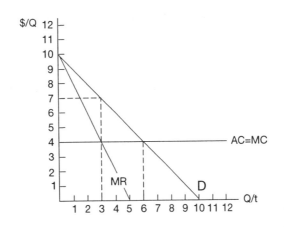

a) Profit = $9. If Q = 3, P = 7 and AC = 4 then profit = Q(P - AC) = 3(7 - 4) = 9.
   Or you can calculate by area, which is really the same thing.

b) Consumer's surplus = $4.50. ½ base * height = ½(3*3) = 4.5.

c) Quantity = 6 Price = 4. Where MC = MV = P.

d) Profit = 0. Since AC = P at this quantity profits are zero.

e) Consumer's surplus = 1/2(6) x 6 = $18.00.

f) Deadweight loss = $4.50. ½[(6-3)*(7-4)] = $4.50.

Question 5.

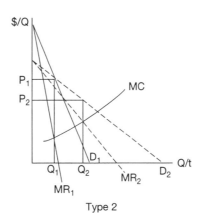

Type 2

THE BIG PICTURE

Chapters 1 through 8 presented the basic microeconomic principles underlying the supply and demand of goods. These principles are absolutely fundamental to microeconomic analysis. Their presentation in the first eight chapters presumed a perfectly competitive market (a market of price taking firms). There are, however, other market structures or models, for example the market structure in which price searching firms operate. Chapters 11 and 12 take up where Chapter 8 left off to fill out the description of market structures in the economic paradigm. Chapter 11 introduces the monopoly model; the other end of the spectrum from perfect competition. Chapter 12 presents the middle ground between perfect competition and monopoly: oligopoly and monopolistic competition.

Monopoly, oligopoly and monopolistic competition all fall under the larger category known as imperfect competition, which, of course, stands in contrast to perfect competition. The model within these broader categories that applies in any industry depends on the market characteristics in which the firm operates. A partial list of characteristics would include: the type of product being produced, the geographic location of the market, the number of competing producers in the market, the number of buyers for the product, and the costs of entry. By no means are these models an exhaustive description of the continuum of economic behavior. By necessity, constructing a theoretical model entails generalizing observed behavior, boiling it down to common elements based on refutable propositions that support the theory. The models presented in this text are general applications that have been found to explain the fundamental behavioral patterns of economic actors and markets.

The study of monopolies and the monopoly model is very involved with the examination of regulated monopolies. As you've learned, monopolists will not voluntarily produce a quantity that is Pareto efficient or market clearing. In markets where it is most efficient to have a single firm serving the entire market (where extreme economies of scale exist -- like utilities), economists attempt to discover appropriate regulatory schemes that improve net economic efficiency by forcing monopolists to produce greater quantities.

REVIEW QUESTIONS

Answers to all review questions appear at the end of this chapter.

PROBLEMS AND EXERCISES
Write your answer in the space(s) provided.

1. The market demand curve for motor oil (liters) is given by P = 53 - Q. Assume that oil is initially produced by a competitive industry in which the long-run supply curve is perfectly elastic at $5 per unit.

a. What output level would be produced by the competitive industry? What would be the price of motor oil? Calculate the consumer's surplus.

b. Now assume that the industry is monopolized but that production costs remain the same (MC = AC = $5). Calculate the profit maximizing price-quantity combination for the monopolist. Calculate the monopolist's profit. Calculate the welfare loss from monopolization.

c. Illustrate your answers on a graph that shows the competitive and monopoly outcomes. Label the areas you have calculated in part a and b.

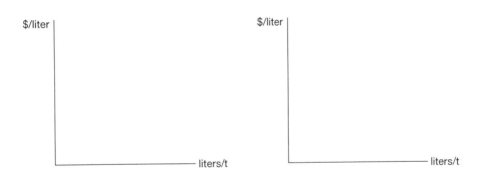

2. The market demand and marginal cost for party hats is illustrated below.

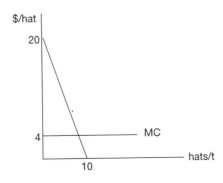

a. If the party hat industry is competitive, what output level would be produced in the market, and what would the market price be?

b. Calculate the amount of consumer surplus with the competitive industry.

c. If the party hat industry was a monopoly, what would the profit maximizing price and quantity be?

d. Calculate consumer surplus, monopoly profit, and deadweight loss under the monopoly.

3. A price searcher (monopoly) produces output at a constant marginal cost of $3 and has no fixed costs. The demand curve facing the price searcher is given as follows:

Price ($)	Quantity Demanded
10	0
9	3
8	6
7	9
6	12
5	15

a. Determine the price searcher's profit maximizing output, price and profit.

b. Show that by producing more output, the firm would decrease its profit.

4. You have invented a new board game called "College - Getting In, Getting Out." It is the only game of its kind, so you have a monopoly. You sell the rights to produce and distribute the game to a company, "Academic Press-ure." This publishing company's market analyst, Rosy Scenario, indicates that she believes the market demand curve for the game is as follows:

Price Per Game	Quantity
$20	70,000
19	80,000
18	90,000
17	100,000
16	110,000
15	120,000
14	130,000
13	140,000

a. If the marginal cost of producing and distributing the game is constant at $8 no matter how many games are produced and sold, and the average variable cost is the same, how many games will Academic Press-ure sell and at what price, to maximize monopoly profits? Assume Rosy's scenario is correct.

b. If you charged the publishing company $500,000 for the rights to the game, how much profit will they make selling at the price and quantity levels you gave in a)? What is the maximum amount the Academic Press-ure would have been willing to pay for the game?

c. You, as inventor and having sold production and distribution rights to Academic Press-ure, have a marginal cost of zero for producing and distributing the game. This marginal cost is the same no matter how many games are sold. The average variable cost to you is also zero no matter how many games are sold. What is the lowest price you would set as a profit-miximizing monopolist?

d. If it is possible for Academic Press-ure to price discriminate among purchasers of the game would the number of games they sell be greater or less than in a)? Who would benefit and who would lose? Is price discrimination a reasonable option in this case? Why or why not?

5. Below are the demand curves for heavy metal music for teenagers and senior citizens.

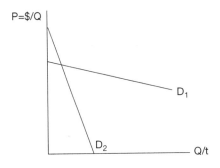

a. Identify (label) which demand curve belongs to which group.
b. What conditions are necessary for a firm selling heavy meatal music to be able to price discriminate?

c. If price discrimination is possible, which group will be charged a higher price? _____

d. Which group is more likely to receive a coupon for heavy metal albums? _____

6. You've just been elected President of the only local golf club. The club is in need of some major repairs and renovations that will require substantial cash. You've determined (below) a demand curve, representative of the typical golfer at the club, and the marginal cost per round of golf.

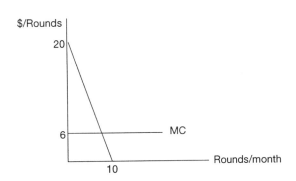

a. The club currently charges $7.00 per round (game). Can you raise the price and increase profits? What is the profit maximizing price per round and quantity of rounds? _____

What are the profits? _____

b. If you do raise green fees, it is advisable that any increase be phased in over several years. In the meantime you are also contemplating a club membership fee. How much could you charge the typical golfer as an annual membership fee? _____

c. What are the total profits then for the course given maximum green fees and club membership fees? _____

d. There is another option that could possibly raise even more money for the golf course, given some consumer's surplus is still realized by golfers. It also involves charging a per round fee and an annual membership. Determine the price per round and the size of the annual fee.

7. This advertisement for Pay Less Drug Stores and Skippers Seafood Restaurants was in the local paper.

> The Skippers and Pay Less Guaranteed Catch! With every fishing equipment purchase of $2.00 or more at Pay Less, you will receive a coupon good for one Skippers Regular Fish Dinner **FREE** with the purchase of one Regular Fish Dinner. Offer good through April 27, 1995 in our Pay Less Sporting Goods Department.

a. Skippers is engaging in a form of price discrimination here. Why does Skippers give the discount to customers of Pay Less only, instead of to customers of any fishing shop in town?

b. Draw the demand curve for Skippers Fish Dinners that is attributable to Payless Fishing Department customers and a second demand curve for all other Fish Dinner consumers. Label the Pay Less demand as D_p and the other demand as D_o. Show and label the price charged and quantity sold to Payless customers as P_p and Q_p, and for that sold to other customers as P_o and Q_o. Assume MC = 0.

$/Q

Q/t

c. Skippers is also price discriminating, charging the same customer regular price for the first dinner and nothing for the second. Given the demand schedules below for two Pay Less/Skippers customers, how many dinners, priced at $4.00 each, would Skippers sell without the coupon deal? _____ For these two customers, do the coupons make a difference and is it a profitable deal for Skippers? Why?

Customer A			Customer B	
Q_d	($) MV		Q_d	($) MV
1	4		1	2.50
2	2		2	1.50
3	0		3	.50

8. For each of the following points on the demand curve facing a bridge-owner who is a nondiscriminating monopolist, calculate the total revenue and the marginal revenue.

Bridge Crossings Per Day	Toll Charged Per Crossing	Total Revenue	Marginal Revenue
98,039	$1.02		
99,010	1.01		
100,000	1.00		
101,010	0.99		
102,041	0.98		

Assume the bridge owner incurs no costs as people cross the bridge. If she sets a price in the range above, does it matter where she sets the price? Explain. What is the elasticity of demand in this range?

9. The Canadian Gadget Company (CGC) sells its product in the domestic market and in the U.S. CGC enjoys a monopoly in the Canadian market due to the existence of a tariff, but CGC is a perfect competitor in the U.S. market. As a result of a Canada-U.S. trade accord, the Canadian tariff is disappearing. What will happen to prices and quantities in Canada and the U.S. as a result of the accord?

10. The municipal government grants a licence to the Goodie Co. to sell Dampfnudel (a Bavarian dessert specialty) at a particular location in the city. The company agrees to pay to the city a licence fee (tax) of "x" per dampfnudel sold. Dampfnudel are produced at a constant MC.
    a. Show the company's profit maximizing price and quantity on a diagram. Indicate the area that represents the company's profit and the area that represents its payment to the city.

$/Dampfnudel

Dampfnudel/month

b. After some time, the company proposes to pay a monthly fee to the city that is equal to what it paid in the previous month. That is, the new fee would be fixed at this amount regardless of the company's sales or profits. This proposal converts the fee into a "fixed cost" or lump sum fee, rather than a per unit fee. Compared to a. above, what would be the effect of this new scheme on:

      1) price and quantity?
      2) consumer welfare?
      3) company profit?
      4) the share of the tax paid by consumers?

11. Illustrate the **net** gain to a monopolist in the diagram below of adopting a monopolist's profit maximizing output level compared to competitive output levels.

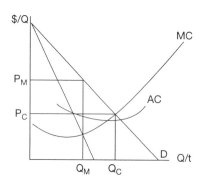

TRUE - FALSE QUESTIONS
Provide a one or two sentence explanation with your answer.

1. A songwriter will want their song to sell for a higher price than the record producer to whom she sells her songs for a fixed percentage of revenues from the commercial sales of the song.

2. One difference between pure monopoly and perfect competition is that the industry demand curve is downward sloping in the monopoly case, and perfectly elastic in the competitive case.

3. A natural monopolist regulated to charge a price equal to marginal cost will lose money.

4. It is possible for price discrimination to increase monopoly output.

5. Microeconomic theory predicts that a monopolist will use inputs less efficiently than a perfectly competitive firm, because of its unique position as single producer in the market.

6. Since the monopolist faces a downward sloping demand curve, a decision to change output quantity will have no effect on the price of the good.

7.   The fundamental reason for the existence of a single firm in an industry (a monopoly) is that there are barriers to entry into that industry for other firms.

8.   A monopolist will <u>always</u> charge a price in the elastic region of the demand curve.

9.   There are a variety of legal or economic institutions, monopoly being one of them, that can cause the economy to move away from economically efficient levels of production.

10.   Monopolists have little incentive and are therefore less likely to bring into production innovations in their good or service.

11.   A profit-maximizing monopolist always produces where MC = MR.

12.   A monopolist may not produce where average costs are minimized, even in the long run.

13.   A monopolist that can discriminate perfectly may not produce the same level of output as would a perfectly competitive industry.

MULTIPLE CHOICE QUESTIONS
Choose the <u>best</u> answer.

The diagram below shows the total demand for tickets to Husky football games, made up of the alumni demand and the student demand. Assume that the University can costlessly distinguish students from alumni and prevent them from reselling tickets, and that the cost to the University of admitting additional spectators is effectively zero, up to the capacity of Husky stadium, which is 62,000. Assume also that the University wants to maximize net revenue from the football program.

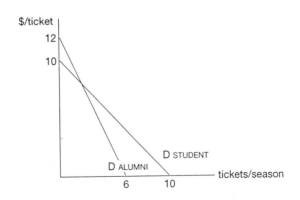

1. The University should charge students a price of
a. 0   b. $3   c. $5   d. $7

2. The University should charge alumni a price of
a.   0
b.   higher than the student price.
c.   lower than the student price.
d.   equal to the student price.

3. If the State of Washington levies a $1,000 lump sum tax on the University's football program, by how much will the University immediately increase the price of football tickets?
a.   0
b.   By an amount equal to the tax.
c.   By an amount less than the tax.
d.   By an amount equal to the tax divided by the number of tickets.

4. If the State of Washington instead levies a $1 per ticket tax on the Husky football program, by how much will the University increase the price of each football ticket?
a.   0
b.   By an amount equal to the tax.
c.   By an amount less than the tax.
d.   By an amount equal to the tax divided by the number of tickets.

5. Your associate has determined the elasticity of demand for a competitive industry and a monopoly. The elasticities of demand that she found were -0.5 and -3.0. Unfortunately, she cannot remember which estimate belongs to which industry. Can you help her out?
a.   No, there is not enough information.
b.   Yes, the competitive industry is the one with -3.0, and the monopoly has -0.5.
c.   Yes, the competitive industry is the one with -0.5 and the monopoly has -3.0.
d.   No, because both industries could possibly have either elasticity.

The diagram below is used to answer questions 6 through 8.

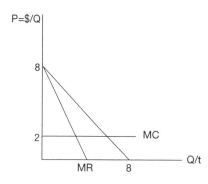

6. A perfect competitor and monopolist would respectively have price and quantity at:
a.   P = 2, Q = 6; P = 5, Q = 3.

b.   P = 2, Q = 8; P = 5, Q = 3.
c.   P = 2, Q = 6; P = 3, Q = 4.
d.   P = 2, Q = 8; P = 3, Q = 5.

7. Consumer surplus under perfect competition and monopoly is respectively:
a. 18 and 3   b. 18 and 4.5   c. 24 and 8   d. 24 and 12

8. Dead weight loss under perfect competition and monopoly is respectively:
a. 18 and 4.5   b. 18 and 9   c. 0 and 4.5   d. 0 and 9

9. A market in which the average total costs of production continually decline with increased output is referred to as:
a.   diminishing returns to scale.
b.   diminishing returns to a variable factor.
c.   a natural monopoly.
d.   a constant cost industry.

Consider the 2 for 1 pizza deals major pizza chains offer customers for questions 10-13.

10. The pizza chains place coupons in the student newspapers offering these deals because
a.   they feel sorry for the University students.
b.   they are identifying the customers with a lower elasticity of demand for pizza.
c.   they are offering a lower price to customers with more substitutes for pizza at that price.
d.   University students tend to like pizza more than most people.

Three demand schedules for pizza are given below:

Mr. Rojo		Mr. Verde		Mr. Azul	
Qd	$MV	Qd	$MV	Qd	$MV
1	3.50	1	3.75	1	6.00
2	2.50	2	2.00	2	3.00
3	1.50	3	.75	3	0.00

11. Assume the pizza dealer charges $6.00 for the first pizza and nothing for the second. Who would redeem the 2-for-1 coupon?
a.   Mr. Rojo and Mr. Verde.
b.   Mr. Verde and Mr. Azul.
c.   Mr. Rojo and Mr. Azul.
d.   All of them.

12. To which customer does the dealer sell more pizza with the 2-for-1 deal than they would pricing each pizza at the average of $3.00?
a. Mr. Rojo   b. Mr. Verde   c. Mr. Azul   d. None of them

13. Which customer gains consumer's surplus on the exchange with the pizza dealer?
a. Mr. Rojo   b. Mr. Verde   c. Mr. Azul   d. None of them

14. Which of these contributes to the existence of monopoly power?
a.   a continuously decreasing long-run average cost curve.

b.   possession of a patent.
c.   control over essential inputs.
d.   all of the above.

15. The marginal revenue curve for a monopolist is
a.   always above the demand curve.
b.   generally below the average cost curve.
c.   the same as the average revenue curve.
d.   always below the demand curve.

16. In which of the following ways is a monopolist different from a perfect competitor?
a.   Average cost will continually drop as output expands.
b.   Price is above marginal revenue.
c.   Average total cost equals average fixed costs plus average variable costs.
d.   The demand curve for the industry has a negative slope.

17. A certain electric utility has a long-run average cost curve that slopes downward throughout the relevant range of production. If regulations require the utility to charge a uniform price equal to marginal cost to all customers, the utility will:
a.   make a positive profit.
b.   break even (zero profit).
c.   incur a loss.
d.   insufficient information to conclude.

18. Doctors can charge different patients different prices because:
a.   everyone at some time requires the services of a doctor.
b.   it is difficult to resell doctor services.
c.   doctors have a good idea about how much you are willing to pay.
d.   b and c.

19. The concept of monopoly is ambiguous because:
a.   anyone can be shown to be a monopolist if the product is defined narrowly enough.
b.   anyone can be shown to be a monopolist if the product is defined broadly enough.
c.   most products are sold by corporations rather than by individuals.
d.   sellers may combine or collude in setting prices.

20. Assume that MR equals MC at 500 units of output. At this output level, a profit maximizing monopoly firm's TFC is $1900 and TVC is $2300. If the price of the product is $10 per unit, the firm should produce,
a. 0 units.   b. 10 units.   c. 50 units.   d. 500 units.

21. In the preceding question, the firm will earn an economic profit of,
a. 0   b. $700   c. $800   d. $1900

22. Authors who sell book rights to a publisher in exchange for royalty fees (a payment per book sold) will want, compared to their publisher who prints and promotes the book,
a.   to charge a lower price and sell more books.
b.   to charge a lower price and sell fewer books.

c.   to charge a higher price and sell fewer books.

d.   to charge the same price but sell more books.

SHORT ANSWER QUESTIONS

1. Why do economists consider society's welfare to be greater in a competitive market than in a monopoly? Under what conditions might a monopoly be preferable to forcing the market to be competitive?

2. Resort hotels commonly charge higher room rates during their peak seasons (e.g., winter months in Florida). City bus services charge higher fares to commuters who ride the bus in peak periods (e.g., 4-6 p.m. on weekdays). What is the principle behind these pricing schemes? How are the two situations the same? How are they different?

3. Does the second statement follow from the first? Why or why not?

     i)   "It is well established result in economics that price is higher and output is lower in a monopolized market than in a competitive market."

     ii)   "Western industrialized countries have experienced recurring bouts of inflation in recent years because of the existence of monopoly power in their respective economies."

4. Why is it most efficient for a single firm to serve the entire market in cases of natural monopoly?

5. In the case of natural monopoly, would a firm agree to charge a P = MC in exchange for a guaranteed monopoly position. Why or why not? Diagram this situation showing the profit or loss.

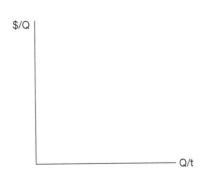

ANSWERS TO REVIEW QUESTIONS

Answers to EXERCISES AND PROBLEMS

1. a. <u>P & Q:</u> P = $5 because P = MC for a competitive firm, and $5 = 53 - Q, Q = 48.
<u>Consumer's Surplus:</u> CS = ½(48) x (53 - 5) = $1152.

b. <u>P & Q:</u> MR = MC, 53 - 2Q = 5 (MR slope is twice the slope of the demand curve). 48 = 2Q,
Q = 24. Enter Q = 24 into the equation for the **demand curve**, P = 53 - Q, P = 53 - 24 = 29.
<u>Profits:</u> Profit = Total Revenue - Total Cost, (29 x 24) - (5 x 24) = $576. <u>Welfare Loss:</u> ½[(29 -
5)(48 - 24)] = $288.

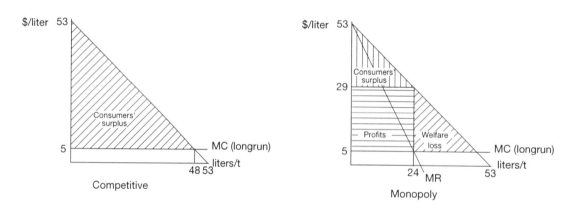

2. a. Derive the equation of the demand curve from the graph. P = a - bQ, where a is the y-intercept
and b is the slope. b = (0-20)/((10-0) = -2. P = 20 - 2Q. P = $4, so 4 = 20 - 2Q. Q = 8.

b. CS = 1/2(8) x (20 - 4) = $64.

c. Determine the equation of the marginal revenue curve, to find out where MR = MC. MR has the
same y-intercept, but twice the slope of the demand curve: P = 20 - 4Q. MC = $4, so 4 = 20 - 4Q,
Q = 4. Enter Q = 4 into the equation for the demand curve for monopoly price, P = 20 - 2(4) = $12.

d. CS = 1/2(4) x (20 - 12) = $16. Profit = (P x Q)-(AC x Q) = $32. Deadweight loss = 1/2(8 -
4)*($12 - $4) = $16.

3. a. Profit maximization occurs where MC = MR. MC = $3 as given. MR is determined by first
calculating total revenue, then MR from TR. MR = change in TR/change in quantity.

TR	MR	
0	0	MR = MC at P = $5 and Q = 15
27	27	Profit = TR - TC. $75 - ($3 x 15)
48	21	Profit = $75 - $45 = $30.
63	15	
72	9	Profit also = Q(P - AC)
75	3	15($5 - $3) = 15 x $2 = $30.

b. Increasing output, say to 18, would imply a decrease in price from $5 to $4. Profit decreases to 18($4 - $3) = $18. Notice how if output quantity were increased further to 21 or 24, then (P - AC) will become less than or equal to zero, making profits equal to zero or negative.

4. a. Answer: $17 for 100,000. You must first calculate TR (P x Q) to get MR (ΔTR/ΔQ). The catch here is that the change in quantity given in the table is per 10,000 games.

TR	MR	
1,400,000	----	MC = $8 per game. MR = $80,000 per
1,520,000	120,000	10,000 games at a price of $17 and
1,620,000	100,000	quantity of 100,000 games.
1,700,000	80,000	
1,760,000	60,000	
1,800,000	40,000	
1,820,000	20,000	
1,820,000	0	

b. Answer: Net Profit = $400,000; maximum willing to pay is < $900,000.
Profit = Q(P - AC) = 100,000($17 - $8). Note that MC = AC when MC or AC are given as constant. Profit = 100,000 x $9 = $900,000. Net profit (i.e. profit minus charge for the rights to the game of $500,000) = $900,000 - $500,000 = $400,000. Academic Press-ure would be willing to pay some amount less than $900,000. It is important to question whether this demand curve is for a single year or for the games "lifetime".   If this were only for a single year and similar demand is anticipated for the future, then the company would be willing to pay some amount up to the present value of the stream of profits from the game.

c. Answer: $13.00 for 140,000.
Set MC = MR to determine your price and quantity levels.

d. If the company can price discriminate they would sell more games than described in a. The seller would gain by capturing more of the consumer's surplus. Price discrimination would not seem to be a reasonable option, because it is difficult to think of how the company could divide the consumers according to their elasticities of demand, and it is difficult to prevent resale of the game by those who would take advantage of the companies price differences.

5. a. D1 seniors; D2 teenagers
b. The firm must face a downward sloping demand curve which implies price searching power, a dividable market based on the different elasticities of demand among the consumer groups, and they must be able to prevent resale by those who can buy at the lower price to those in the higher price group.
c. Teenagers
d. Seniors

6. a. Yes you can raise the price to P = $13 and Q = 3.5 rounds per month. Profits are $24.50. The equation of the demand curve is P = 20 - 2Q. The equation for the MR curve is therefore P = 20 - 4Q. MC = MR where $6 = 20 - 4Q. This comes out as 4Q = 14, Q = 3.5. Substituting in Q = 3.5 into the demand equation gives, P = 20 - 2(3.5) = $13. Profit is Q(P - AC), 3.5(13 - 6) = $24.50

b. You could charge the typical golfer a membership fee that is anything less than the total amount of their consumer surplus at the profit maximizing quantity identified in (a). In this case that amount is $1/2(3.5) \times (20 - 13) = \$12.25$. Thus, you could charge the typical golfer something less than $12.25 per month.

c. Total profits are $24.50 + $12.25 = $36.75 per month.

d. The other option is to competitively price each round of golf but charge a larger membership fee approximating the value of each member's total consumer surplus. Price = $6.00 and quantity = 7 rounds per month. $P = 20 - 2Q$; $6 = 20 - 2Q$, $Q = 7$. Consumer Surplus = $1/2(7) \times (\$20 - \$6) = 3.5 \times 14 = \$49$ per month. The membership fee in this case would be some amount less than $49 per month. Total profit in this case would be $49.00 per month.

7. a. Skippers is offering them 1/2 price dinners, a lower price than regular, because these customers are expected to have more elastic demand curves than other potential Skippers customers. Customers of Pay Less generally have a lower income then people who would shop at more expensive fishing stores, and they would therefore be more willing to substitute away from the regularly priced fish dinner. They have close substitutes, including the fish they may catch themselves. Additionally, with a lower income the relative value of their time is less, so they are more willing to devote time to clipping coupons and shopping around for the best price.

b. With MC = 0, MC=MR where the MR line for each demand curve would cross the quantity axis.

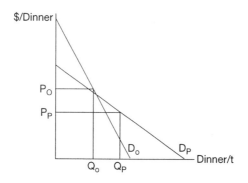

c. Skippers would only sell one dinner without the coupon deal to customer A, because her marginal value of $4.00 is equal to the cost of the regularly priced dinner. The coupon deal does make a difference because now customer A will still buy the dinner, and customer B will also buy a dinner. Customer B's MV is not high enough to buy one $4.00 dinner, but his total value for 2 dinners ($2.50 + $1.50) is equal to the cost of the two dinners with the coupon. This is a profitable deal for Skippers as long as the average cost of producing the dinners does not exceed the average price of $2.00 per dinner.

8. When MC=0, the profit maximizing strategy is to maximize TR. Since profit = TR - TC, if costs are zero then maximizing TR is the same as maximizing profit.

Bridge Crossings Per Day	Toll Charged Per Crossing	Total Revenue	Marginal Revenue
98,039	$1.02	99999.8	Approx:
99,010	1.01	100000.1	.0003
100,000	1.00	100000.0	.0001
101,010	0.99	99999.9	.0001
102,041	0.98	100000.1	.0003

In this case marginal revenue per single car crossing is incredibly small and virtually no different from the marginal revenue received at any particular price level. It makes no significant difference where she sets the price within this range. The elasticity of demand in this range is approximately -1 or unitary elastic demand.

9. The price of gadgets in Canada will decrease when the tariff disappears, and quantity demanded will increase. Competition should lower the price to MC. There is no reason to expect a change in the price and quantity in the United States.

10. a.

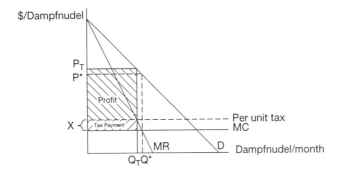

b. The change to the fixed fee would lead to:
1) a decrease in price and an increase in quantity.
2) an increase in consumer surplus.
3) an increase in company profit.
4) since a lump sum tax does not change the price to sonsumers in the short run, they would pay less of this tax.

11. Profit in either equals TR - TC. In the monopoly case producing output Q_M at price P_M, total revenue equals area B + C + D and total cost area D. In the competitive case producing output Q_C at price P_C, total revenue equals area C + D + F + G and total cost area D + G. Thus rents for the monopolist include area B but at the expense of area F. It is a net gain in profit, otherwise they wouldn't produce at that level. Area E and F are a net loss to society, that is deadweight loss. As you can see, however, it depends on the slope of the demand curve and the shape of the cost curves to determine how much better off, or relatively how little better off the monopolist is relative to the perfectly competitive case.

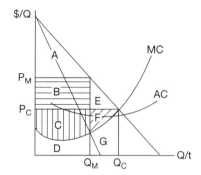

Answers to TRUE - FALSE QUESTIONS

1. False. The record producer, having a monopoly over the songs of the performer will profit maximize by offering a quantity at a price where MC = MR. Total revenues would increase, though profits would decrease, by offering a greater quantity at a lower price, which is what the songwriter would prefer.

2. False. The industry demand curve is downward sloping in both cases. The perfectly competitive <u>firm</u> faces a perfectly elastic demand at the price level.

3. True. Since a natural monopolist produces in the downward sloping portion of its average cost curve, marginal cost is below average cost in this range. A firm receiving a price equal to marginal cost would therefore not be covering its average costs of producing the good, and would therefore be losing money.

4. True. First degree price discrimination, if possible, would lead a monopolist to produce a level of output that otherwise exceeds their profit maximizing quantity.

5. False. Microeconomic theory predicts that monopolists will use inputs in the same way as perfectly competitive firms, so that the value of their marginal product is equal to their wage.

6. False. The downward sloping, market demand curve ensures that a change in quantity will result in a change in price.

7. True. If a firm is making profits and there are no barriers to entry, other firms will enter the market and destroy the monopoly position. The monopolist maintains its position because of one or several barriers to other firms.

8. False. This is true for regular monopoly pricing. But a regulated monopolist, or first degree price discrimination, for example, could result in a price in the inelastic portion of the demand curve.

9. True. Monopoly is one of several institutions, such as taxation, regulation, and others which lead the economy away from a Pareto efficient point.

10. False. Monopolists have the same array of incentives as other firms to bring new products and innovations into production. The alternative view ignores the law of demand and the various options that

exist to a monopolist for increasing prices to capture profits from the new product.

11. True. Production at an output level where MC = MR leads to the greatest profits, because up to that point the monopolist is receiving more per additional unit produced than it costs him to produce that unit.

12. True. The production decision is not tied to the firms average costs, but to its marginal costs.

13. False. A monopolist that can discriminate perfectly will produce the same level of output as a perfectly competitive industry, because the monopolist would be extracting rents on each unit produced up to the point where the monopolists marginal costs equaled the marginal value of the consumer.

Answers to MULTIPLE CHOICE QUESTIONS

1. c	6. a	11. c	16. b	21. c
2. b	7. b	12. a	17. c	22. a
3. a	8. c	13. c	18. d	
4. c	9. c	14. d	19. a	
5. c	10. c	15. d	20. d	

Answers to SHORT ANSWER QUESTIONS

1. Economists consider society's welfare to be greater under a competitive market because all gains from exchange are exhausted. Under a monopoly, there is usually a distortion from the optimal, efficient price and quantity, leaving unacquired gains from trade. It is only in the case of a natural monopoly, where a single firm will prove to be the least cost producer of the good, that a monopoly is preferable to forcing the market to be competitive.

2. The principle behind these pricing schemes is price discrimination based on the consumer's price elasticity of demand for the good in question. City bus services often have a monopoly on public transportation in their service areas, so commuters who must get to work have little choice but to pay the higher fares in peak periods. Similarly, those seeking the warmth of Florida in the middle of winter have relatively few options, without paying for international travel. Therefore their demand is less elastic and the resort hotel owners capitalize on this situation. Beyond the similar notions of peak and off-peak usage, the two situations are similar in that both the resort hotels and the bus service have some degree of monopoly or price searching power (i.e., they can affect the price of the good they provide). They are different in that the demand for bus service is more inelastic than for hotels, because there are fewer substitutes for busses. The two also differ in that the bus service is more of a monopoly. Generally there is only one public transportation network in a community. Finally, the supply of bus service is far more flexible than hotel service. The bus service can bring additional busses into service if needed whereas the hotel cannot add more rooms in the short run.

3. No. Inflation is an increase in the general price level (i.e., all goods) from a previous period. A price increase from a monopolist could be part of an inflationary trend, but that sort of price increase is the result of a different set of circumstances, for example rising costs of production. The establishment of a high price for a good by a monopolist is an increase in the price of this good *relative* to the price of all other goods in the economy. Consumers respond to the high price of a monopolist by reducing their consumption, as they do according to the law of demand with all goods.

4. Natural monopolies exist when the market characteristics of decreasing average cost for all producers exist throughout the possible range of output demanded by consumers. In other words there aren't enough consumers demanding the good to get the producer out of the range where his average costs are decreasing. For example, the producer's average costs are decreasing until they hit their low point at 120, but the quantity demanded at any price never exceeds 100 and firms will lose money producing any more than 90 units. This sets up the situation where one producer, supplying all 90 units is the least cost way for society to achieve that output. One producer in this case ensures that this firm is producing at the lowest average cost possible.

If two or more firms were fighting over the market, then they might each end up with half or one third of the market. Since they all have similar, decreasing average cost curves, if each of three firms are producing a quantity of 30 units, they will all be producing at higher costs (at higher positions on their AC curves) than the single firm producing all 90 units.

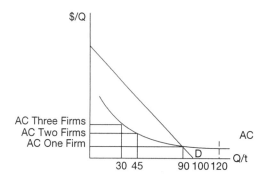

5. No. To produce at P = MC would mean the firm would lose money. By definition MC is less than AC in a natural monopoly. Since profit = Q(P - AC), and P = MC < AC, profit would be negative.

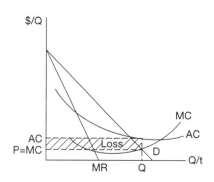

CHAPTER 12
Imperfect Competition

PRINCIPAL GOALS

1.0 Understand the continuum of market structures between perfect competition and monopoly. (Objectives 1.1, 1.2)

2.0 Recognize the distinguishing characteristics of monopolistic competition. (Objective 2.1)

3.0 Recognize the distinguishing characteristics of oligopoly. (Objective 3.1)

4.0 Be familiar with some of the concerns of antitrust legislation. (Objective 4.1)

OBJECTIVES
Answers to bold-faced questions appear at the end of the dialogue.

"Have you seen the Diner's latest ads Mo?" They feature Karl, dressed all in black, with a stubble beard and his usual bored, bemused, 'I am old beyond my years' look. The caption reads, "Meatloaf -- what this country was built on."

"This country was built on meatloaf? No wonder New York is sinking. What are all the rigs in Texas drilling for? Tomato sauce?"

"Apparently corny sells well. Some of the other fast food joints are putting meatloaf on the menu. I think it's sort of a retro fad, a tofu backlash. But Jim thinks he's a genius."

"Some genius. Before he had a monopoly on meatloaf in the University District. Now it's available on every streetcorner."

"I know," said Ginny. "At first he advertised just to increase the demand for meatloaf. Now I think he realizes he has to focus just on his product somehow, and advertise that it's different from all the others."

"The only one not to use real meat?"

"I was thinking more along the lines of winning Seattle's Best Meatloaf contest last month."

OBJECTIVE 1.1 List the characteristics that distinguish market models.

"You realize Ginny, that this means Jim is operating in a monopolistically competitive market. He and his meatloaf are somewhere between pure monopoly and perfect competition."

"Did you get the impression from Chapter 12 that most industries do lie somewhere in between? I mean, you can always define the product or location narrowly enough to call something a monopoly, but in reality it seems like most firms face some competition, and most products are somewhat differentiated."

"Do you think that's the key to distinguishing market structures then?" asked Mo. "By the number of firms and their relationship, and product differentiation?"

"Those are two characteristics. But I think the costs of entry and exit are also important for any short and long run distinctions, and the number of buyers and cost structure also play a role."

OBJECTIVE 1.2 Recognize definitions for the important new vocabulary.

Question 1. Match the term with its definition(s). Write out definitions for any undefined terms.

a. imperfect competition
c. collusion
e. price fixing
g. product differentiation
i. horizontal merger
k. trust
m. predatory pricing
o. tie-in sales

b. oligopoly
d. cartel
f. monopolistic competition
h. contestability
j. vertical merger
l. antitrust policy
n. block booking

_____ the practice of bundling several goods together as an indivisable package which the buyer can take all together or not at all.

_____ the existence of which permits firms a certain degree of price searching power.

_____ the practice of selling one, usually less desired, good by combining it as a package with another, usually more desired, good.

_____ the act of setting and maintaining prices for goods at certain levels, especially by the mutual agreement of competing firms.

_____ an agreement by two or more firms engaged in different stages of a single, but larger production process to form a single, integrated firm.

_____ an industry in which the same basic product (i.e. it serves the same basic function) is produced by many firms, but each individual firm's product possesses some unique characteristics, making it distinguishable from the other products offered by the industry.

_____ the act of conspiring to coordinate prices and/or output levels among firms with the purpose of gaining monopoly benefits.

_____ an association of firms with the purpose of gaining monopoly benefits through collusion.

_____ a market structure which exhibits the qualities that a producer faces a downward sloping demand curve for their product, which is not identical to the goods produced by other producers in the industry, though essentially the same basic good.

_____ an industry in which many firms possess some degree of price-searching power due to the differentiation of their products.

_____ the creation of or observation of different qualities and attributes in a given product.

_____ in the United States a series of legislation directed towards eliminating and preventing the formation and activities of trusts.

_____ the ability to enter and exit quickly a market at low or no cost.

_____ an industry in which only a few price searching firms produce a similar good.

_____ a group of firms from the same industry combined by corporate investors (usually including the owner(s) of the largest firm(s) in the particular industry), who have acquired a controlling interest in these firms. These investors then form a leadership group to operate the firm in a manner that seeks to achieve monopoly profits and control over the industry.

_____ a strategy designed to drive weaker firms out of business by forcing them to sell their product at a price below their cost of production.

_____ an agreement by two firms producing a similar product to form a single firm.

OBJECTIVE 2.1 Identify the distinguishing characteristics of monopolistic cometition.

"So the Diner is in a monopolistically competitive market because in the shortrun, the unique product gives Jim some monopoly rents, but in the long run, other establishments can enter the market in response to these profits and offer meatloaf on their menu. I mean, how much can it cost to start up a meatloaf entree?"

"And entry will continue until the marginal firm is making zero economic profit," continued Ginny. "Which makes me wonder how this differs from perfect competition in the long run."

"I think," said Mo, "that although both have zero profit long run equilibriums, the perfectly competitive firm is at the minimum of their average cost curve because all their products are the same, whereas for the monopolistically competitive firm with a differentiated product, the zero profit equilibrium will be where P = AC, but not min AC."

"What does product differentiation have to do with being at the minimum of the AC curve?"

"It puts slope into the demand curve the firm faces. In other words, it means it has some price searching power in the sense that if it raises its price slightly it loses some, but not all sales, like a perfect competitor would."

"That's true," Ginny said. "Jim would lose some business if he raised the price of meatloaf by 50 cents, but not all his business. It is, after all, Karl's unique recipe served in the only true U-district Diner by yours truly. But I'm still not making the connection with minimum AC's."

"Just try drawing a downward sloping demand curve that's tangent to a U-shaped average cost curve (the tangency means P = AC so the zero profit conditions holds). You can't draw it at the minimum, whereas you can't draw a horizontal demand curve tangent anywhere but the bottom of the curve."

Question 2. Do what Mo says: draw a downward sloping and horizontal demand curve, each tangent to the same U-shaped average cost curve. Compare the price and quantity at the zero profit (P=AC) tangencies for the two-curves.

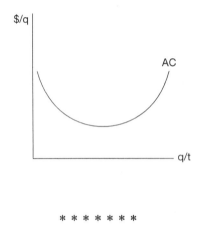

* * * * * * *

"Eureka! I see it. So the monopolistically competitive firm will produce less output and have a higher price in the long run equilibrium than a perfectly competitive firm with the same cost curves."

Question 3. Diagram a clothing boutique (monopolistically competitive) earning short run profits. Suppose a competitor opens up a store across the street. What do you expect to happen to the demand curve that the original boutique faces? Draw the long run equilibrium for this firm earning zero economic profit.

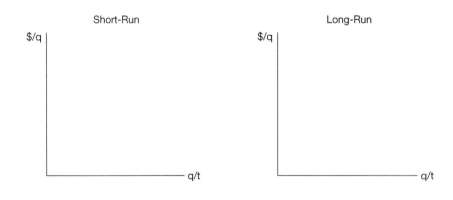

* * * * * * *

OBJECTIVE 3.1 **Identify the conditions making collusion more difficult for oligopolistic firms.**

"As a fellow firm-owner I sympathize with Jim. You know that obnoxious guy who sits in the first row and constantly tries to score Brownie points with Silberberg?"

"Sure, his name is Thorsten. Silberberg seems to find him annoying."

"Well I find him more than annoying Ginny. I've found out he's starting up a CD exchange."

"Oh dear. That could affect what you can charge for membership, especially if he tries to undercut you. Do you have anything to protect your market position?"

"Only my current customer list," said Mo. "You need a critical mass to make these exchanges work; they're like telephones -- their value depends on the number of other people participating."

"Why don't you two collude and agree to set a high price. You can call your cartel OPECD, Organization of People Exchanging CD's."

"Because Ginny, that's a stupid name, and it would mean having to talk to the guy. Besides, it's illegal."

"I can hear those customers walking away. Is that a Nancy Sinatra tune they're humming from their latest Thorsten CD exchange? Wait, I think I've got it, something about boots being made for walkin'..."

"It wouldn't work anyway," said Mo, "I don't trust him. Even though we could monitor each other's fees I wouldn't put it past him to start offering side deals and signing bonuses to people, like one month's free membership or something."

"Not a bad idea. Why don't you offer free math tutoring with yours?" suggested Ginny.

"Don't you see, once we both start trying to undercut the agreement the whole thing unravels and neither one of us makes any profit."

"Why is there such an incentive to cheat when total profits would be higher with collusion? This reminds me of the prisoner's dilemma in Chapter 9."

"It must be exactly the same principle." Mo said. "Total profits are higher with collusion, but each of us can do better than our half of the profits if we can cheat and get away with it."

"And that's because each of you faces a more elastic demand curve than the market in total, since you're each selling a product that's a substitute for the other's. So if one of you lowers your price slightly, you could increase sales dramatically. And since we know from chapter 11 that the monopoly price is on the elastic portion of the demand curve, a price decrease is matched by a greater percentage increase in sales, so total revenues will rise."

"Quite so Ginny. Besides, if we both cooperated and earned some profit there's nothing we can do to prevent other people entering the business and starting their own exchange. Then we have to either bring them into the cartel or let them steal all our business."

"So what would make colluding easier?"

"Well it makes more sense if we can keep other people out. After that I think it's largely a matter of removing the incentive to cheat."

"Which means making it more likely that you get caught cheating."

"Right," said Mo, "so things that make detecting cheating easier make the cartel more stable: like good price information on one another, fewer firms, and similar sized firms. Also, you don't want any basis for members changing their price that they may try to attribute to a slightly different product, different costs, shifting demand or technological change."

Question 4. Rank the following markets according to where collusion would be easiest: airlines _____, retail gas stations _____, video stores _____, banking _____, personal computer manufacturers _____. Explain your ranking.

* * * * * * *

"So oligopolists can vary on all these characteristics?" asked Ginny.

"I think so. The only thing that really distinguishes their market is that there are a few sellers whose fortunes are highly dependent."

Question 5. Into which market model would you place the following industries? Airlines _____, aircraft manufacturers _____, travel agents _____, tour operators _____, passenger rail service _____. Explain your reasoning.

* * * * * * *

"Maybe you could merge?" suggested Ginny.

"That's less apealling than colluding. Besides horizontal mergers are also subject to antitrust scrutiny."

OBJECTIVE 4.1 List some concerns of antitrust legislation.

"I doubt that the Justice department is really going to be interested in your CD exchange Mo."

"You never know. Now that they've finished with Microsoft they may have some time on their hands. And lots of practices are illegal that you might not suspect."

"You mean beyond collusion and attempts to monopolize markets?"

"I'm thinking of specific practices like price discrimination, predatory pricing, and deceptive advertising."

"Like Jim claiming America was built on meatloaf?" asked Ginny. "I thought the Sherman Act just dealt with monopoly power."

"It does. But there are several other acts that make up the antitrust laws. The Sherman Act in 1890 was followed by the Clayton Act and Federal Trade Commission Act in 1914, the Robinson-Patman Act in 1936, the Wheeler-Lea Act in 1938, and the Celler-Kefauver Act in 1950."

"Do they all promote competition?" asked Ginny.

"Well, judging by Silberberg opinions are mixed. On the one hand you can be penalized for pricing too high, like a monopoly, but on the other hand the Robinson-Patman Act can penalize firms for selling at prices that are *below* their competitors."

"Ah-ha, sounds like they were written by lawyers ensuring their future employment. Maybe you should just get out of business Mo, and go to law school. Seems like that's where the money is."

"Thanks -- I'd rather join forces with Thorsten."

ANSWERS TO DIALOGUE QUESTIONS

Question 1. Vocabulary: n, g, o, e, j, f, c, d, a, f, g, l, h, b, k, m, i.

Question 2. With the same AC curve, a monopolistic competitor would produce less and charge a higher price than a perfect competitor.

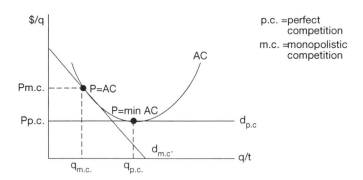

Question 3. The appearance of new competitors would shift the firm's demand curve in and make it more elastic until the AC curve was just tangent to the demand curve indicating a long-run zero profit equilibrium.

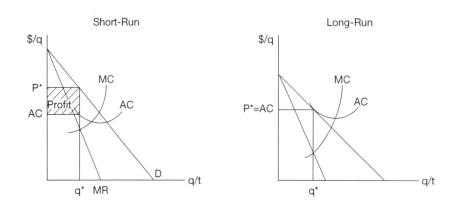

Question 4. From easiest to collude to most difficult: airlines <u>3</u>, retail gas stations <u>1</u>, video stores <u>4</u>, banking <u>2</u>, personal computer manufacturers <u>5</u>. Your ranking may differ, but I thought retail gas was the easiest to collude in because demand is stable, prices are posted, the product is homogeneous, there are only a few major firms, and entry is difficult (you need a supplier). For banking and airline the same conditions apply though the product can be differentiated more, and demand for various services differs. Video stores offer a pretty homogeneous product, but collusion is less attractive because there are so many firms to monitor and entry into the industry is so easy, making profits from collusion short term. Collusion in the computer business is more difficult because of differentiated products and technological change.

Question 5. Airlines: <u>monopolistically competitive</u> or <u>oligopoly</u>. Airlines differ in routes, schedules, and service, and certainly face downward sloping demand curves. In Canada there are only two major airlines, and the industry would be closest to an oligopoly. In the U.S. there are more firms, but their actions are still quite dependent on those of their rivals, and entry is difficult because of limited landed rights at airports. Aircraft manufacturers: <u>oligopoly</u>, with only a few worldwide their actions are linked to their rival's. Travel agents: <u>perfect</u> or <u>monopolistic competition</u>. There are many, they offer a fairly homogeneous service, and entry is relatively low cost making firms close to price takers. Tour operators: <u>monopolistically competitive</u>. Similar to travel agents but perhaps with a more differentiatied product. Passenger rail service: <u>monopoly</u>. Most geographic areas only have one service giving them a local monopoly.

THE BIG PICTURE

Imperfect competition describes a market structure that differs from perfect competition. Within the structure of imperfect competition are monopoly, oligopoly and monopolistic competition models. Most firms operate within an imperfectly competitive market structure. Even more specifically most firms operate within the monopolistically competitive model of imperfect competition. This is the case because observation reveals that the characteristics of most firm's products (like toothpaste for example), the number of competing firms in the market, the number of buyers for the product, and the cost or barriers of entry into the market faced by new firms all indicate that this is the predominant market model in the world's market economies, such as the United States, Canada, most of Europe, Japan, etc. Remember, to identify which type of market structure a firm operates in you must look at the characteristics of the market itself.

One distinguishing characteristic of firms in imperfectly competitive markets is that they face downward sloping demand curves, as opposed to the flat demand curve faced by firms in the perfectly competitive model. This implies that these firms have some control over the price at which they sell their good in the short-run. This power derives from the firms ability to differentiate their product from those of their competitors; something perfectly competitive firms are unable to do, thus giving them no control over the market price. A firm operating in the monopoly model, by definition, has a unique product due to a variety of potential conditions such as patent, geographic location, possession of a unique resource, etc. Firms operating in oligopoly or monopolistic comptetion models have less power than monopolists, but more than perfectly competitive firms.

The power of a monopolistic competitor to influence the market price means that a firm can influence the conditions faced by other firms through its own behavior. For example, firm A's decision to reduce output in the hopes of gaining higher profits, may induce firm B to enter the market with its own product. Is this a wise move then for firm A? Because oligopoly and monopolistically competitive markets consist of firms which act, react and thereby influence the price and behavior of the other firms in the market, economists use game theory, which you learned about in Chapter 9, to analyze the behavior of these firms.

REVIEW QUESTIONS

Answers to all review questions appear at the end of this chapter.

PROBLEMS AND EXERCISES
Write your answer in the space(s) provided.

1. Identify the market structure(s) that have the characteristic given below. Choose from perfect competition, monopoly, natural monopoly, oligopoly and monopolistic competition. (Note: there may be more than one answer per characteristic)

a. $P = $ min AC in long run equilibrium.
b. Downward sloping industry demand curve.
c. Continuously decreasing long run average cost curve over the relevant range of output.
d. $P = MC$.
e. Interdependence among firms that may lead to collusive behavior.
f. Price greater than average cost in long run equilibrium.
g. Absolute value of the price elasticity of demand less than one at the market price.
h. $P > MR$.

2. Assume there are ten identical firms in a market. Fixed costs are zero and each operates at a constant $MC = \$10.00$. The market (inverse) demand for their product is $P = 40 - Q$.
a. If this market is competitive, what will the market price be and how much will be sold?
b. What is the value of consumer surplus?
c. If the firms collude, what price will be charged and what quantity will be sold?
d. What is consumer surplus if the firms collude?
e. How much profit will each firm make if market profits are divided evenly?
f. How much in dollars is the monopoly distortion (dead weight loss) of the output chosen in c.?

3. Your company wants to try to get into the toothpaste or the oatmeal industries.
a. Who would your competition be in each case? Write down the brands (or some of them) and types of toothpaste and oatmeal your company would face as competition.

b. Which of these (toothpaste or oatmeal) is more homogenous and which is more differentiated?
c. Does the degree of product differentiation have any bearing on your company's ability to introduce a new brand? Explain why or why not.

d. Given your answer in c., what would make it difficult to break into either industry and what would your company have to do to succeed in either case?

e. Finally, assume for the moment that the U.S. market demand for toothpaste and oatmeal are identical. If you could succeed into either of these industries, in which industry would you expect your profits to be larger? Explain your reasoning. (Hint: Think about the advantages/disadvantages a differentiated product gives a producer over a non-differentiated product).

4. Canada's merger guidelines are based on overall welfare gains, and place less emphasis than the U.S. Federal Trade Commission (FTC) on the effect the merger might have on consumer prices.
a. How might a merger increase total welfare (consumer plus producer surplus) but still result in a higher consumer price?

Illustrate a market where total welfare is higher under a monopoly than perfect competition, but where price increases to the consumer.

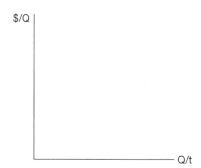

b. Why might Canada favor this approach more than the U.S.? (Hint: contrast market sizes.)

c. How might the U.S.- Canada Free Trade Agreement affect Canada's guidelines?

TRUE - FALSE QUESTIONS
Provide a one or two sentence explanation with your answer.

1.   In imperfectly competitive markets, firms can compete on many margins other than the price of the good.

2.   Oligopolies are illegal in the U.S.

3.   With equal AC curves, a perfect competitor charges a lower price and produces more output in LR equilibrium than a monopolistic competitor.

4.   Advertising and location are forms of nonprice competition.

5.   Cartels are legal in some countries.

6.   One difference between oligopolies and perfect competition is that the industry demand curve is downward sloping for an oligopoly.

7.   Differentiated products are a dominant characteristic of oligoplies.

8.   A primary difference between monopolistic competition and monopoly is the low cost of entry in monopolistic competition.

9.   Advertising and brand names always increase the cost to consumers of making a purchase.

10.   In reality, most firms are most closely described by an oligopolistic or monopolistically competitive market structure.

11.   Oligopolies and monopolies are price searchers, while perfect and monopolistic competitors are price takers.

12.   Product differentiation is the primary characteristic that allows firms to sustain long run profits.

13.   In general entry is more costly in monopoly than oligopoly.

14.   Even with the same costs, when a perfect competitor and a monopolistic competitor are earning zero economic profit in long run equilibrium, there will be dead weight loss in the monopolistically competitive market.

MULTIPLE CHOICE QUESTIONS
Choose the best answer.

1. If we were looking for evidence that an industry was best characterized as a price-taking, rather than a price-searching industry, we would check to see if:
a.   the industry demand curve was downward sloping.
b.   marginal costs were upward sloping.
c.   diminishing returns were present for the industry.
d.   prices were equal to marginal costs for each firm.

2. Firms selling in price searchers' markets
a.   refrain from producing certain units that could be provided at a cost below what buyers are willing to pay.
b.   are free from the constraints that competition imposes.
c.   make more money than firms selling in price takers' markets.
d.   sell fewer goods if they are allowed to charge different prices to different consumers.

3. A highly profitable cartel arrangement among sellers contains the seeds of its own destruction because
a.   a monopoly arrangement is more unstable than an oligopoly arrangement.
b.   a price maintained above each cartel member's marginal cost is an incentive to offer secret price reductions to attract additional business.
c.   net revenue for the cartel as a whole could be increased by producing where marginal revenue equals marginal cost for each cartel member.
d.   monopoly agreements will, in the long run, reduce net revenue to zero.

4. If the firms in a market all charge the same price, and all change prices together, this implies:
a.   it is a perfectly competitive market.
b.   it is an oligopolistic market with a price leader.
c.   there is a price collusion and legal action is necessary.
d.   any or all of the above.

5. Which of the following is true of a monopolistic competitor in the long run?
a.   P > MR.
b.   MR = MC.
c.   P = minimum AC.
d.   a. and b.
e.   All of the above.

6. Which of the following is not true of a monopolistic competitor in the long run?
a.   P = AC.
b.   MR = MC.
c.   AC > minimum AC.

d.   none of the above.

7. Which of these is likely to lessen the chance of collusion among oligopolists?
a.   a small number of oligopolists.
b.   low costs of entry.
c.   unenforced or weak anti-trust laws.
d.   effective means of policing pricing policies of other oligopolists.

8. For the monopolistically competitive firm in the diagram below, long-run equilibrium can occur only at the quantity indicated by point
a. A   b. B   c. C   d. D

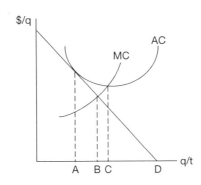

9. Cartels are unstable arrangement because:
a.   they are always illegal and may be dissolved if discovered.
b.   they require trust.
c.   they require members to lower their price which may not be individually beneficial.
d.   firm's demand curves are more elastic than the industry, leading to an incentive to cheat.

10. Suppose that a perfect competitor and a monopolistic competitor faced the same cost curves. Then it would be true that, in long-run equilibrium, the monopolistic competitor would:
a.   produce less at higher average cost.
b.   produce more at higher average cost.
c.   make lower economic profit.
d.   make higher economic profit.

11. Which of these is likely to INCREASE the chance of collusion among oligopolists?
a.   low barriers to entry.
b.   unstable demand conditions.
c.   fairly large number of oligopolists.
d.   unenforced or weak anti-trust laws.
e.   b and d.

12. Your assistant estimated two price elasticities for the competitive and monopoly market she was studying: -4.0 and -0.8. Which of the following must be true?

a.   -4.0 is for the competitive market and -0.8 for the monopoly.
b.   -0.8 is for both markets.
c.   -0.8 is for the competitive market and -4.0 for the monopoly.
d.   none of the above.

Use the diagram below to answer questions 13 through 16.

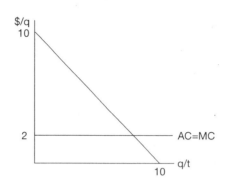

13. If this market is competitive, what will the market price be and how much will be sold?
a.   P = 2, Q = 8
b.   P = 2, Q = 4
c.   P = 3, Q = 7
d.   P = 4, Q = 6
e.   P = 5, Q = 5.

14. If the firms in this market successfully collude, what will the market price be, and how much will be sold?
a.   P = 2, Q = 8
b.   P = 2, Q = 4
c.   P = 3, Q = 7.
d.   P = 6, Q = 4.
e.   P = 5, Q = 5.

15. What will be the monopoly profit in the case of collusion?
a. 8   b. 16   c. 24   d. 32

16. What is the CHANGE in consumer surplus from the competitive case to the monopoly case?
a. 8   b. 16   c. 24   d. 32

17. Brand names may
a.   increase monopoly power.
b.   lower costs to consumers.
c.   signal higher product quality.
d.   a and c.
e.   all of the above.

18. Product differentiation exists
a.   because people have different tastes.
b.   because people have different incomes.
c.   because advertisers try to change preferences.
d.   a and b.
e.   all of the above.

SHORT ANSWER QUESTIONS

1. Speculate on how lower trade barriers might affect antitrust action against domestic firms with monopoly power.

2. In response to depressed aluminum prices resulting from a glutted market since Russia redirected its aluminum production into exports, Russia and the West's aluminum smelters recently signed an agreement to cut capacity. Since the governments negotiated the agreement, the U.S. Justice Department ruled that the cartel did not violate antitrust laws. Western aluminum smelters, however, are concerned that the Russian smelters are not reducing production by the agreed upon amount. What are the characteristics that make collusion particularily easy in this industry? What factors make collusion difficult? Why is there an incentive for the Russian smelters not to cut capacity as much as agreed upon?

3. Some economists believe that the Canadian market can only support one major airline, and that the government should therefore grant a monopoly license to one carrier. As a result, over the past few years Canada's two major airlines, Air Canada and Canadian Air, have been vying for market share, hoping to be the largest airline in the event the government restricts the market to one carrier. This competition included prolonged discount fares that put both airlines in a loss position. Canadian Air accused Air Canada of trying to drive them out of the market by predatory pricing.

a. How might you distinguish predatory pricing from normal competitive behavior?
b. During this same period Air Canada bought more planes and operated with excess capacity. Why might Canadian see this as further evidence?
c. Predatory pricing can be an irrational strategy if firms can re-enter the market as monopoly pricing behavior begins. Why might this market not be quite so amenable to re-entry?

4. Is a large number of firms necessary for a competitive market?

ANSWERS TO REVIEW QUESTIONS

Answers to PROBLEMS AND EXERCISES

1. a. P = min AC in LR equilibrium: perfect competition.
    b. Downward sloping industry demand curve: all models.
    c. Continuously decreasing long run average cost curve over the relevant range of output: natural monopoly.
    d. P = MC: perfect competition.
    e. Interdependence among firms that may lead to collusive behavior: oligopoly.
    f. Price greater than average cost in long run equilibrium: monopoly or oligopoly (may also be natural monopoly depending on how/if it is regulated).
    g. Absolute value of the price elasticity of demand less than one at the market price: possible under perfect competition only. Price searchers only price in the elastic portion of the demand curve.
    h. P > MR: all price searchers, monopolistic competition, oligopoly, and monopoly (including natural monopoly).

2. a. The market price will be $10, equal to MC, and 30 units will be sold. See the diagram below.
    b. Consumer's surplus is .5($30 * 30) = $450.
    c. With collusion, the monopoly price of $25 will be charged, with 15 units sold.
    d. Consumer's surplus falls to .5($15 * 15) = $112.50.
    e. $225 profit divided equally will be $22.50 per firm.
    f. Deadweight loss is .5($15 * 15) = $112.50.

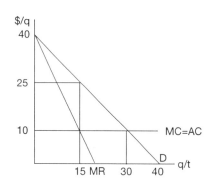

3. a. Toothpaste competitors: Crest, Pepsodent, Gleem, Arm and Hammer, Colgate, AIM, Macleans,...
Toothpaste Types (they contain various combinations of the following attributes): paste, gel, tube, pump, mint flavor, regular flavor, cavity preventing additives, plaque fighting additives, tartar build-up preventing additives, anti-bacterial additives, whitening agents, baking soda, others....

Oatmeal competitors: Quaker Oats, Old Mill Oats,...
Oatmeal types: regular, quick cooking,...

b. Oatmeal is more homogenous and toothpaste more differentiated.

c. Product differentiation refers to the attributes of the product. The fact that a product is differentiated does not significantly hinder other companies from introducing similar but also slightly differentiated products. Absent the protection of a patent, it might be just as easy for a company to produce a new brand of toothpaste, complete with its own set of attributes, as a new brand of oats, which are more inherently difficult to differentiate. Therefore, without more in-depth analysis of the two industries, there is no reason to assume the toothpaste industry is more difficult to enter than the oatmeal industry or vice versa.

d. What would make it difficult in either industry is the presence of dominant brand name products (Crest and Quaker Oats) to which many consumers have significant loyalty. Their pre-existing brand names and reputations may represent a significant barrier to entry for your company. To overcome this barrier would require your company to win over some minimum number of consumers to your brand. This is normally accomplished through advertising. It would help if your company already had a good name in hygiene products for the toothpaste, or breakfast cereals in the case of oatmeal (e.g. Kelloggs).

e. Barring any collusive activity, we might expect profits to be higher in the differentiated industry in the short-run; though profit always just depends on the difference between price and average cost. Differentiation ensures that the producer faces a downward sloping demand curve, and thus has some control over price like a monopolist. This source of profits is only available in the short-run, however, as the existence of profits will entice other producers into the market eventually eliminating those rents.

4. a. The higher price will always reduce consumer's surplus, but if costs are reduced significantly by the merger, for example, through economies of scale or efficiency gains, the increase in producer rent may outweigh the deadweight loss resulting from the reduced output of a monopolist. In the diagram below, if S is the supply curve with a competitive market, and MC is the marginal cost curve of a single, more efficient (merged) firm, the lost gains from trade with the monopoly deadweight loss are smaller than the additional rent from producing at a lower cost. Total welfare increases, since it is just the sum of consumer's surplus and producer's rent.

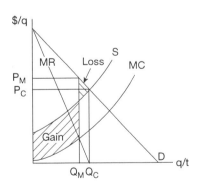

b. Some economists would argue that Canada has tended to judge mergers on net efficiency (welfare) gains rather than just consumer's surplus because of a desire to exploit more economies of scale in our smaller domestic market.

c. Free trade increases the size of the relevant market. That is, the market is now North America rather than Canada or the U.S, making any economies of scale easier to realize by expanding into the U.S.

Answers to TRUE - FALSE QUESTIONS

1. True. Nonprice competition occurs in the form of quality, location, hours, service, etc.

2. False. Oligopolies are a market structure model, neither legal or illegal. Collusion, common within oligopolistic markets, is illegal in the U.S.

3. True. The LR equilibrium of the perfect competitor occurs at the minimum of the AC curve, which results in a lower price and larger quantity than the equilibium (to the left) of the monopolistic competitor.

4. True. Advertising and convenient locations are ways other than low prices of attracting customers.

5. True. Witness OPEC.

6. False. The industry demand curve is downward sloping in both models. The firm demand curve is horizontal in perfect competition.

7. False. Products may be differentiated or homogeneous in oligoplies. The dominant characteristic is a few sellers concerned with their rival's behavior.

8. True. Low entry costs, or contestability, imply zero profit in the long run for monopolistic competition, unlike monopolies.

9. False. Both advertising and brand names can provide valuable information to consumers that lowers their total cost (including time and search costs) of making a purchase. Advertising can also make markets more competitive, lowering the price to consumers.

10. True. Perfect competition and monopoly are extreme examples, both of which seldom appear in pure form.

11. False. Firms in oligopolies, monopolies, and monopolistic competitors are price searchers as all face downward sloping demand curves.

12. False. The cost of entry (barriers to entry) is the primary characteristic that allows firms to sustain long run profits.

13. True. Entry may be costly or not in oligopoly, but high entry costs is one of the distinguishing features of monopoly.

14. True. The deadweight loss in the monopolistic competitor case arises from price exceeding MC (and MR). For a perfectly competitive firm, P = MR so P = MC when MC = MR.

Answers to MULTIPLE CHOICE QUESTIONS

1. d	4. d	7. b	10. a	13. a	16. c
2. a	5. d	8. a	11. d	14. d	17. e
3. b	6. d	9. d	12. c	15. b	18. d

Answers to SHORT ANSWER QUESTIONS

1. Lower trade barriers can enlarge the relevant market for considering market power. For example, Boeing might be considered to have monopoly power domestically in the production of aircraft, but worldwide they have several competitors including the European company Airbus.

2. Collusion is particularily easy in this industry because of the limited number of firms, homogenous product, and high costs of entry. It is easy to keep track of the players, and prices should not deviate as a result of product differentiation. Fluctuating demand caused by economic cycles, and the political and cultural differences across countries may make monitoring and disciplining firms that deviate from the agreement difficult. Each smelter has an incentive to try to increase production to sell more output at the higher cartel price. If they can cheat and get away with it, their individual profits will be higher than their share of the pie under the cartel arrangement.

3. a. Predatory pricing is very dificult to distinguish from normal competitive behavior unless you have evidence that the firm is pricing below their MC's with the intent of driving the other firm out of the market.
b. Excess capacity allows Air Canada to easily increase their output (flights) and lower fares. Normally firms would not want to operate with such excess capacity because it is costly when the planes are idle.
c. Re-entry might have been barred by the government which was already contemplating a single licensed carrier, making predatory pricing, if successful, a potentially profitable strategy for Air Canada in this case.

4. A large number of firms does not guarantee a competitive market, but it makes collusion more difficult. Two non-colluding firms, however, are sufficient for competition (but not the perfectly competitive model, because with only two firms in the market they would be price searchers).

CHAPTER 13
Labor Markets

OBJECTIVES
Answers to bold-faced questions appear at the end of the dialogue.

"Mo, I want you to have all my old econ notes if I meet an early demise."

"Gee, thanks a heap Ginny. Any special reason why you think the end is near?"

"Meatloaf. I'm working so many extra shifts since Jim won the contest that I think I'm going to collapse. Which reminds me, I've got to go to work in about an hour."

"It's 10:00 at night! Is the Diner open 24 hours now?"

"No, I've got to go to a meeting Karl set up so his union representative could speak to us about joining."

"He's still pushing that?" said Mo. "You should show him this chapter, so he can see how inadvisable it is for people like you to join the union."

"I know. What are we going to do, go on strike for higher wages? Jim would get rid of us all and hire all new people in about a second. But the movement has gained new life with these ridiculous hours."

"Maybe he thinks the union will help you socially. I don't think it can do much for you economically."

"I think he just likes the idea of unions and workers joining together. You know all of the historical imagery associated with the common man struggling to lead a humane existence. You know Karl Mo."

"Yes, he's a bit of a dreamer. Smart guy, but a dreamer."

"Unfortunately completely unrealistic about what motivates people and why things are the way they are. I don't know, I'll just go to the meeting and hear what this guy has to say."

"Maybe we can come up with a couple of tough questions from Chapter 13 you can ask this guy?"

OBJECTIVE 1.1 Recognize definitions for the important new vocabulary.

Question 1. Match the term with its definition(s). Write out definitions for any undefined terms.

a. wage income
b. nonwage income
c. in-kind income
d. income effect
e. substitution effect
f. derived demand
g. labor market
h. compensating wage differentials
i. time series data
j. cross section data
k. longitudinal/panel data
l. labor unions
m. collective bargaining

_____ data which record the similarities and differences among various groups in a single time period, while simultaneously recording the changes within the groups over several time periods.

_____ that portion of a change in the quantity of labor supplied attributable exclusively to an absolute change in income.

_____ non-monetary income produced by working in the market or in non-market activity.

_____ the market in which labor is exchanged for wages.

_____ income produced by working in the market for monetary compensation, payed at hourly, weekly, monthly or annual rates.

_____ data which are gathered on a single group or category of information over several time periods.

_____ the process by which unions negotiate with one or more firm managers over wages, benefits and other work conditions for all workers represented by the union.

_____ data which record the similarities and differences among various groups and/or categories of information in a single time period.

_____ the demand for inputs that stems, ultimately, from consumer's demand for goods produced with those inputs.

_____ monetary income derived from sources other than working in the labor market.

_____ an amount added to the competitive wage rate in certain cases to attract workers to a job.

_____ associations of workers, organized according to industry or type of work, formed to act collectively for increasing wages or improving working conditions.

_____ that portion of the impact on the quantity of labor supplied attributable to a change in the relative price of labor versus leisure.

* * * * * * *

"I had the impression that this material is not all that different from what we've been doing," Mo said. "The biggest difference is that when the commodity being exchanged is labor, you and I are now the suppliers rather than the consumers."

OBJECTIVE 1.2 Derive the supply of labor from an individual's willingness to trade their time for wages.

"I know. That plus the fact that the price in this chapter is the wage. And it's so true, if it weren't for that wage I would not give up my leisure time."

"I hadn't really thought of labor like this before: as an exchange occurring in a market at given prices according to people's marginal value for leisure. I always thought people just had to work and tried to find the best, highest paying job they could. You work 8 or 10 hours per day, take your two weeks vacation -- visit the relatives, go to Disneyland, you know."

"It is sort of like that," Ginny said, "but isn't the point that some people won't work 12 hour days, no matter what the wage, is. They think it's more important to be home with their families, or travelling, or something, so their marginal value of leisure -- or non-market work -- is higher than somebody who is willing to put in those kind of hours for the money or other perceived benefits."

"So our preferences for work and leisure differ, but for each individual diminishing marginal value for leisure still holds. Like the woman's marginal value schedule for oysters in Chapter 4, as she sells more of her stock of oysters her marginal value for the next oyster increases."

"Exactly. If hours of work were allocated in one hour increments people would supply exactly the number of hours of labor that makes their marginal value of leisure equal to the wage they receive. That way the opportunity cost of taking an hour of leisure is equal to the wage, which is equal to the marginal value for that hour of leisure."

"Well, they have to be equal," Mo said. "If they weren't, then it would be in the best interest of that person to either take more leisure or work more, whichever has the higher value to them."

Question 2. Beginning at a stock of 48 leisure hours for B, determine the quantity of labor B would supply to A, who pays according to his own marginal value of leisure.

Weeks	A's ($/hr) MV	B's ($/hr) MV
8	10.00	12.50
16	9.50	10.50
24	9.00	9.50
32	8.50	9.00
40	8.00	8.75
48	7.50	8.50

Question 3. Consider three people: Mrs. June Cleaver, wife of Ward, mother of Wally and Beaver Cleaver -- the classic model of the 1950's-60's homemaker. Vincent Van Gogh, the brilliant, obsessive and perennially poor painter, and Lee Iacocca, former CEO for the Chrysler Corporation.

a. Distribute the 24 hours in each of June, Vincent, and Lee's day between market, non-market, leisure and sleep hours. Make your best estimate as to their marginal value for each of these activities given their opportunity costs.

June: M _____, NM _____, L _____, S _____
Vincent: M _____, NM _____, L _____, S _____
Lee: M _____, NM _____, L _____, S _____

b. What happens to your estimate if each person had the opportunity to work in the market for 50% more. How many hours more would they each trade into market work?

June: M _____, NM _____, L _____, S _____
Vincent: M _____, NM _____, L _____, S _____
Lee: M _____, NM _____, L _____, S _____

For whom is the percentage increase the greatest? Explain why.

c. From their initial position, what would you expect if they experienced a 50% decrease in their "hourly wage"? Is it clear that Iacocca and Van Gogh would reduce their market work by the same amount or in the same proportion? Explain why or why not.

June: M _____, NM _____, L _____, S _____
Vincent: M _____, NM _____, L _____, S _____
Lee: M _____, NM _____, L _____, S _____

* * * * * * *

"Hey, maybe this is a good time to ask a quick question on that 'backward bending' supply curve of labor," Ginny said, "the curve includes this backward "C" shaped part right?"

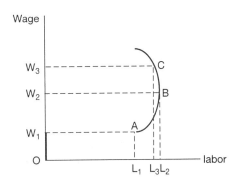

"Yes. From 0 to w_1 no labor is supplied. At w_1 the supplier of labor decides to go to work, and L_1 units are supplied."

"But it requires an increase in wages to w_2 to increase labor beyond that point," said Ginny.

OBJECTIVE 1.3 Work through the income and substitution effects on the supply of labor stemming from changes in wages.

"Did you understand why the curve bends back on itself like that?" Mo asked.

"Yes, I think so. It's because of the income and substitution effects that occur when there is an increase in wages."

"So which is it?"

"Which is what?"

"Which effect makes the curve bend back on itself like that?"

"The income effect makes.... Is this some kind of quiz?"

"No, I just think this is important and I was hoping you would explain it so I can see if I understand it."

"Right," Ginny said sceptically. "Maybe we should just think of an example."

"An example. Okay, how about figuring out the income and substitution effects of winning $10 million in the lottery?"

"Winning the lottery doesn't change your price of trading leisure for labor, better known as your wage, so there is no substitution effect. The substitution effect only comes into play when there is a change in the price. There is a huge income effect though. If most people won 10 million smackers they would quit working and convert all of that work time back into leisure."

"But now this gets at something I thought I understood. I understood the income effect also to be related to a change in price by way of either increasing or decreasing your purchasing power. In addition I thought there was a second, pure income effect from things like winning the lottery or just getting a wage increase."

"I see what you're saying," Ginny said. "If the price of food goes down then you will spend less on the same amount of food and have more money in your pocket to buy other things."

"Right, that's the change in purchasing power, which for all practical purpose is the same as an increase in income, in this case."

"If I recall correctly, you're absolutely right, but Silberberg said that most of the time that kind of purchasing power, income effect is ignored because it's usually quite small and the effect is spread out over all the other things you buy. Besides this is labor we're talking about, not the price of peaches or some other good. Don't you think those kinds of goods are affected differently than labor, where a change in the wage *is* a change in income?"

"Yes, that's a good point," Mo said. "So graphically, that wasn't a very good example. How about if you were to get a $5.00 an hour raise at work?"

"Now we're talking. That would be great, but I'll have to think about this in terms of my normal work schedule. Would I work more or less? I am definitely on the labor supply curve and since the price of trading my time from leisure to labor just went up, as a supplier of labor I would be inclined to sell more hours to Jim. One more shift a week at that wage and I'd be about $250.00 richer a month, not counting tips."

"So the substitution effect is to work more hours," Mo said, "because the price increase leads you to sell more of your time to Jim."

"Correct. Just like any other supplier, if the price increases I will supply more. I substitute out of leisure into more labor in search of the big payola. Now the question is, is the income effect greater than the substitution effect?"

"Right, because you are getting paid more for the hours you already devote to work, your income has increased."

"That's right, hey wait a minute," Ginny said. "Even without any more hours I'd already be making $100 more than I do now. That's pretty good."

"So what are you going to do? Take the extra shift or settle for the $100 increase in income?"

"You sound like a game show host. I'd probably just keep the same hours, since I'm in school. The extra income is enough to pay my bills and let me spend more time studying. If it wasn't for school, I'd be racking up those hours."

"That's it. It's all over. You heard it here folks, Ginny's income effect appears to have offset her substitution effect. Her supply curve does bend, oops, I guess it just straightens out. Working fewer hours would have bent you backwards, but you get the point."

"Yes, well it was a tough decision and I'd just like to thank my mother and father and all the people who've helped me out along the way, my good friend Mo, Gene Silberberg for the textbook..."

"Hey, let's not get carried away."

Question 4. Identify whether the number of hours you would be willing to work would increase or decrease in response to the following situations. (indicate these with various sized up and down arrows in the spaces provided; e.g., large arrows outweigh small arrows) Separate this response into an income and substitution effect (assume no backward bend in the supply curve).

a. Because of hard times you have been asked to take a 20% wage reduction to save everyone's job at the factory. Income: _____ Substitution: _____ .

b. Your 17 year old daughter informs you that she has been accepted into the top ranked astro-physics program in the country, she neglects to inform you that it is also one of the most expensive universities in the country at $22,000 a year tuition. Income: _____   Substitution: _____

c. In an attempt to find spiritual fulfilment, you join a religious group that demands 40% of your gross annual income as a tithe. Income: _____   Substitution: _____

d. On your twenty-seventh birthday your parents visit you in Africa, where you are posted as a Peace Corps Volunteer, and inform you that they have been hiding the fact that they are billionaires. They like the way you have turned out as a person and have decided to top up your hourly Peace Corps wage to $100 for every hour you work. Income: _____   Substitution: _____

OBJECTIVE 2.1 **Derive the demand for labor from a firm's calculation of the value of the marginal product of employing an additional worker.**

"So that's the supply of labor," Mo said, "how about the demand for labor?"

"Well the interesting thing to me is that even though the roles are reversed with firms as the consumer of labor, and individuals as the suppliers, the principles of basing your decision to consume or supply on the marginal value of the good still hold."

"How's that?"

"I guess that wasn't completely clear. What I'm trying to say is that when you buy some good, like a pair of Levi's, your decision to consume is based on your marginal value for the jeans. When a firm decides to consume more labor their decision is similarly based on the *value* of the marginal product from the labor."

"I see what you're saying, now," Mo said. "Sure. For any output demand will be based on the consumer's marginal value for that good, but for an input market it's the value of the output from the input that is crucial."

"Exactly. The value of the output that some firm gets from adding a worker had better be greater or at least equal to the cost of adding the worker -- which would be the wage paid to that worker. If the firm anticipated that the value of the output was going to be less than the wage, it would not demand the additional worker, so to speak."

"So, just like before, in Chapter 7, the firm will hire labor to the point where the value marginal product of labor equals the wage."

"Yep. And they'll hire all factor inputs up until the point where the additional output received from that input, per dollar, is equal among all of the inputs the firm employs."

Question 5. Given that firms will hire inputs, including two categories of labor, to the point where,

$$\frac{MP_1}{w_1} = \frac{MP_2}{w_2}.$$

If the wage for input 1 increases, show the results of this for the quantities of input 1 and 2 hired. Assume diminishing marginal product has occurred.

OBJECTIVE 3.1 Demonstrate (using graphs and prose descriptions) the consequences of laws, licences and unions on the labor market as a whole and on individual sectors of the labor market.

"Now when we sum up all of the individual supply and demand curves we get the market supply and demand curves. And as I understand it these curves respond to shocks in a similar way as all the other supply and demand curves we've been studying."

"Yes, like the minimum wage case," Mo said. "That's exactly like the price floor examples we worked through before."

"And how about cases where licensing things like doctors or even hairstylists, puts a ceiling on supply The same is true for making it illegal to hire illegal aliens."

"We should work on a couple of these to make sure we can handle the curves. I think it's especially important that we think about the effects these things have on the price and quantities of smaller groups of workers, like he did with the skilled workers when the minimum wage changes."

"For example," Ginny said, "what is the effect on local labor of the United States changing its immigration law to allow a greater flow of seasonal labor from Mexico?"

"You're talking about agricultural workers here right? That will mean an increase in supply of these workers, so the curve will shift outward along the quantity axis; the wage will fall and farmers will increase the quantity demanded of labor. It will look like this:

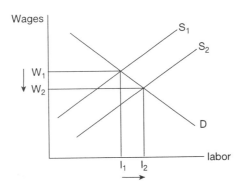

"Okay, wages fall from their previous level, but what about the effect on the quantity of local workers hired? It seems to me that some of them are going to get passed over as the new workers who are willing to work for lower wages enter the market."

"You're right," Mo said, "but I don't think we can tell exactly what the proportion of local to immigrant workers will be, because we can't know whether some of the local workers will take a wage reduction thereby keeping their jobs. How about the effect of unionization?"

"You mean going from no union at all to creating a union?"

"Yes, I guess. I was actually thinking of this example Adam was telling me about, where government offices have a certain type of worker that is unionized and another that is not. The executive level people are not unionized, but most of the other people are. It was interesting, I thought, because for a lot of things these people can do the same work."

"You're getting at whether there are fewer of these union workers than there might be and more executives than there might be if there were no unions distorting the wage scale?"

"Hey, you catch on quick."

"Well, every now and again," Ginny said. "But what is the question? What is the effect of unionization in these government offices on the quantity of executives and union people hired?"

"Something like that. The union shifts the supply curve to the left, raising wages and reducing quantity."

"So, you would hire fewer union people," Ginny said. "Would you hire more non-union executives?"

"I think so. That wage increase for union workers would lead to an increase in demand for non-union workers for the work areas where they are substitutable."

"I agree, though I don't think that you would hire one new executive for every non-executive position since they aren't perfect substitutes."

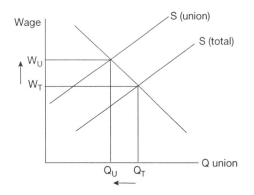 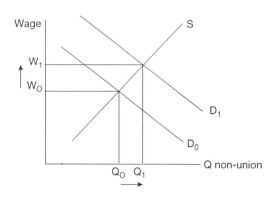

"Okay Ginny, here's a question for you. What is the effect on your job of unionization when there are about 30,000 substitutes willing to take your place and no legal protection enforcing your position?"

"Would that be a sudden, swift decrease in demand for my services?"

"Correct, would you care to graph that?"

"No, I think I get the picture."

ANSWERS TO DIALOGUE QUESTIONS

Question 1. Vocabulary: k, d, c, g, a, i, m, j, f, b, h, l, e.

Question 2. B would supply 24 weeks of work to A, because for up to 24 weeks, A, based on her marginal value, is willing to pay B a wage that exceeds her marginal value for her time. To solve this problem you must read A's marginal value schedule from 0 to 8 to 16, etc. and B's from 48 to 40 to 32, etc., as A is gaining work hours and B is trading away her stock of leisure hours.

Question 3. Although your distribution of hours may differ slightly the positions among the three people should be the same as below.

a.
$$\text{June: } M = 0, NM = 10, L = 6, S = 8$$
$$\text{Vincent: } M = 14, NM = 3, L = 1, S = 6$$
$$\text{Lee: } M = 14, NM = 0, L = 4, S = 6$$

b.
$$\text{June: } M = 6, NM = 8, L = 2, S = 8$$
$$\text{Vincent: } M = 16, NM = 3, L = 0, S = 5$$
$$\text{Lee: } M = 15, NM = 0, L = 3, S = 6$$

June would increase her hours the most, because she has the greatest possible marginal gain from entering the market. Vincent and Lee are already working at near maximum possible hours, so their marginal value of leisure is probably quite big, even facing a 50% wage increase.

c.
$$\text{June: } M = 0, NM = 10, L = 6, S = 8$$
$$\text{Vincent: } M = 12, NM = 3, L = 2, S = 7$$
$$\text{Lee: } M = 10, NM = 0, L = 6, S = 8$$

No, it is not clear that Vincent and Lee would change by the same amount or in the same proportion. Despite their similar distribution of hours, they will have different marginal value schedules. Moreover, they will have different preferences for work, or their work. One might imagine Lee Iacocca having a much greater price sensitivity than Van Gogh, who basically lived on gifts from his brother to continue his painting, and loved to paint.

Question 4. a. Income effect: ⇑, substitution effect: ↓
b. Income effect: ⇑, substitution effect: 0
c. Income effect: ↑, substitution effect: ↓
d. Income effect: ↓, substitution effect: ↑

Question 5. If the wage for input 1 increases, this decreases the overall value of the left-hand side of the equation. For example, if $MP_1 = 1$ and w_1 increases from 1 to 2 then the overall value of the expression changes from 1/1 to 1/2. To return the whole equation to equilibrium, either the numerator of the left-hand side expression must change in proportion to the change in wages or the value of the right side of the equation must also decrease.

Looking at the latter case first, reducing the right-hand expression can be achieved either by increasing the wage of input 2 or decreasing the marginal productivity of input 2. It is unlikely that any firm would just raise wages, so the solution must lie in the numerator. The solution lies in hiring more of input 2, which, because of diminishing marginal product, lowers MP_2.

The same effect can be achieved by reducing the quantity (i.e., letting go, laying off, etc.) of input 1, thus moving higher up on the marginal product curve. With diminishing marginal product, the MP of the last unit would be greater than the one currently employed.

THE BIG PICTURE

The thing to remember when you are analyzing labor markets is that they behave in accordance with the same principles as the other markets you've studied, such as the perfectly competitive markets for various goods (although the market for labor can also be imperfectly competitive, such as baseball). There is supply and there is demand. If the price of the good changes, then a change in quantity supplied or demanded results. Any outside changes, such as technology or changes in related markets will cause the curves to shift. A piece of cake.

Having said that, also remember that the roles change in the labor market. The supplier is the individual, the consumer is the firm. Moreover, the good in question is an input, a factor of production. Labor is something that is used to produce other goods that consumers want directly. There is no inherent demand for labor in the marketplace that isn't based on the demand consumers have for finished goods. So the demand for labor is a second order, or derived, demand, one step removed from the direct demand of previous chapters.

All in all, studying the labor market is really a separate field of inquiry within microeconomics, sharing a place among other fields addressing inputs, such as capital markets, natural resource economics and land economics. There are also separate fields addressing output markets, like agriculture economics, or the basic structure of various sectors of the economy as in industrial organization economics (anti-trust concerns). If you were drawing the family tree of economics, labor market economics would be a branch on the input side, stemming from the trunk of the basic microeconomics principles you have learned.

REVIEW QUESTIONS

Answers to all review questions appear at the end of this chapter.

PROBLEMS AND EXERCISES
Write your answer in the space(s) provided.

1. Below are the marginal value schedules of Vijay Singh, an electrical engineer with a medium-sized telecommunications company. He earns $48,000 a year which translates into a wage of $25.00 per hour, but he cannot work less than 8 hours per day, and he is paid nothing for overtime.

a. Indicate at what levels of the three types of activity Vijay would gain the greatest benefits during his 17 waking hours (he sleeps 7 hours per night). Hint: since he is limited to 17 hours, work down his non-market schedule and up (from the bottom of) his leisure hours.

Hrs	Market ($wage)	Hrs	Non-Market ($MV)	Hrs	Leisure ($MV)
1	25	17	5	1	68
2	25	16	10	2	64
3	25	15	15	3	60
4	25	14	20	4	56
5	25	13	25	5	52
6	25	12	30	6	48
7	25	11	35	7	44
8	25	10	40	8	40
9	0	9	45	9	36
10	0	8	50	10	32
11	0	7	55	11	28
12	0	6	60	12	24
13	0	5	65	13	20
14	0	4	70	14	16
15	0	3	75	15	12
16	0	2	80	16	8
17	0	1	85	17	4

b. If Mr. Singh could work additional hours at $25/hour, would he choose to extend his work day beyond 8 hours?

2. Suppose the inverse demand for labor in a particular clothing factory is P = 12 - Qd, and labor supply is P = .5Qs, where P is the hourly wage and Q is labor hours per shift.
a. Calculate the equilibrium hourly wage and number of labor hours.

b. The province of Quebec just announced an increase in their minimum wage to $6.00/hour. At that wage, the quantity of labor hours demanded is _____, the quantity of labor hours supplied is _____, and the surplus of labor hours is _____.

c. Illustrate this market below, indicating the minimum wage, Qs, Qd, and the surplus.

```
$/hour |
       |
       |
       |
       |
       |
       |
       |_____ hour/shift
```

d. Suggest some ways in which the factory might allocate its resources to deal with the wage increase. What groups of workers probably benefit from the wage control, and what groups may be harmed?

3. Suppose the (inverse) demand for labor at a fast food restaurant is P = 10 - .75Qd, and the supply curve for labor is the same as at the clothing factory. Is this demand curve more or less elastic than the demand curve in question 2? Without doing any calculations, where would you expect labor hour cutbacks to be higher in response to the minimum wage? _____. Why?

Confirm your expectations by calculating the labor hours surplus in the fast food restaurant. Show this surplus on your diagram above.

4. Show the effects of legislation requiring businesses to pay a larger proportion of their employees health care costs. What is the effect on the demand for labor?

```
$/employee |
           |
           |
           |
           |
           |
           |_____ employees/team
```

5. One of the more contentious points in the baseball strike of 1994 was the owners' desire to put a cap on player salaries. The cap would take the form of a maximum limit on the total amount any team could spend on their 25 player roster. The player's union vigorously opposed this idea, demanding instead to

permit individual players to bargain for the highest salary the market would allow without restrictions. Show these two bargaining positions on a graph below. Is the salary cap a wage floor or a wage ceiling? Describe the benefits and costs of each proposal for both players and owners. Note that in reality each player's value to the team varies widely.

TRUE - FALSE QUESTIONS
Provide a one or two sentence explanation with your answer.

1. We would anticipate that a person who receives an increase in non-wage income (e.g. winning the lottery) would take less leisure than if they received a comparable increase in wage income.

2. If the price of labor (the wage) changes there will be a substitution effect and an income effect on a person's consumption of leisure.

3. If there is no change in the relative price of labor and leisure, then there is no substitution effect.

4. If there is a change in the relative price of labor and leisure, then there can be no income effect.

5. Leisure is an inferior good.

6. It is the individual's labor supply curve that is backward bending; the market supply curve for labor is positively sloped.

7. A minimum wage law will decrease the quantity of labor demanded more the higher the elasticity of demand for labour in the industry.

8. A minimum wage law will decrease the quantity of labor demanded more the higher the elasticity of demand for the output of the industry.

9.	A minimum wage law will decrease the quantity of labor demanded more the greater the proportion of total costs this labor accounts for in the industry.

10.	The substitution effect of a wage increase will always induce a person to work more hours.

MULTIPLE CHOICE QUESTIONS
Choose the <u>best</u> answer.

1. If a new technology comes on line that increases the productivity of a firm's workers, the firm will
a.	hire more workers.
b.	let some workers go.
c.	keep the same number of workers.
d.	raise the workers' wages.

2. The net effect of an increase in an individual's wages is always that
a.	they work more hours.
b.	they work fewer hours.
c.	they work the same number of hours.
d.	none of the above.

3. An individual will seek to engage in wage, non-wage and leisure activities to the point where their marginal value per hour spent on each is equal among all three activities. This practice is based on which of the following?
a.	utility maximization
b.	the fact that there are only 24 hours in a day
c.	individual preference for more income and more leisure.
d.	all of the above

4. If you want to analyze the effects of wage changes on the number of hours worked by white collar and blue collar workers you would need
a.	panel data.
b.	cross sectional data.
c.	time series data.
d.	b and c.

5. If you want to analyze the effect of the industrial revolution on agricultural labor supply from 1840 to 1860 in the United States, you would need
a.	panel data.
b.	cross sectional data.
c.	time series data.
d.	all of the above.

6. The elasticity of demand for a factor of production depends on
a.	the value placed on leisure.
b.	the availability of substitutes.

c.   the share of total costs the factor accounts for.

d.   b and c.

7. The difference between labor and other factors of production is that

a.   labor services have an opportunity cost.

b.   labor usually costs more.

c.   labor is governed by maximizing behavior.

d.   a and c.

8. Which of the following is least likely to be a result of minimum wages laws?

a.   automated phone systems.

b.   longer hours.

c.   self-service counters.

d.   increased management.

9. If daycare costs continue to rise, we would expect to see

a.   fewer couples having children.

b.   each couple having fewer children.

c.   more couples choosing to have one spouse stay at home.

d.   a and b.

e.   all of the above.

10. The answer to question 9 is based on

a.   diminishing marginal product.

b.   rising marginal costs..

c.   the law of demand.

d.   social norms.

11. The million dollar salaries commanded by top Hollywood actors arise from

a.   the actor's union.

b.   the opportunity cost of these individuals.

c.   the greed of these individuals.

d.   nonreplicable resources.

e.   a, b, and d.

12. Despite the high fee some of these actors earn, many of them turn down jobs and choose not to work full-time. This suggests:

a.   they value an additional day of leisure more than their daily fee.

b.   they are facing diminishing marginal product of their labor.

c.   their supply curve is not backward bending yet.

d.   they want to keep demand for their product inelastic by appearing selectively.

13. If you want to analyze differences in hourly wages between white collar and blue collar workers you would need

a.   panel data.

b.   cross sectional data.

c.   time series data.

d.   b and c.

SHORT ANSWER QUESTIONS

1. "Companies just want to replace their workers with machines and robots, so that they don't have to pay benefits or anything." Evaluate this statement.

2. Out of the millions of men between the ages of 18 and 30, there are only about 350 professional basketball players in the NBA. These people are clearly unique individuals, with rare abilities -- their salaries are evidence of this. Yet even with so few people skilled enough to be in the pool of NBA players, how can some players like Hakeem Olajuwon, Charles Barkley and Shaquille O'Neill make 10 and 20 times the salary that other NBA players make?

3. Many hockey fans accused the New York Ranger's of buying the 1993 Stanley Cup by signing a number of superstars, much as the Yankees were accused of buying baseball's World Series in the late 1970s. Consider that most hockey arenas hold around 15,000 fans, and sell out, whereas the average baseball stadium might hold around 55,000 fans, and has empty seats. All else equal, in which sport would the marginal return of signing a superstar be greater? In which sport would more than one superstar likely be signed?

4. Labor is an input into the production process which produces final goods, much like capital and land. Capital and land, however, have positively sloped supply curves in all price and quantity ranges. Labor has a backward bending supply curve (i.e., its slope changes from positive to negative as price increases). Why is labor's supply curve backward bending and what is it about labor as an input that would explain this difference?

5. The Government of Canada is considering changing the tax rules on retirement savings plans (RRSP). Currently, money invested in a RRSP (similar to the Individual Retirement Account (IRA) in the United States) is not taxed and interest or dividend income generated by these retirement investments and savings is also not taxed provided the money is not withdrawn from the plan. When the individual retires and begins to draw out the money, then this is taxed as regular income. If the government decides to tax this retirement money, what do you foresee happening to people's decisions about how much they work now and how many years they work throughout their lives?

ANSWERS TO REVIEW QUESTIONS

Answers to PROBLEMS AND EXERCISES

1. a. Mr. Singh is best off if, after supplying his 8 hours a day to the market, he splits his remaining 9 hours into 4 hours of non-market activity (MV = \$20), and 5 hours of leisure (MV = \$20).
b. Yes. Since Mr. Singh's hourly wage of \$25 exceeds his MV of \$20 for an hour of leisure or non-market activity, if possible he would choose to work more than 8 hours.

2. a. Q = 8, P = 4
b. The quantity of labor hours demanded is 6, the quantity of labor hours supplied is 12, and the surplus of labor hours is 6.
c.

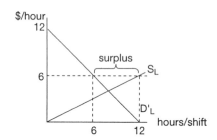

d. Discriminate more on experience, affecting young people, women returning to the work force, and certain groups of immigrants; Substitute capital for labor where possible; Change full-time workers to part-time to avoid paying benefits; Don't pay overtime if legal.

3. This demand curve is more elastic than the demand curve in question 2, therefore a greater change in quantity demanded, that is, a greater cutbacks in labor hours is expected in the restaurant. The quantity of labor offered remains 12 because the supply curve is unchanged. The quantity of labor demanded is 6 = 10 - .75Qd, Qd = 5.33, so the surplus is 6.67 labor hours, .67 hours greater than in the factory.

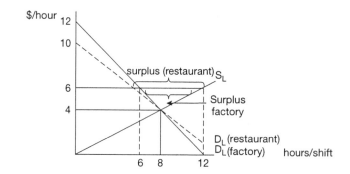

4. If businesses are required to pay a greater proportion of employee benefits this increases their per unit costs like a tax, and would decrease the demand for labor (which could also be shown as a decrease in supply -- i.e. an increase in the price of an input). The before-benefit wage to employees would decrease (their nominal wage, w) but their after-benefit wage (w + b) would increase. The number of employees would decrease.

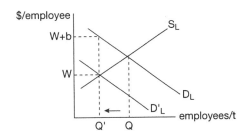

5. The salary cap is a wage ceiling, above which total salaries are not to rise.

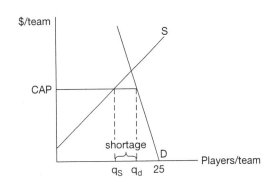

The baseball situation is odd given the unique nature of the talent and individual employment contracts. The graph indicates a very inelastic demand curve, indicating that up to a certain total salary level any change in price will not lead to a change in the quantity demanded by team owners. The players' supply curve, as a whole, may also be quite inelastic over most salary ranges, especially considering that some play for many reasons in addition to their pecuniary salary. Any given individual may have a more elastic supply curve.

Under the owners' salary cap proposal the overall wages paid to players will be below the market clearing price level. In a normal market situation this would create a shortage of workers. It is doubtful, however, that many players will quit baseball because of this salary cap, indicating that their individual contracts are at least equal to their marginal value of leisure and better than any alternative market wage they could get being an salesman, sports bar owner, coach, etc.

Answers to TRUE - FALSE QUESTIONS

1. False. We would anticipate more leisure in the non-wage case. The income effect of both the wage and non-wage increase in income is to reduce work hours. The increase in wage, however, also induces a substitution effect to work more hours because the cost of leisure has increased. There is no substitution effect in the non-wage case, because there was no direct change in the relative price of work and leisure, the wage.

2. True. A change in relative prices always induces a substitution effect. Any corresponding change in purchasing power is called the income effect.

3. True. A substitution effect only results from a change in relative prices.

4. False. There will be an income and substitution effect whenever relative prices change, though if they go in opposite directions they may cancel each other out. Substitution and income effects just separate out how much of a change in consumption is due to a relative price change and how much is due to a resulting change in purchasing power.

5. False. Leisure is considered a normal good, based on empirical observations of behavior by those who receive pure income increases. These people tend to increase their consumption of leisure as their income increases.

6. True. It is assumed that increases in market wages will result in an increasing number of workers entering the labor force, though any given individual may actually supply less labor as the market wage increases.

7. True. The higher the elasticity of demand for labor, the easier it is to substitute out of labor and into other inputs whose relative price has not risen.

8. True. The higher the elasticity of demand for the output, the more consumers will substitute away from the final product in response to price increases from increased labor costs.

9. True. The greater the share of total costs that labor accounts for, the more likely the firm will be more responsive to price (wage) increases.

10. True. Only the income effect may, on net, result in a person working fewer hours after a wage increase.

Answers to MULTIPLE CHOICE QUESTIONS

1. a	6. d	11. d
2. d	7. c	12. a
3. d	8. b	13. b
4. a	9. e	
5. c	10. c	

Answers to SHORT ANSWER QUESTIONS

1. The statement reflects a common sentiment, that is partly true and partly false. In the first case it reflects a misunderstanding of the nature of capital. Capital can either be a substitute for or a complement to labor. Not all "machines and robots" replace labor. Second, companies want to maximize profit. To achieve this they combine inputs (labor and capital) to produce a good. While it is true that firms are willing to substitute capital for labor, they are equally willing to substitute labor for capital. In either case firms are only willing to do so when it will lead to productivity gains. The firm will hire a mix of inputs to the point where the marginal product per dollar cost of all inputs are equal. If an advance in technology displaces this equilibrium, then the firm will seek to adjust its hiring of inputs so as to restore the equilibrium.

2. Shaq, Sir Charles, and Hakeem the Dream make the big money because the value of their marginal product to the owners is that much higher than these other players. In this case the marginal product is measured in terms of revenue for the franchise as much as statistics on the court. In addition to helping a team make the playoffs and win championships, the big names attract fans to see games and buy souvenirs and other merchandise, and they make it lucrative, through advertising revenue, for television to pay money for the rights to broadcast games featuring these players.

3. Since the return from signing a superstar is, among other things, the number of additional fans that player can attract, this would tend to be higher for a baseball team that had empty seats to fill. For a hockey team already selling out each game, a superstar might only increase the price they could charge per seat, or television rights. Likewise, hiring each additional superstar brings diminishing marginal returns, so it is again more likely that a baseball team would hire more superstars than a hockey team.

4. The labor supply curve will bend backwards if the income effect of an increase in hourly wages outweighs the substitution effect and induces the person to actually work fewer hours (and vice versa for a wage decrease). That is, a positively sloped curve means an increase in hourly wages induces an increase in the number of hours someone is willing to work. Leisure becomes more costly. But suppose you are a doctor an your hourly income rises to $150. At some point, the increase in your income from these wage increases may induce you to work fewer hours, because you are now so wealthy that you feel you can engage in more leisure (leisure is often quite income elastic).

5. Retirement savings are an effort to shift current consumption to the future as described in Chapter 10. If the tax rules change so that the government taxes the invested money and the interest income generated by the investment, an individual's income will decrease. This decrease is similar to a decrease in wage since take home pay will be reduced; thus it creates both a substitution and an income effect. The substitution effect is to work fewer hours and eventually to retire sooner, because the opportunity cost of taking leisure has decreased. The income effect will run opposite to the substitution effect, leading people to increase their work hours and prolong their working lives, provided tax and income conditions remain roughly constant. This is because leisure is a normal good -- as income increases/decreases we anticipate that individuals will consume more/less leisure.

CHAPTER 14
The Macro Economy

THE BIGGER PICTURE

Microeconomists exercise considerable license with the axioms of behavior. They are forever looking at markets that are made up of hundreds, thousands even millions of consumers. For example, economists interested in the market for television programs are dealing with many producers and millions of consumers, the same with running shoes, pharmaceuticals, insurance policies, almost anything you can think of. Indeed, it is difficult to think of a market where there is only a single consumer. Yet, as you have now had thoroughly embedded into your consciousness, the behavioral postulates, which serve as the foundation of microeconomics, pertain exclusively to the individual. Silberberg points this out in Chapter 2 on page 35,

> It's important to note that the proposed postulates of behavior are all about *individual* preferences, not group preferences. Although economics rarely focuses on only what single individuals do, being more concerned with the consequences of the combined actions of individuals, the behavioral postulates are all about individual behavior, not about what groups do. The reason, simply put, is that there is little reason to believe we can successfully model the preference of groups.

Individual preferences cannot with any consistancy be aggregated to the macroeconomic level. This means that the behavioral postulates that support microeconomist's propositions do not transfer with the same rigor to the field of macroeconomics. There is no macro equivalent, for example, to the most powerful postulate of microeconomic theory: the law of demand. Nonetheless, each individual in the macro economy is still presumed to operated according to the axioms of chapter two, which also gives macroeconomists a considerable amount of mileage.

Macroeconomists work with aggregate markets that make up "the economy". Instead of observing the price in one market, macroeconomists observe the general price level and the overall increases or decreases in it (i.e., inflation and deflation). Instead of studying a single firm's decision to hire inputs like labor, macroeconomists study the economy-wide labor market and changes in broad measures of employment (e.g. the unemployment rate). And instead of measuring the output of a single firm or factory, macroeconomists measure the Gross National Product or the value of all goods and services produced in the entire economy.
Interest rates, and the supply and demand for money play a prominent role in macroeconomic theory, and their relationship to the general price level and economic activity is discussed.

Additionally there are other influences that must be accounted for in macroeconomic theory. For example, the pool of buyers and sellers in the economy now includes foreign interests in the forms of imports and exports, into and out of the economy. And, as Silberberg describes in his section on the Great Depression of the 1930's, actions taken in one national economy can influence other national economies.

This highlights another difference. Although government actions affect markets in microeconomic theory, the discussion is usually limited to its role of delineating property rights, or enacting taxes, quotas, or price controls. In macroeconomics, government's influence and role is more prominent. Government's are major consumers of goods and labor, and suppliers of services. Even more significantly the national government is the superintendent of fiscal and monetary policies. The effect of these policies is the subject of continuous debate, and unlike microeconomics, has led to several competing schools of thought.

Thus, macroeconomists work at a different level of the economy, they make different kinds of assumptions, and they have developed other models to explain the movements and changes of the economy as a whole. Nonetheless, an increasing number of these models still build upon the foundations of the economic paradigm, and you will find that the principles of microeconomics that you take from this class continue to offer insight into the workings of markets and economic behavior.

EPILOGUE

(Somewhere in the Library...)

"Hey Mo, how's it going?"

"Ginny, I was just thinking about you and economics."

"Ugh, you had to bring that up."

"What are you going to do?"

"Study my butt off between now and the exam of course. I've got two papers and two exams to finish up, but I'm actually in a lot better shape than I was around mid-terms. I told Jim that I needed more time off this week and next for school."

"No, I mean are you going to drop out? You know the first year is the hardest psychologically, with all the adjustments and everything. Once you get through that, then it's just a lot of work."

"I suppose so. I guess I'm still thinking about it. But I'm going to talk to this guy again about the watershed work and see if I can start part-time. Then over the summer I can see what my options are. I still have to earn some money to pay for my dorm room and the bad cafeteria food that comes with it."

"So does that mean you'll be back next semester?" Mo asked.

"Probably... But not for sure."

"Well let me put it this way, did you register for classes?"

"Well...yes I did."

"Excellent! Did you register for Macro?"

"Yes," Ginny replied quietly.

"You like economics don't you?" Mo pressed. "You're going to get a Masters degree or a Ph.D. in environmental economics and save the world."

"Maybe I will and maybe I won't. I refuse to be pigeon-holed at such a young age. Besides I want to take this thing one semester at a time. What about you? You're going to become the head of some huge corporation. You'll probably be the head of some huge *polluting* corporation and I'm going to have to come after you."

"No way. My companies will all be environmentally sensitive. They'll be models for the rest of the corporate world."

"Okay, I'll take your word for it -- for now. Did you sign up for macro?" Ginny asked.

"Of course. But I have to, it's required for my business degree."

"Geez, people like you drive me crazy. You have such certainty about what you're doing. How come you're so sure you want to go into business?"

"Well, when you grow up like I did it's hard to think you have the same choices as other people. I think a lot about how I can get a job that will give me some security and enough income to help my mother out when she gets too old to work. I guess college for me is more of a place to get the skills and credentials I need to get a good job. I just decided that business was the best way to do that, since I like numbers, and I have my Mom as a role model."

"Wow, you're an amazing person Mo."

"Well thanks, but I admire you for your social concerns."

"Hey are we going to get together and go over this stuff before the exam?" Ginny asked.

"I think we have to. Why don't you come over to our house? You can meet my mother. We can study. And knowing that you're going to be there will ensure that Adam will be lurking around, which will work well if we have any questions. I promise not to let him lurk too long or too close."

"That's okay, he's starting to grow on me. How about Saturday afternoon? The exam is Monday right?"

"Yes, 8:30 - 11:30."

"Whew that's a brutal time slot."

"I know, but it will be over with quick. Saturday afternoon sounds great. Call me, or I'll call you if something comes up."

"Great, okay."